Volume 23! Thanks for choosing to take
this one home!

I wrote a comment in an issue of *Weekly Shonen
Jump* a while back about having sticker phobia,
but then I remembered all the fans who've
sent me fan mail decorated with stickers. That
comment probably hurt them...

I'm sorry I ever wrote that.

I've got a second stomach for fan letters, and I
always get such a kick out of reading them.

KOHEI HORIKOSHI

MY HERO ACADEMIA

23

SHONEN JUMP Manga Edition

STORY & ART KOHEI HORIKOSHI

TRANSLATION & ENGLISH ADAPTATION **Caleb Cook**
TOUCH-UP ART & LETTERING **John Hunt**
DESIGNER **Julian [JR] Robinson**
SHONEN JUMP SERIES EDITOR **John Bae**
GRAPHIC NOVEL EDITOR **Mike Montesa**

BOKU NO HERO ACADEMIA © 2014 by Kohei Horikoshi
All rights reserved.
First published in Japan in 2014 by SHUEISHA Inc., Tokyo.
English translation rights arranged by SHUEISHA Inc.

Printed in the U.S.A.

Published by VIZ Media, LLC
P.O. Box 77010
San Francisco, CA 94107

10 9 8 7 6 5 4 3 2 1
First printing, February 2020

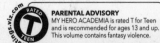

My Hero Academia vol. 23

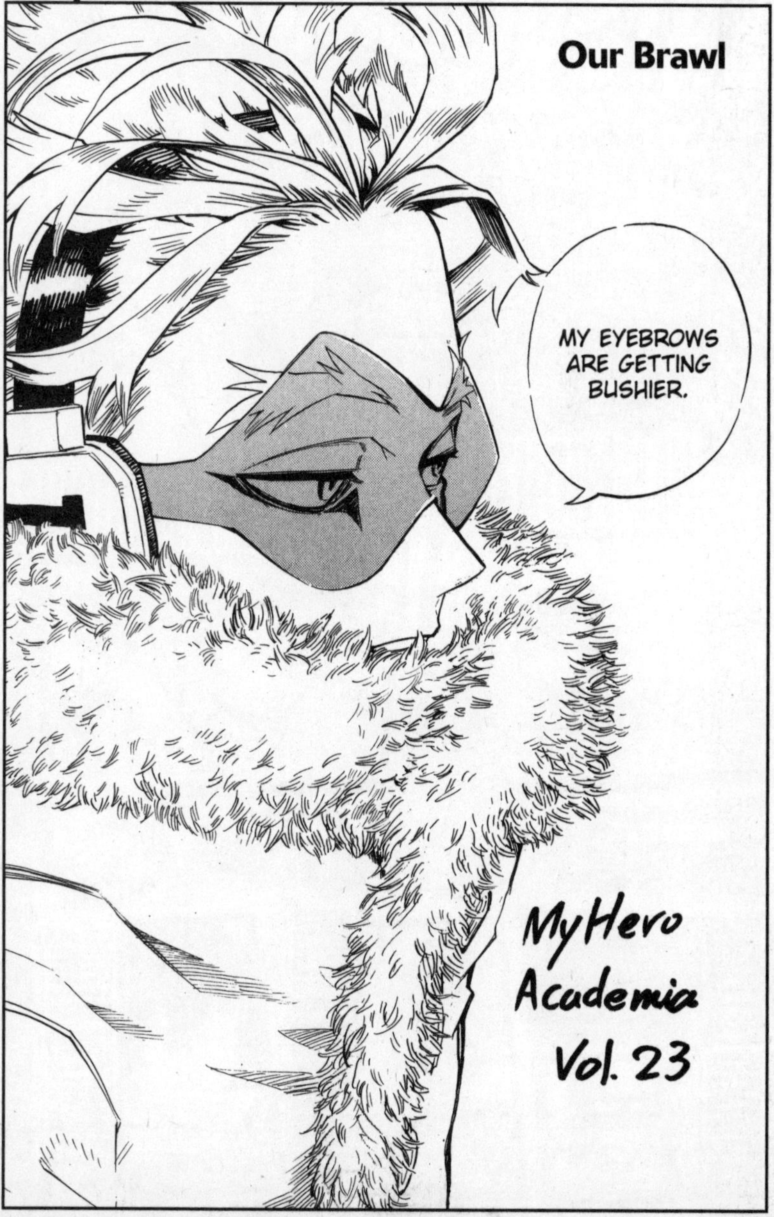
Our Brawl
MY EYEBROWS ARE GETTING BUSHIER.
My Hero Academia Vol. 23

KOHEI HORIKOSHI

KATSUKI BAKUGO'S CHARACTER INTROS!!

Horikoshi didn't have much time to draw new art for these intro pages, so Bakugo was chosen to take over instead! Why Bakugo, you ask?! Because his lack of dark and shaded spots mean he's easy to draw even without lots of ink and tone! So c'mon, Bakugo! Go ahead and introduce these characters for readers new to the series!

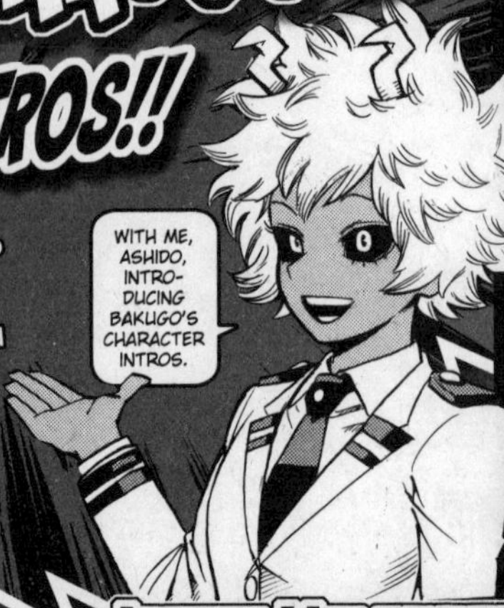
WITH ME, ASHIDO, INTRODUCING BAKUGO'S CHARACTER INTROS.

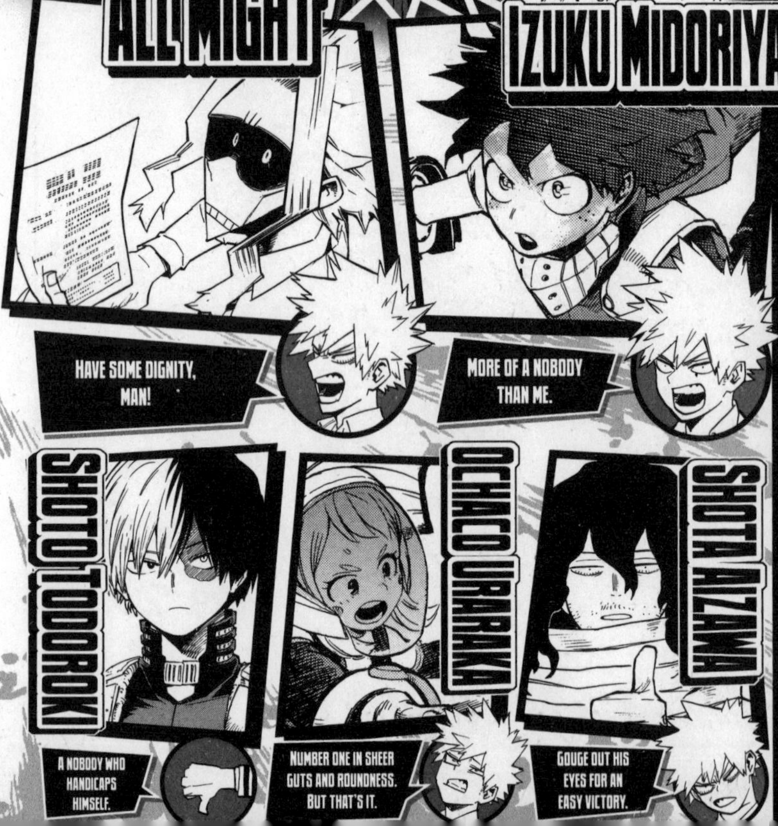
IZUKU MIDORIYA
MORE OF A NOBODY THAN ME.
ALL MIGHT
HAVE SOME DIGNITY, MAN!
SHOTA AIZAWA
GOUGE OUT HIS EYES FOR AN EASY VICTORY.
OCHACO URARAKA
NUMBER ONE IN SHEER GUTS AND ROUNDNESS. BUT THAT'S IT.
SHOTO TODOROKI
A NOBODY WHO HANDICAPS HIMSELF.

One day, people began manifesting special abilities that came to be known as "Quirks," and before long, the world was full of superpowered humans. But with the advent of these exceptional individuals came an increase in crime, and governments alone were unable to deal with the situation. At the same time, others emerged to oppose the spread of evil! As if straight from the comic books, these heroes keep the peace and are even officially authorized to fight crime. Our story begins when a certain Quirkless boy and lifelong hero fan meets the world's number one hero, starting him on his path to becoming the greatest hero ever!

STORY

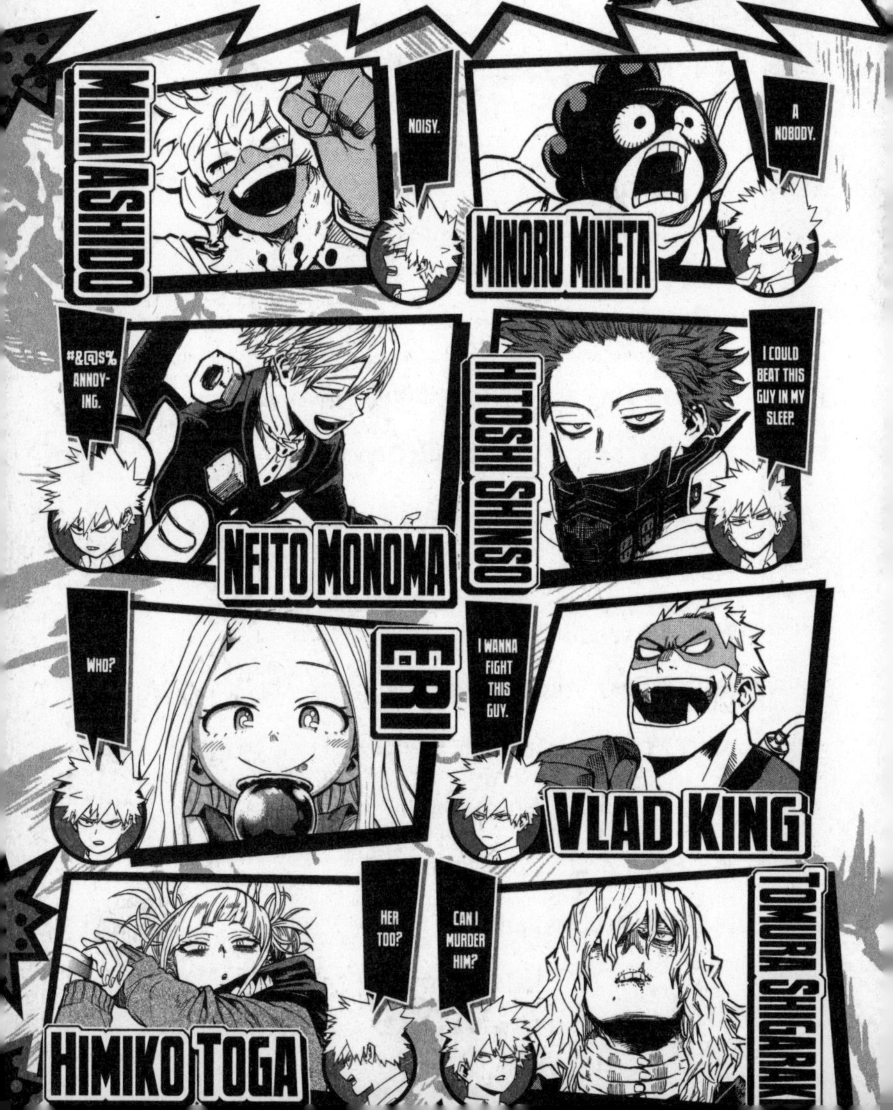

MINORU MINETA
A NOBODY.
MINA ASHIDO
NOISY.
HITOSHI SHINSO
I COULD BEAT THIS GUY IN MY SLEEP.
NEITO MONOMA
#&@$% ANNOY-ING.
VLAD KING
I WANNA FIGHT THIS GUY.
ERI
WHO?
TOMURA SHIGARAKI
CAN I MURDER HIM?
HIMIKO TOGA
HER TOO?

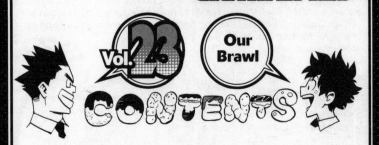

MY HERO ACADEMIA

Vol. 23

Our Brawl

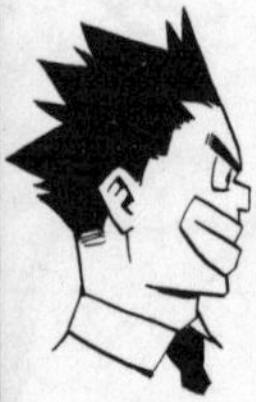

CONTENTS

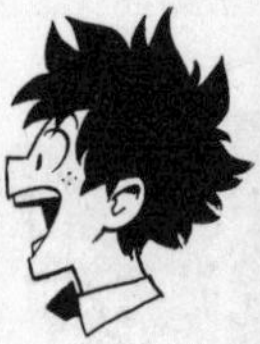

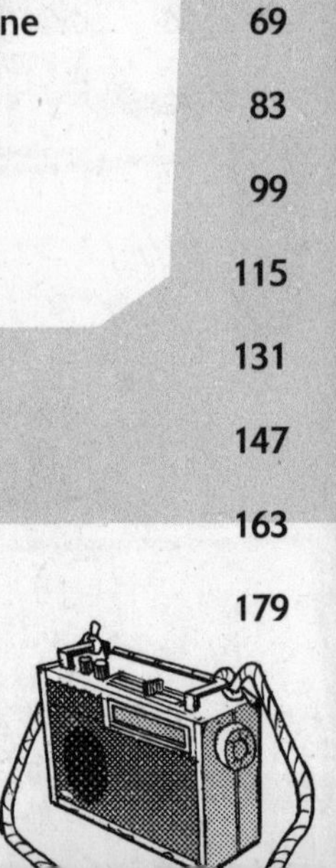

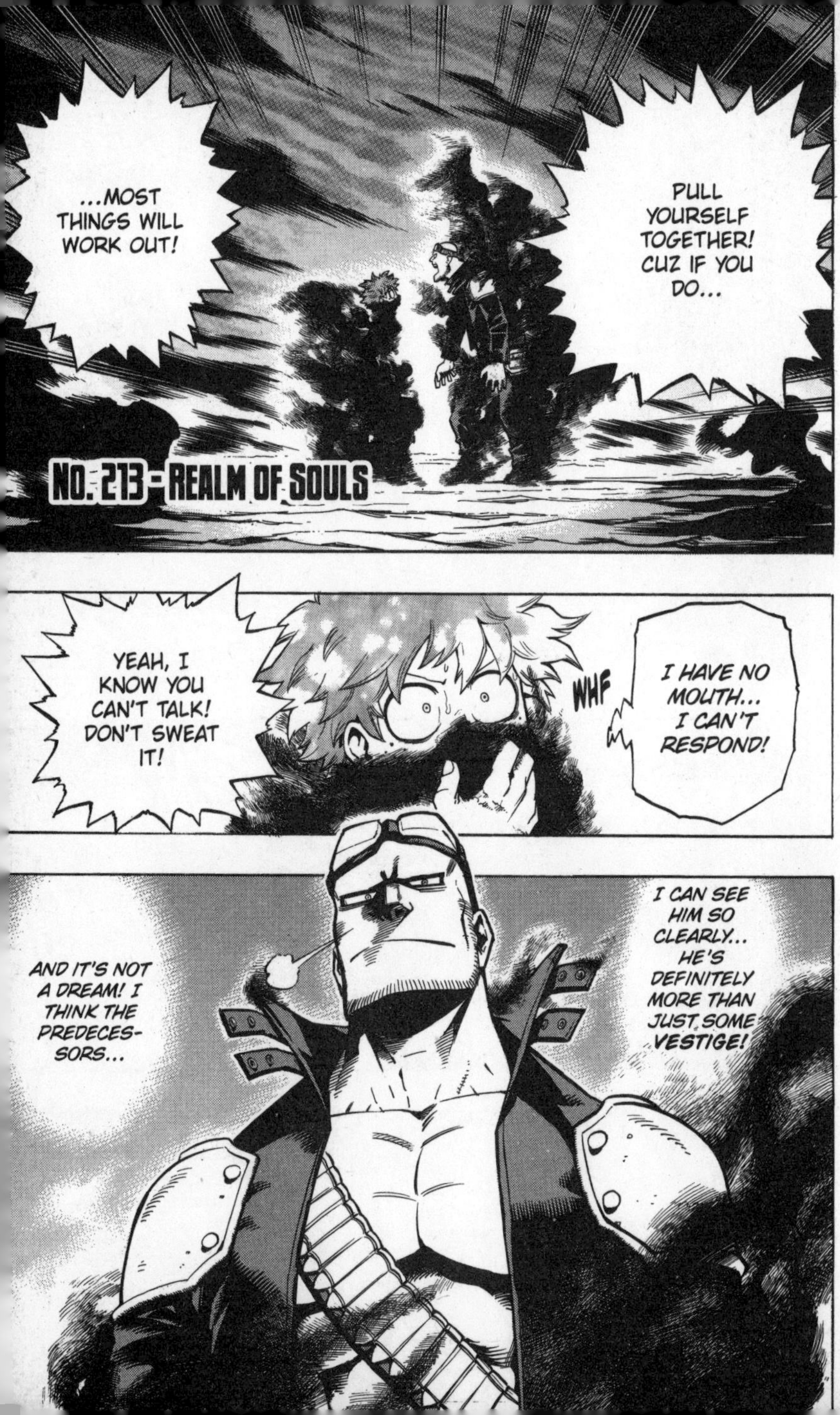
PULL YOURSELF TOGETHER! CUZ IF YOU DO...
...MOST THINGS WILL WORK OUT!
No. 213 - REALM OF SOULS
I HAVE NO MOUTH... I CAN'T RESPOND!
WHF
YEAH, I KNOW YOU CAN'T TALK! DON'T SWEAT IT!
I CAN SEE HIM SO CLEARLY... HE'S DEFINITELY MORE THAN JUST SOME VESTIGE!
AND IT'S NOT A DREAM! I THINK THE PREDECES-SORS...

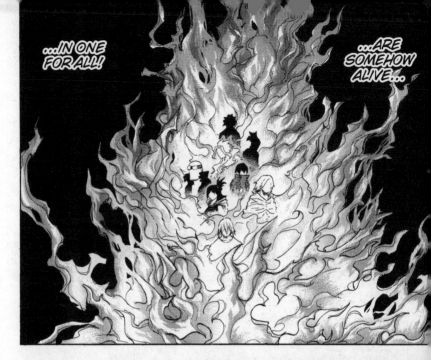

...IN ONE FOR ALL!

...ARE SOMEHOW ALIVE...

HRM? LOOKS LIKE I'M SHORT ON TIME...

BUT LISTEN UP, KIDDO!

AS FOR THAT POWER THAT JUST EXPLODED OUTTA YOU...

THAT'S MY QUIRK!

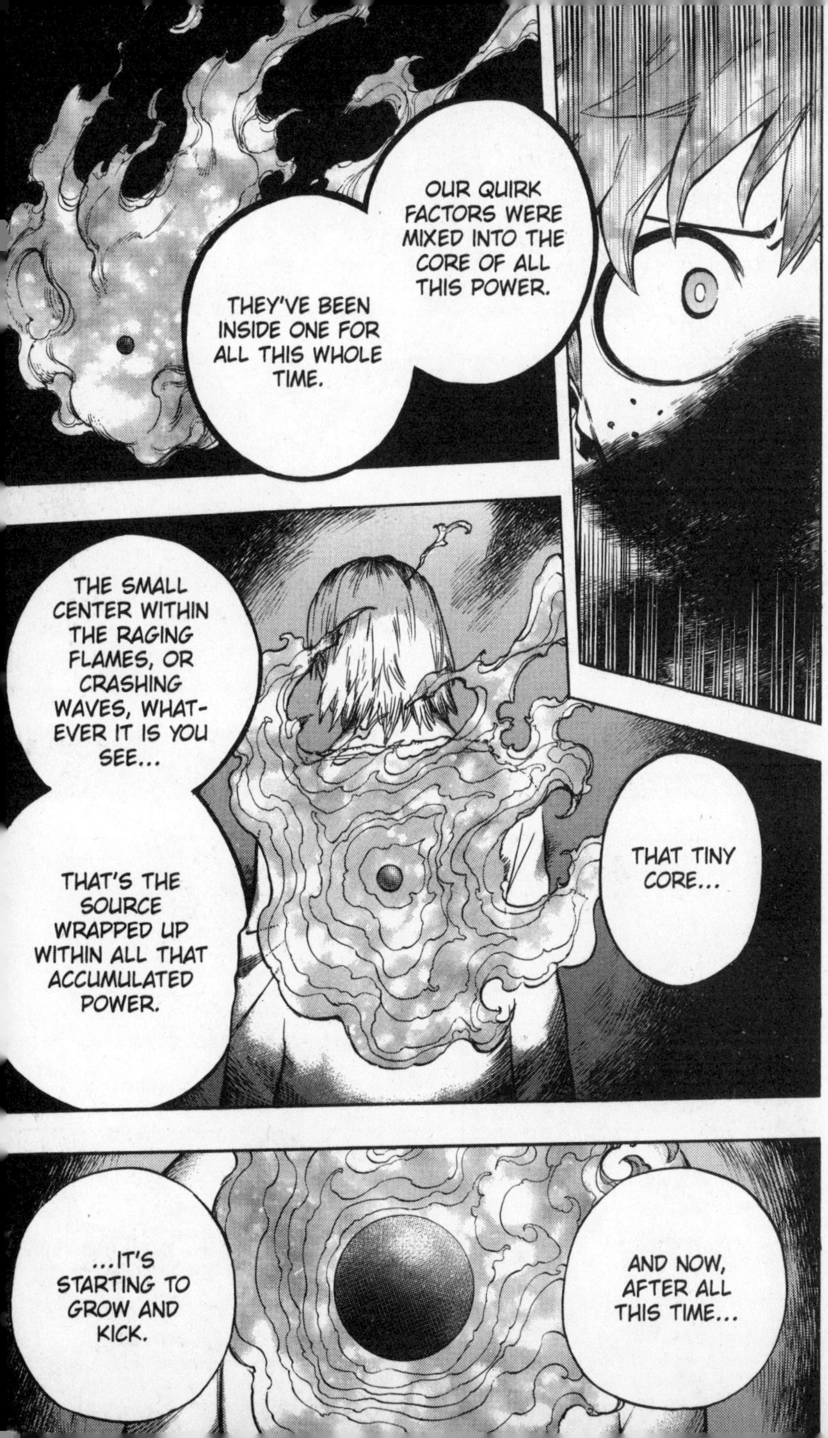
OUR QUIRK FACTORS WERE MIXED INTO THE CORE OF ALL THIS POWER.
THEY'VE BEEN INSIDE ONE FOR ALL THIS WHOLE TIME.
THE SMALL CENTER WITHIN THE RAGING FLAMES, OR CRASHING WAVES, WHAT-EVER IT IS YOU SEE...
THAT'S THE SOURCE WRAPPED UP WITHIN ALL THAT ACCUMULATED POWER.
THAT TINY CORE...
AND NOW, AFTER ALL THIS TIME...
...IT'S STARTING TO GROW AND KICK.

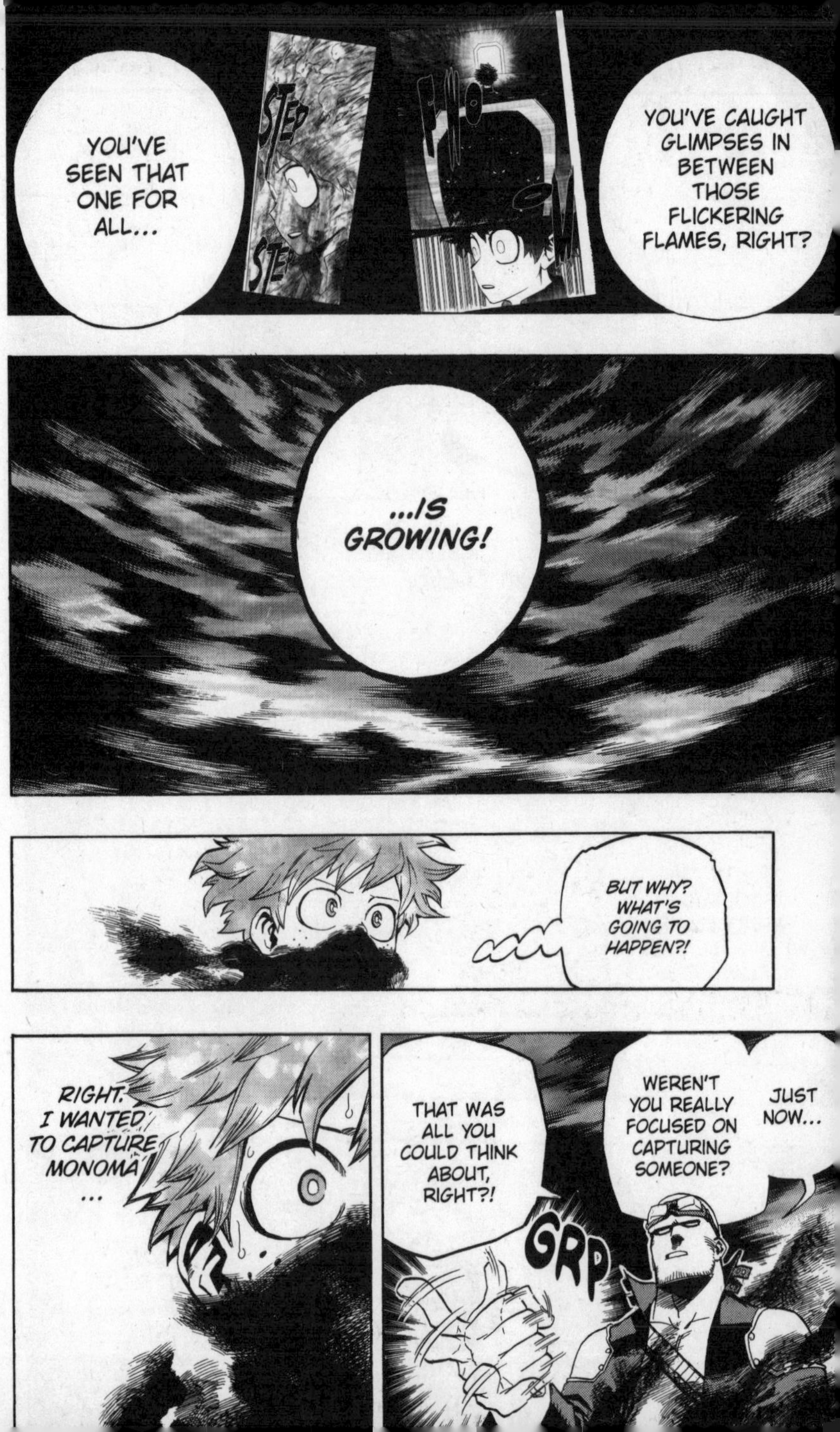
YOU'VE CAUGHT GLIMPSES IN BETWEEN THOSE FLICKERING FLAMES, RIGHT?
STEP
STEP
YOU'VE SEEN THAT ONE FOR ALL...
...IS GROWING!
BUT WHY? WHAT'S GOING TO HAPPEN?!
JUST NOW...
WEREN'T YOU REALLY FOCUSED ON CAPTURING SOMEONE?
THAT WAS ALL YOU COULD THINK ABOUT, RIGHT?!
GRP
RIGHT. I WANTED TO CAPTURE MONOMA ...

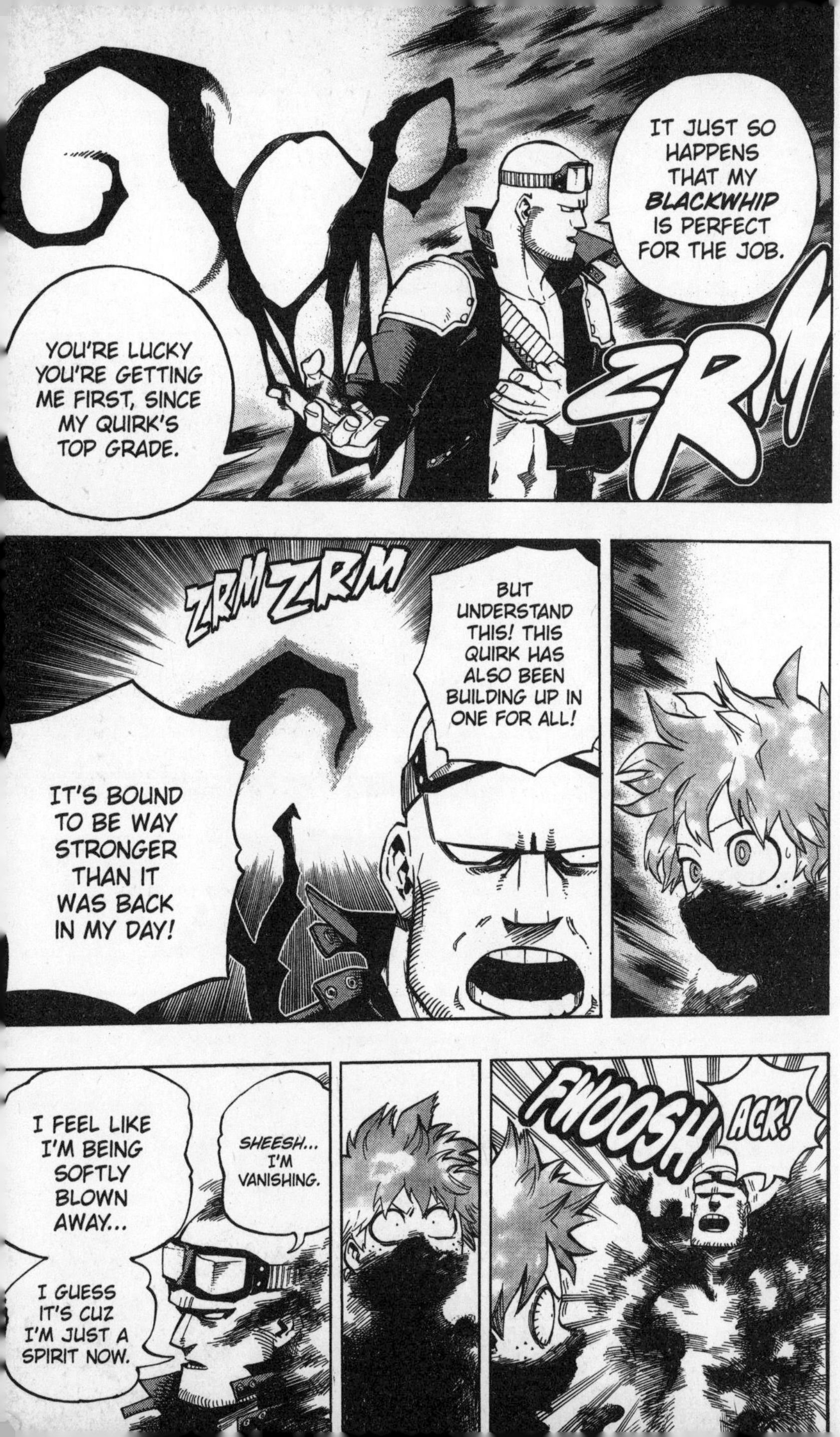
IT JUST SO HAPPENS THAT MY BLACKWHIP IS PERFECT FOR THE JOB.
ZRM
YOU'RE LUCKY YOU'RE GETTING ME FIRST, SINCE MY QUIRK'S TOP GRADE.
BUT UNDERSTAND THIS! THIS QUIRK HAS ALSO BEEN BUILDING UP IN ONE FOR ALL!
ZRM ZRM
IT'S BOUND TO BE WAY STRONGER THAN IT WAS BACK IN MY DAY!
ACK!
FWOOSH
SHEESH... I'M VANISHING.
I FEEL LIKE I'M BEING SOFTLY BLOWN AWAY...
I GUESS IT'S CUZ I'M JUST A SPIRIT NOW.

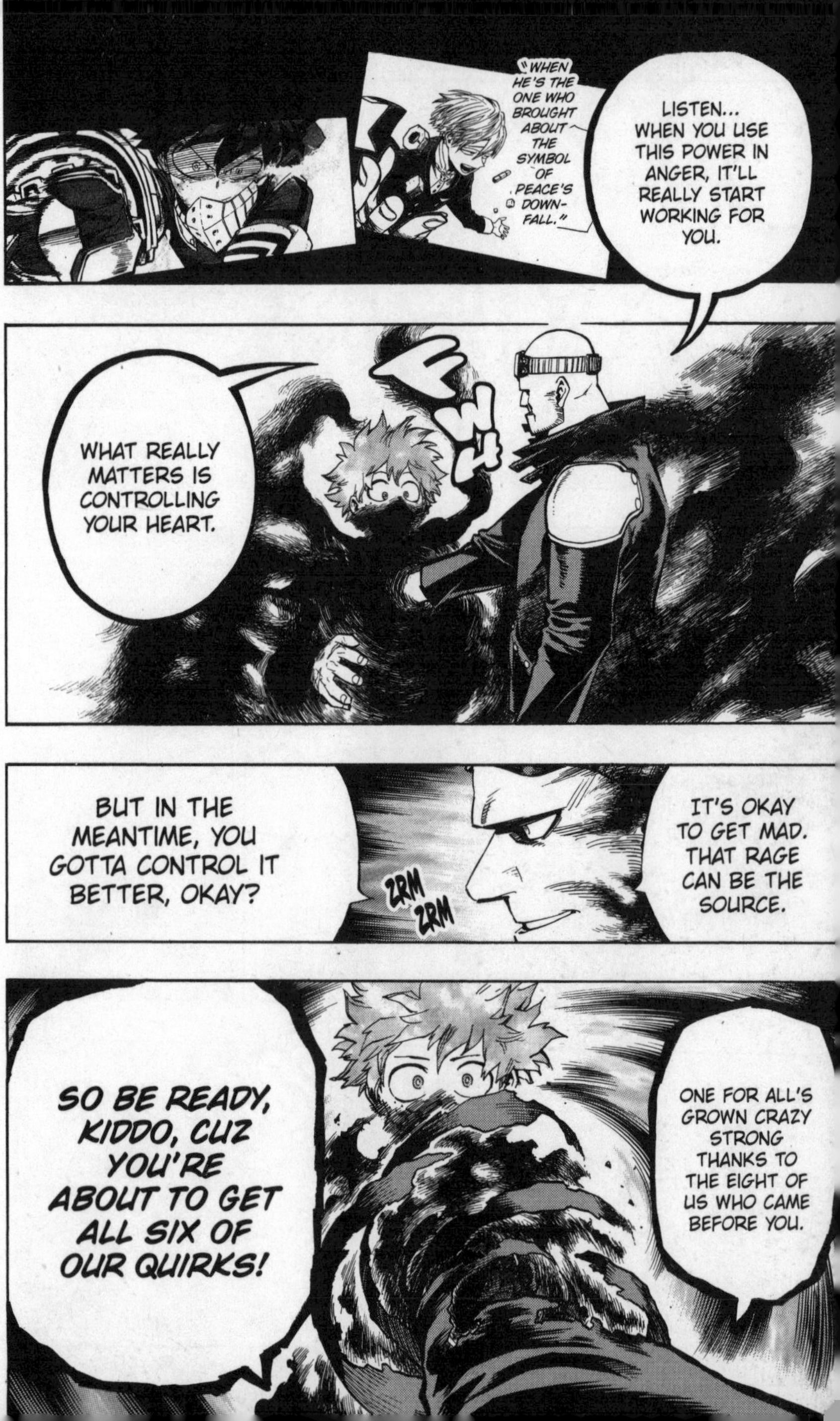
LISTEN... WHEN YOU USE THIS POWER IN ANGER, IT'LL REALLY START WORKING FOR YOU.
"WHEN HE'S THE ONE WHO BROUGHT ABOUT THE SYMBOL OF PEACE'S DOWNFALL."
WHAT REALLY MATTERS IS CONTROLLING YOUR HEART.
IT'S OKAY TO GET MAD. THAT RAGE CAN BE THE SOURCE.
ZRM ZRM
BUT IN THE MEANTIME, YOU GOTTA CONTROL IT BETTER, OKAY?
ONE FOR ALL'S GROWN CRAZY STRONG THANKS TO THE EIGHT OF US WHO CAME BEFORE YOU.
SO BE READY, KIDDO, CUZ YOU'RE ABOUT TO GET ALL SIX OF OUR QUIRKS!

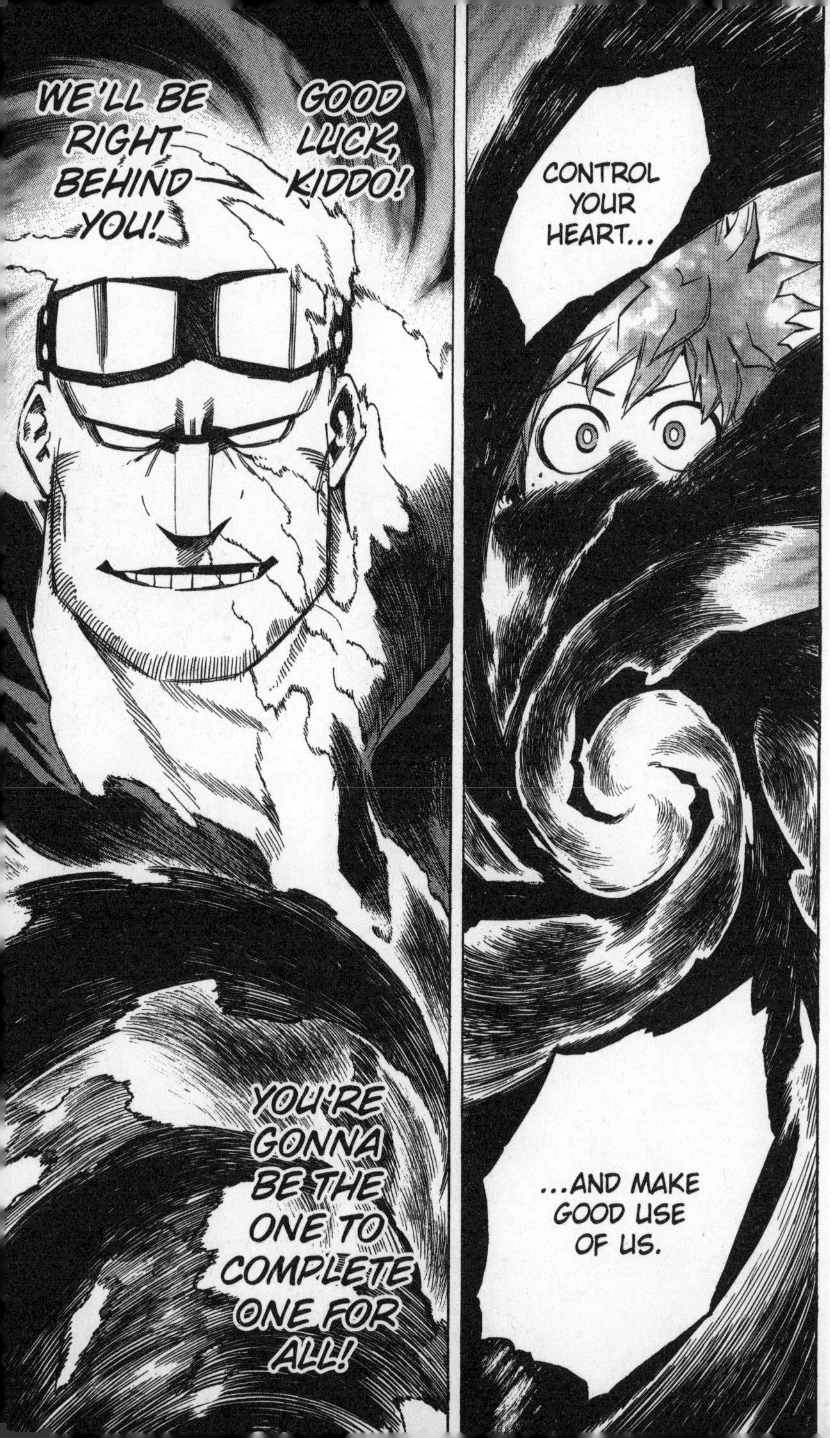
CONTROL YOUR HEART...
...AND MAKE GOOD USE OF US.
GOOD LUCK, KIDDO!
WE'LL BE RIGHT BEHIND YOU!
YOU'RE GONNA BE THE ONE TO COMPLETE ONE FOR ALL!

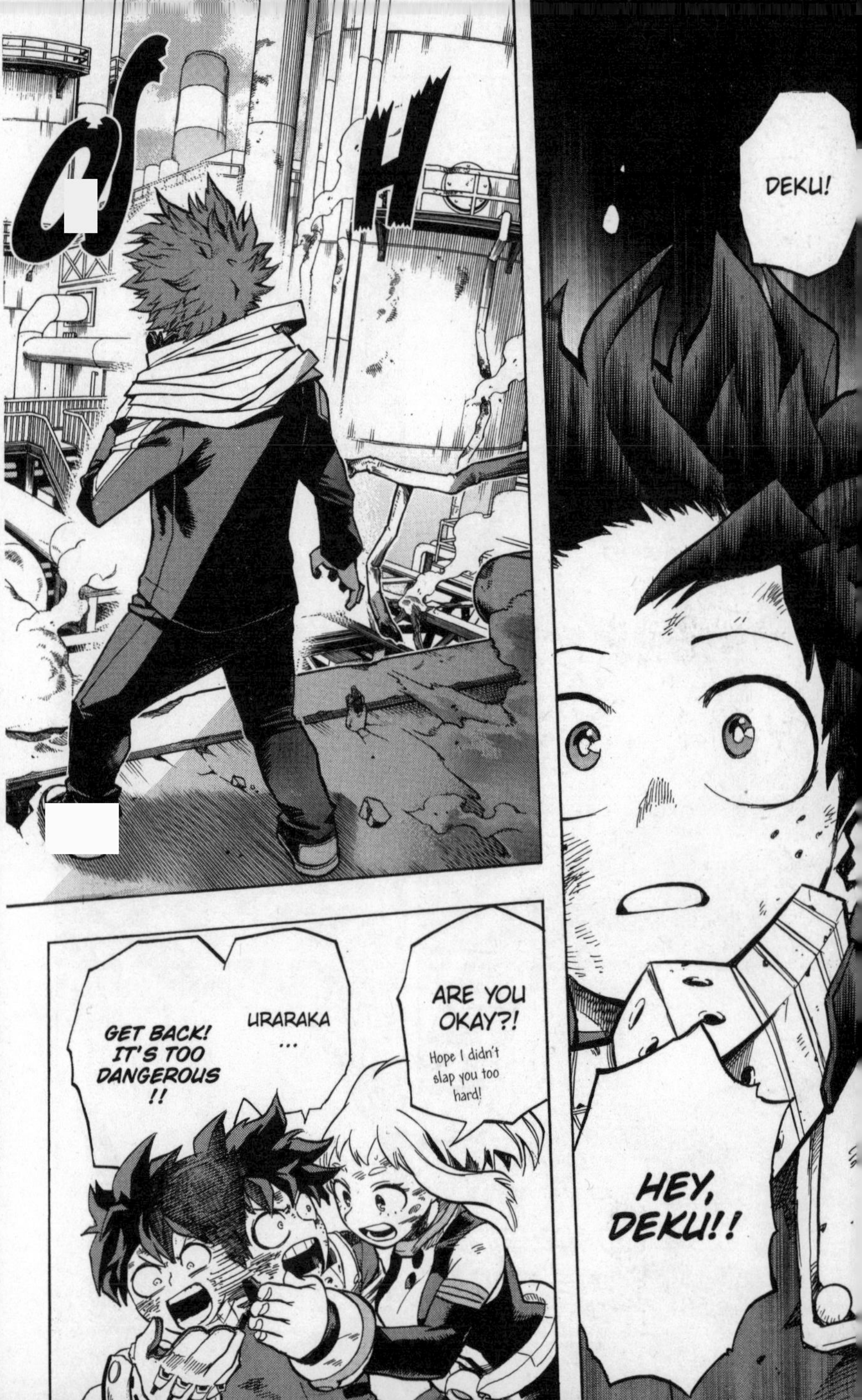
DEKU!
HEY, DEKU!!
ARE YOU OKAY?!
Hope I didn't slap you too hard!
URARAKA ...
GET BACK! IT'S TOO DANGEROUS !!

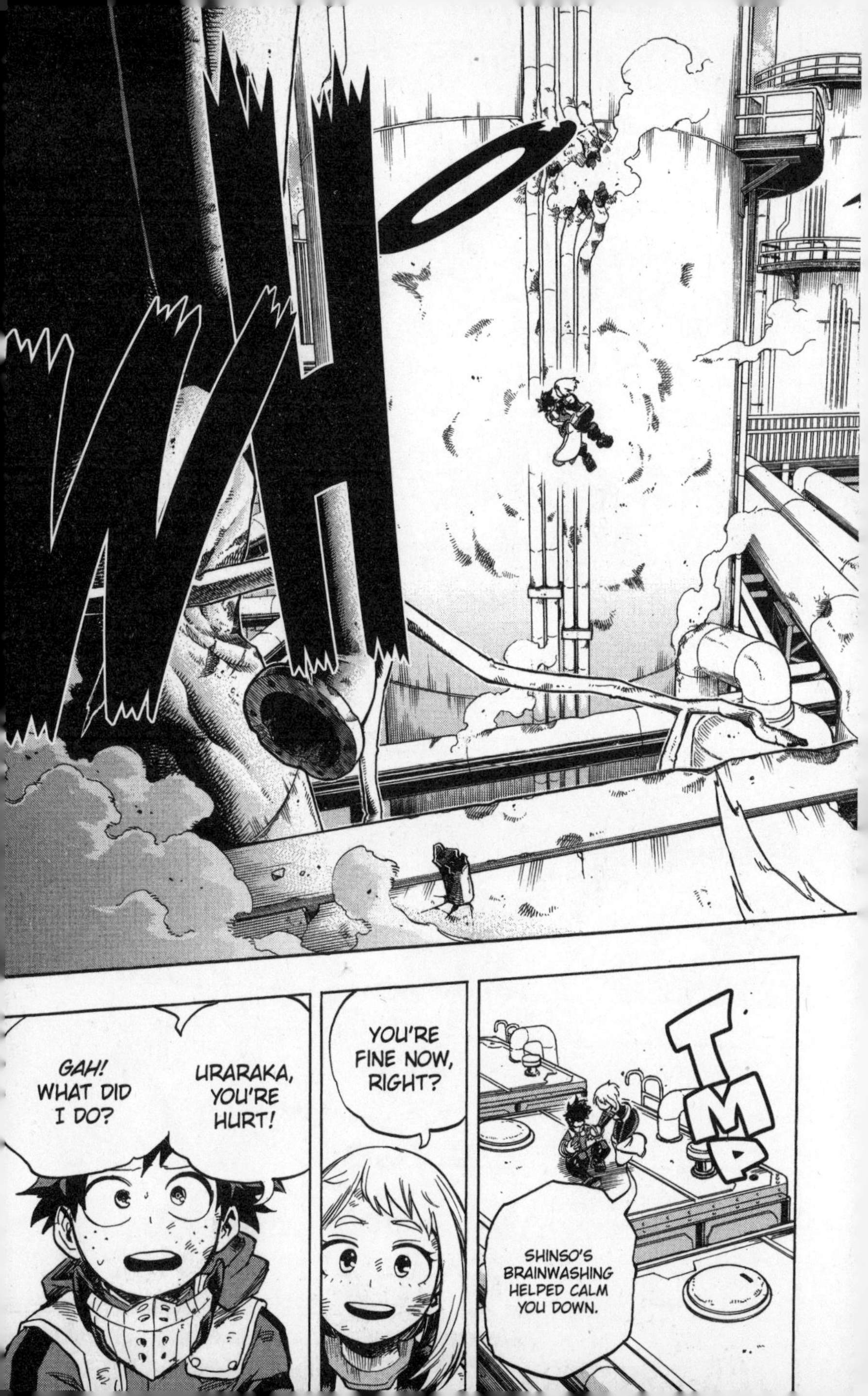
TMP
SHINSO'S BRAINWASHING HELPED CALM YOU DOWN.
YOU'RE FINE NOW, RIGHT?
URARAKA, YOU'RE HURT!
GAH! WHAT DID I DO?

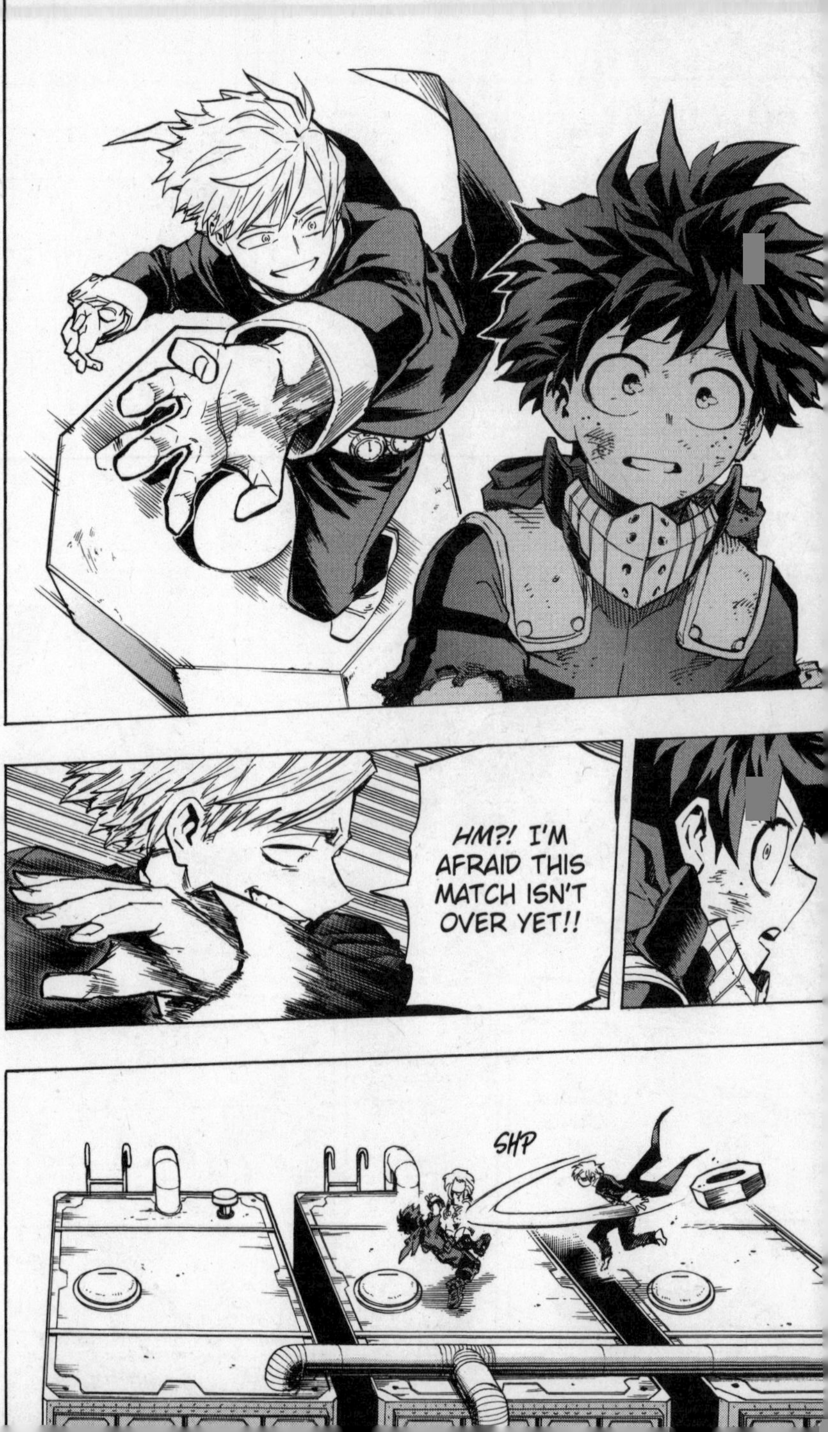
HM?! I'M
AFRAID THIS
MATCH ISN'T
OVER YET!!
SHP

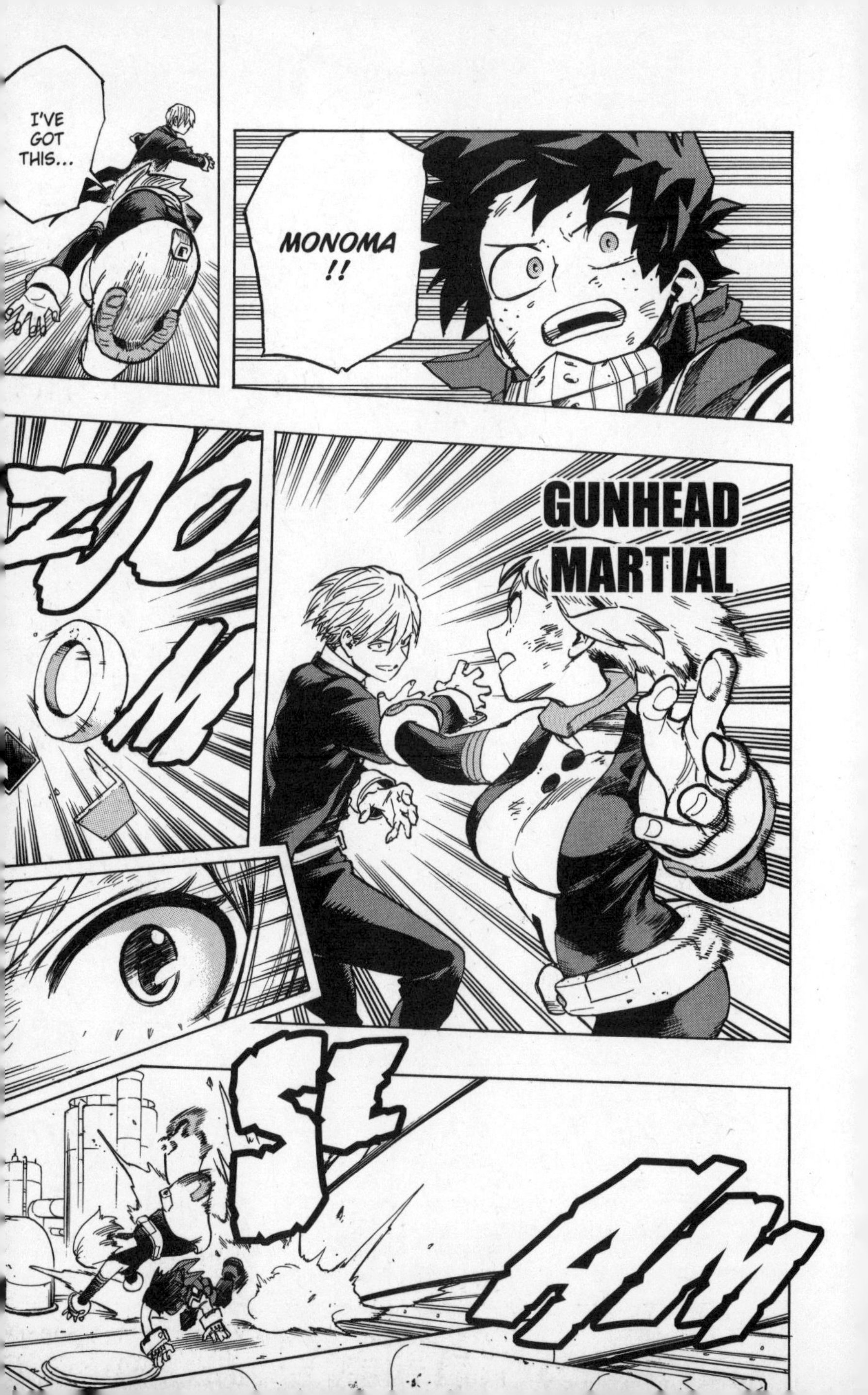
MONOMA !!
I'VE GOT THIS...
GUNHEAD MARTIAL
ZOOOM
SLAM

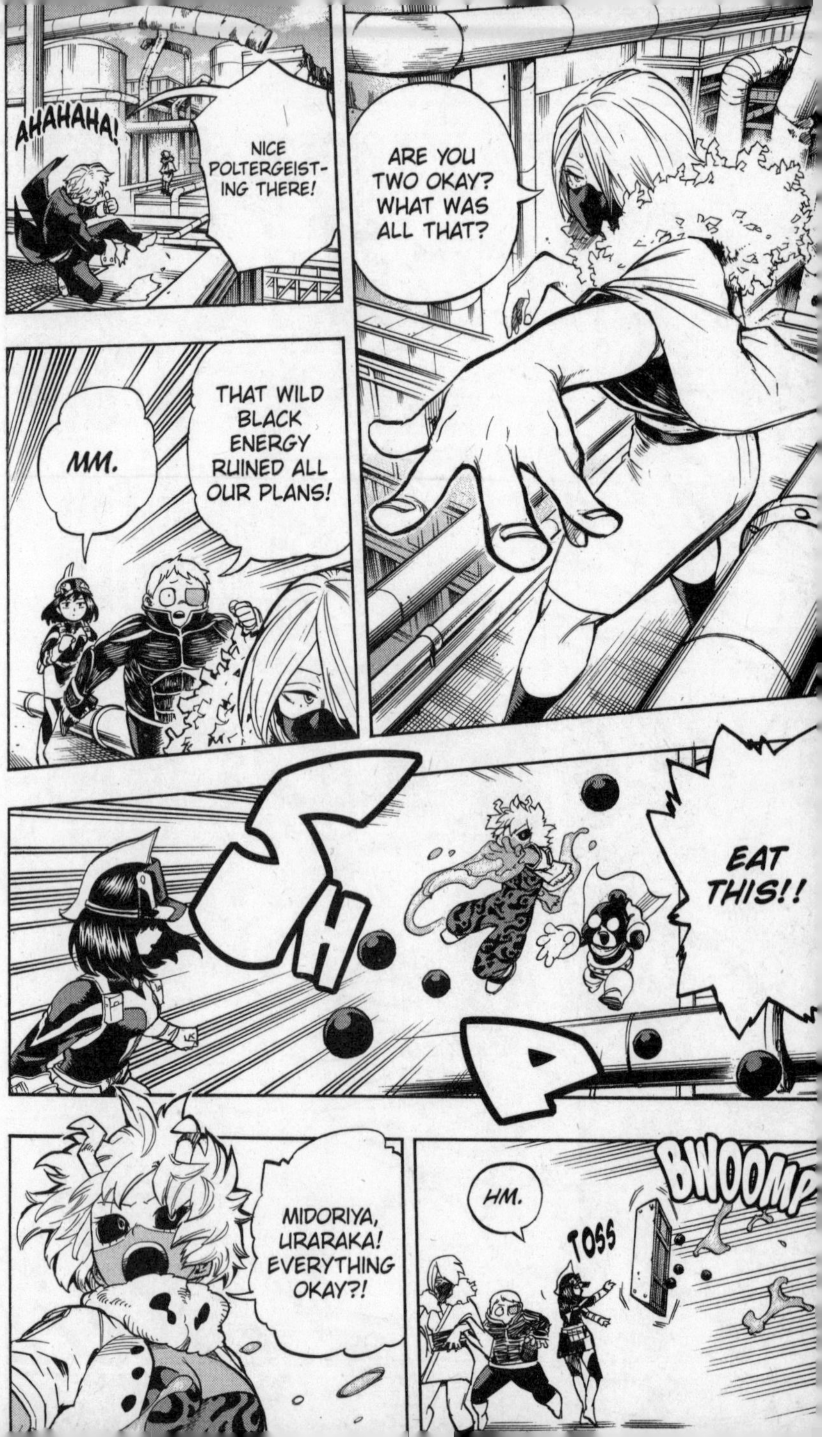
ARE YOU TWO OKAY? WHAT WAS ALL THAT?
NICE POLTERGEIST-ING THERE!
AHAHAHA!
THAT WILD BLACK ENERGY RUINED ALL OUR PLANS!
MM.
EAT THIS!!
BWOOMP
HM.
TOSS
MIDORIYA, URARAKA! EVERYTHING OKAY?!

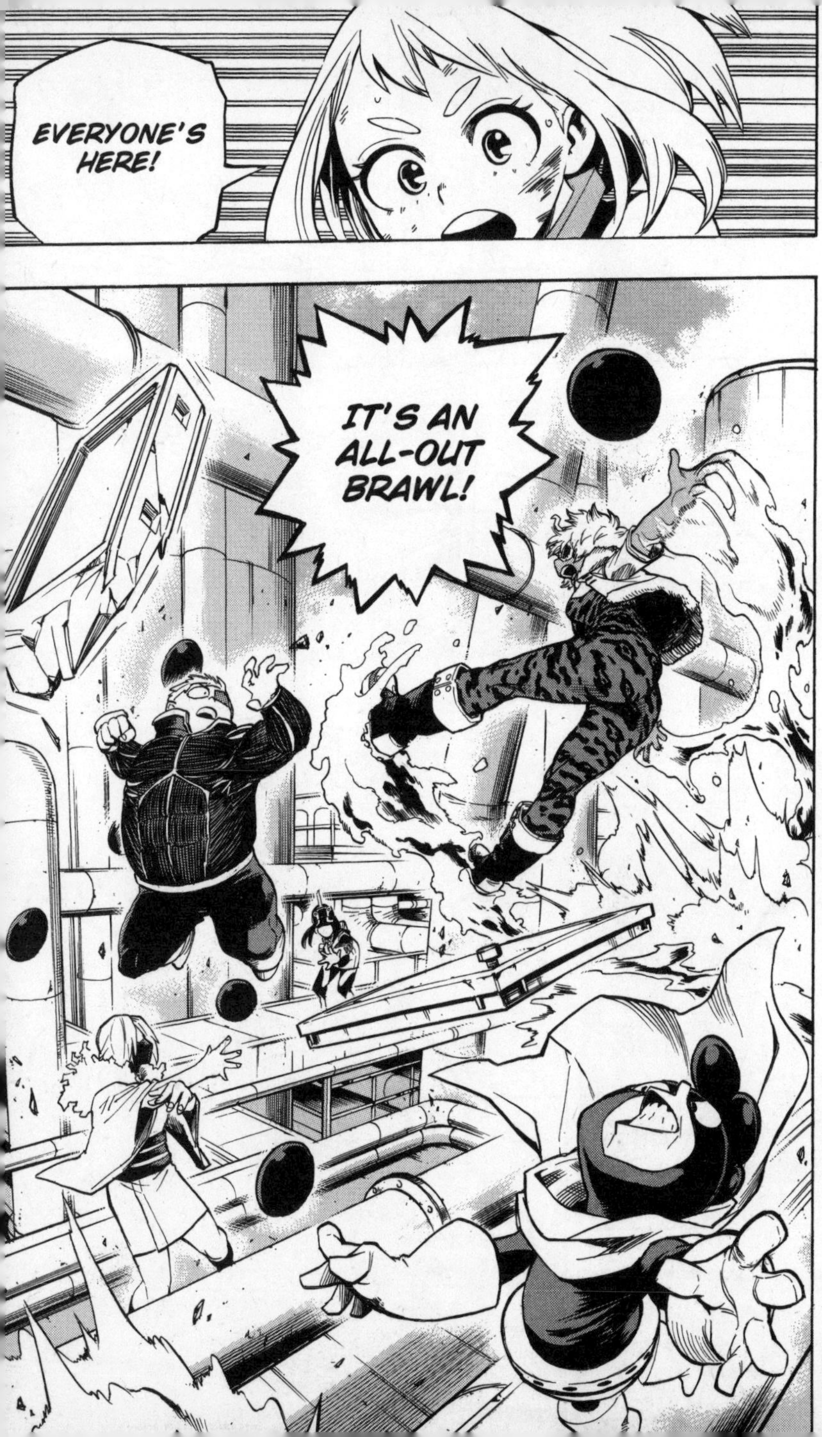
EVERYONE'S HERE!
IT'S AN ALL-OUT BRAWL!

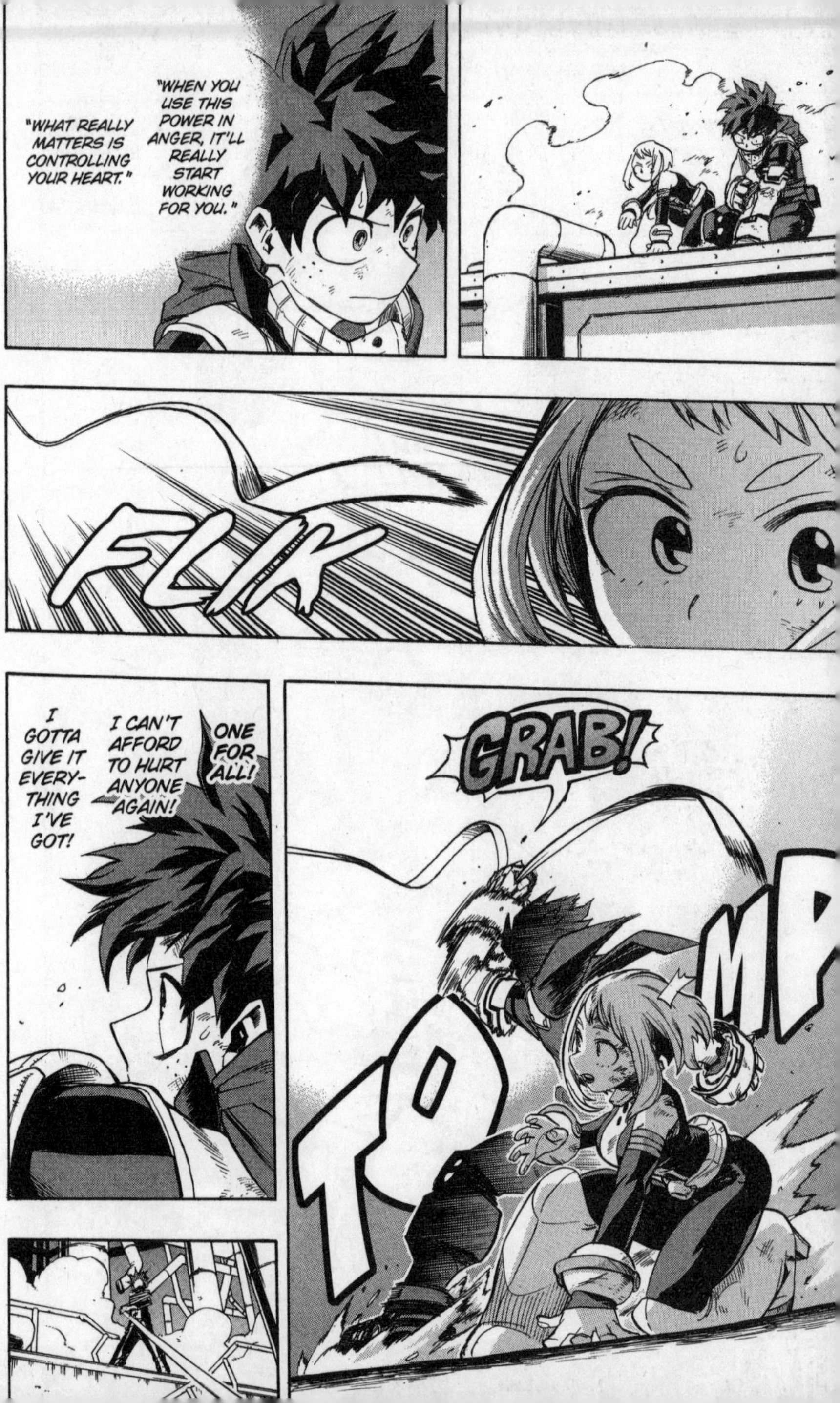
"WHEN YOU USE THIS POWER IN ANGER, IT'LL REALLY START WORKING FOR YOU."
"WHAT REALLY MATTERS IS CONTROLLING YOUR HEART."
FLIK
GRAB!
TOMP
ONE FOR ALL!
I CAN'T AFFORD TO HURT ANYONE AGAIN!
I GOTTA GIVE IT EVERYTHING I'VE GOT!

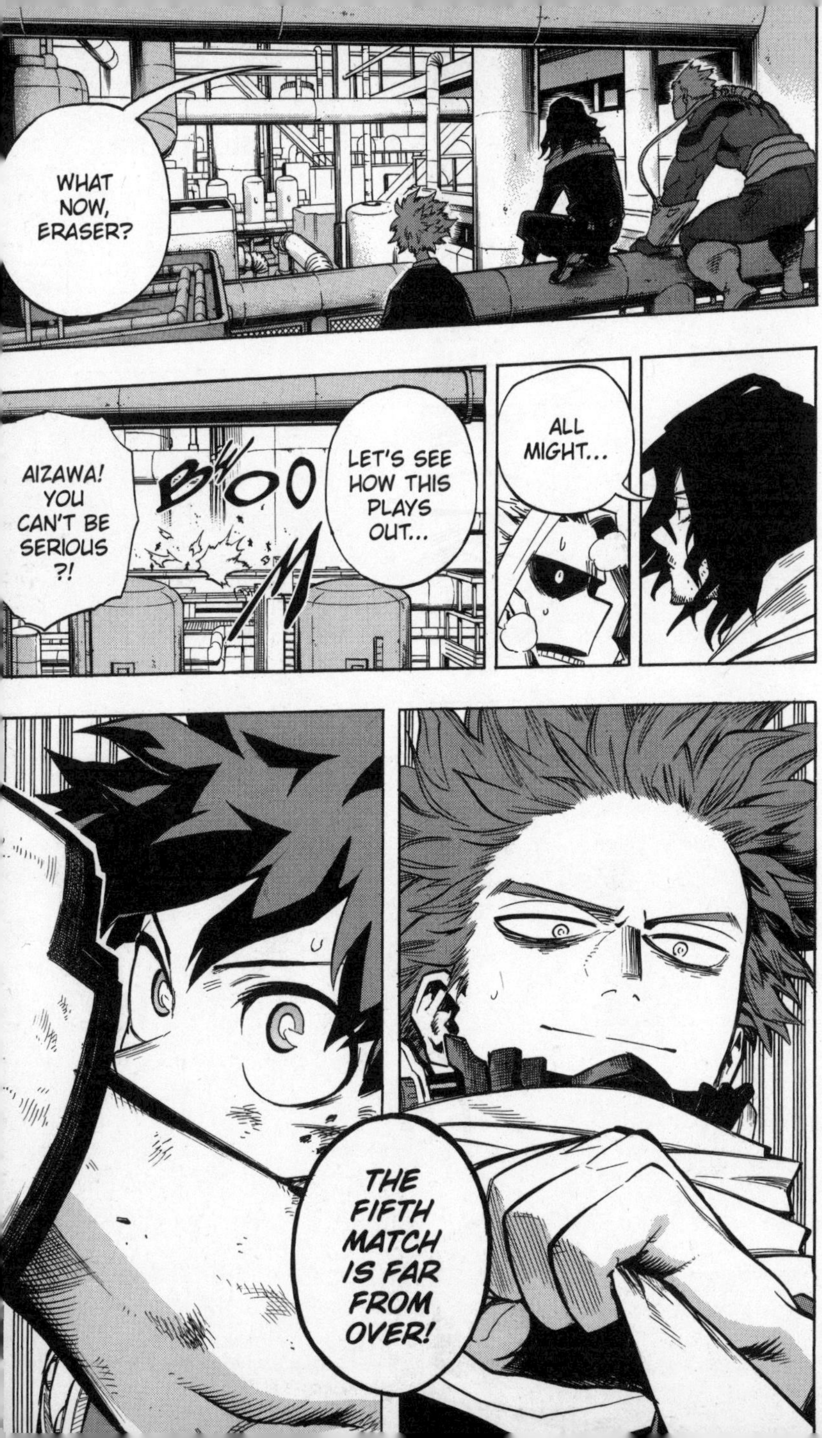
WHAT NOW, ERASER?
ALL MIGHT...
LET'S SEE HOW THIS PLAYS OUT...
BOOM
AIZAWA! YOU CAN'T BE SERIOUS?!
THE FIFTH MATCH IS FAR FROM OVER!

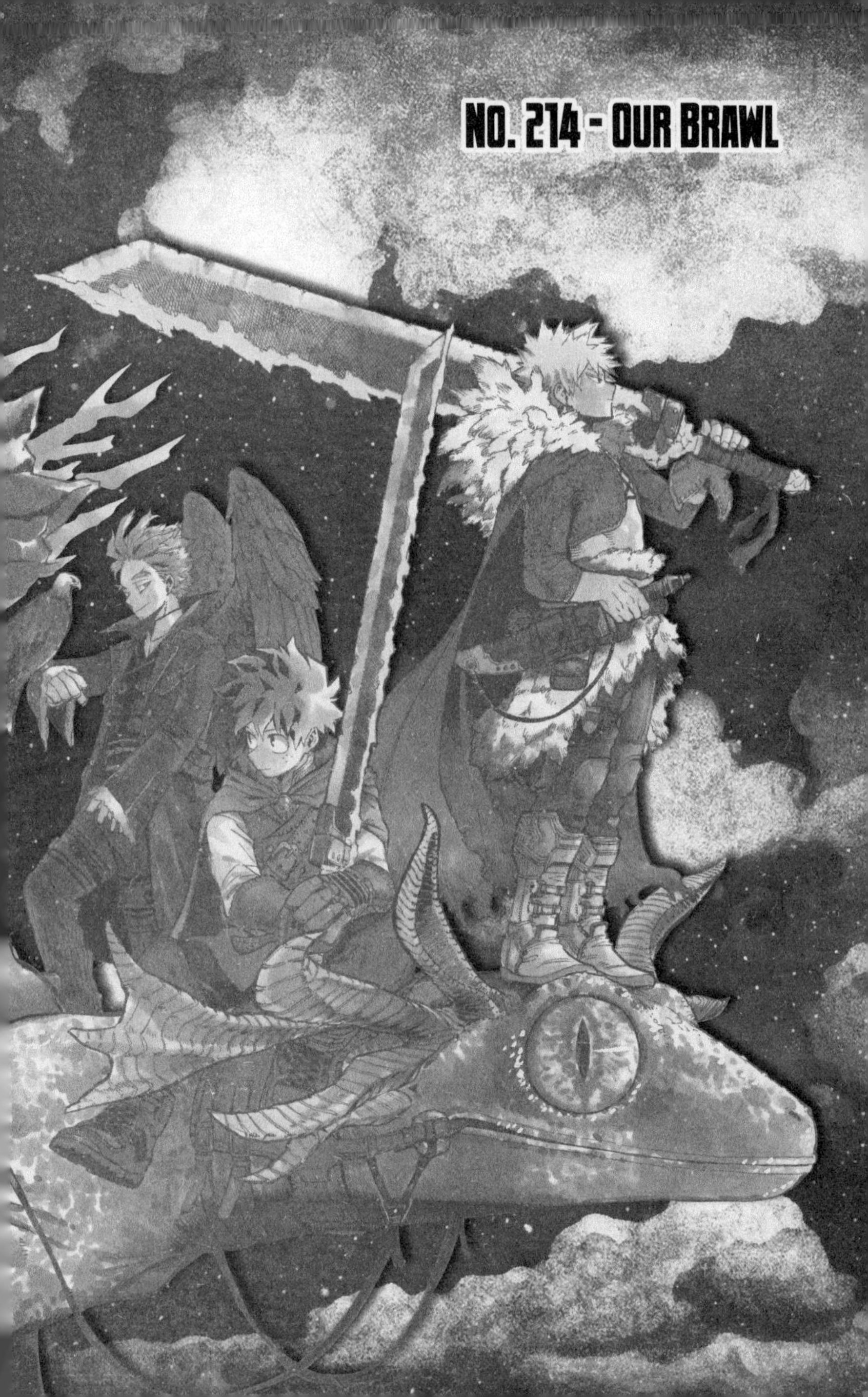
No. 214 - Our Brawl

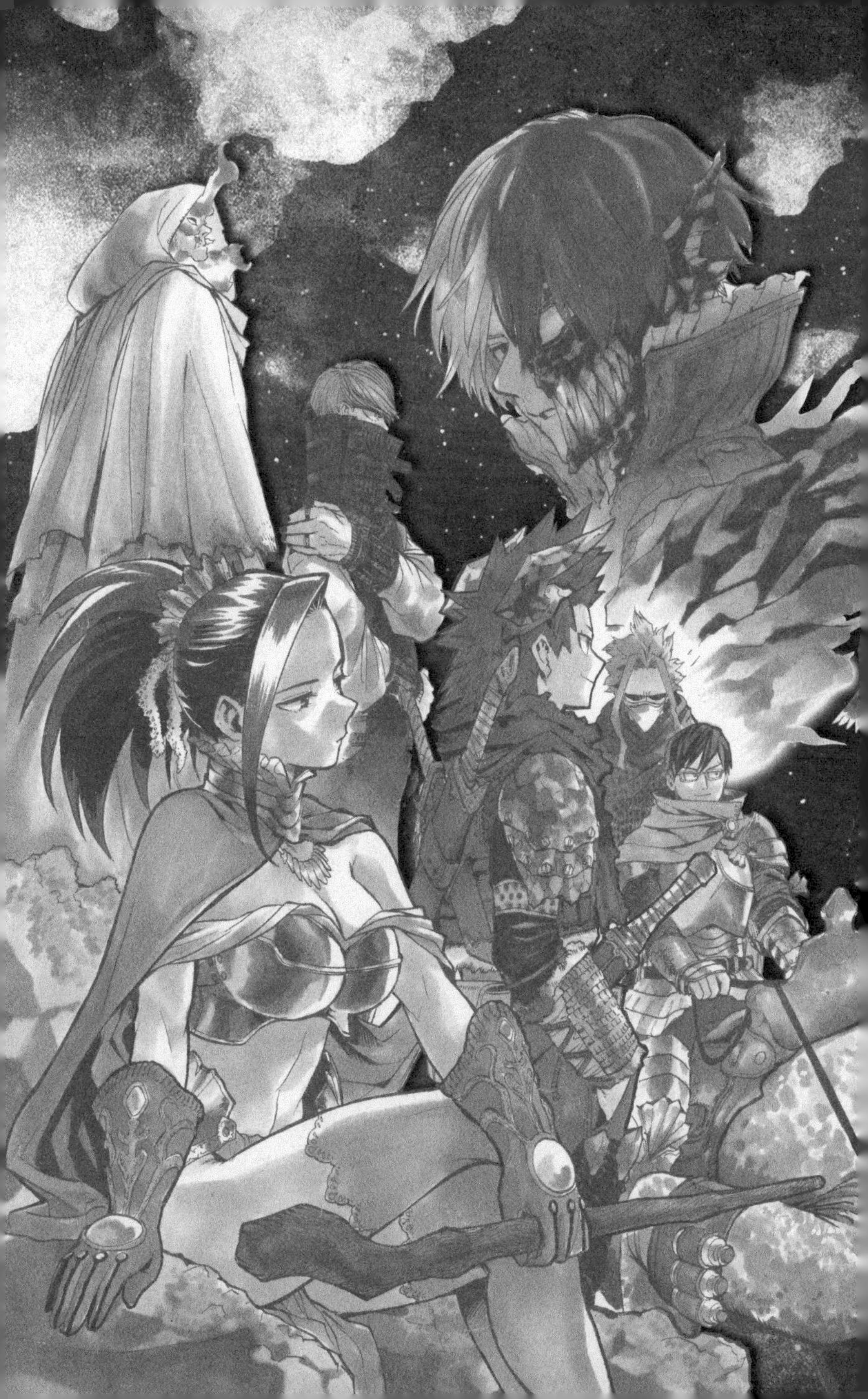

MY HERO ACADEMIA

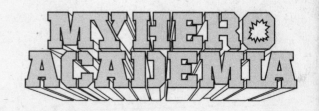

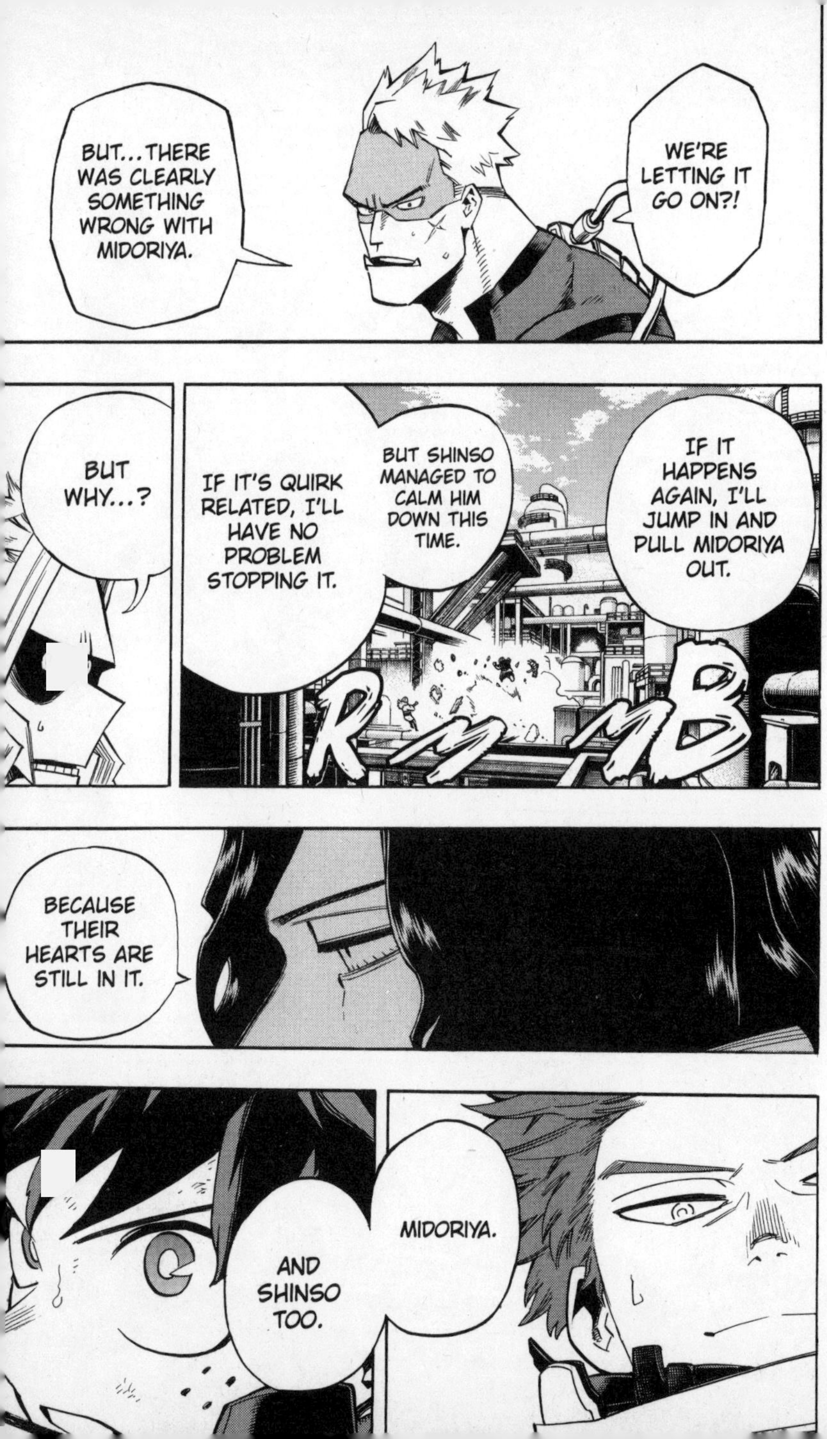
WE'RE LETTING IT GO ON?!
BUT...THERE WAS CLEARLY SOMETHING WRONG WITH MIDORIYA.
IF IT HAPPENS AGAIN, I'LL JUMP IN AND PULL MIDORIYA OUT.
BUT SHINSO MANAGED TO CALM HIM DOWN THIS TIME.
IF IT'S QUIRK RELATED, I'LL HAVE NO PROBLEM STOPPING IT.
RMMB
BUT WHY...?
BECAUSE THEIR HEARTS ARE STILL IN IT.
MIDORIYA.
AND SHINSO TOO.

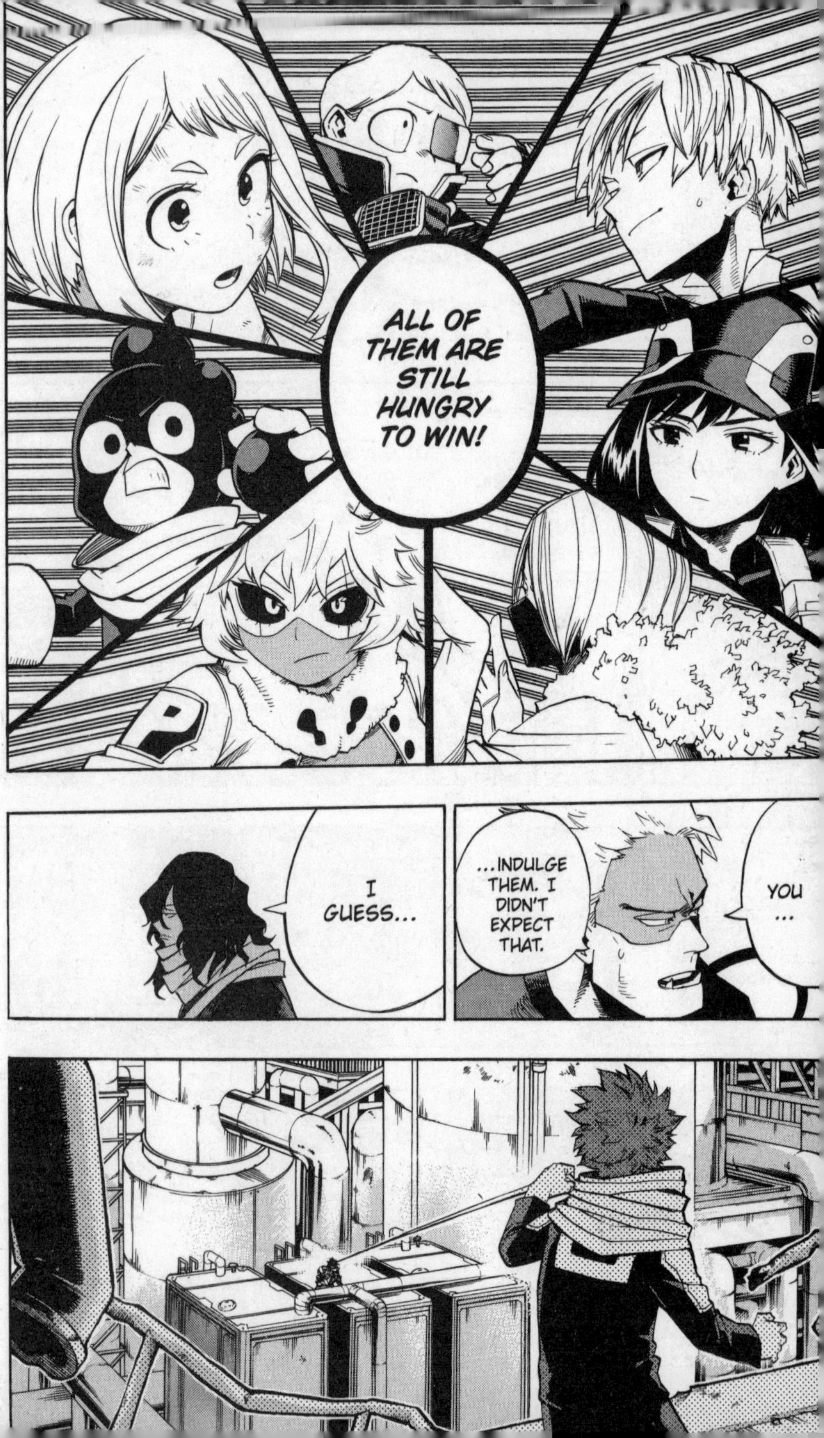
ALL OF THEM ARE STILL HUNGRY TO WIN!
YOU ...
...INDULGE THEM. I DIDN'T EXPECT THAT.
I GUESS...

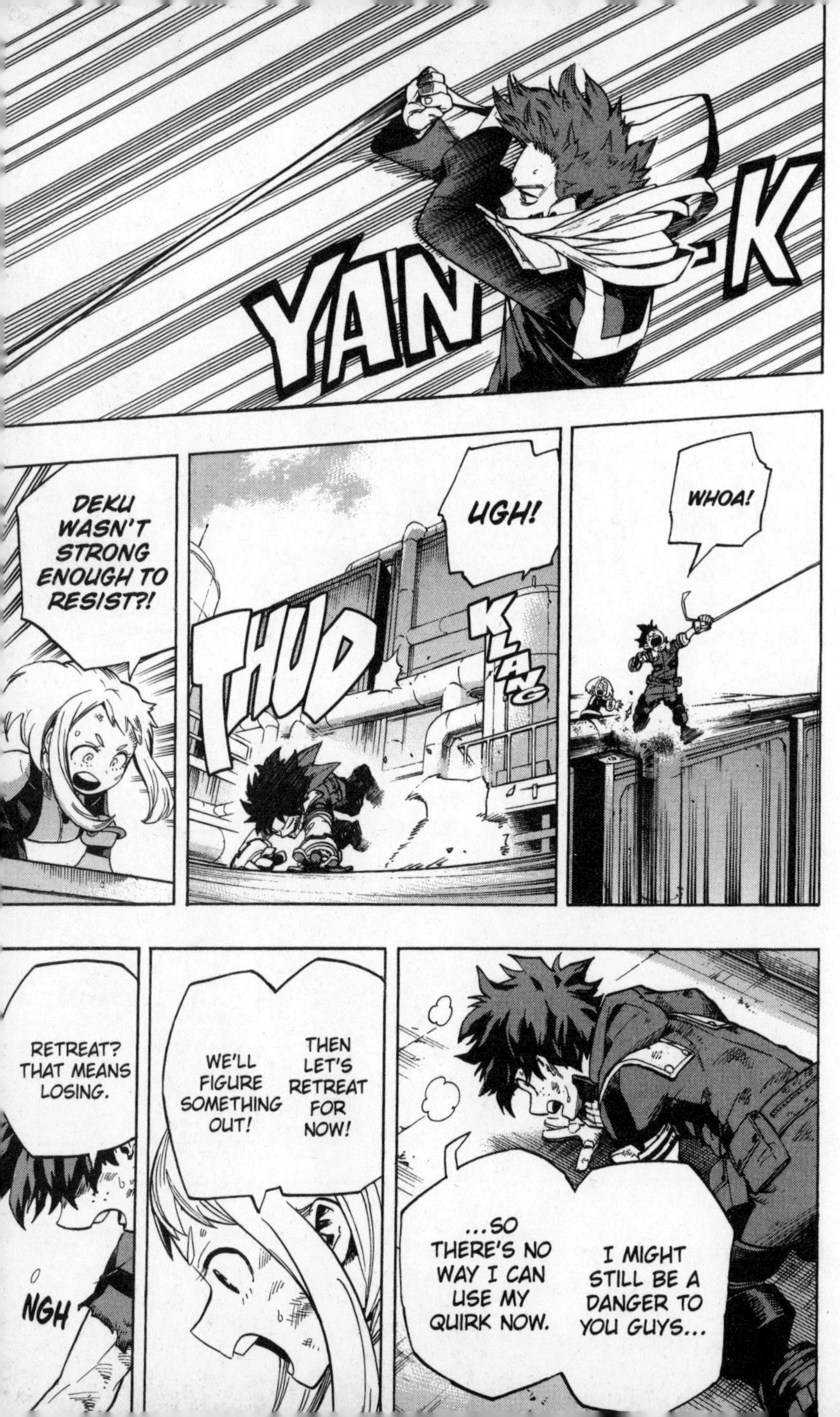
YANK
WHOA!
UGH!
KLANG
THUD
DEKU WASN'T STRONG ENOUGH TO RESIST?!
I MIGHT STILL BE A DANGER TO YOU GUYS...
...SO THERE'S NO WAY I CAN USE MY QUIRK NOW.
THEN LET'S RETREAT FOR NOW!
WE'LL FIGURE SOMETHING OUT!
RETREAT? THAT MEANS LOSING.
NGH

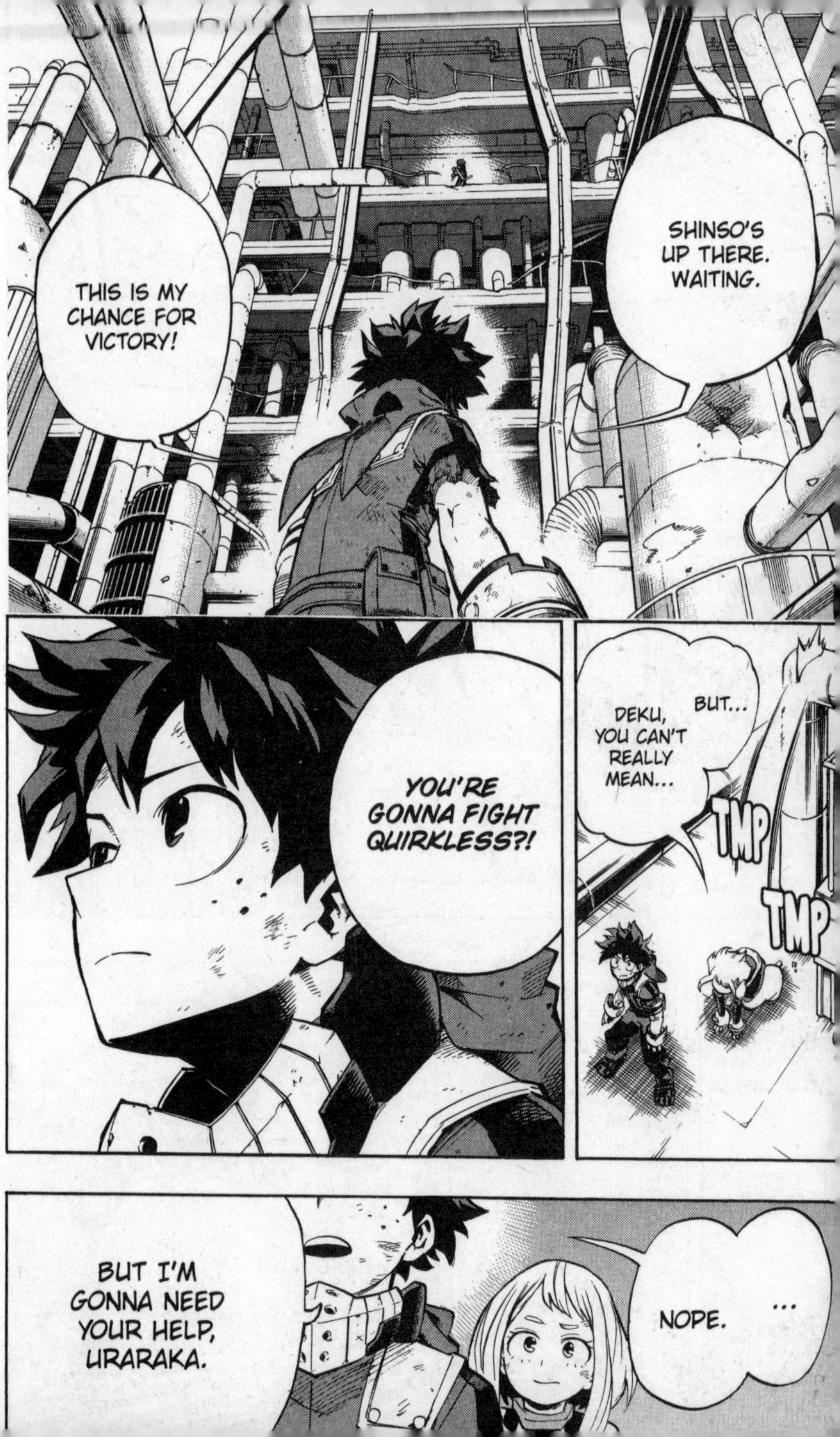
SHINSO'S UP THERE. WAITING.
THIS IS MY CHANCE FOR VICTORY!
BUT...
DEKU, YOU CAN'T REALLY MEAN...
TMP
TMP
YOU'RE GONNA FIGHT QUIRKLESS?!
...
NOPE.
BUT I'M GONNA NEED YOUR HELP, URARAKA.

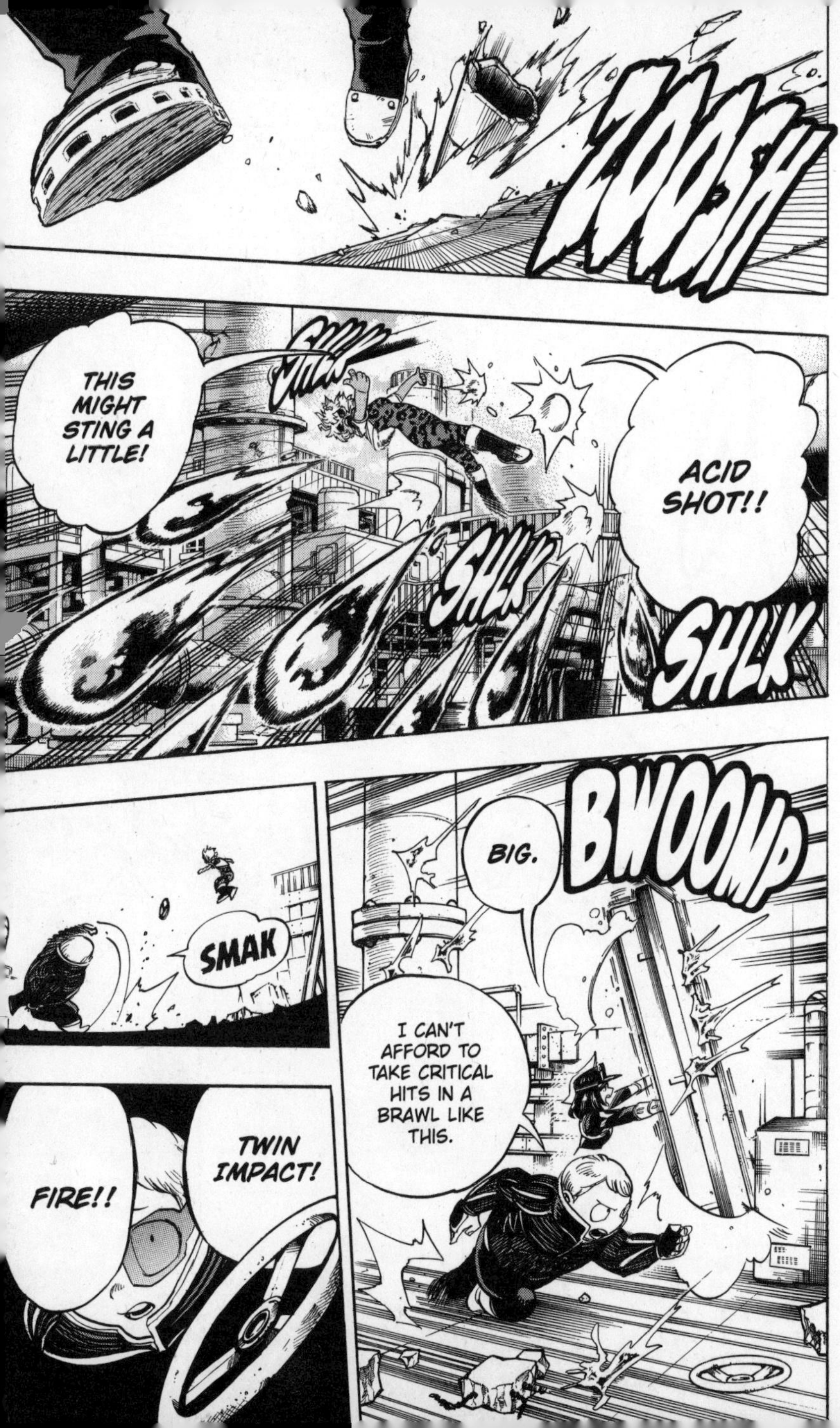

SHLK
ACID SHOT!!
SHLK
SHLK
THIS MIGHT STING A LITTLE!
BWOOMP
BIG.
I CAN'T AFFORD TO TAKE CRITICAL HITS IN A BRAWL LIKE THIS.
SMAK
TWIN IMPACT!
FIRE!!

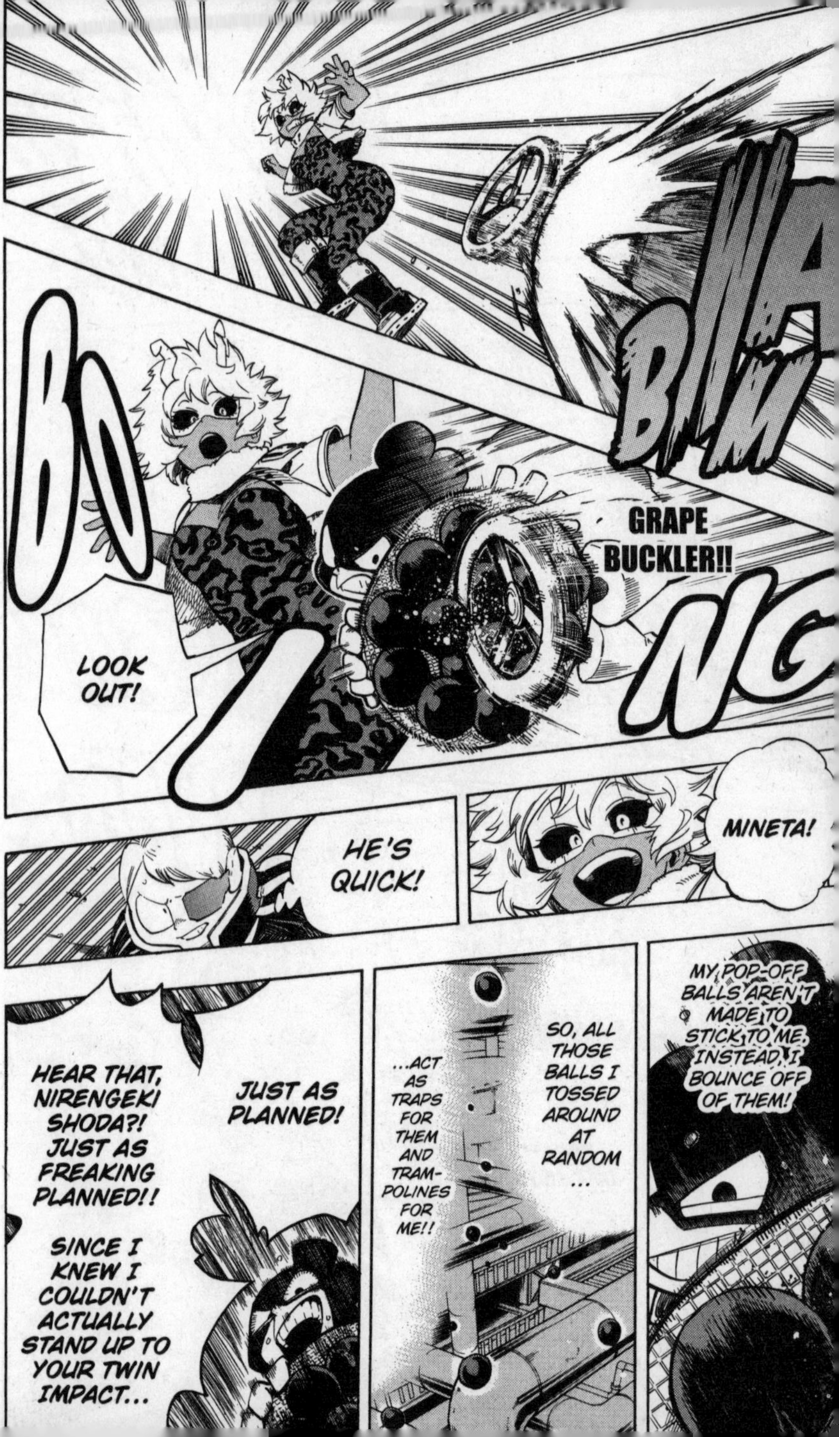
GRAPE BUCKLER!!
LOOK OUT!
MINETA!
HE'S QUICK!
MY POP-OFF BALLS AREN'T MADE TO STICK TO ME. INSTEAD, I BOUNCE OFF OF THEM!
SO, ALL THOSE BALLS I TOSSED AROUND AT RANDOM...
...ACT AS TRAPS FOR THEM AND TRAMPOLINES FOR ME!!
JUST AS PLANNED!
HEAR THAT, NIRENGEKI SHODA?! JUST AS FREAKING PLANNED!!
SINCE I KNEW I COULDN'T ACTUALLY STAND UP TO YOUR TWIN IMPACT...

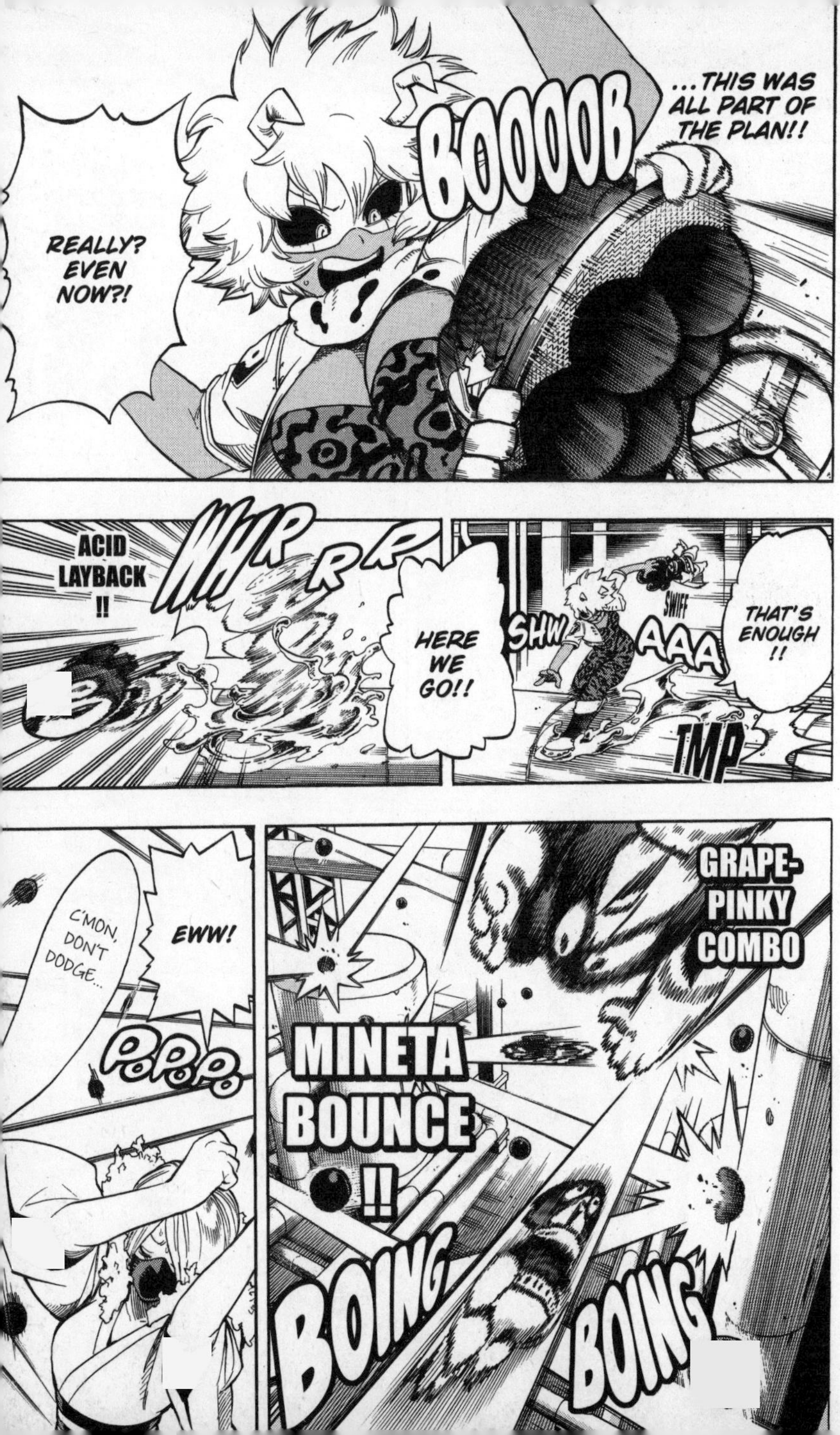
...THIS WAS ALL PART OF THE PLAN!!
BOOOOB
REALLY? EVEN NOW?!
THAT'S ENOUGH!!
SWIFF
AAA
SHW
TMP
HERE WE GO!!
WHIRRR
ACID LAYBACK!!
GRAPE-PINKY COMBO
MINETA BOUNCE!!
BOING
BOING
EWW!
C'MON, DON'T DODGE...
POPOPO

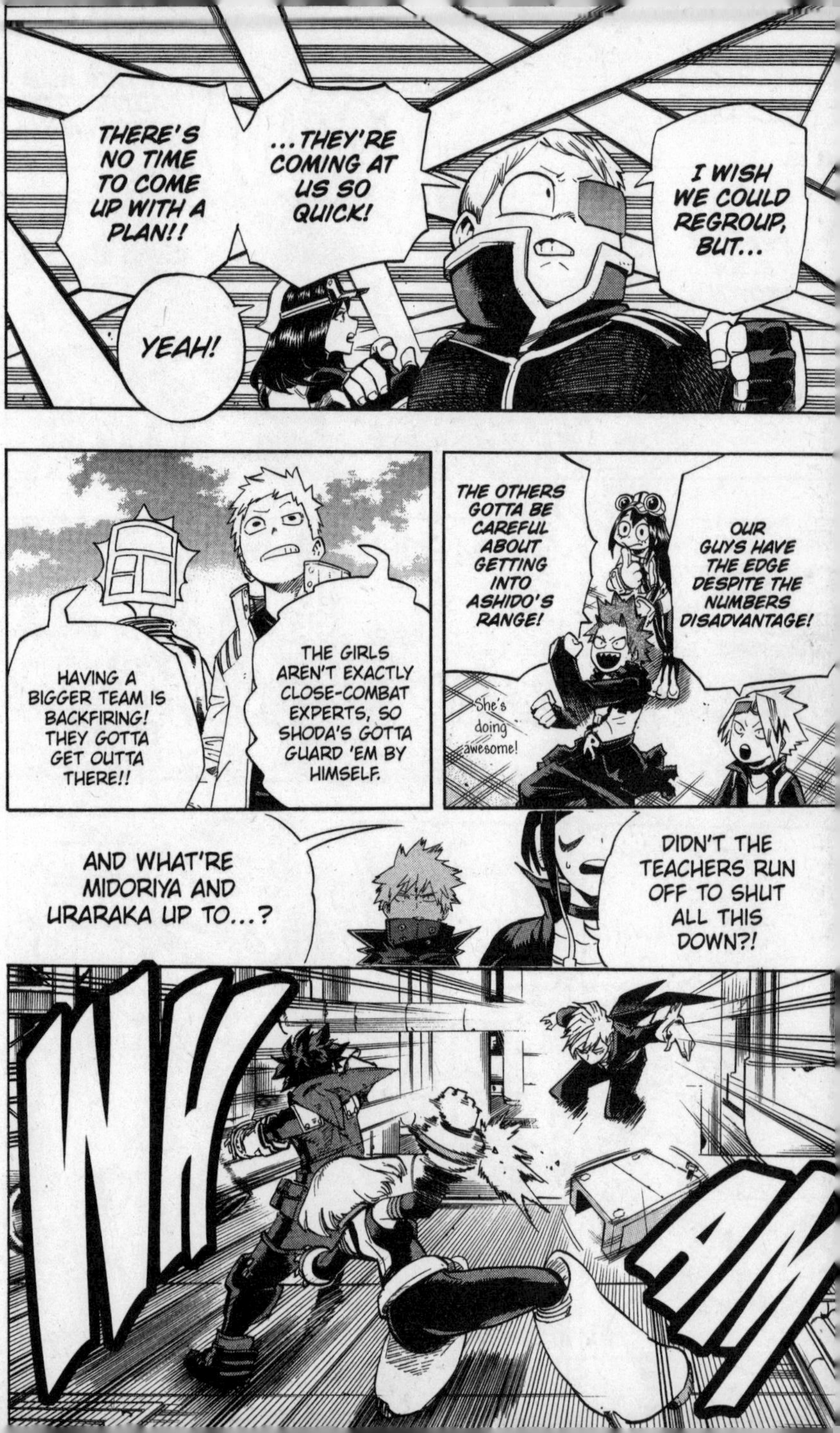
I WISH WE COULD REGROUP, BUT...
...THEY'RE COMING AT US SO QUICK!
THERE'S NO TIME TO COME UP WITH A PLAN!!
YEAH!
OUR GUYS HAVE THE EDGE DESPITE THE NUMBERS DISADVANTAGE!
THE OTHERS GOTTA BE CAREFUL ABOUT GETTING INTO ASHIDO'S RANGE!
She's doing awesome!
THE GIRLS AREN'T EXACTLY CLOSE-COMBAT EXPERTS, SO SHODA'S GOTTA GUARD 'EM BY HIMSELF.
HAVING A BIGGER TEAM IS BACKFIRING! THEY GOTTA GET OUTTA THERE!!
DIDN'T THE TEACHERS RUN OFF TO SHUT ALL THIS DOWN?!
AND WHAT'RE MIDORIYA AND URARAKA UP TO...?
WHAM

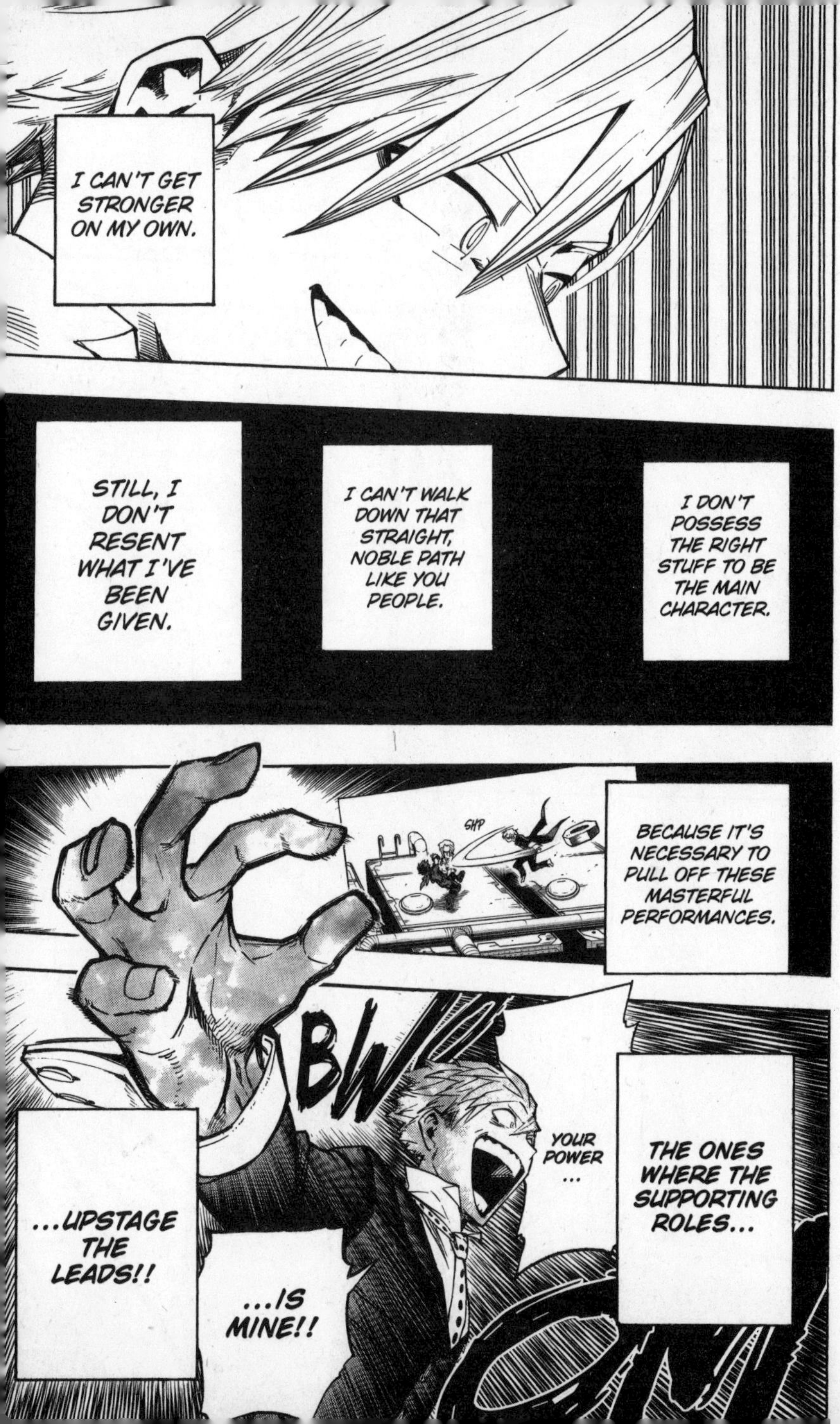
I CAN'T GET STRONGER ON MY OWN.
I DON'T POSSESS THE RIGHT STUFF TO BE THE MAIN CHARACTER.
I CAN'T WALK DOWN THAT STRAIGHT, NOBLE PATH LIKE YOU PEOPLE.
STILL, I DON'T RESENT WHAT I'VE BEEN GIVEN.
BECAUSE IT'S NECESSARY TO PULL OFF THESE MASTERFUL PERFORMANCES.
SHP
THE ONES WHERE THE SUPPORTING ROLES...
YOUR POWER ...
BW
...UPSTAGE THE LEADS!!
...IS MINE!!

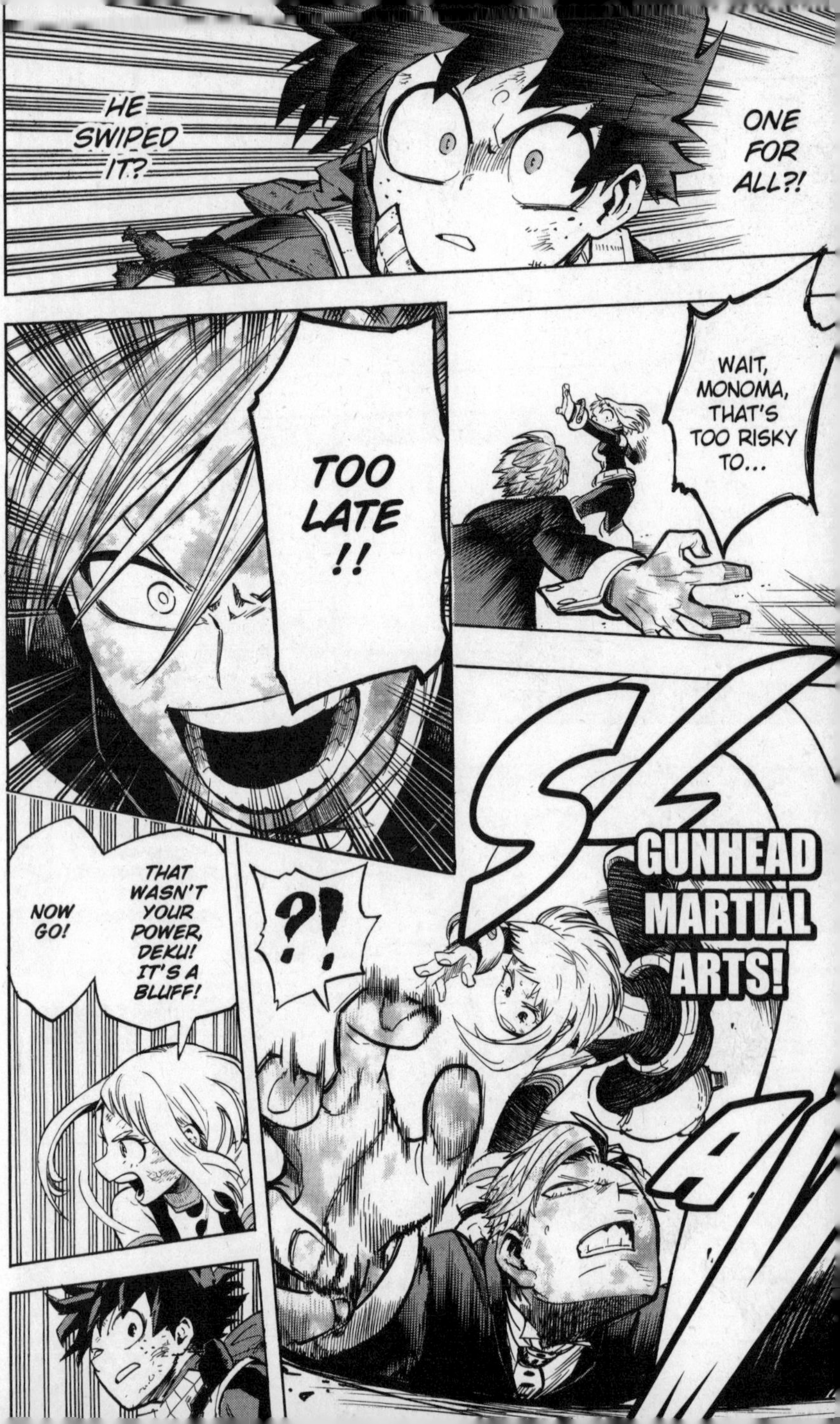
ONE FOR ALL?!
HE SWIPED IT?
WAIT, MONOMA, THAT'S TOO RISKY TO...
TOO LATE!!
GUNHEAD MARTIAL ARTS!
?!
THAT WASN'T YOUR POWER, DEKU! IT'S A BLUFF!
NOW GO!

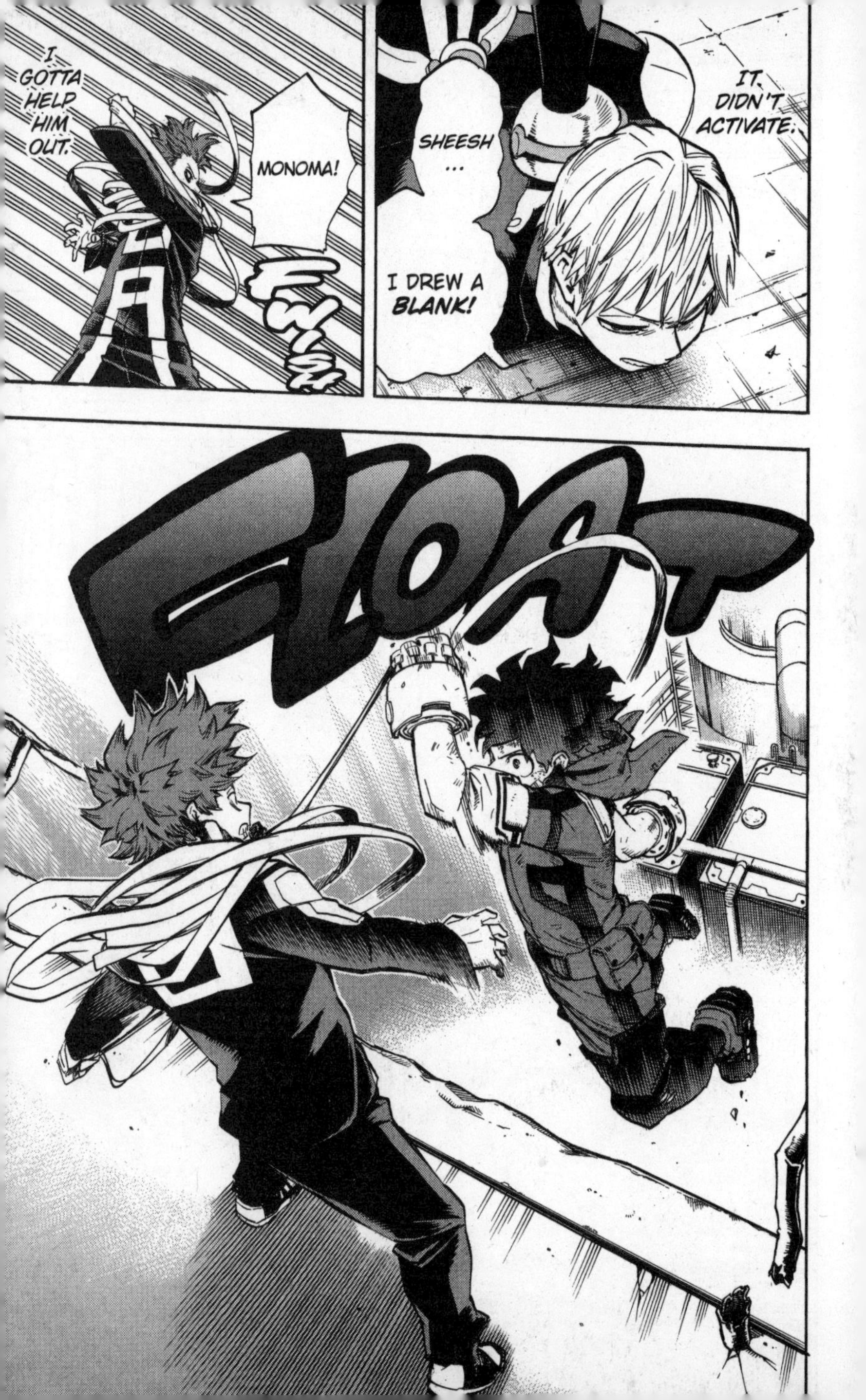
IT. DIDN'T ACTIVATE.
SHEESH ...
I DREW A BLANK!
MONOMA!
I GOTTA HELP HIM OUT.
FLOAT

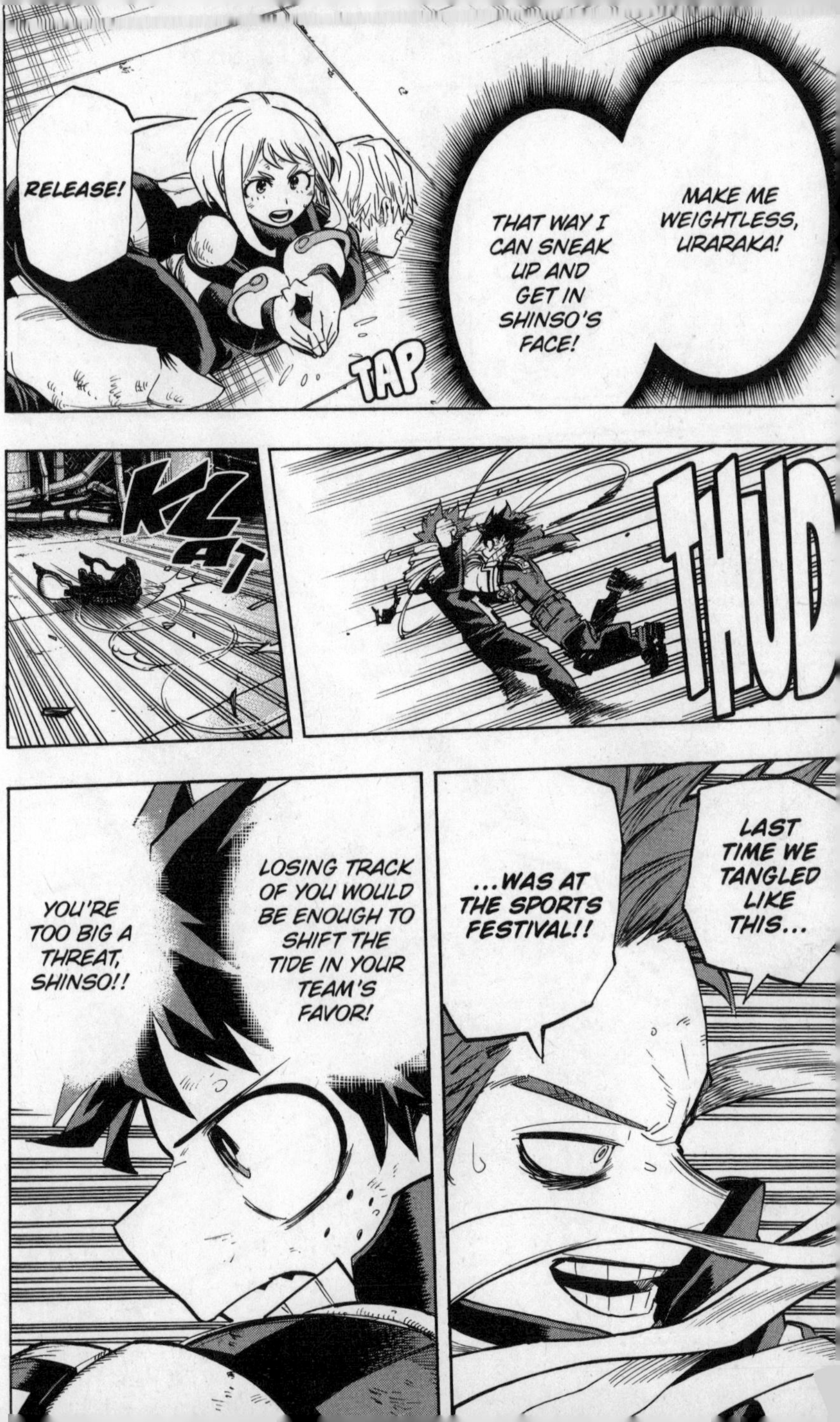
MAKE ME WEIGHTLESS, URARAKA!
THAT WAY I CAN SNEAK UP AND GET IN SHINSO'S FACE!
TAP
RELEASE!
THUD
KLAT
LAST TIME WE TANGLED LIKE THIS...
...WAS AT THE SPORTS FESTIVAL!!
LOSING TRACK OF YOU WOULD BE ENOUGH TO SHIFT THE TIDE IN YOUR TEAM'S FAVOR!
YOU'RE TOO BIG A THREAT, SHINSO!!

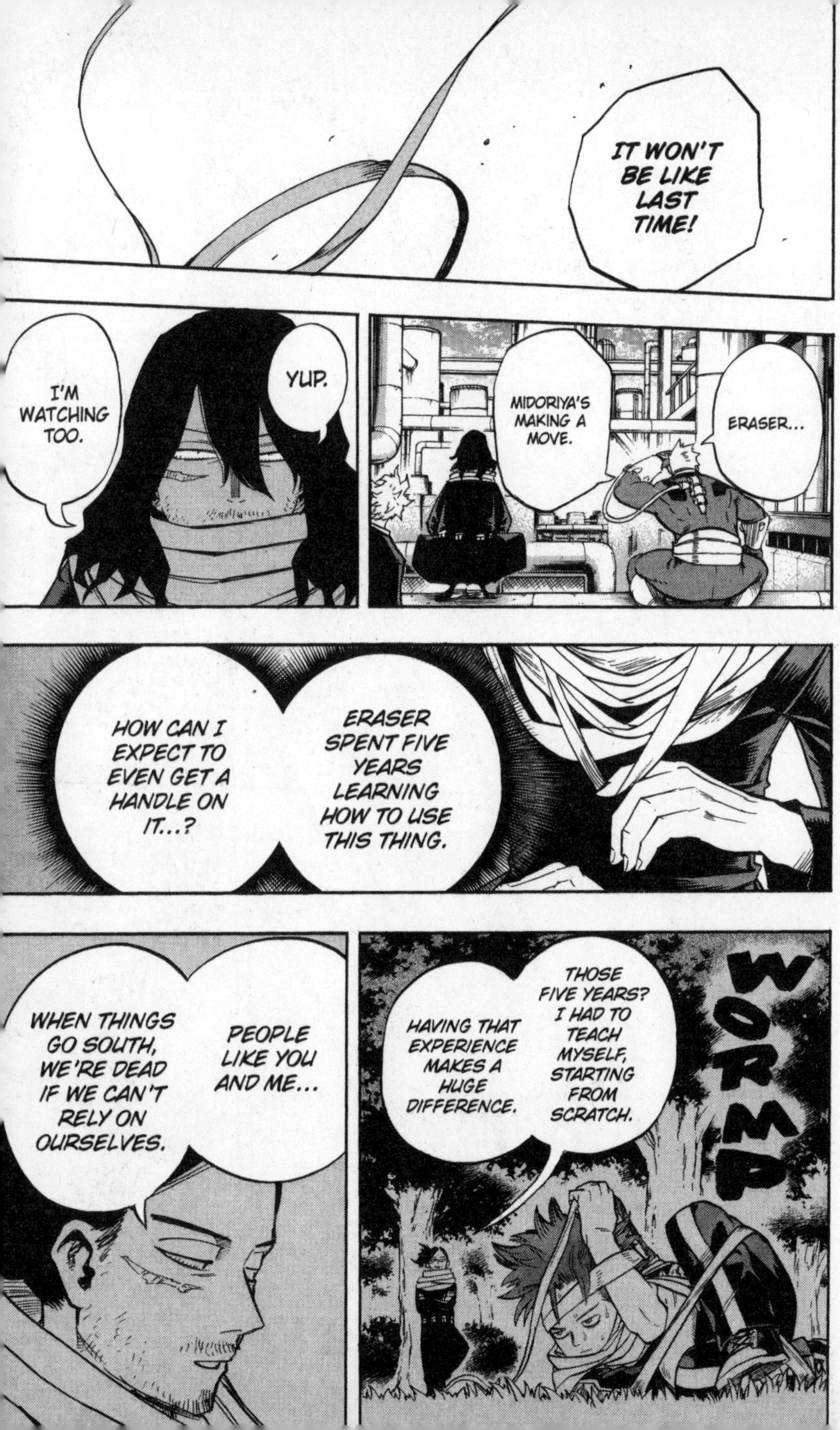
IT WON'T BE LIKE LAST TIME!
ERASER...
MIDORIYA'S MAKING A MOVE.
YUP.
I'M WATCHING TOO.
ERASER SPENT FIVE YEARS LEARNING HOW TO USE THIS THING.
HOW CAN I EXPECT TO EVEN GET A HANDLE ON IT...?
WORMP
THOSE FIVE YEARS? I HAD TO TEACH MYSELF, STARTING FROM SCRATCH.
HAVING THAT EXPERIENCE MAKES A HUGE DIFFERENCE.
PEOPLE LIKE YOU AND ME...
WHEN THINGS GO SOUTH, WE'RE DEAD IF WE CAN'T RELY ON OURSELVES.

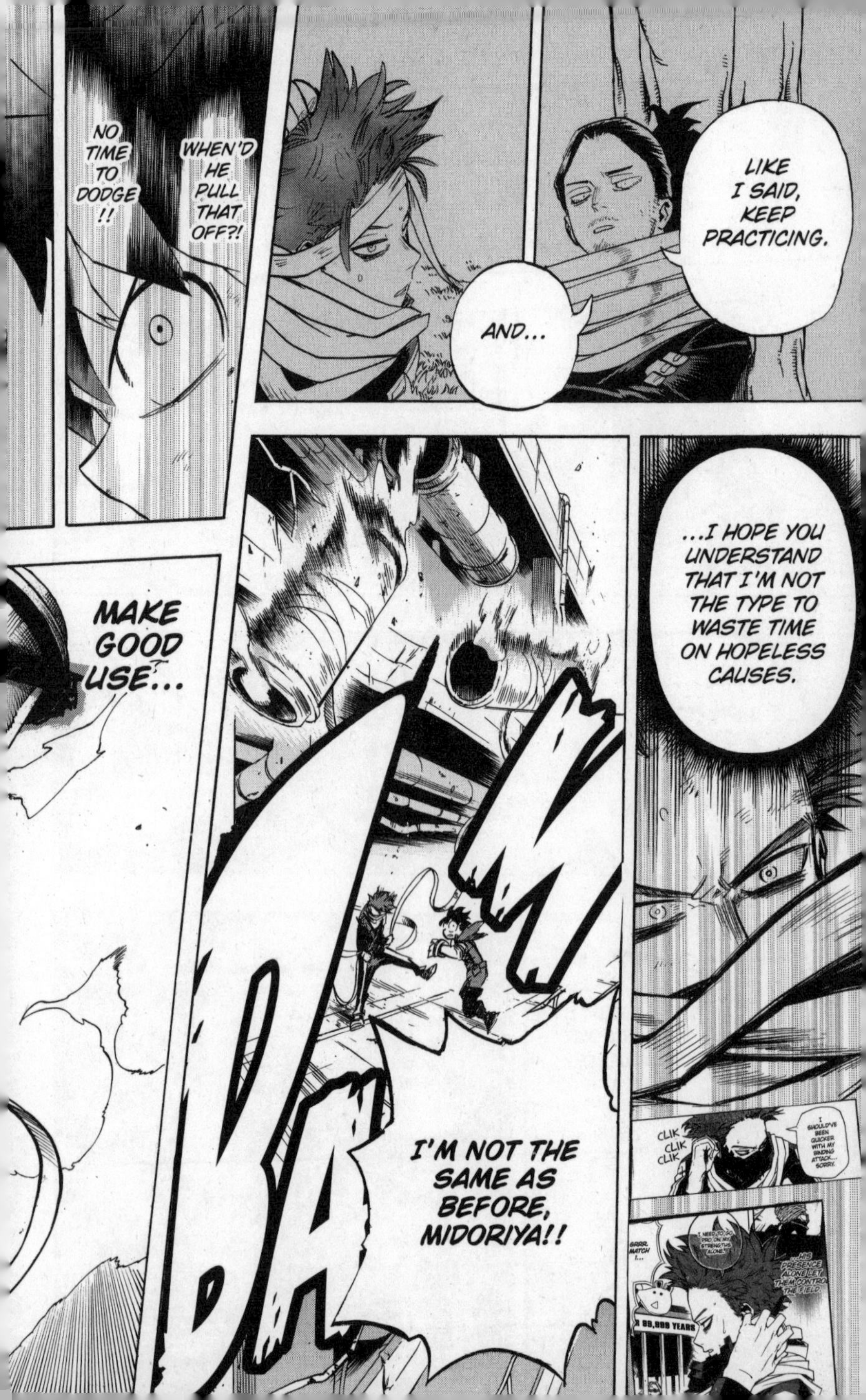
LIKE I SAID, KEEP PRACTICING.
AND...
NO TIME TO DODGE!!
WHEN'D HE PULL THAT OFF?!
...I HOPE YOU UNDERSTAND THAT I'M NOT THE TYPE TO WASTE TIME ON HOPELESS CAUSES.
I SHOULD'VE BEEN QUICKER WITH MY BINDING ATTACK... SORRY.
CLIK CLIK CLIK
...HIS PRESENCE ALONE LET THEM CONTRO THE FIELD.
I NEED TO GO PRO ON MY STRENGTHS ALONE.
GRRR. MATCH I...
99,999 YEARS
BAM
I'M NOT THE SAME AS BEFORE, MIDORIYA!!
MAKE GOOD USE...

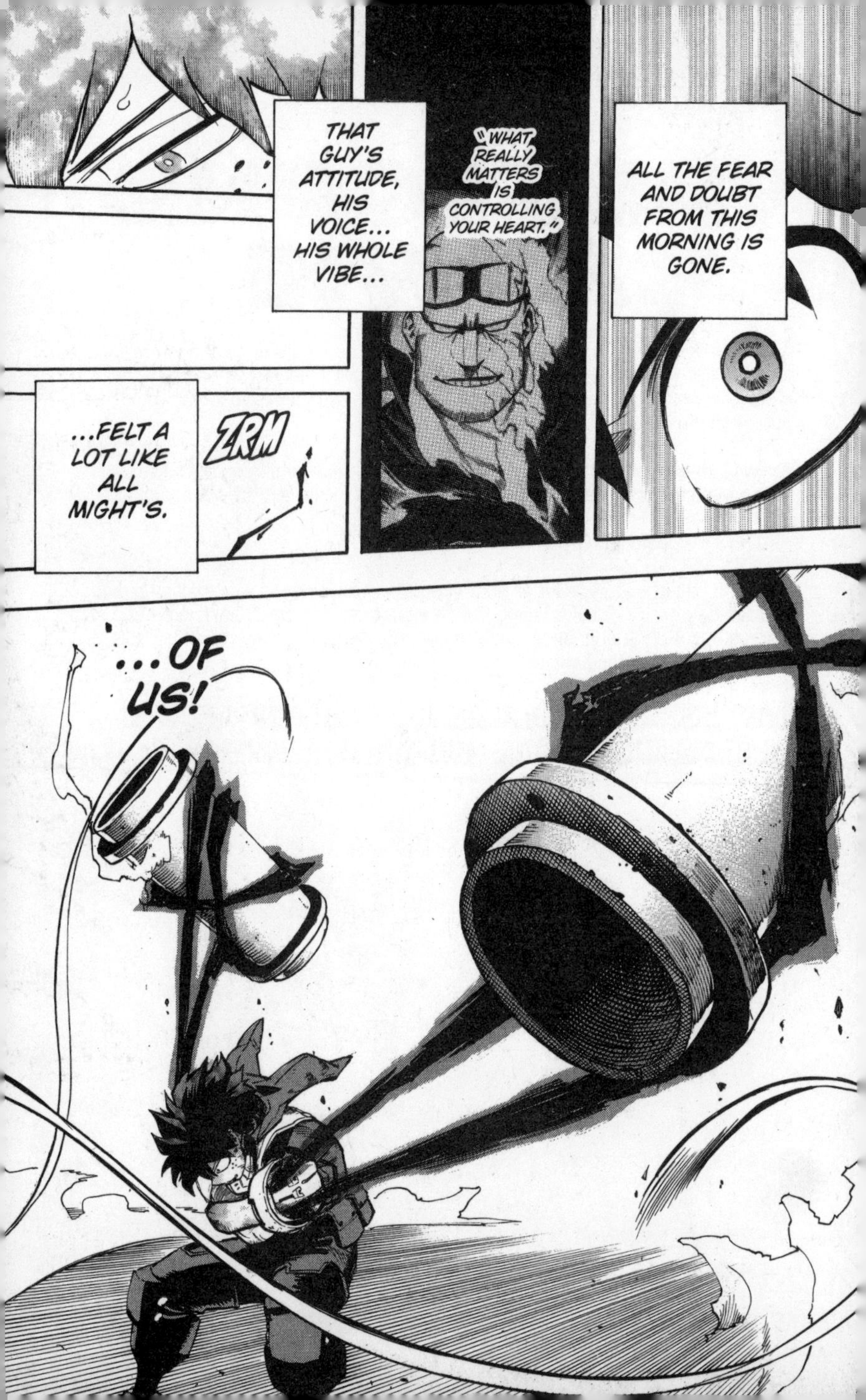
ALL THE FEAR AND DOUBT FROM THIS MORNING IS GONE.
"WHAT REALLY MATTERS IS CONTROLLING YOUR HEART."
THAT GUY'S ATTITUDE, HIS VOICE... HIS WHOLE VIBE...
...FELT A LOT LIKE ALL MIGHT'S.
ZRM
...OF US!

THE SECOND MOVIE

As I write this, it's 5:52 a.m. on March 31, 2019. They're going to announce the name of Japan's new imperial era in about 30 hours. I wonder what they'll choose? I hope they go with "onigiri era" or "bread era" because those would just put me in the mood for a snack. I guess I'm hungry.

Anyway, they've announced that *My Hero Academia* is getting a second movie! When the first movie came out last year, I thought, "This is it! My life has peaked!"

And now it's peaking AGAIN!

So thank you to everyone for all your support! I was involved with the first movie to a fair degree, but they're letting me be even more involved this time around. It also seems like the animation staff are pouring everything they've got into this, so I hope you're all getting excited!

The Second Movie: releasing winter of year 0 of whatever they end up calling this new era!!

P.S. They're calling the new era "Reiwa."
4/1/2019

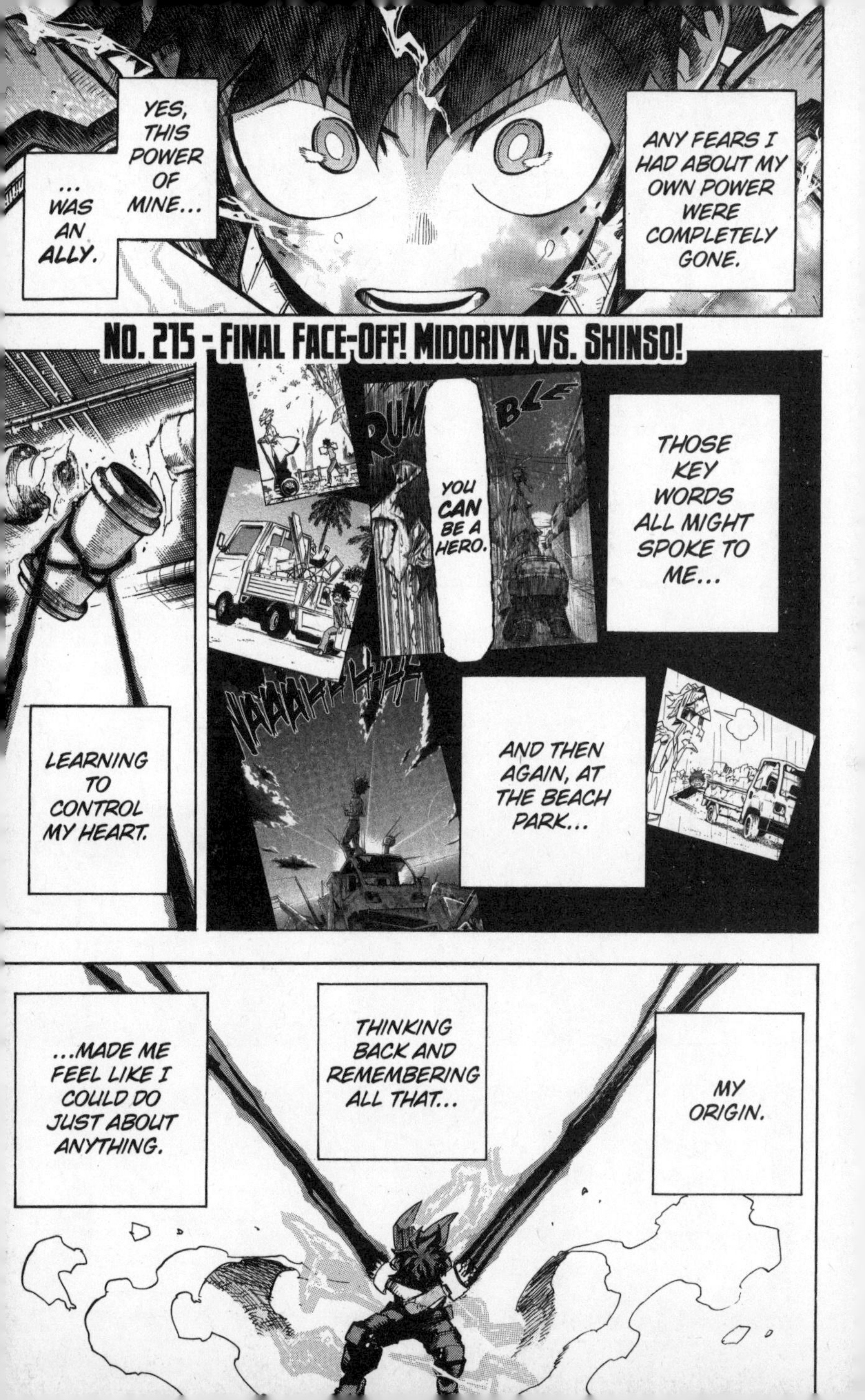
ANY FEARS I HAD ABOUT MY OWN POWER WERE COMPLETELY GONE.
YES, THIS POWER OF MINE...
...WAS AN ALLY.
NO. 215 - FINAL FACE-OFF! MIDORIYA VS. SHINSO!
THOSE KEY WORDS ALL MIGHT SPOKE TO ME...
RUMBLE
YOU CAN BE A HERO.
AND THEN AGAIN, AT THE BEACH PARK...
WAAAHHHH
LEARNING TO CONTROL MY HEART.
MY ORIGIN.
THINKING BACK AND REMEMBERING ALL THAT...
...MADE ME FEEL LIKE I COULD DO JUST ABOUT ANYTHING.

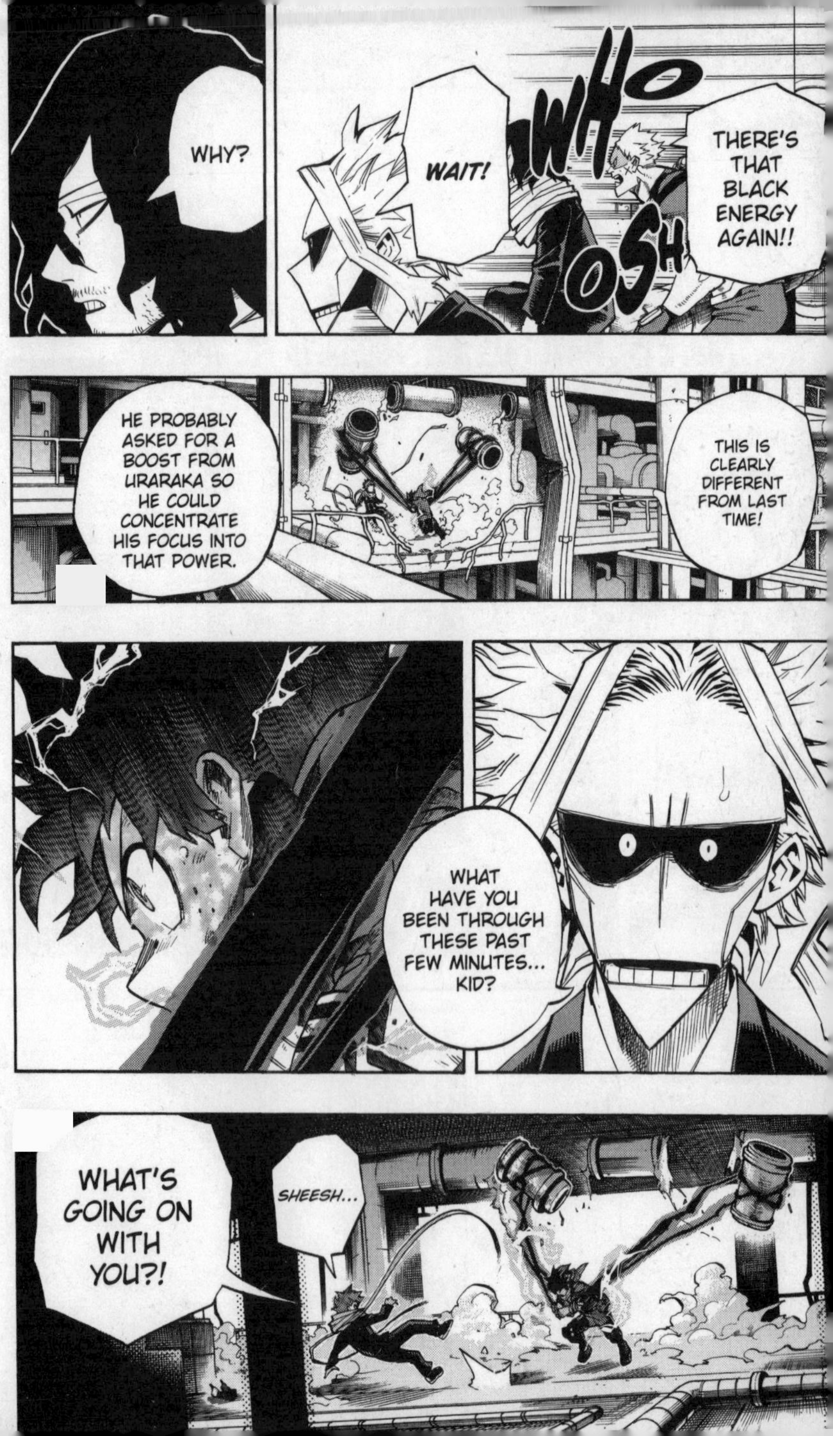
THERE'S THAT BLACK ENERGY AGAIN!!
WHOOSH
WAIT!
WHY?
THIS IS CLEARLY DIFFERENT FROM LAST TIME!
HE PROBABLY ASKED FOR A BOOST FROM URARAKA SO HE COULD CONCENTRATE HIS FOCUS INTO THAT POWER.
WHAT HAVE YOU BEEN THROUGH THESE PAST FEW MINUTES... KID?
SHEESH...
WHAT'S GOING ON WITH YOU?!

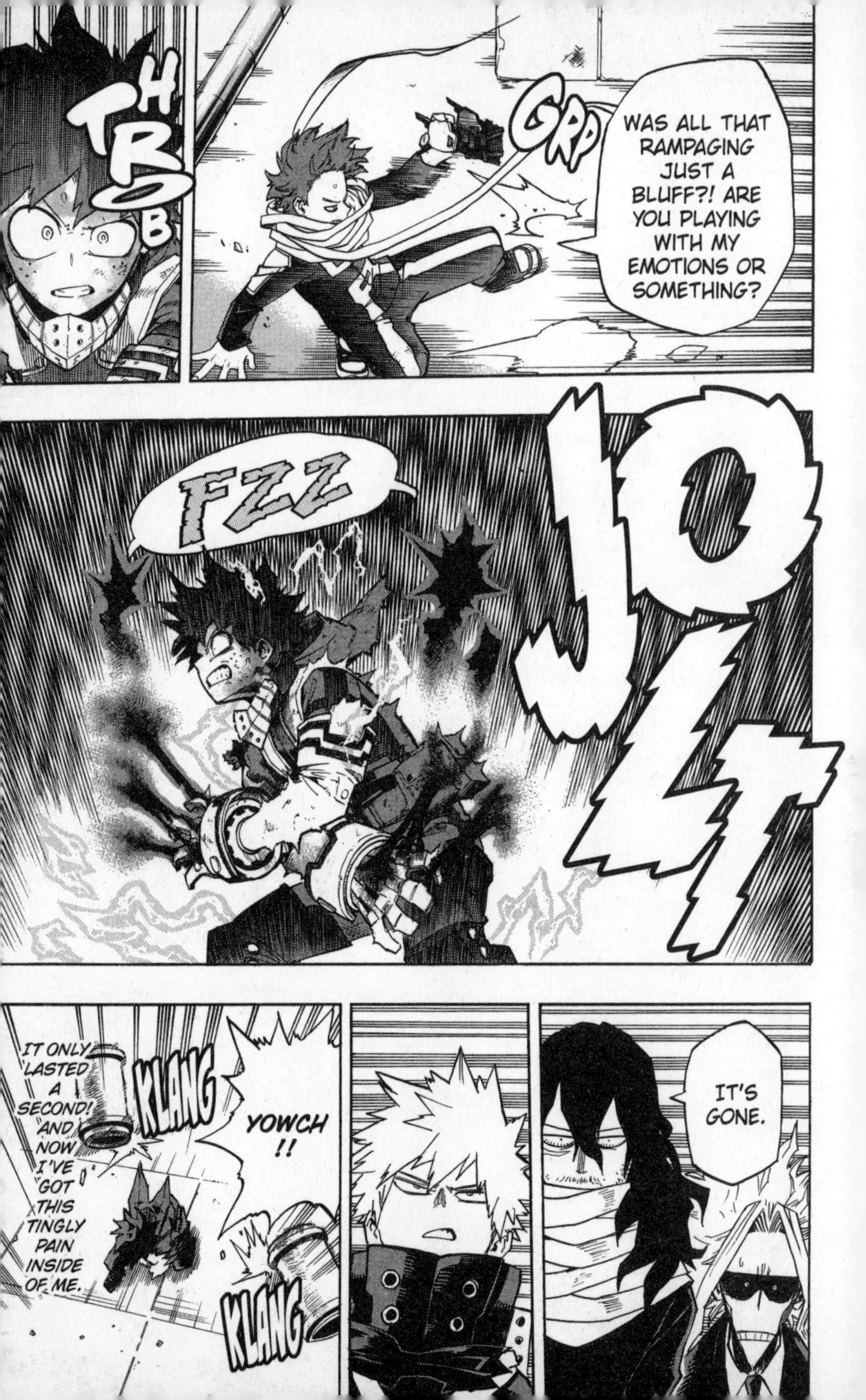
WAS ALL THAT RAMPAGING JUST A BLUFF?! ARE YOU PLAYING WITH MY EMOTIONS OR SOMETHING?
GRP
THROB
JOLT
FZZ
IT'S GONE.
KLANG
YOWCH!!
IT ONLY LASTED A SECOND! AND NOW I'VE GOT THIS TINGLY PAIN INSIDE OF ME.
KLANG

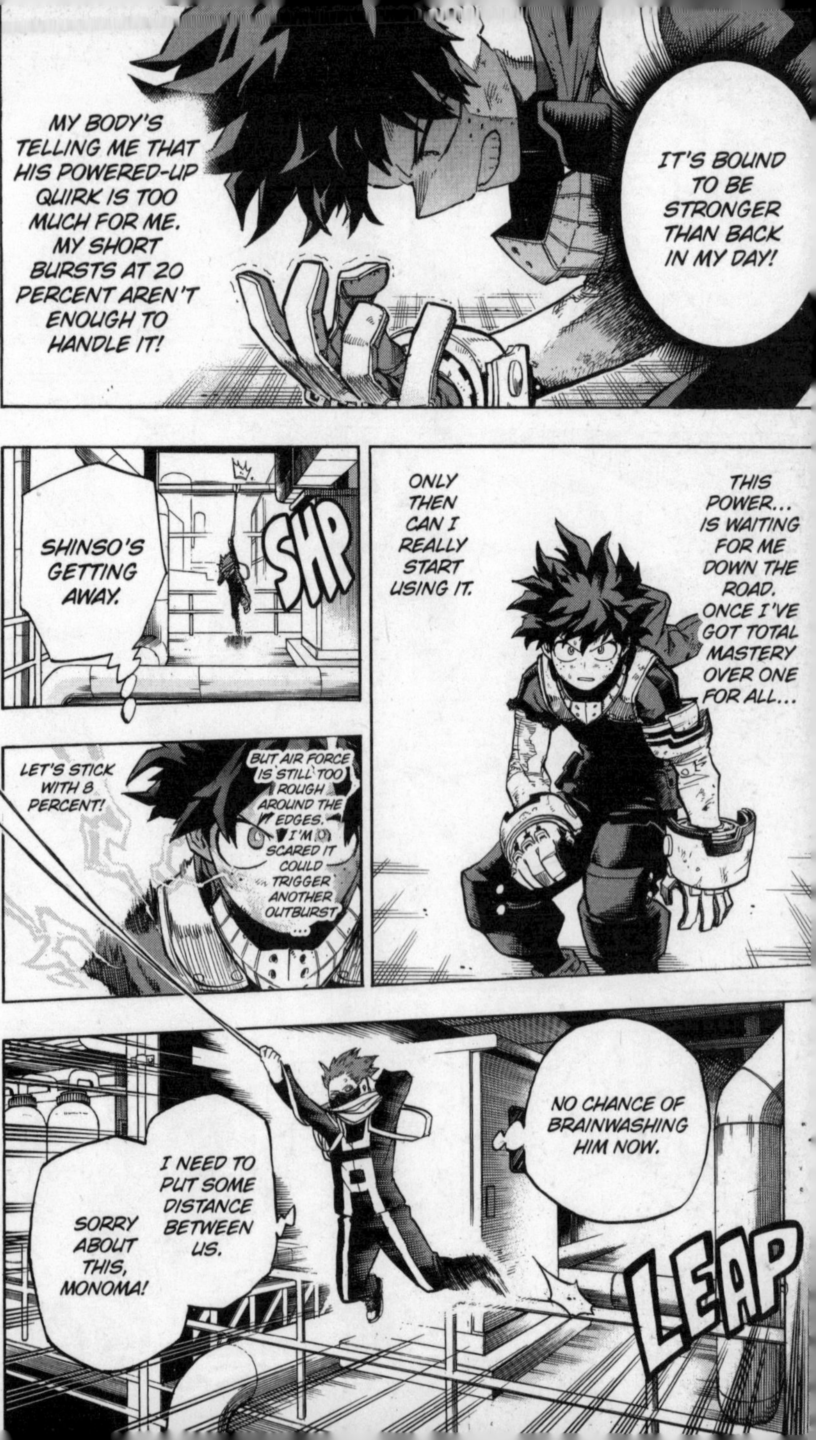
IT'S BOUND TO BE STRONGER THAN BACK IN MY DAY!
MY BODY'S TELLING ME THAT HIS POWERED-UP QUIRK IS TOO MUCH FOR ME. MY SHORT BURSTS AT 20 PERCENT AREN'T ENOUGH TO HANDLE IT!
THIS POWER... IS WAITING FOR ME DOWN THE ROAD. ONCE I'VE GOT TOTAL MASTERY OVER ONE FOR ALL...
ONLY THEN CAN I REALLY START USING IT.
SHP
SHINSO'S GETTING AWAY.
BUT AIR FORCE IS STILL TOO ROUGH AROUND THE EDGES. I'M SCARED IT COULD TRIGGER ANOTHER OUTBURST...
LET'S STICK WITH 8 PERCENT!
NO CHANCE OF BRAINWASHING HIM NOW.
LEAP
I NEED TO PUT SOME DISTANCE BETWEEN US.
SORRY ABOUT THIS, MONOMA!

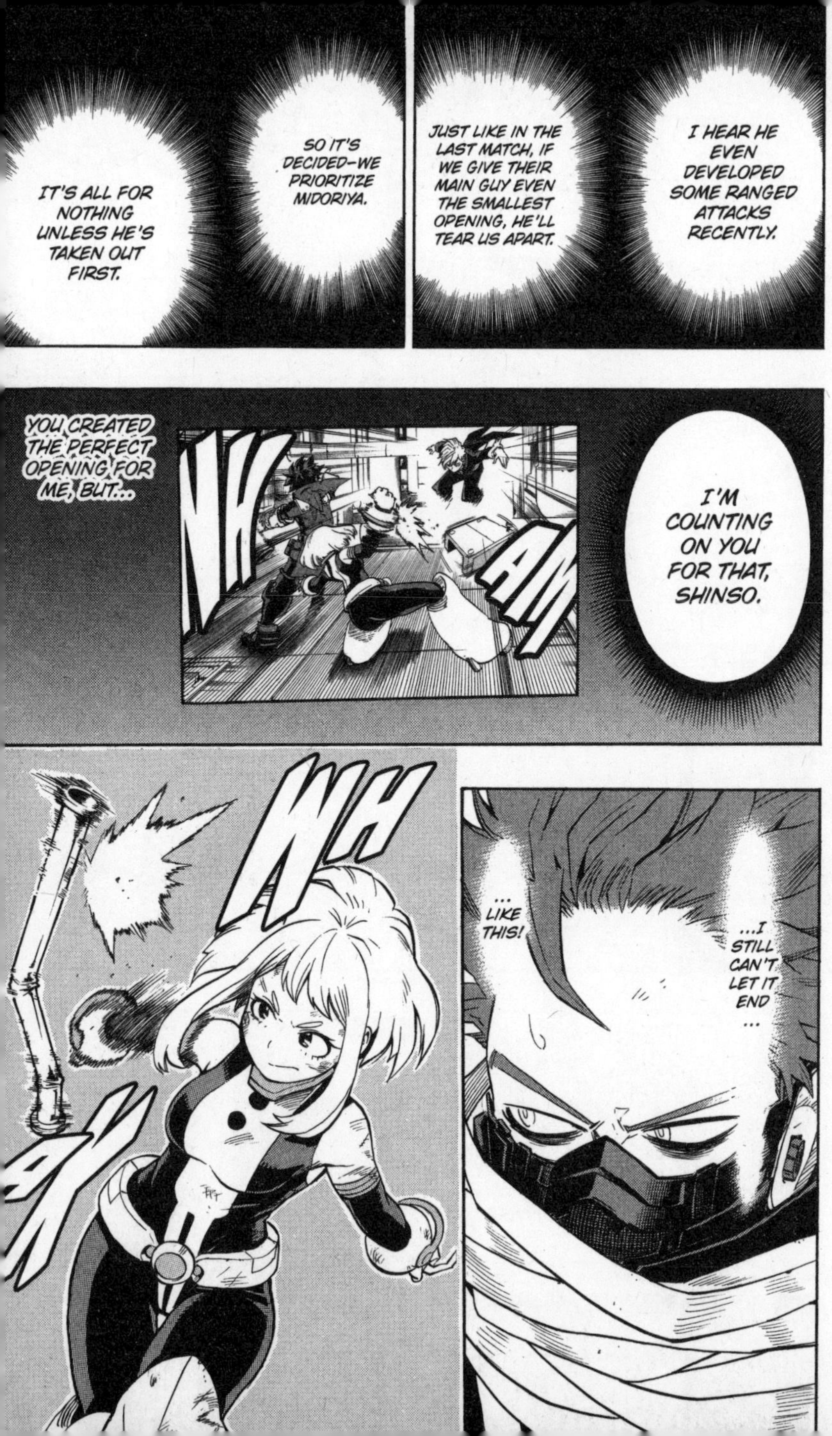
I HEAR HE EVEN DEVELOPED SOME RANGED ATTACKS RECENTLY.
JUST LIKE IN THE LAST MATCH, IF WE GIVE THEIR MAIN GUY EVEN THE SMALLEST OPENING, HE'LL TEAR US APART.
SO IT'S DECIDED—WE PRIORITIZE MIDORIYA.
IT'S ALL FOR NOTHING UNLESS HE'S TAKEN OUT FIRST.
I'M COUNTING ON YOU FOR THAT, SHINSO.
YOU CREATED THE PERFECT OPENING FOR ME, BUT...
...I STILL CAN'T LET IT END...
...LIKE THIS!

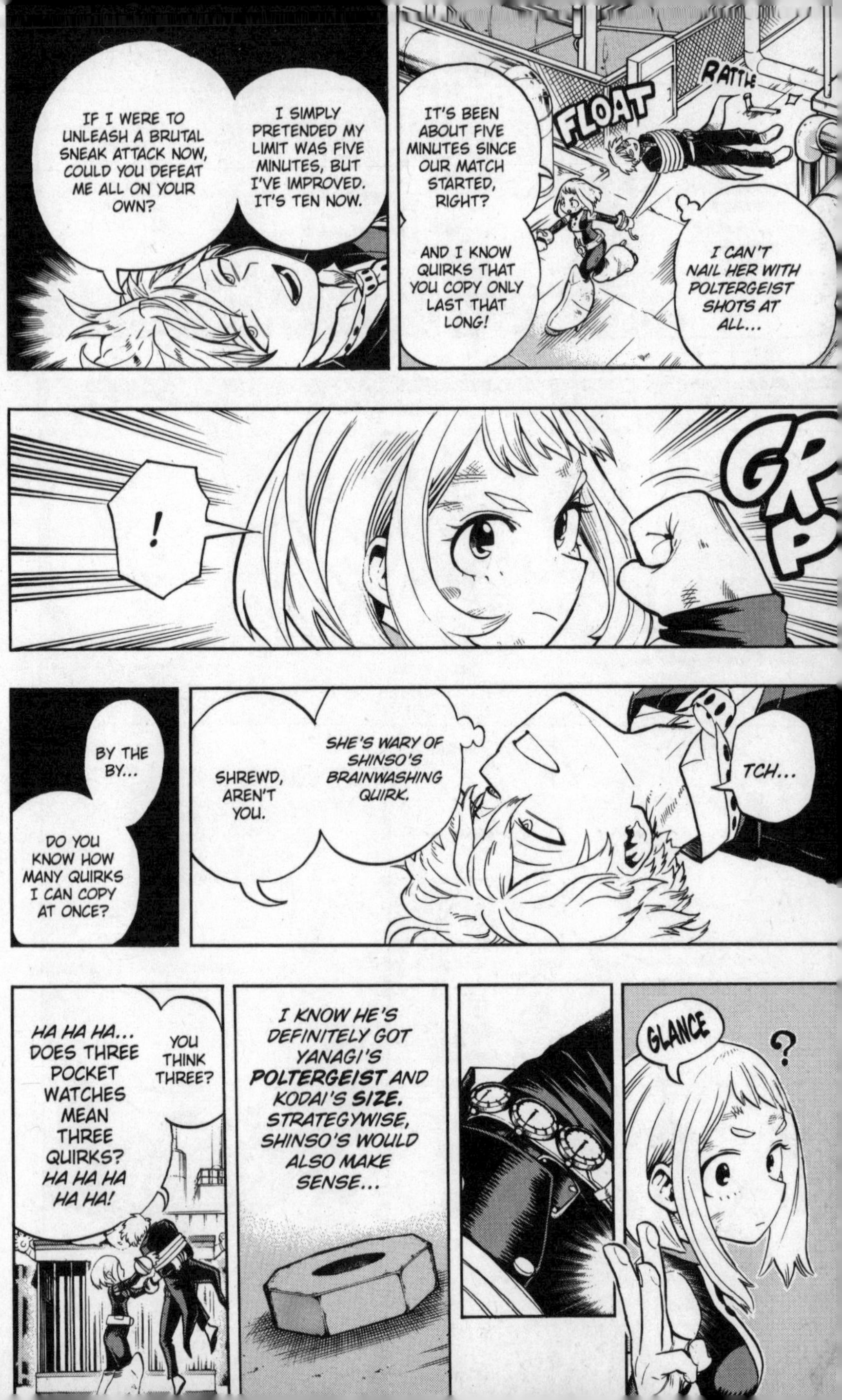

FLOAT
RATTLE
IT'S BEEN ABOUT FIVE MINUTES SINCE OUR MATCH STARTED, RIGHT?
AND I KNOW QUIRKS THAT YOU COPY ONLY LAST THAT LONG!
I CAN'T NAIL HER WITH POLTERGEIST SHOTS AT ALL...
I SIMPLY PRETENDED MY LIMIT WAS FIVE MINUTES, BUT I'VE IMPROVED. IT'S TEN NOW.
IF I WERE TO UNLEASH A BRUTAL SNEAK ATTACK NOW, COULD YOU DEFEAT ME ALL ON YOUR OWN?
GRIP
!
TCH...
SHE'S WARY OF SHINSO'S BRAINWASHING QUIRK.
SHREWD, AREN'T YOU.
BY THE BY...
DO YOU KNOW HOW MANY QUIRKS I CAN COPY AT ONCE?
GLANCE
?
I KNOW HE'S DEFINITELY GOT YANAGI'S **POLTERGEIST** AND KODAI'S **SIZE.** STRATEGYWISE, SHINSO'S WOULD ALSO MAKE SENSE...
YOU THINK THREE?
HA HA HA... DOES THREE POCKET WATCHES MEAN THREE QUIRKS? HA HA HA HA HA!

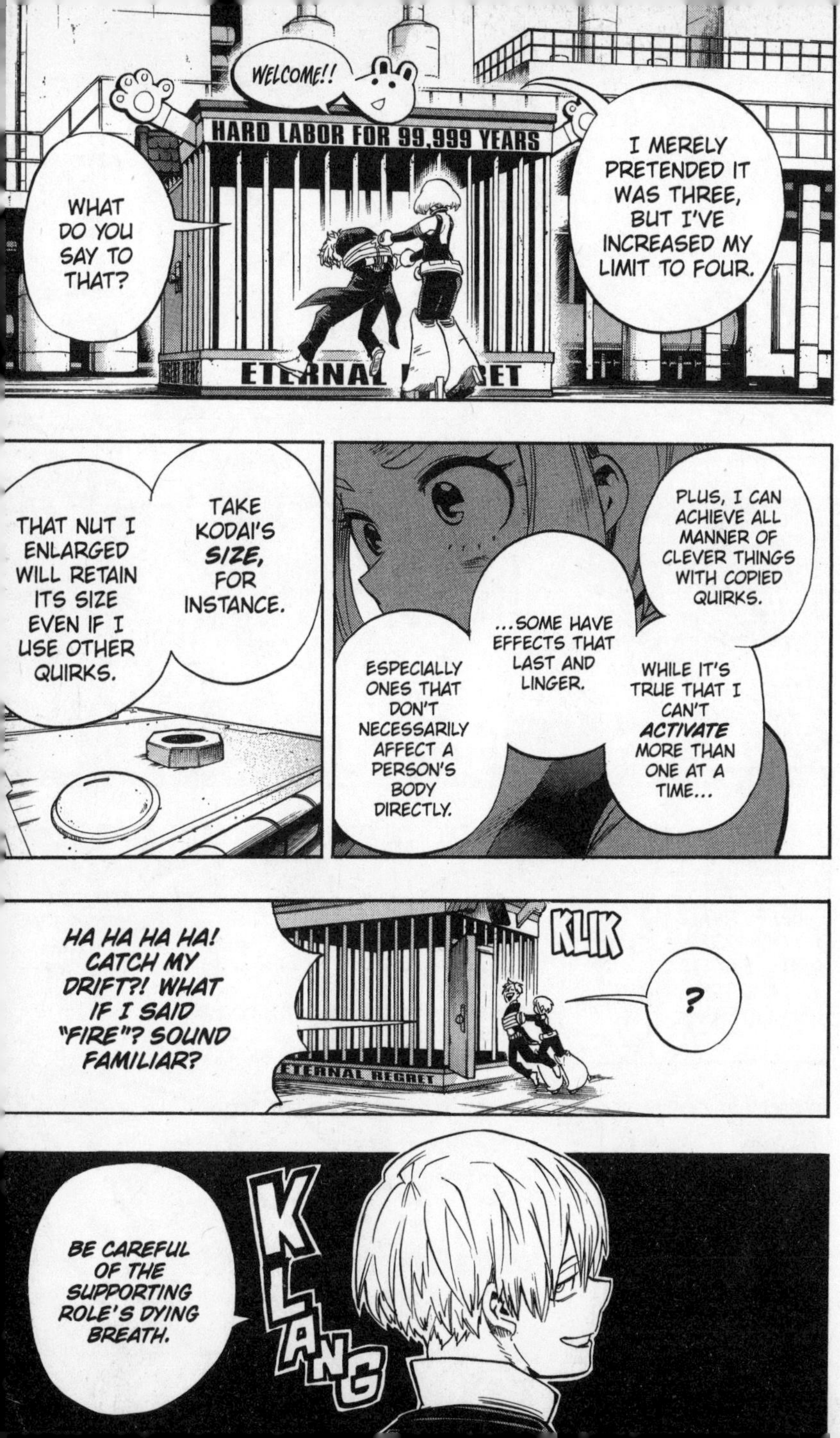
WELCOME!!
HARD LABOR FOR 99,999 YEARS
I MERELY PRETENDED IT WAS THREE, BUT I'VE INCREASED MY LIMIT TO FOUR.
WHAT DO YOU SAY TO THAT?
PLUS, I CAN ACHIEVE ALL MANNER OF CLEVER THINGS WITH COPIED QUIRKS.
WHILE IT'S TRUE THAT I CAN'T ACTIVATE MORE THAN ONE AT A TIME...
...SOME HAVE EFFECTS THAT LAST AND LINGER.
ESPECIALLY ONES THAT DON'T NECESSARILY AFFECT A PERSON'S BODY DIRECTLY.
TAKE KODAI'S SIZE, FOR INSTANCE.
THAT NUT I ENLARGED WILL RETAIN ITS SIZE EVEN IF I USE OTHER QUIRKS.
KLIK
?
HA HA HA HA! CATCH MY DRIFT?! WHAT IF I SAID "FIRE"? SOUND FAMILIAR?
ETERNAL REGRET
KLANG
BE CAREFUL OF THE SUPPORTING ROLE'S DYING BREATH.

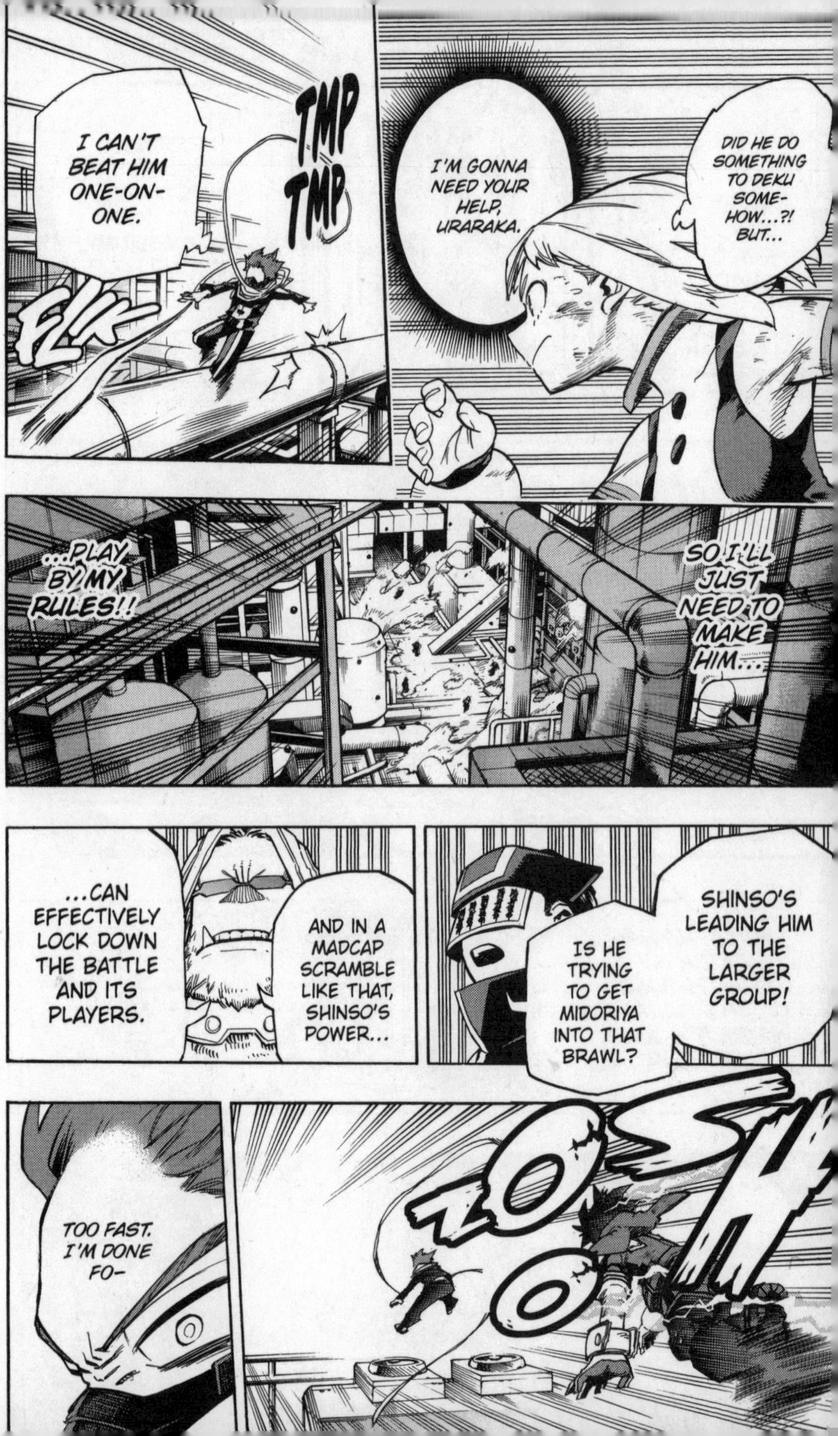
DID HE DO SOMETHING TO DEKU SOME-HOW...?! BUT...
I'M GONNA NEED YOUR HELP, URARAKA.
TMP TMP
I CAN'T BEAT HIM ONE-ON-ONE.
FLIK
SO I'LL JUST NEED TO MAKE HIM...
...PLAY BY MY RULES!!
SHINSO'S LEADING HIM TO THE LARGER GROUP!
IS HE TRYING TO GET MIDORIYA INTO THAT BRAWL?
AND IN A MADCAP SCRAMBLE LIKE THAT, SHINSO'S POWER...
...CAN EFFECTIVELY LOCK DOWN THE BATTLE AND ITS PLAYERS.
ZOOSH
TOO FAST. I'M DONE FO-

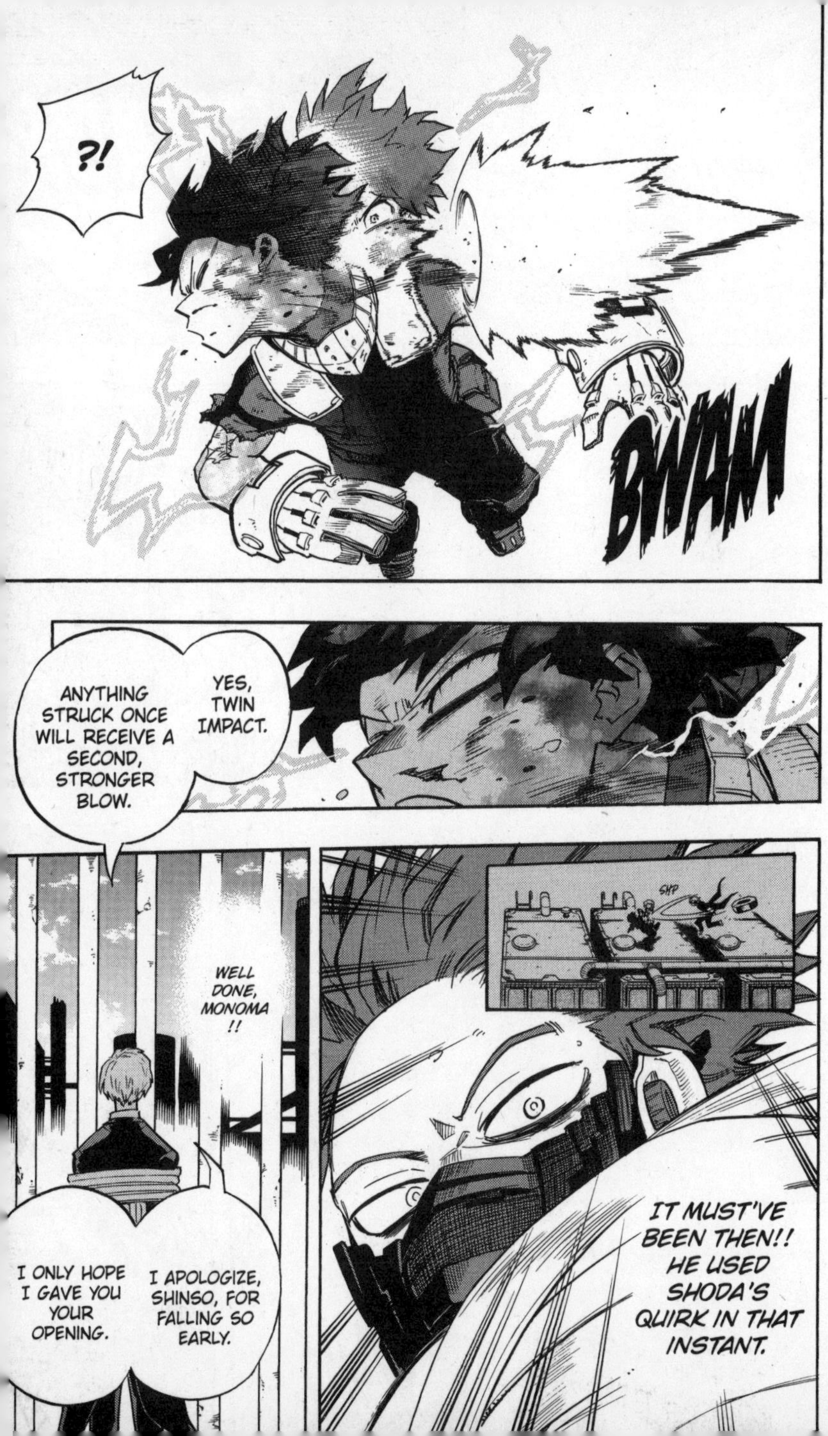
?!
BWAM
YES, TWIN IMPACT.
ANYTHING STRUCK ONCE WILL RECEIVE A SECOND, STRONGER BLOW.
SHP
IT MUST'VE BEEN THEN!! HE USED SHODA'S QUIRK IN THAT INSTANT.
WELL DONE, MONOMA!!
I APOLOGIZE, SHINSO, FOR FALLING SO EARLY.
I ONLY HOPE I GAVE YOU YOUR OPENING.

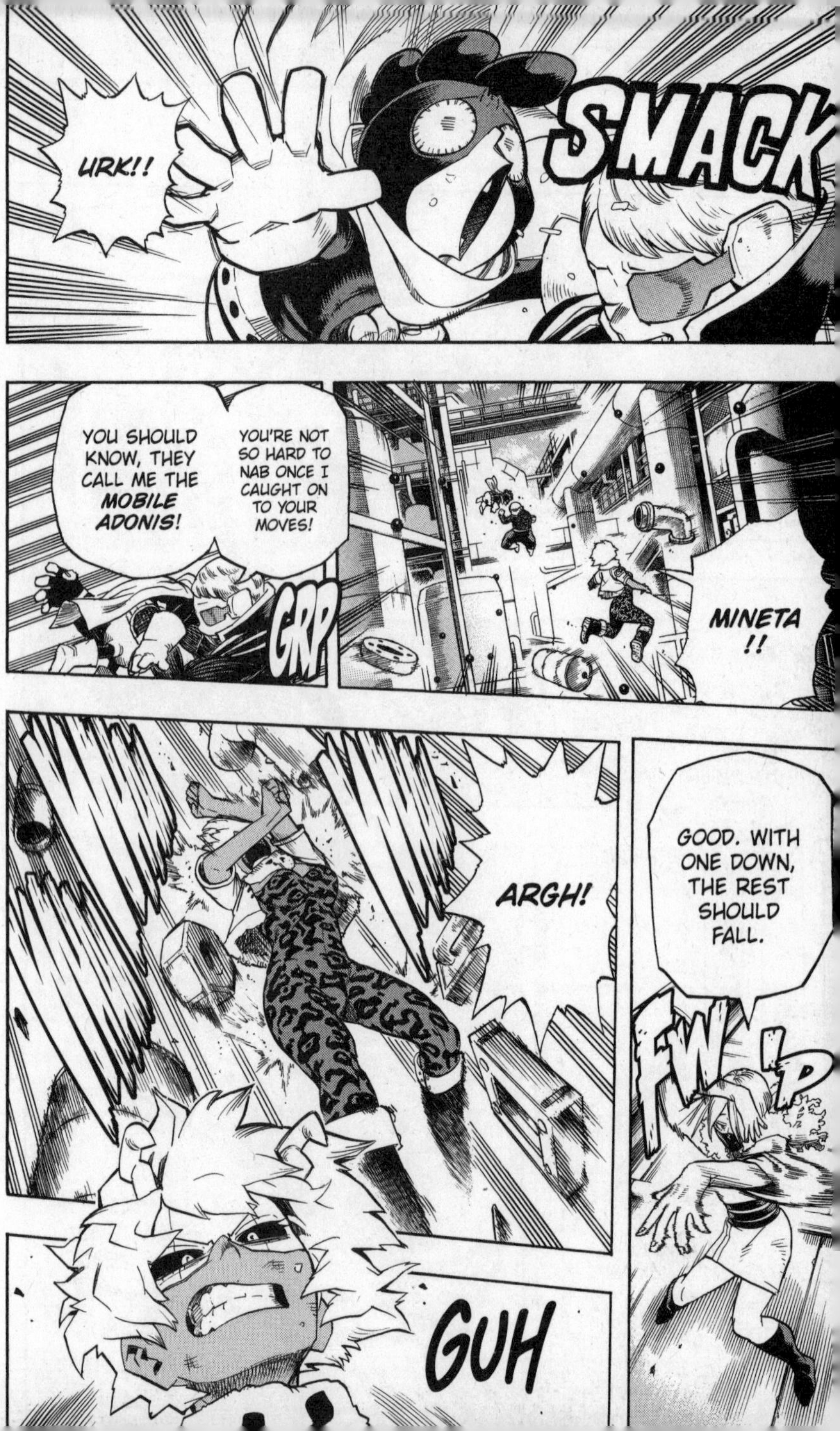
SMACK
URK!!
MINETA!!
YOU'RE NOT SO HARD TO NAB ONCE I CAUGHT ON TO YOUR MOVES!
YOU SHOULD KNOW, THEY CALL ME THE MOBILE ADONIS!
GRP
GOOD. WITH ONE DOWN, THE REST SHOULD FALL.
FW'P
ARGH!
GUH

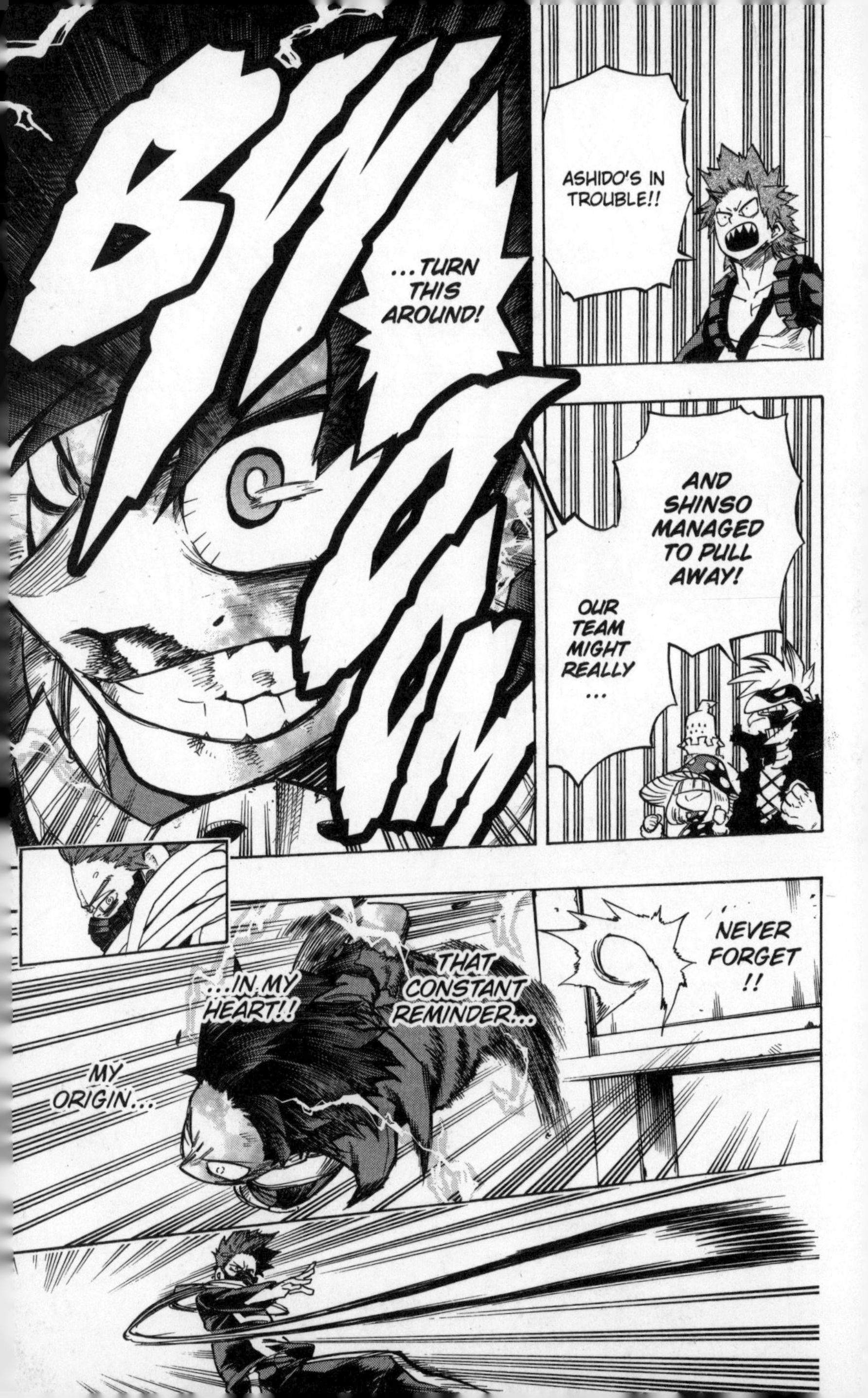
ASHIDO'S IN TROUBLE!!
AND SHINSO MANAGED TO PULL AWAY!
OUR TEAM MIGHT REALLY ...
...TURN THIS AROUND!
NEVER FORGET!!
THAT CONSTANT REMINDER...
...IN MY HEART!!
MY ORIGIN...

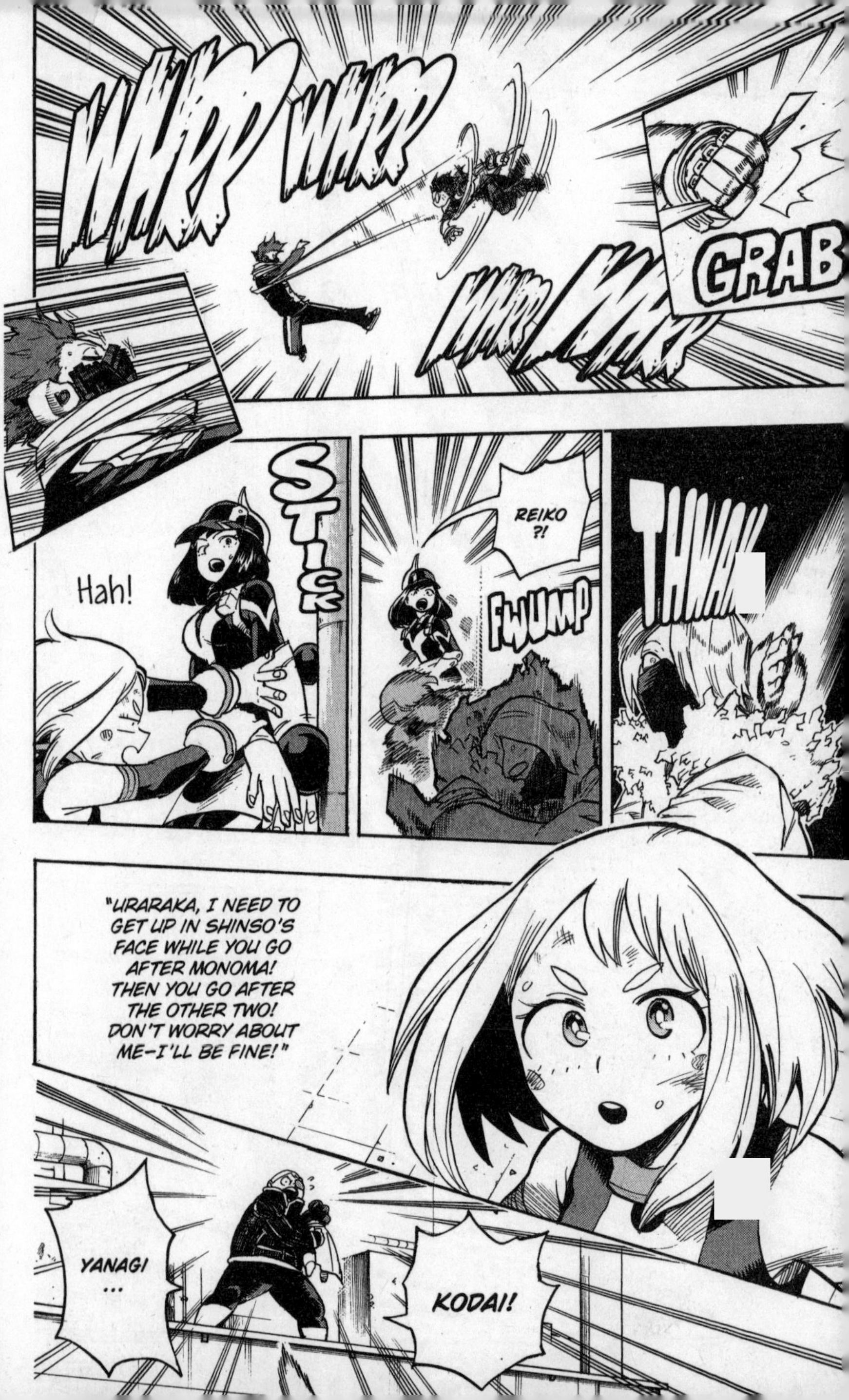
GRAB
REIKO ?!
FWUMP
STICK
Hah!
"URARAKA, I NEED TO GET UP IN SHINSO'S FACE WHILE YOU GO AFTER MONOMA! THEN YOU GO AFTER THE OTHER TWO! DON'T WORRY ABOUT ME—I'LL BE FINE!"
KODAI!
YANAGI ...

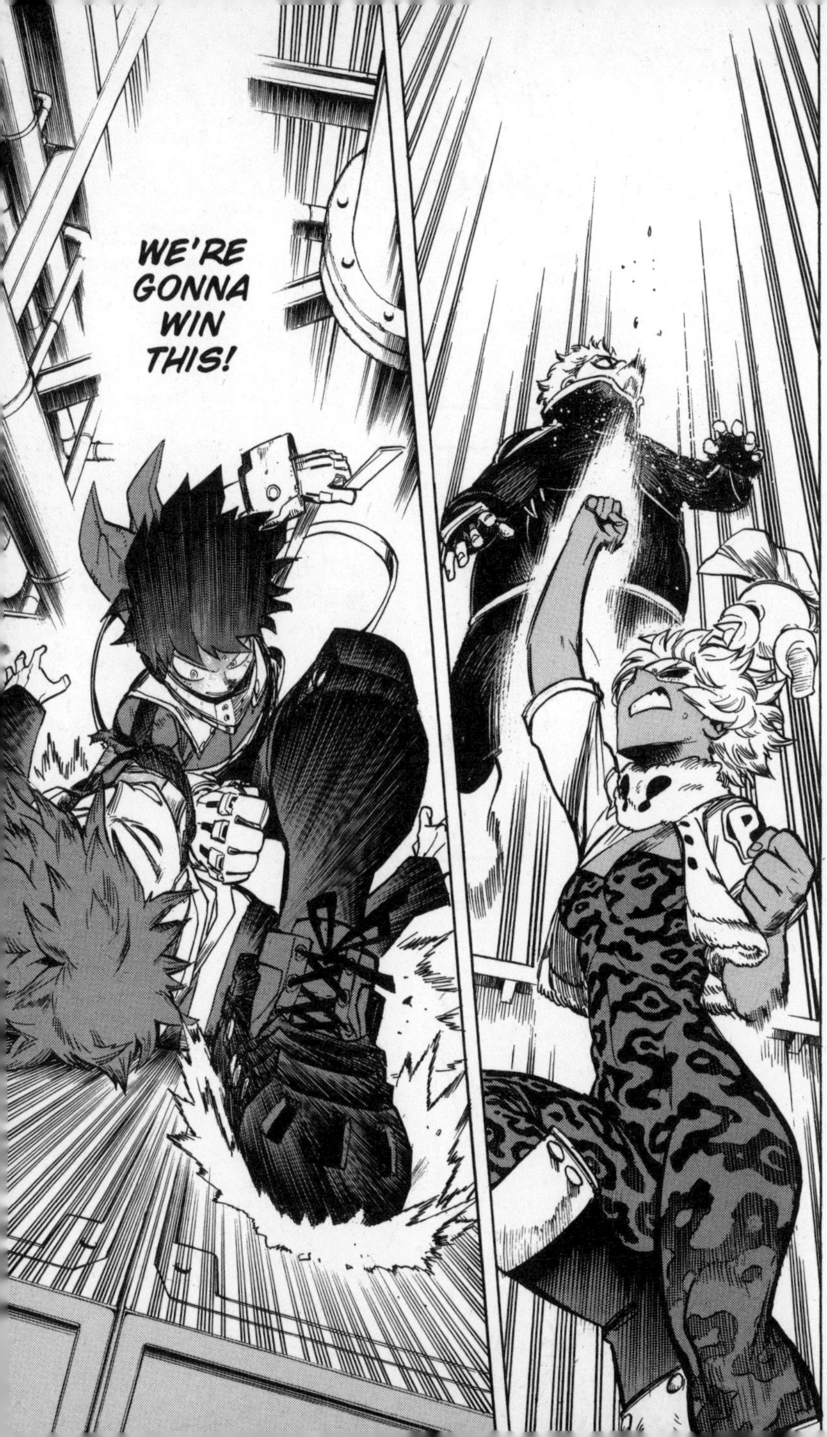
WE'RE GONNA WIN THIS!

REIKO YANAGI (15)

STREET CLOTHES

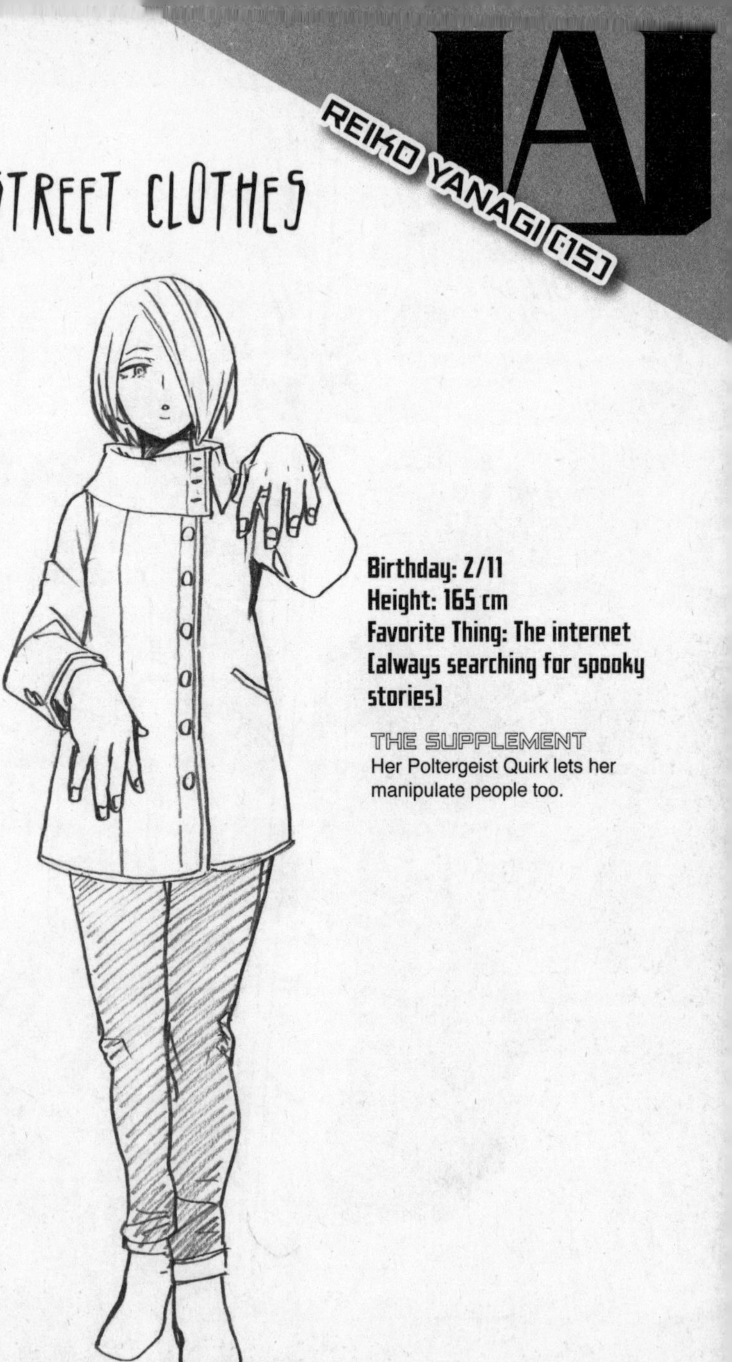

Birthday: 2/11
Height: 165 cm
Favorite Thing: The internet (always searching for spooky stories)

THE SUPPLEMENT

Her Poltergeist Quirk lets her manipulate people too.

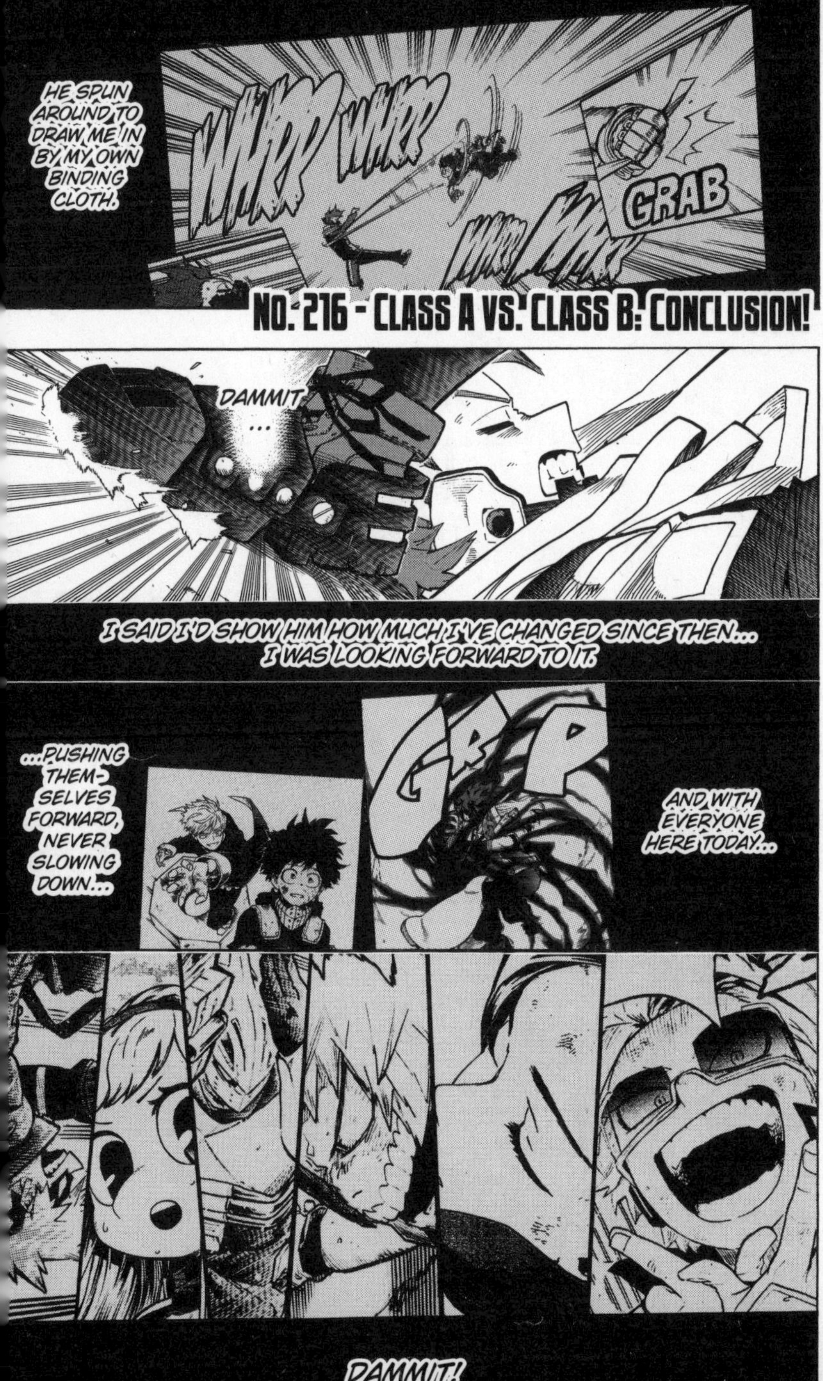
GRAB
WHIRR WHIRR
HE SPUN AROUND TO DRAW ME IN BY MY OWN BINDING CLOTH.
NO. 216 - CLASS A VS. CLASS B: CONCLUSION!
DAMMIT...
I SAID I'D SHOW HIM HOW MUCH I'VE CHANGED SINCE THEN... I WAS LOOKING FORWARD TO IT.
AND WITH EVERYONE HERE TODAY...
GRAP
...PUSHING THEMSELVES FORWARD, NEVER SLOWING DOWN...
DAMMIT!

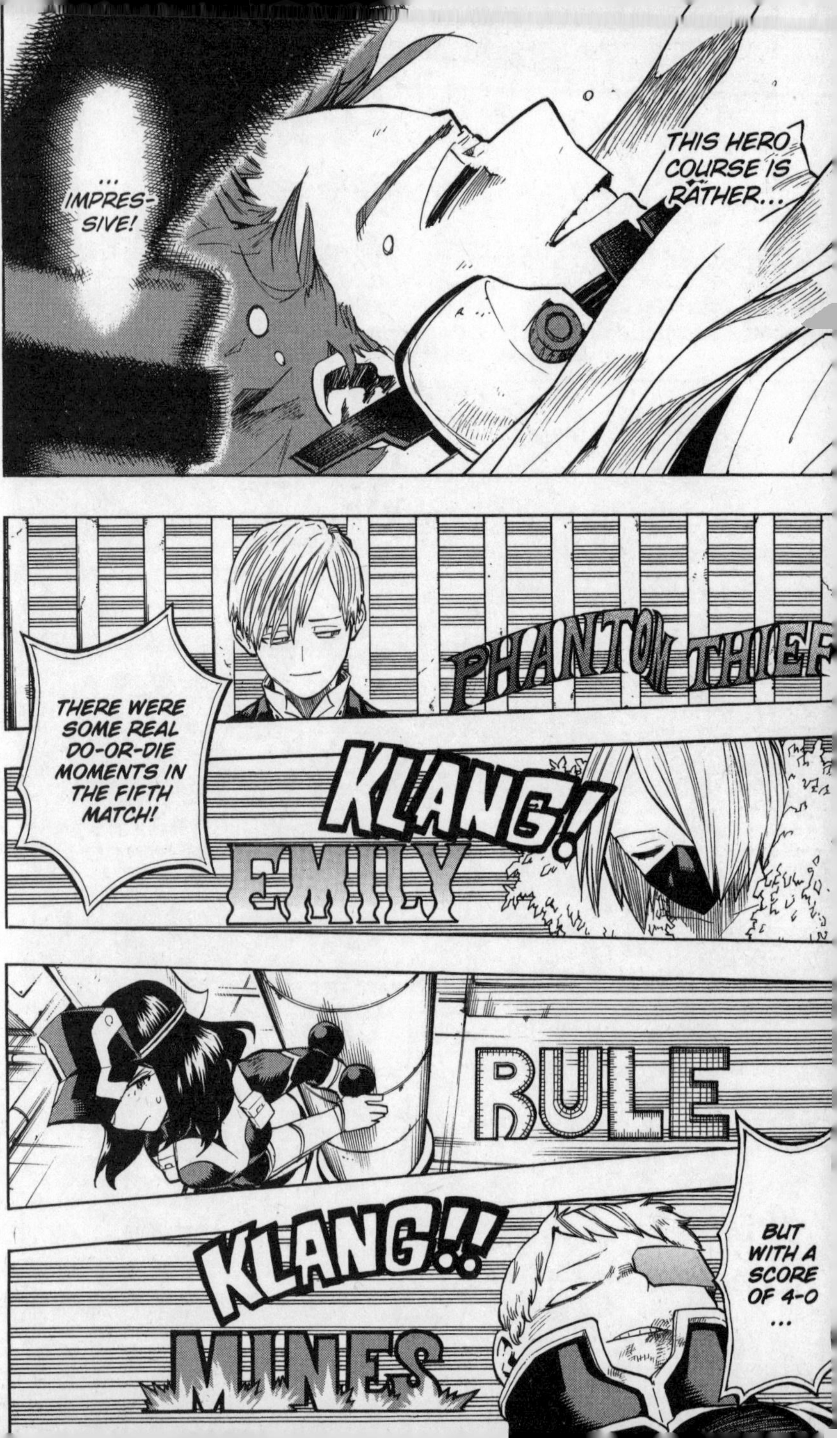
THIS HERO COURSE IS RATHER...
... IMPRESSIVE!
PHANTOM THIEF
THERE WERE SOME REAL DO-OR-DIE MOMENTS IN THE FIFTH MATCH!
KLANG!
EMILY
RULE
BUT WITH A SCORE OF 4-0 ...
KLANG!!
MINES

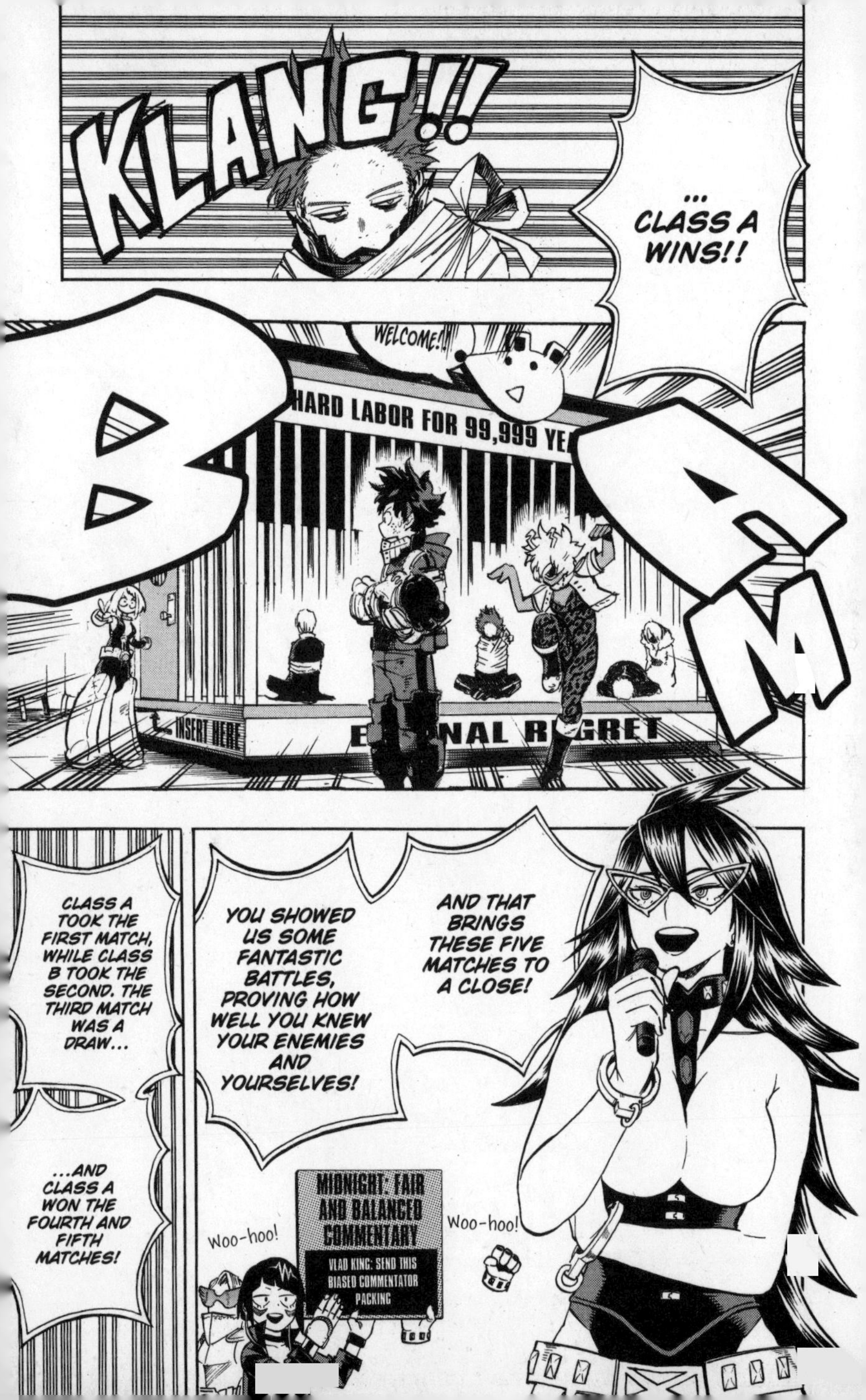
...CLASS A WINS!!
KLANG!!
BAM
WELCOME!!!
HARD LABOR FOR 99,999 YE
INSERT HERE
NAL R GRET
AND THAT BRINGS THESE FIVE MATCHES TO A CLOSE!
YOU SHOWED US SOME FANTASTIC BATTLES, PROVING HOW WELL YOU KNEW YOUR ENEMIES AND YOURSELVES!
Woo-hoo!
MIDNIGHT: FAIR AND BALANCED COMMENTARY
VLAD KING: SEND THIS BIASED COMMENTATOR PACKING
Woo-hoo!
CLASS A TOOK THE FIRST MATCH, WHILE CLASS B TOOK THE SECOND. THE THIRD MATCH WAS A DRAW...
...AND CLASS A WON THE FOURTH AND FIFTH MATCHES!

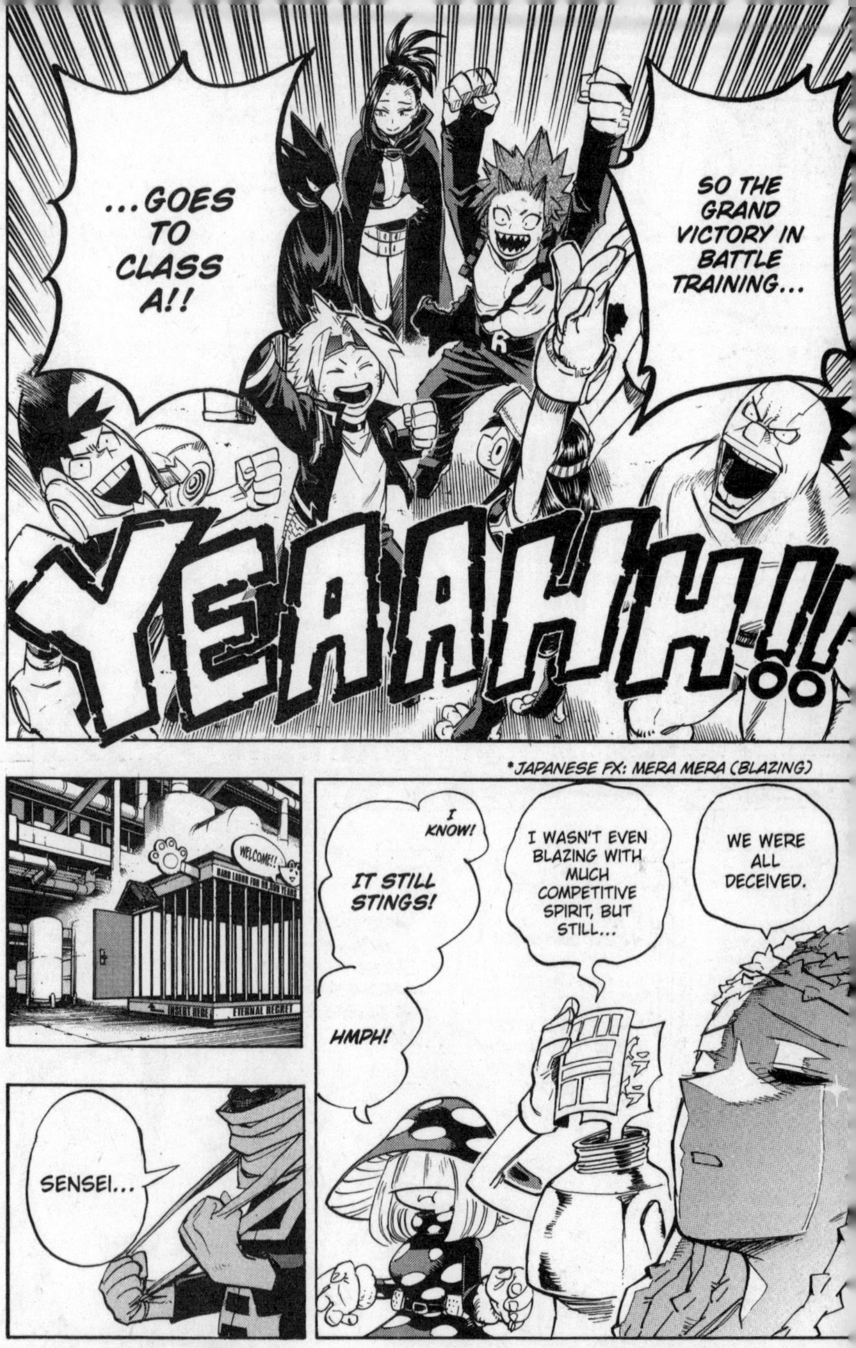
SO THE GRAND VICTORY IN BATTLE TRAINING...
...GOES TO CLASS A!!
YEAAHH!!
WE WERE ALL DECEIVED.
I WASN'T EVEN BLAZING WITH MUCH COMPETITIVE SPIRIT, BUT STILL...
I KNOW!
IT STILL STINGS!
HMPH!
WELCOME!!
INSERT HERE
ETERNAL REGRET
SENSEI...

*JAPANESE FX: MERA MERA (BLAZING)

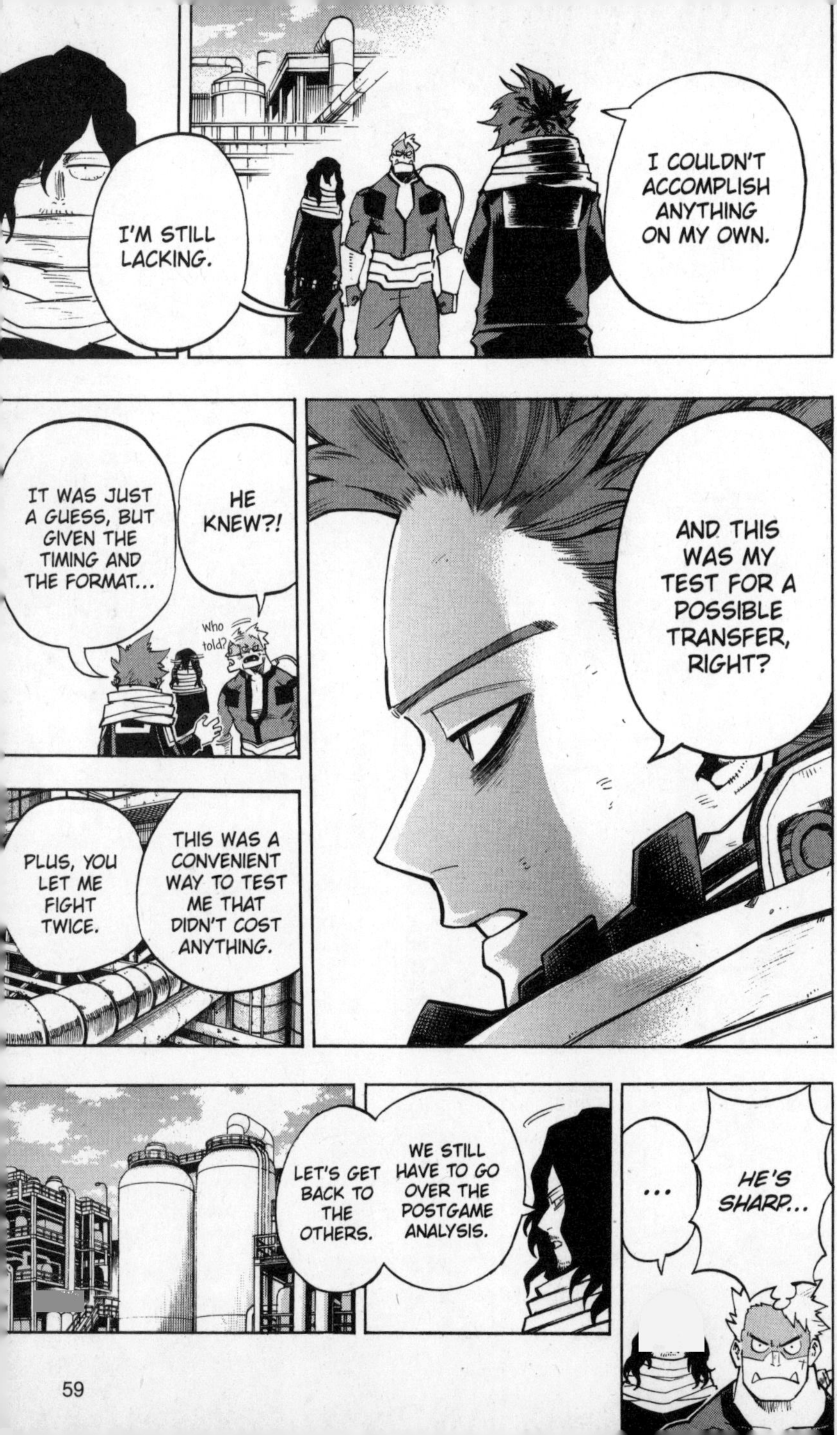
I COULDN'T ACCOMPLISH ANYTHING ON MY OWN.
I'M STILL LACKING.
AND THIS WAS MY TEST FOR A POSSIBLE TRANSFER, RIGHT?
HE KNEW?!
Who told?
IT WAS JUST A GUESS, BUT GIVEN THE TIMING AND THE FORMAT...
THIS WAS A CONVENIENT WAY TO TEST ME THAT DIDN'T COST ANYTHING.
PLUS, YOU LET ME FIGHT TWICE.
HE'S SHARP...
...
WE STILL HAVE TO GO OVER THE POSTGAME ANALYSIS.
LET'S GET BACK TO THE OTHERS.

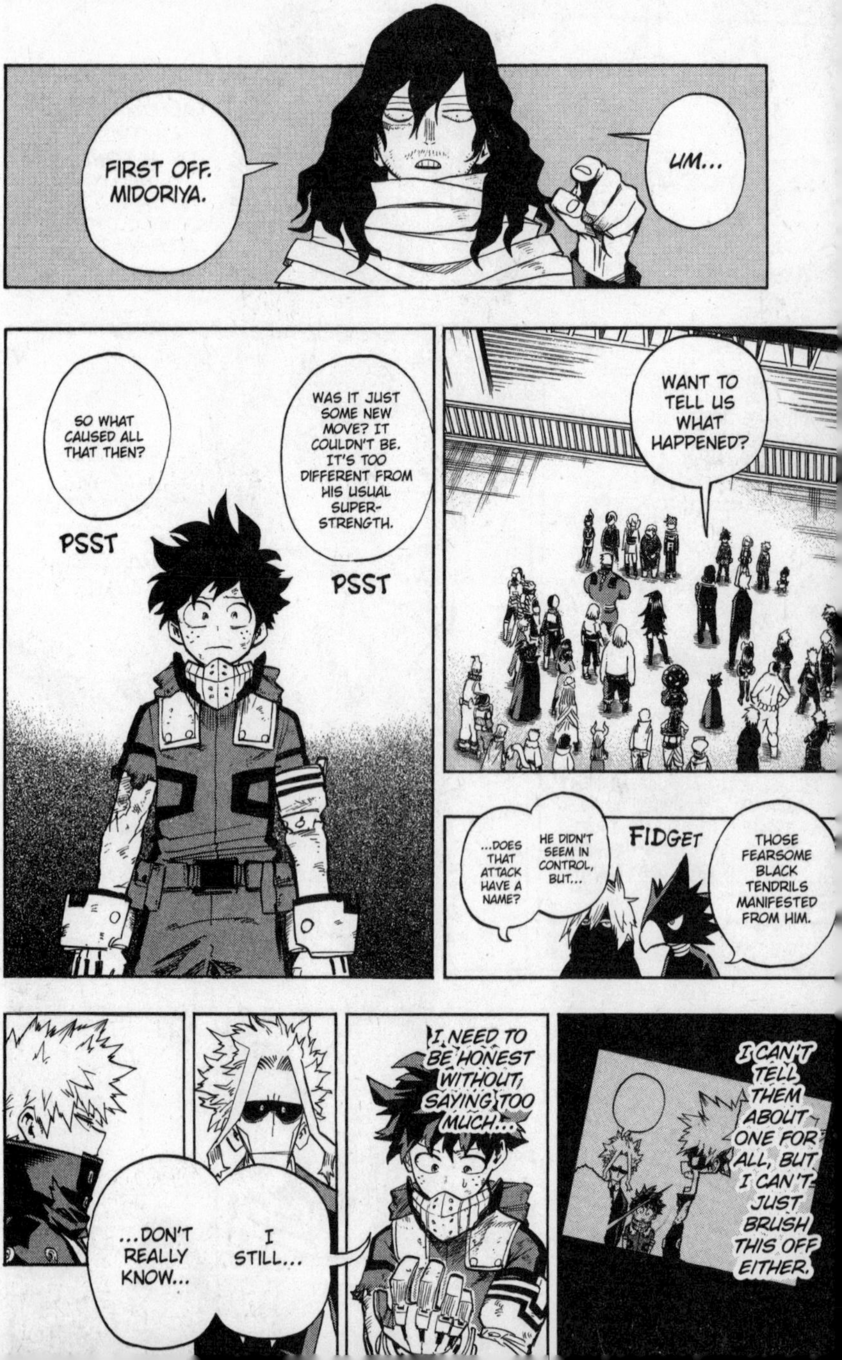
UM...
FIRST OFF. MIDORIYA.
WANT TO TELL US WHAT HAPPENED?
THOSE FEARSOME BLACK TENDRILS MANIFESTED FROM HIM.
FIDGET
HE DIDN'T SEEM IN CONTROL, BUT...
...DOES THAT ATTACK HAVE A NAME?
WAS IT JUST SOME NEW MOVE? IT COULDN'T BE. IT'S TOO DIFFERENT FROM HIS USUAL SUPER-STRENGTH.
PSST
SO WHAT CAUSED ALL THAT THEN?
PSST
I CAN'T TELL THEM ABOUT ONE FOR ALL, BUT I CAN'T JUST BRUSH THIS OFF EITHER.
I NEED TO BE HONEST WITHOUT SAYING TOO MUCH...
I STILL...
...DON'T REALLY KNOW...

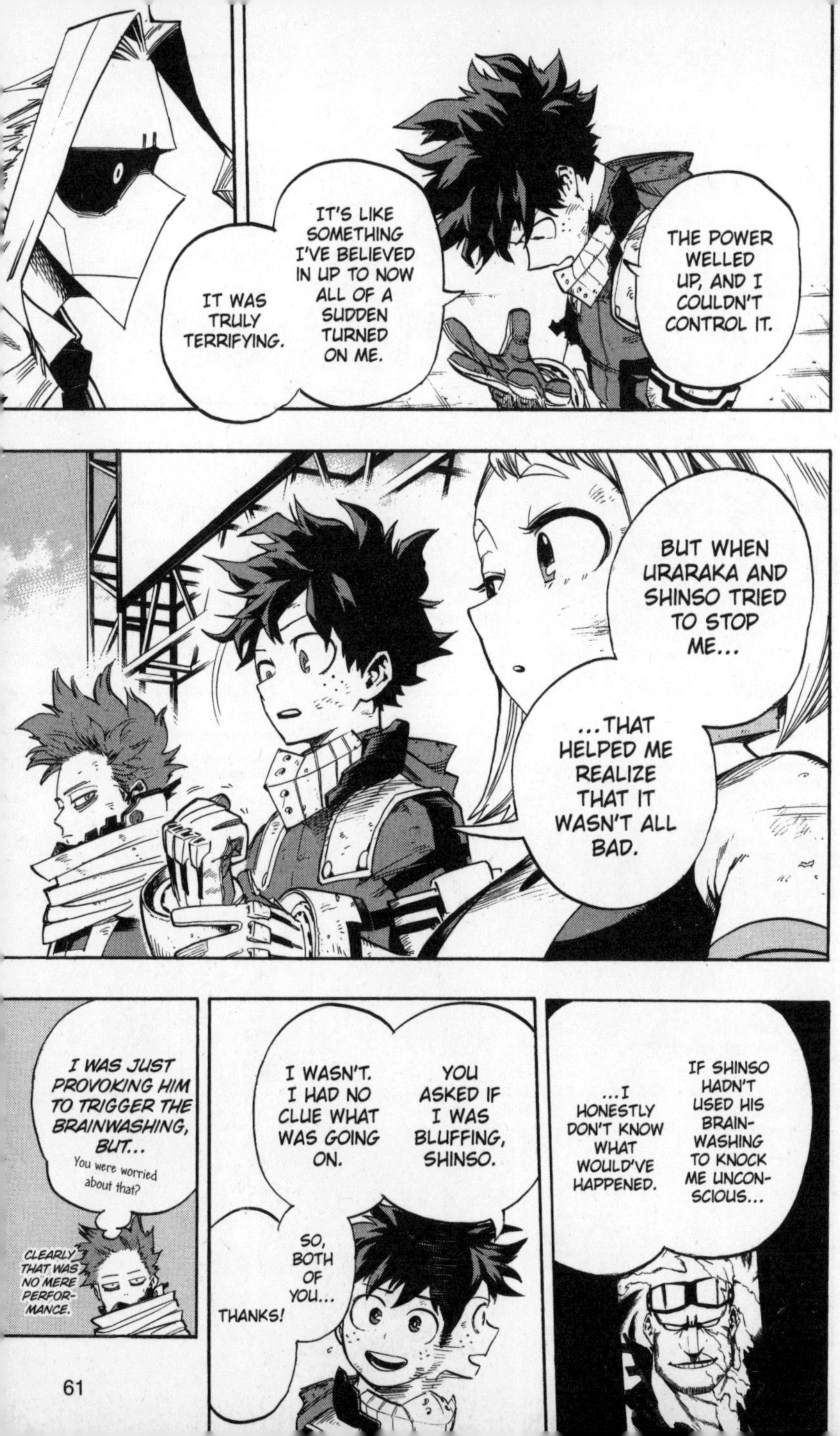
THE POWER WELLED UP, AND I COULDN'T CONTROL IT.
IT'S LIKE SOMETHING I'VE BELIEVED IN UP TO NOW ALL OF A SUDDEN TURNED ON ME.
IT WAS TRULY TERRIFYING.
BUT WHEN URARAKA AND SHINSO TRIED TO STOP ME...
...THAT HELPED ME REALIZE THAT IT WASN'T ALL BAD.
IF SHINSO HADN'T USED HIS BRAIN-WASHING TO KNOCK ME UNCON-SCIOUS...
...I HONESTLY DON'T KNOW WHAT WOULD'VE HAPPENED.
YOU ASKED IF I WAS BLUFFING, SHINSO.
I WASN'T. I HAD NO CLUE WHAT WAS GOING ON.
SO, BOTH OF YOU...
THANKS!
I WAS JUST PROVOKING HIM TO TRIGGER THE BRAINWASHING, BUT...
You were worried about that?
CLEARLY THAT WAS NO MERE PERFORMANCE.

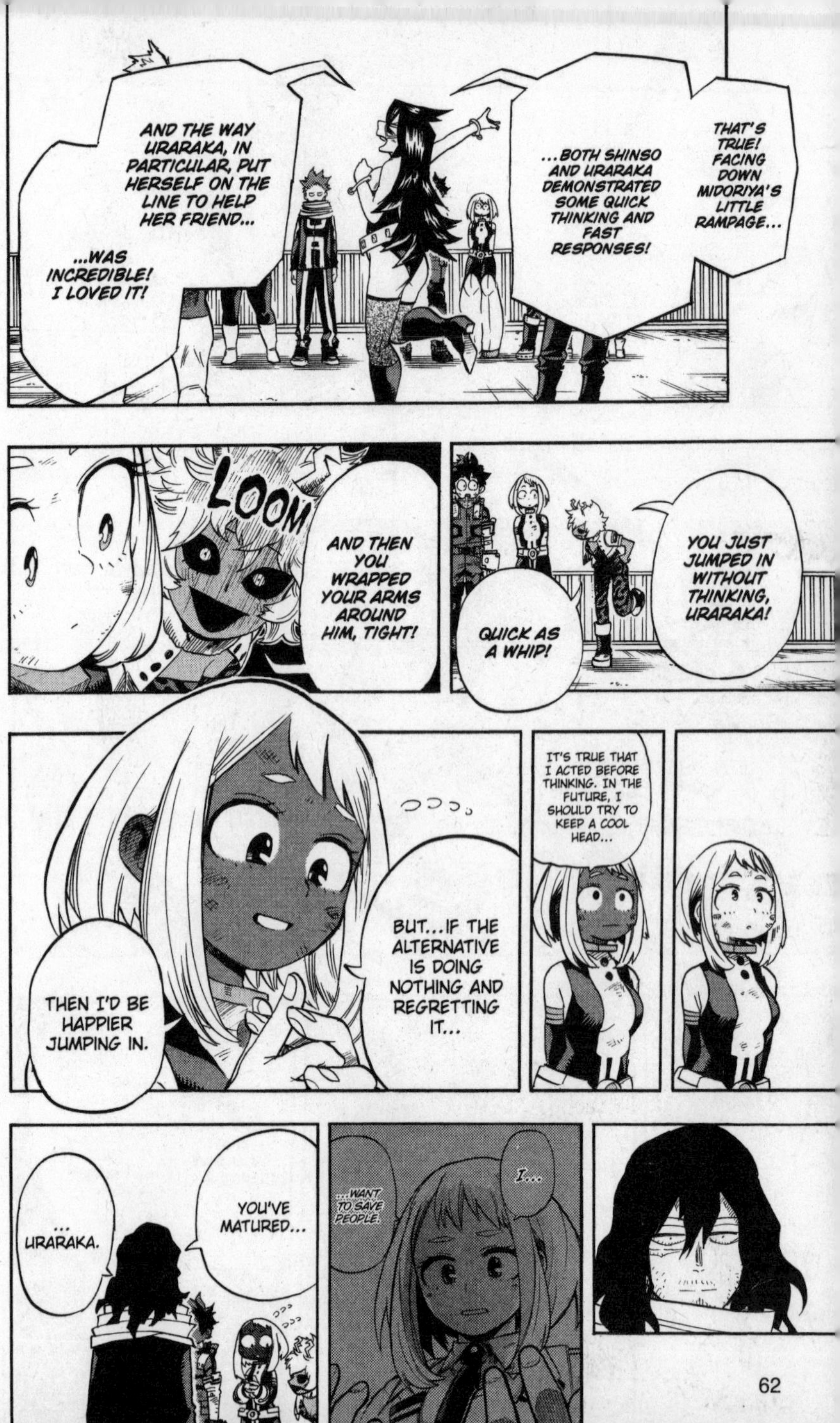
THAT'S TRUE! FACING DOWN MIDORIYA'S LITTLE RAMPAGE...
...BOTH SHINSO AND URARAKA DEMONSTRATED SOME QUICK THINKING AND FAST RESPONSES!
AND THE WAY URARAKA, IN PARTICULAR, PUT HERSELF ON THE LINE TO HELP HER FRIEND...
...WAS INCREDIBLE! I LOVED IT!
YOU JUST JUMPED IN WITHOUT THINKING, URARAKA!
QUICK AS A WHIP!
LOOM
AND THEN YOU WRAPPED YOUR ARMS AROUND HIM, TIGHT!
IT'S TRUE THAT I ACTED BEFORE THINKING. IN THE FUTURE, I SHOULD TRY TO KEEP A COOL HEAD...
BUT...IF THE ALTERNATIVE IS DOING NOTHING AND REGRETTING IT...
THEN I'D BE HAPPIER JUMPING IN.
I...
...WANT TO SAVE PEOPLE.
YOU'VE MATURED...
... URARAKA.

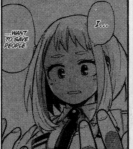

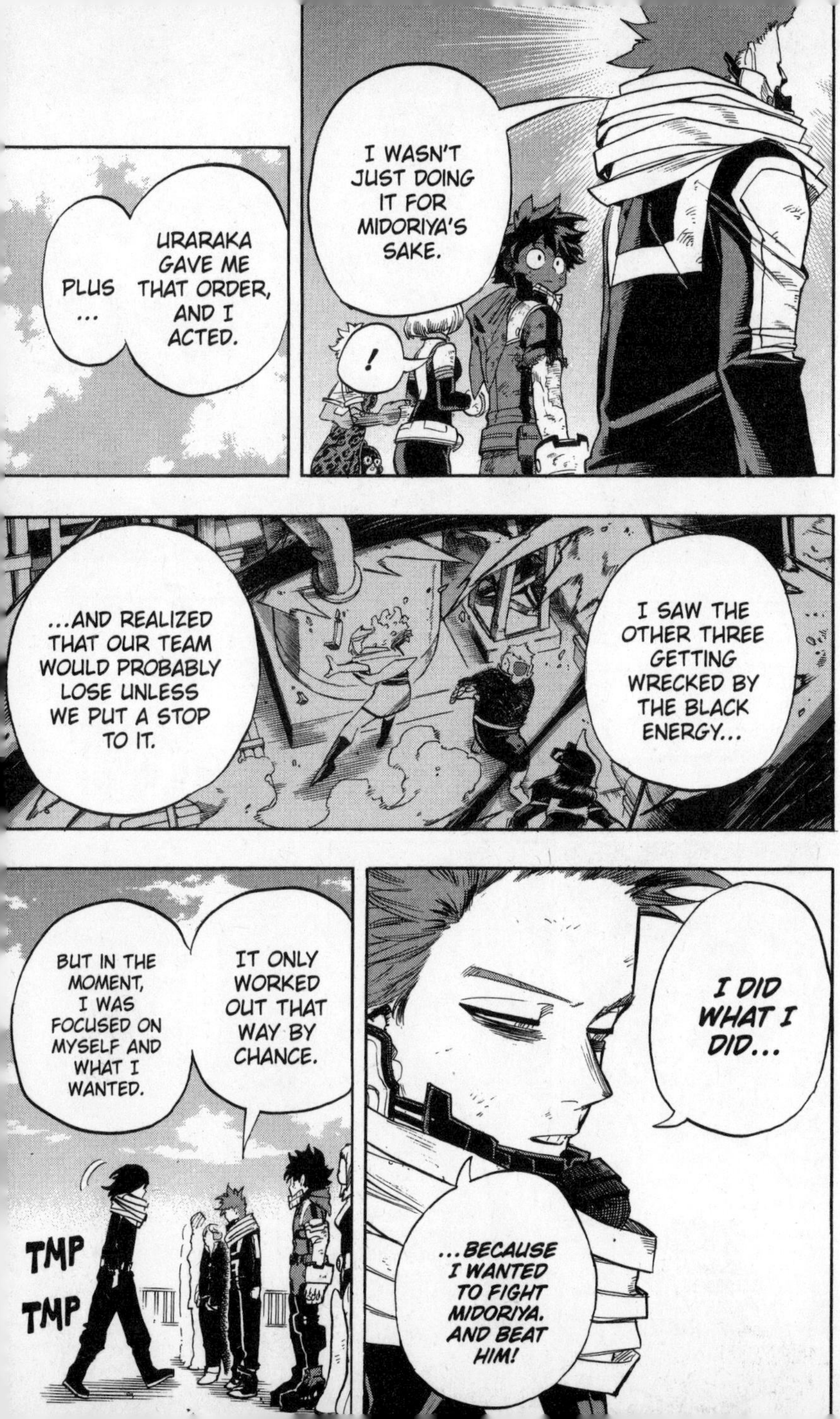
I WASN'T JUST DOING IT FOR MIDORIYA'S SAKE.
!
URARAKA GAVE ME THAT ORDER, AND I ACTED.
PLUS ...
I SAW THE OTHER THREE GETTING WRECKED BY THE BLACK ENERGY...
...AND REALIZED THAT OUR TEAM WOULD PROBABLY LOSE UNLESS WE PUT A STOP TO IT.
I DID WHAT I DID...
...BECAUSE I WANTED TO FIGHT MIDORIYA. AND BEAT HIM!
IT ONLY WORKED OUT THAT WAY BY CHANCE.
BUT IN THE MOMENT, I WAS FOCUSED ON MYSELF AND WHAT I WANTED.
TMP
TMP

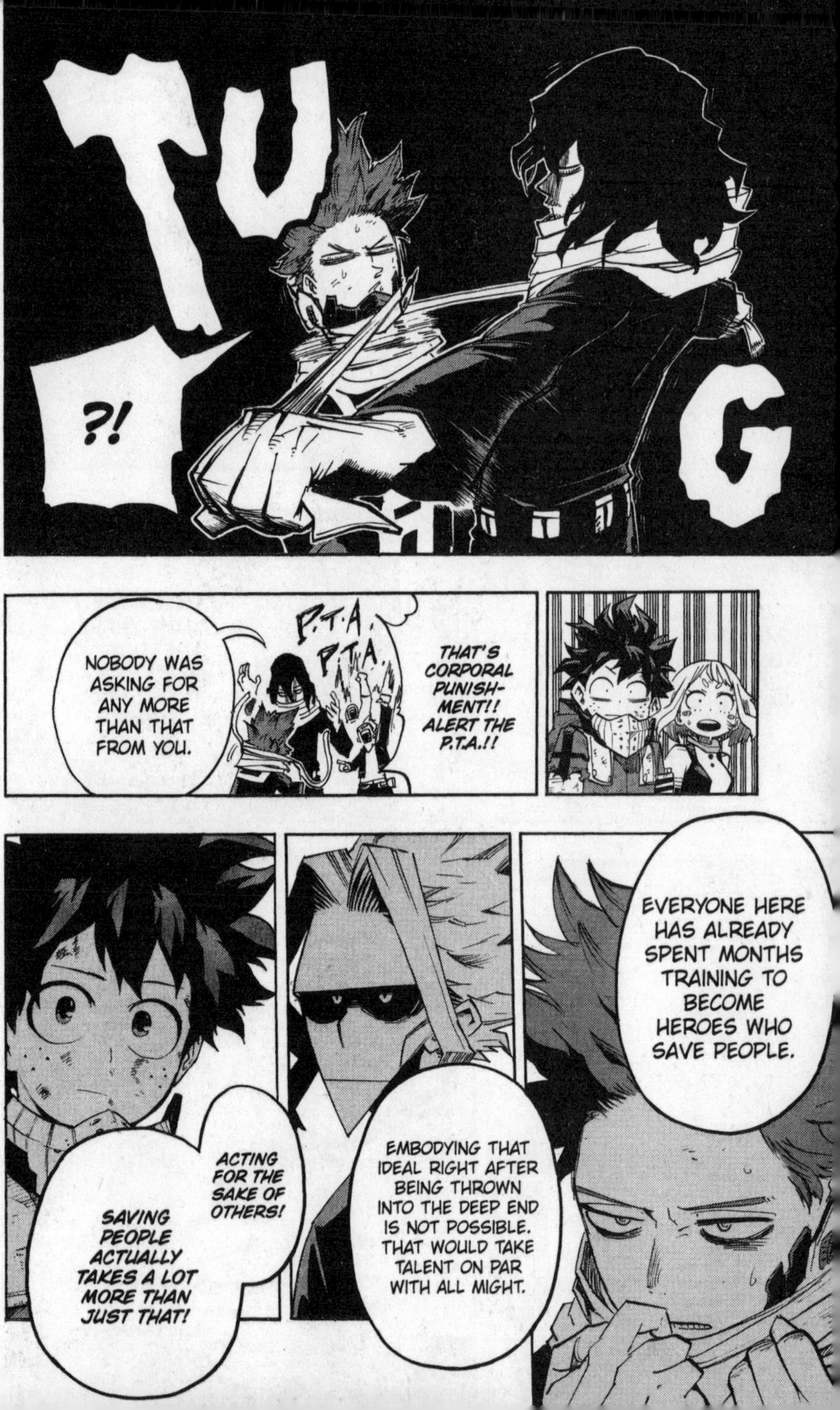
TUG
?!
THAT'S CORPORAL PUNISHMENT!! ALERT THE P.T.A.!!
P.T.A. P.T.A.
NOBODY WAS ASKING FOR ANY MORE THAN THAT FROM YOU.
EVERYONE HERE HAS ALREADY SPENT MONTHS TRAINING TO BECOME HEROES WHO SAVE PEOPLE.
EMBODYING THAT IDEAL RIGHT AFTER BEING THROWN INTO THE DEEP END IS NOT POSSIBLE. THAT WOULD TAKE TALENT ON PAR WITH ALL MIGHT.
ACTING FOR THE SAKE OF OTHERS!
SAVING PEOPLE ACTUALLY TAKES A LOT MORE THAN JUST THAT!

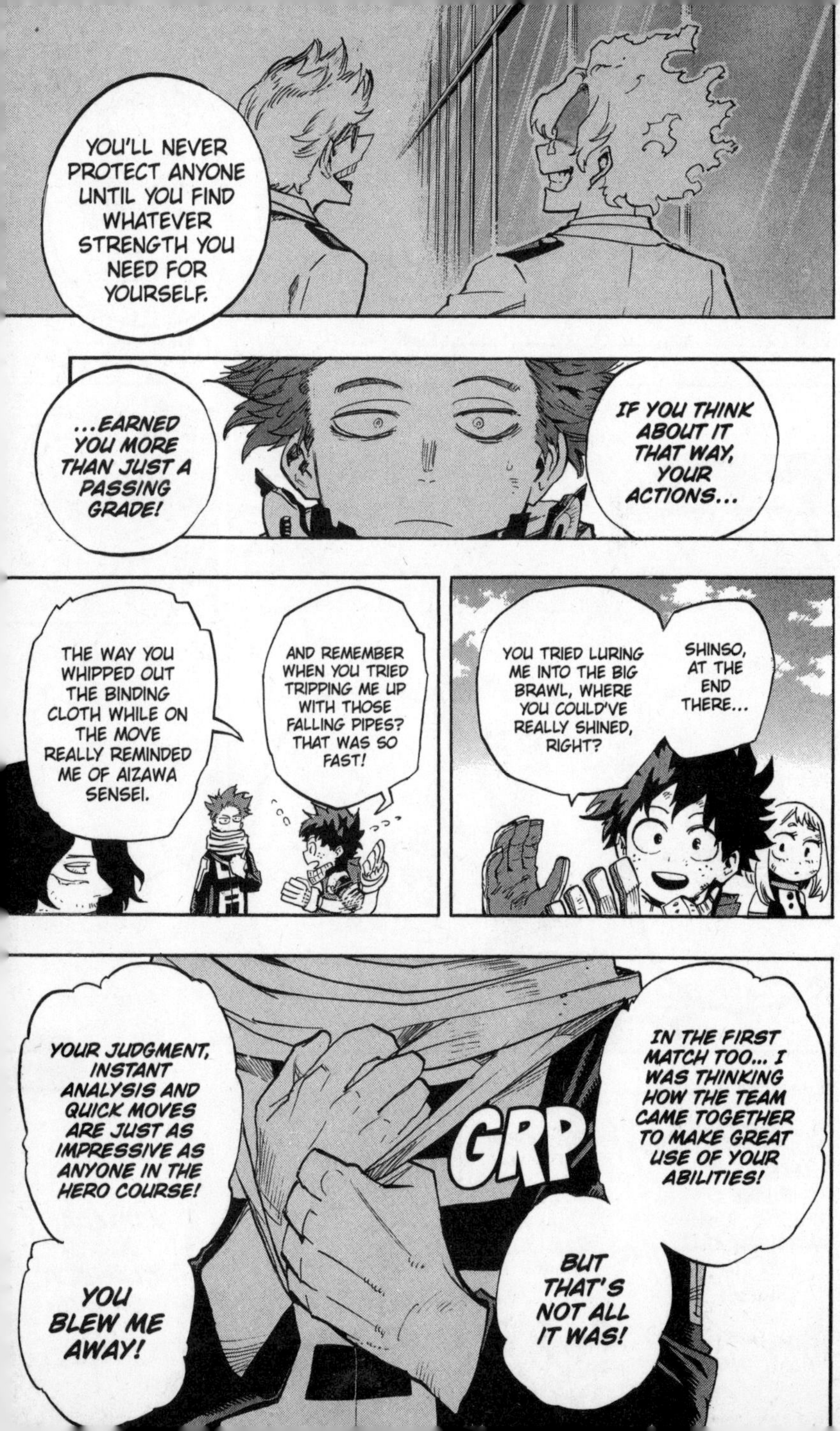
YOU'LL NEVER PROTECT ANYONE UNTIL YOU FIND WHATEVER STRENGTH YOU NEED FOR YOURSELF.
IF YOU THINK ABOUT IT THAT WAY, YOUR ACTIONS...
...EARNED YOU MORE THAN JUST A PASSING GRADE!
SHINSO, AT THE END THERE...
YOU TRIED LURING ME INTO THE BIG BRAWL, WHERE YOU COULD'VE REALLY SHINED, RIGHT?
AND REMEMBER WHEN YOU TRIED TRIPPING ME UP WITH THOSE FALLING PIPES? THAT WAS SO FAST!
THE WAY YOU WHIPPED OUT THE BINDING CLOTH WHILE ON THE MOVE REALLY REMINDED ME OF AIZAWA SENSEI.
IN THE FIRST MATCH TOO... I WAS THINKING HOW THE TEAM CAME TOGETHER TO MAKE GREAT USE OF YOUR ABILITIES!
YOUR JUDGMENT, INSTANT ANALYSIS AND QUICK MOVES ARE JUST AS IMPRESSIVE AS ANYONE IN THE HERO COURSE!
GRP
BUT THAT'S NOT ALL IT WAS!
YOU BLEW ME AWAY!

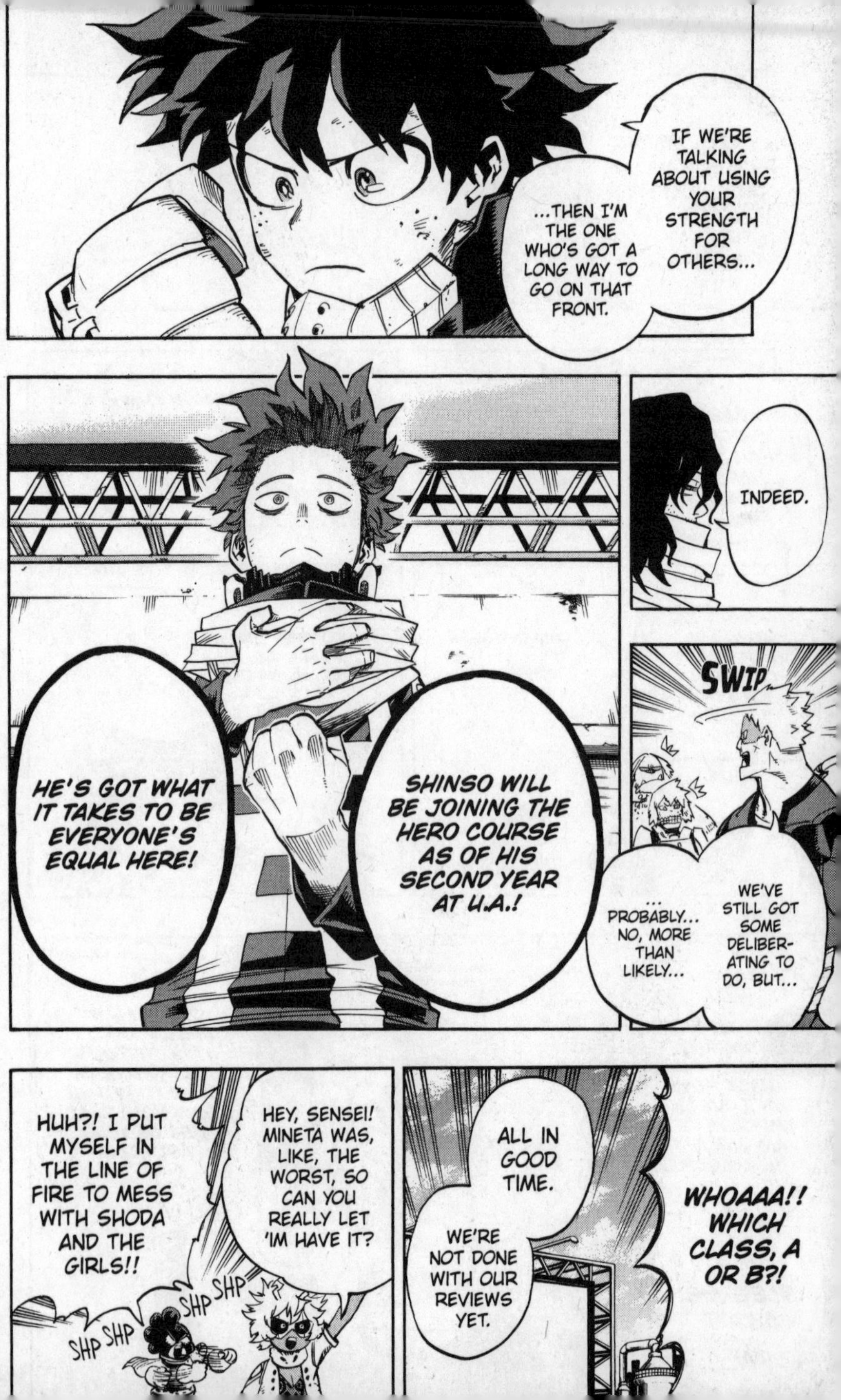
IF WE'RE TALKING ABOUT USING YOUR STRENGTH FOR OTHERS...
...THEN I'M THE ONE WHO'S GOT A LONG WAY TO GO ON THAT FRONT.
INDEED.
SWIP
WE'VE STILL GOT SOME DELIBER-ATING TO DO, BUT...
... PROBABLY... NO, MORE THAN LIKELY...
SHINSO WILL BE JOINING THE HERO COURSE AS OF HIS SECOND YEAR AT U.A.!
HE'S GOT WHAT IT TAKES TO BE EVERYONE'S EQUAL HERE!
WHOAAA!! WHICH CLASS, A OR B?!
ALL IN GOOD TIME.
WE'RE NOT DONE WITH OUR REVIEWS YET.
HEY, SENSEI! MINETA WAS, LIKE, THE WORST, SO CAN YOU REALLY LET 'IM HAVE IT?
HUH?! I PUT MYSELF IN THE LINE OF FIRE TO MESS WITH SHODA AND THE GIRLS!!
SHP SHP SHP SHP

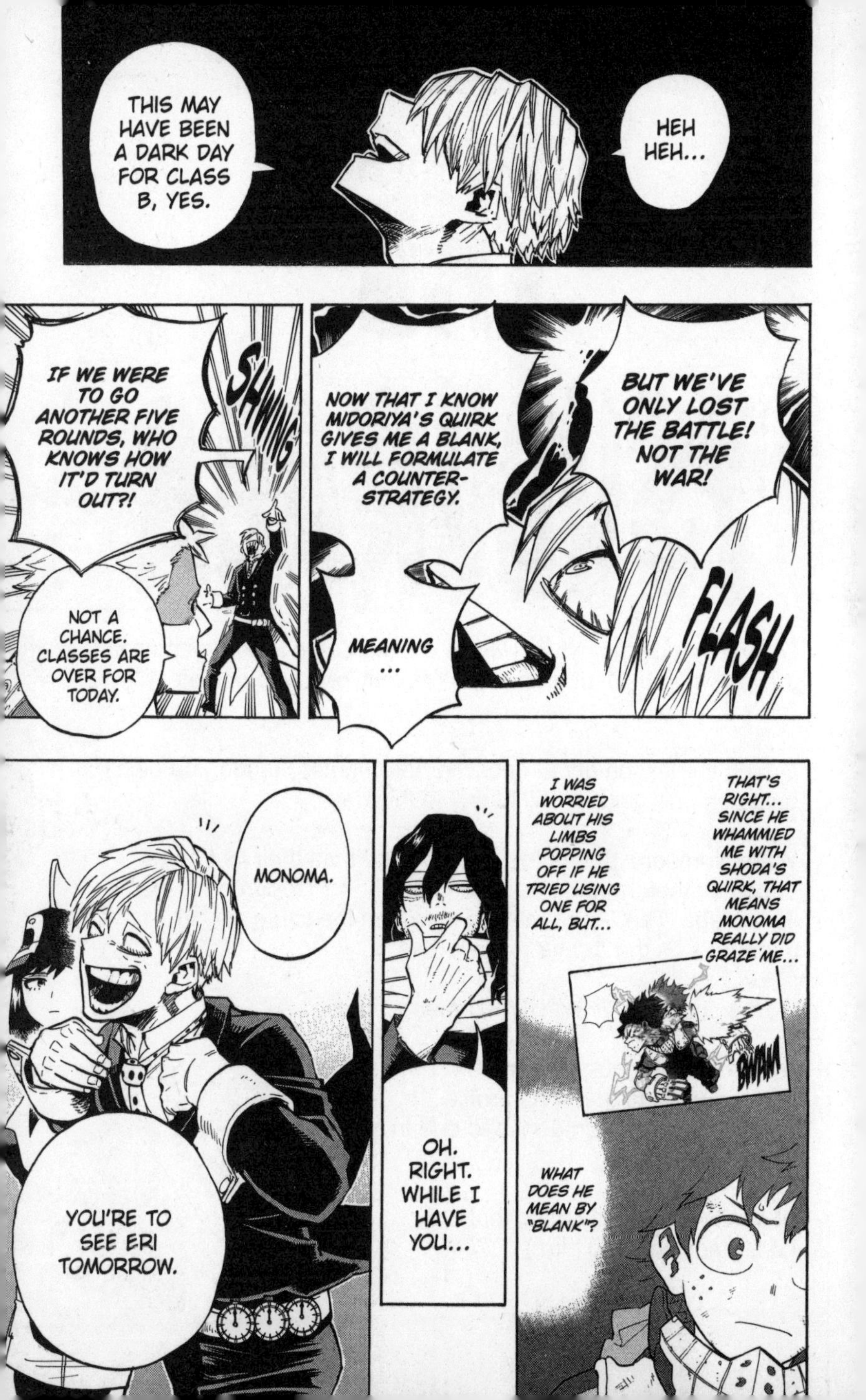
HEH HEH...
THIS MAY HAVE BEEN A DARK DAY FOR CLASS B, YES.
BUT WE'VE ONLY LOST THE BATTLE! NOT THE WAR!
FLASH
NOW THAT I KNOW MIDORIYA'S QUIRK GIVES ME A BLANK, I WILL FORMULATE A COUNTER-STRATEGY.
MEANING...
IF WE WERE TO GO ANOTHER FIVE ROUNDS, WHO KNOWS HOW IT'D TURN OUT?!
SHWING
NOT A CHANCE. CLASSES ARE OVER FOR TODAY.
THAT'S RIGHT... SINCE HE WHAMMIED ME WITH SHODA'S QUIRK, THAT MEANS MONOMA REALLY DID GRAZE ME...
I WAS WORRIED ABOUT HIS LIMBS POPPING OFF IF HE TRIED USING ONE FOR ALL, BUT...
BWOHA
WHAT DOES HE MEAN BY "BLANK"?
OH. RIGHT. WHILE I HAVE YOU...
MONOMA.
YOU'RE TO SEE ERI TOMORROW.

THE TSUBURABA

Did you notice that when I wrote out the Class B hero names in the last volume, Tsuburaba was the only one who got left out...?

During the lesson about deciding hero names, Tsuburaba didn't settle on one, and he still hasn't to this day.

When someone defers the decision like that, their last name becomes their hero name automatically, so Tsuburaba is just Tsuburaba. The "-buraba" part is written the same way in Japanese as the "brava" in La Brava.

How wonderful!! Brava! Erm, I mean...bravo!

By the way, Tsuburaba is a powerful enough dude to get TWO profile pages—one in volume 10 and one in volume 21.

(It totally slipped my mind that I'd already covered him.)

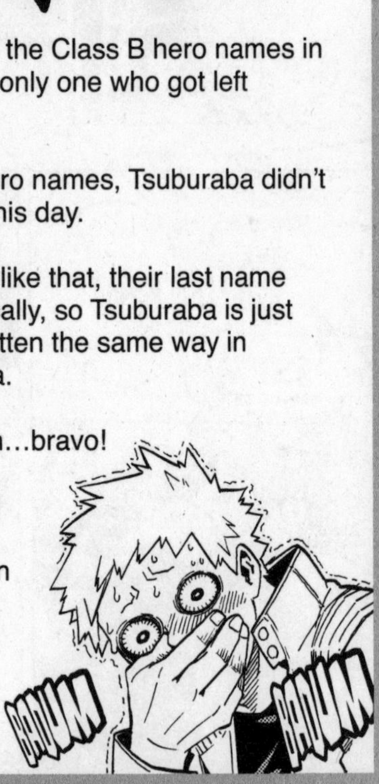
BADUM
BADUM

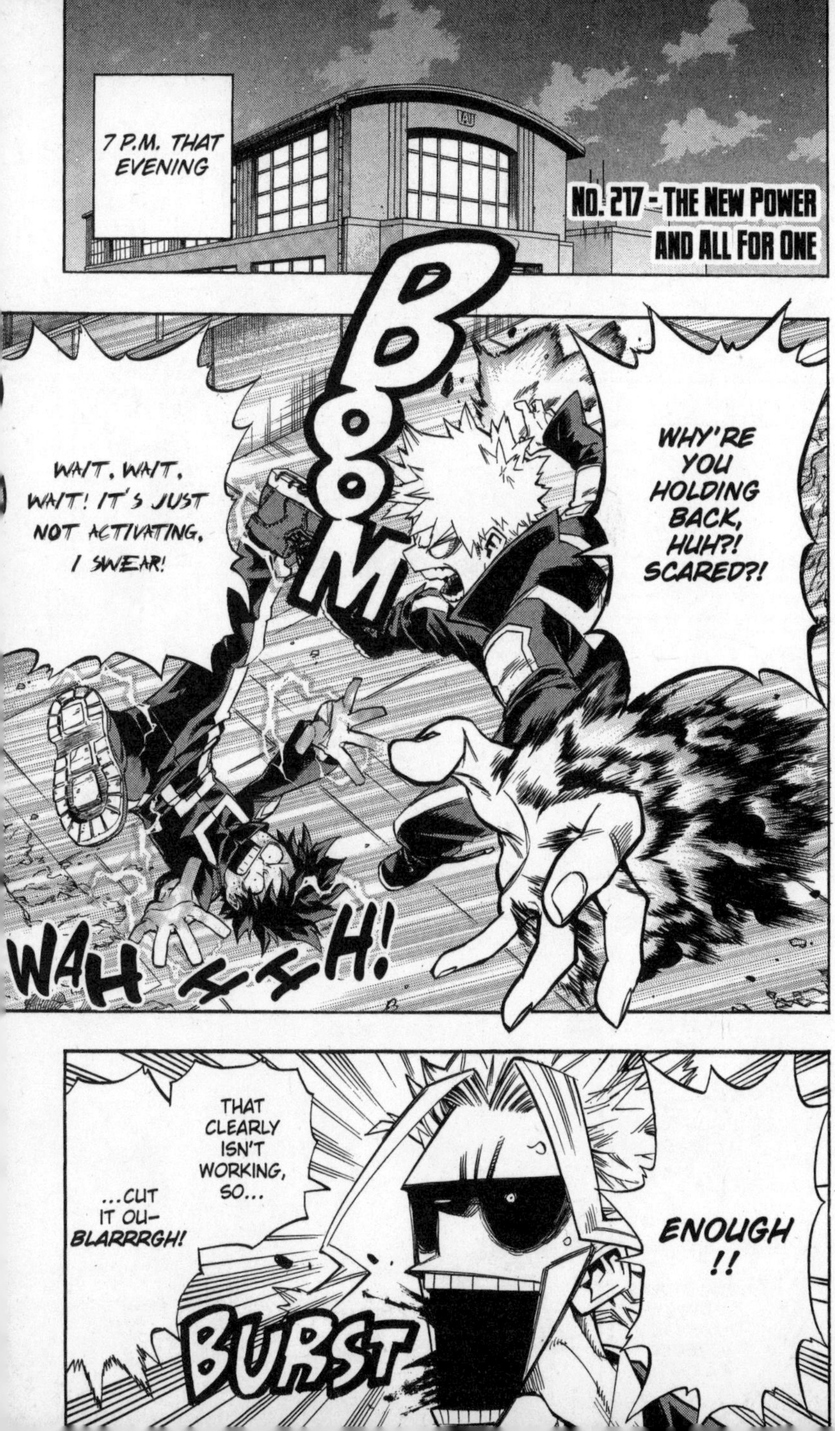
7 P.M. THAT EVENING
NO. 217 - THE NEW POWER AND ALL FOR ONE
WHY'RE YOU HOLDING BACK, HUH?! SCARED?!
BOOM
WAIT, WAIT, WAIT! IT'S JUST NOT ACTIVATING, I SWEAR!
WAHHHH!
ENOUGH!!
THAT CLEARLY ISN'T WORKING, SO...
...CUT IT OU- BLARRRGH!
BURST

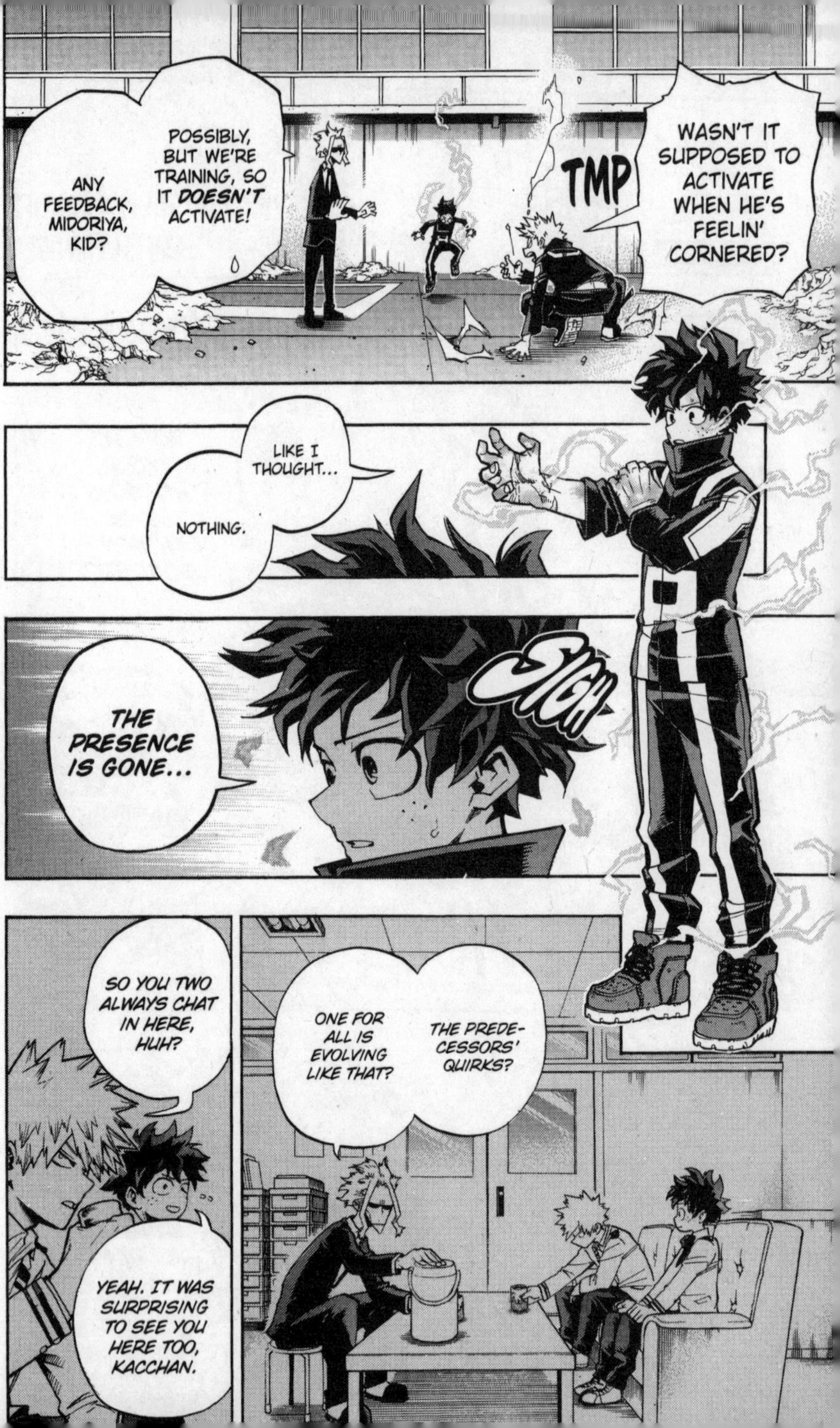
WASN'T IT SUPPOSED TO ACTIVATE WHEN HE'S FEELIN' CORNERED?
TMP
POSSIBLY, BUT WE'RE TRAINING, SO IT DOESN'T ACTIVATE!
ANY FEEDBACK, MIDORIYA, KID?
LIKE I THOUGHT...
NOTHING.
SIGH
THE PRESENCE IS GONE...
THE PREDE-CESSORS' QUIRKS?
ONE FOR ALL IS EVOLVING LIKE THAT?
SO YOU TWO ALWAYS CHAT IN HERE, HUH?
YEAH. IT WAS SURPRISING TO SEE YOU HERE TOO, KACCHAN.

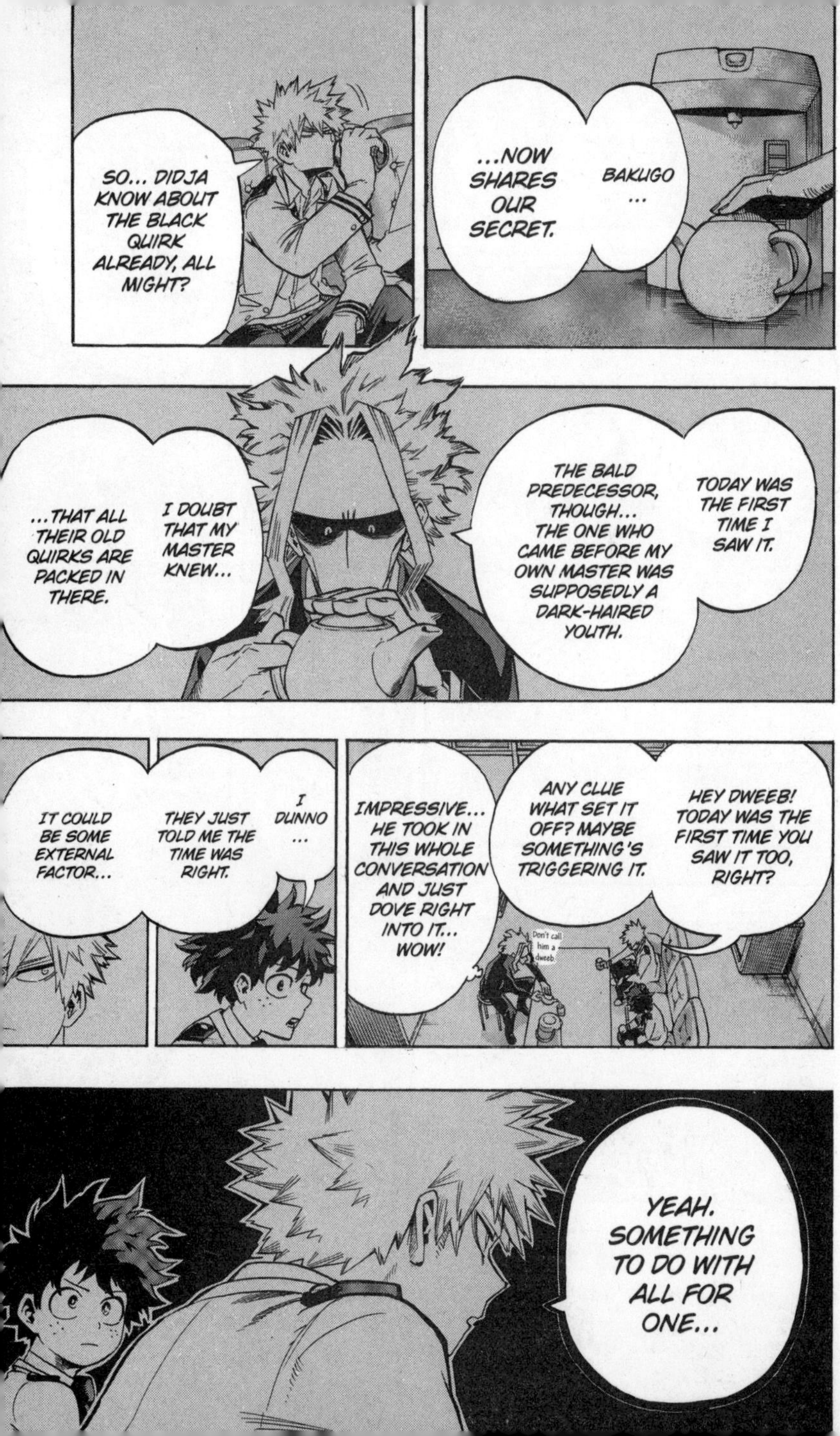
BAKUGO ...
...NOW SHARES OUR SECRET.
SO... DIDJA KNOW ABOUT THE BLACK QUIRK ALREADY, ALL MIGHT?
TODAY WAS THE FIRST TIME I SAW IT.
THE BALD PREDECESSOR, THOUGH... THE ONE WHO CAME BEFORE MY OWN MASTER WAS SUPPOSEDLY A DARK-HAIRED YOUTH.
I DOUBT THAT MY MASTER KNEW...
...THAT ALL THEIR OLD QUIRKS ARE PACKED IN THERE.
HEY DWEEB! TODAY WAS THE FIRST TIME YOU SAW IT TOO, RIGHT?
ANY CLUE WHAT SET IT OFF? MAYBE SOMETHING'S TRIGGERING IT.
Don't call him a dweeb.
IMPRESSIVE... HE TOOK IN THIS WHOLE CONVERSATION AND JUST DOVE RIGHT INTO IT... WOW!
I DUNNO ...
THEY JUST TOLD ME THE TIME WAS RIGHT.
IT COULD BE SOME EXTERNAL FACTOR...
YEAH. SOMETHING TO DO WITH ALL FOR ONE...

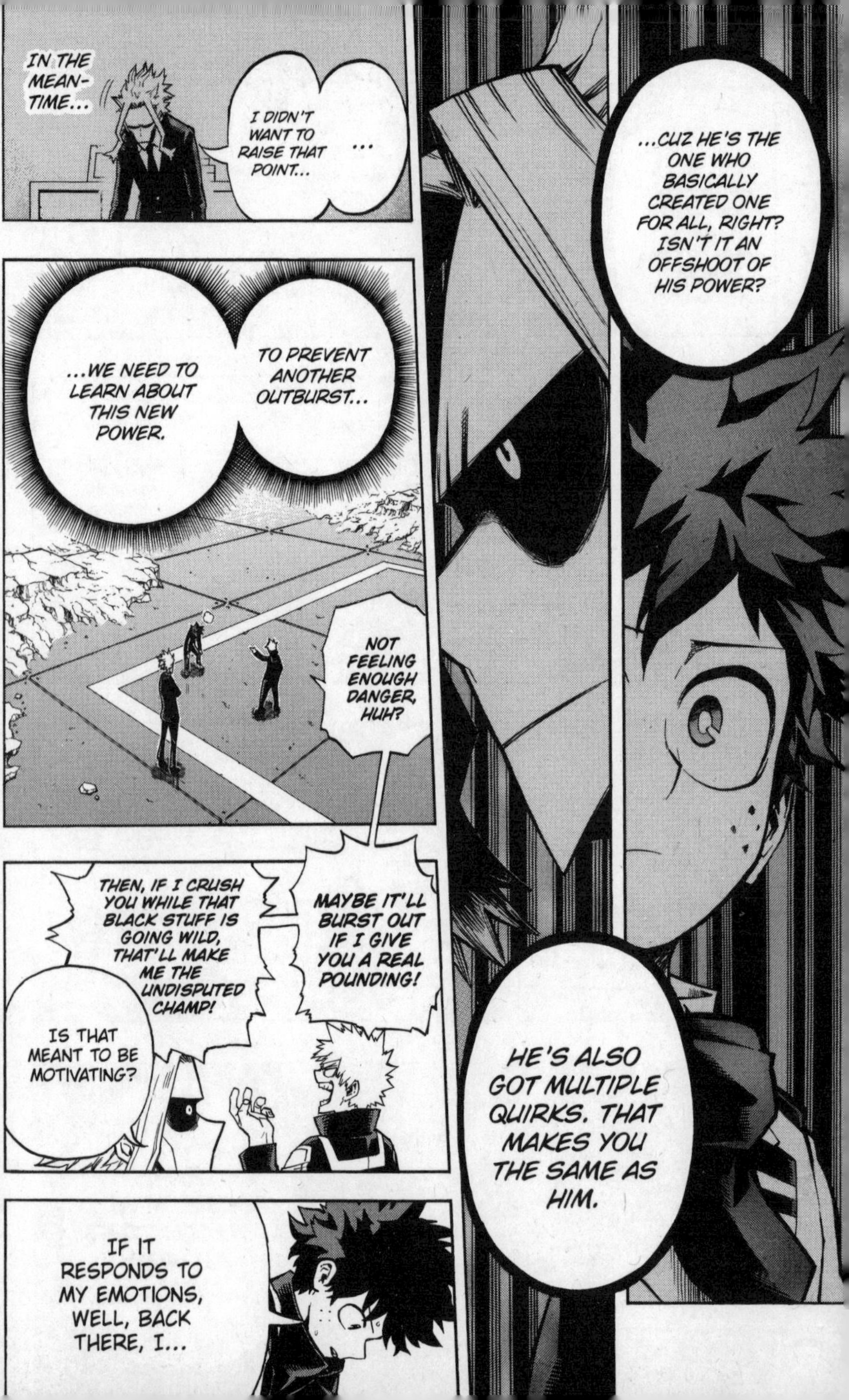
...CUZ HE'S THE ONE WHO BASICALLY CREATED ONE FOR ALL, RIGHT? ISN'T IT AN OFFSHOOT OF HIS POWER?
HE'S ALSO GOT MULTIPLE QUIRKS. THAT MAKES YOU THE SAME AS HIM.
...
I DIDN'T WANT TO RAISE THAT POINT...
IN THE MEAN-TIME...
TO PREVENT ANOTHER OUTBURST...
...WE NEED TO LEARN ABOUT THIS NEW POWER.
NOT FEELING ENOUGH DANGER, HUH?
MAYBE IT'LL BURST OUT IF I GIVE YOU A REAL POUNDING!
THEN, IF I CRUSH YOU WHILE THAT BLACK STUFF IS GOING WILD, THAT'LL MAKE ME THE UNDISPUTED CHAMP!
IS THAT MEANT TO BE MOTIVATING?
IF IT RESPONDS TO MY EMOTIONS, WELL, BACK THERE, I...

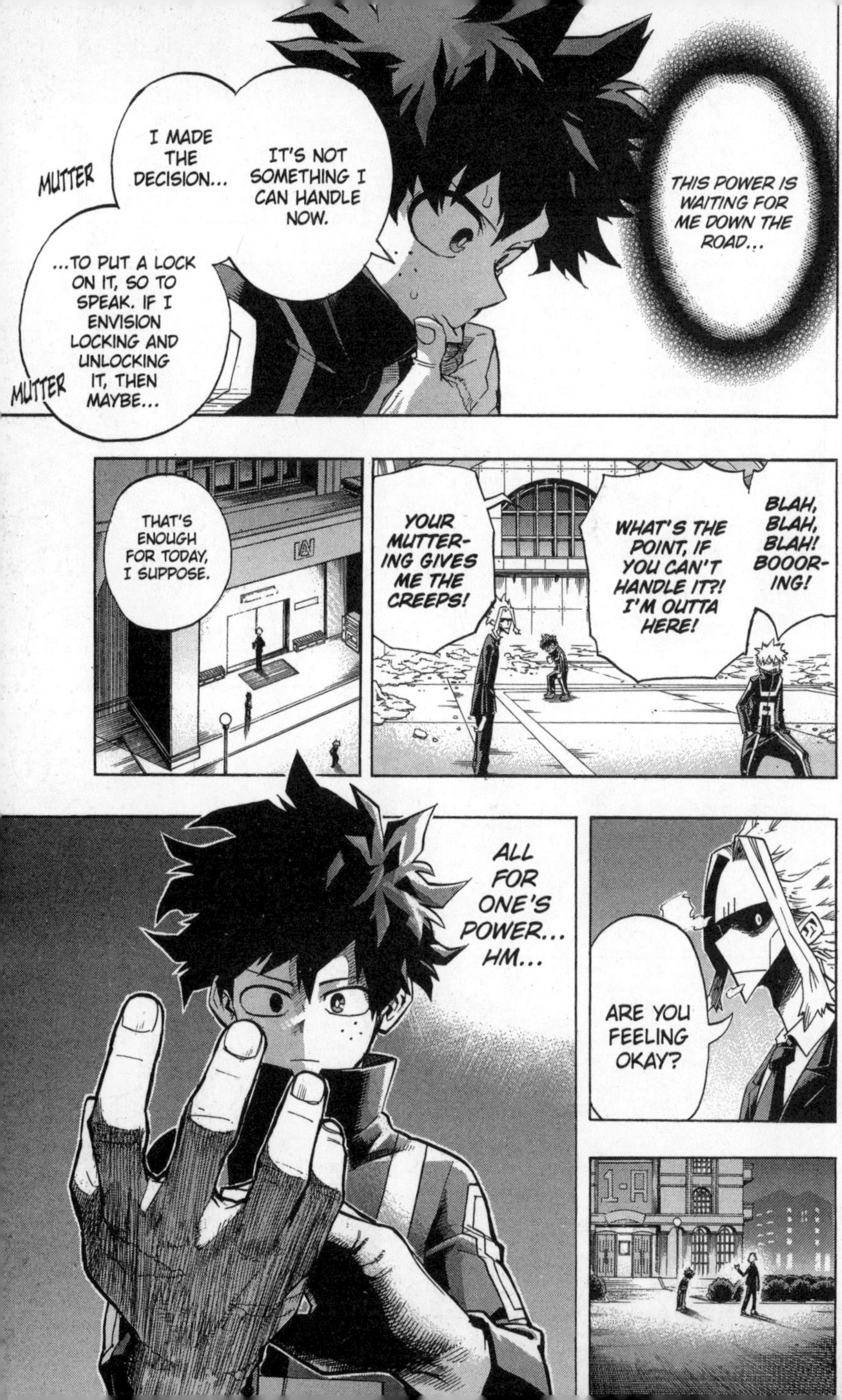
THIS POWER IS WAITING FOR ME DOWN THE ROAD...
IT'S NOT SOMETHING I CAN HANDLE NOW.
I MADE THE DECISION...
MUTTER
...TO PUT A LOCK ON IT, SO TO SPEAK. IF I ENVISION LOCKING AND UNLOCKING IT, THEN MAYBE...
MUTTER
BLAH, BLAH, BLAH! BOOOR-ING!
WHAT'S THE POINT, IF YOU CAN'T HANDLE IT?! I'M OUTTA HERE!
YOUR MUTTER-ING GIVES ME THE CREEPS!
THAT'S ENOUGH FOR TODAY, I SUPPOSE.
ARE YOU FEELING OKAY?
1-A
ALL FOR ONE'S POWER... HM...

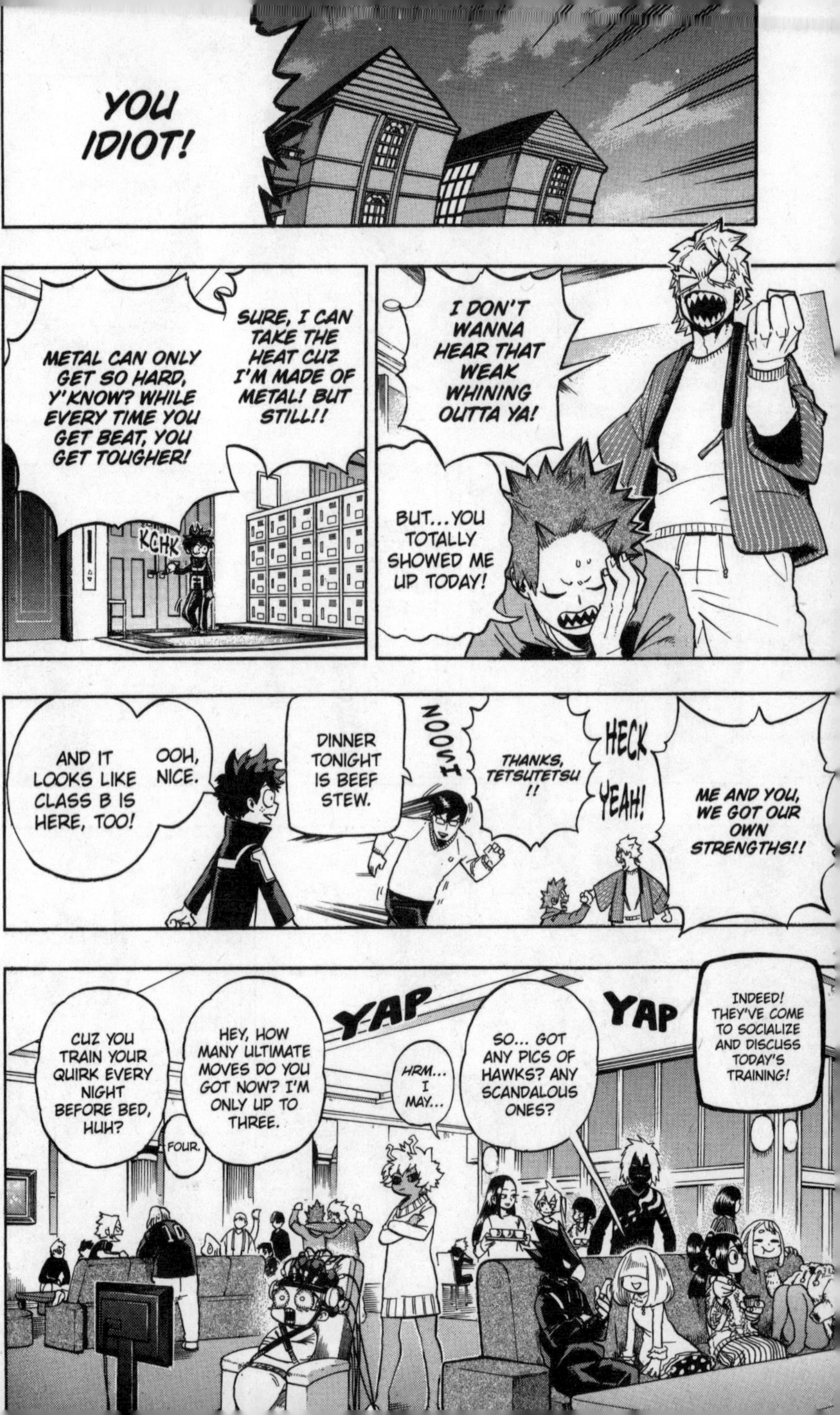

YOU IDIOT!
I DON'T WANNA HEAR THAT WEAK WHINING OUTTA YA!
BUT... YOU TOTALLY SHOWED ME UP TODAY!
SURE, I CAN TAKE THE HEAT CUZ I'M MADE OF METAL! BUT STILL!!
METAL CAN ONLY GET SO HARD, Y'KNOW? WHILE EVERY TIME YOU GET BEAT, YOU GET TOUGHER!
KCHK
ME AND YOU, WE GOT OUR OWN STRENGTHS!!
HECK YEAH!
THANKS, TETSUTETSU!!
WOOSH
DINNER TONIGHT IS BEEF STEW.
OOH, NICE.
AND IT LOOKS LIKE CLASS B IS HERE, TOO!
INDEED! THEY'VE COME TO SOCIALIZE AND DISCUSS TODAY'S TRAINING!
YAP
YAP
SO... GOT ANY PICS OF HAWKS? ANY SCANDALOUS ONES?
HRM... I MAY...
HEY, HOW MANY ULTIMATE MOVES DO YOU GOT NOW? I'M ONLY UP TO THREE.
FOUR.
CUZ YOU TRAIN YOUR QUIRK EVERY NIGHT BEFORE BED, HUH?

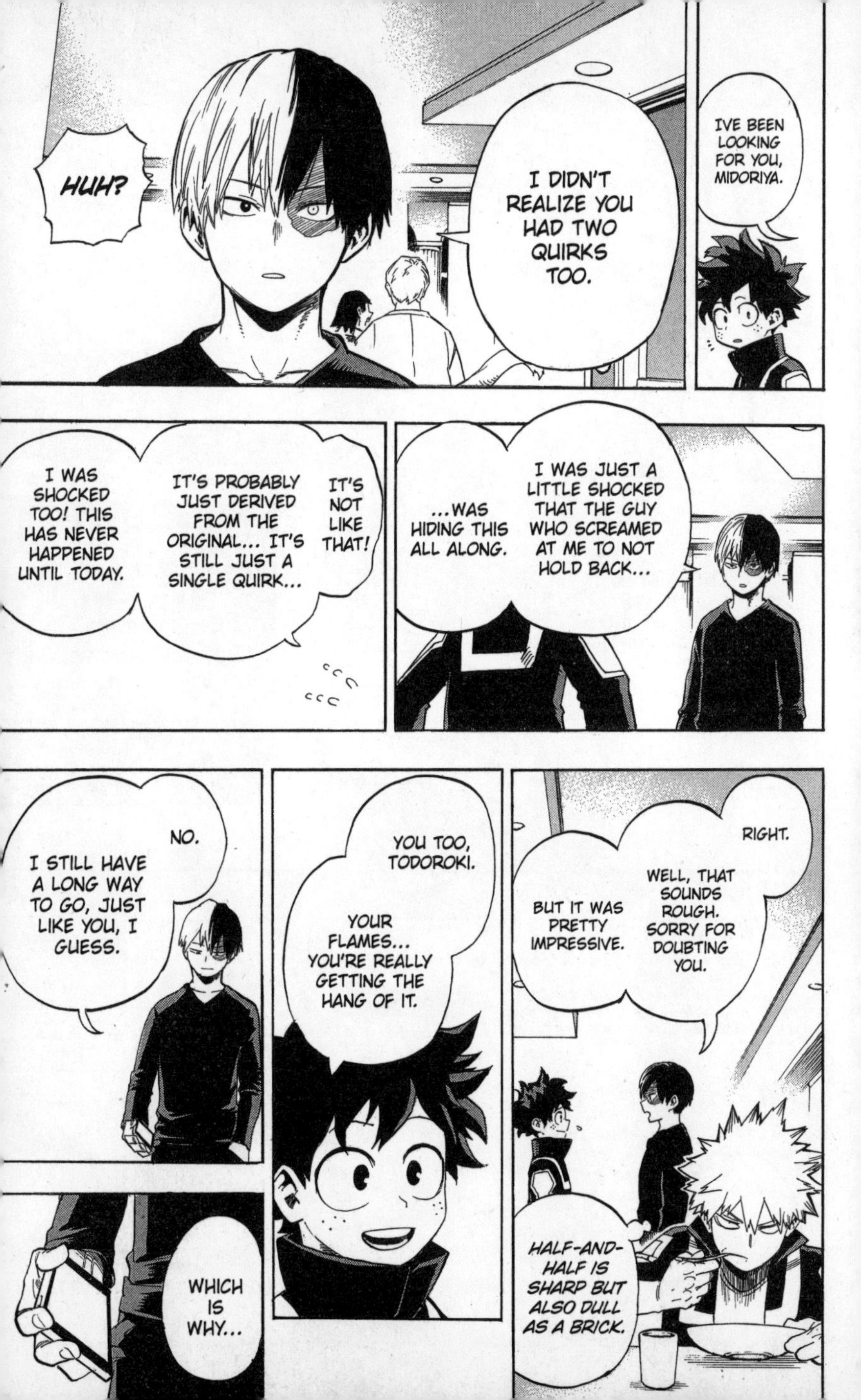
IVE BEEN LOOKING FOR YOU, MIDORIYA.
I DIDN'T REALIZE YOU HAD TWO QUIRKS TOO.
HUH?
I WAS JUST A LITTLE SHOCKED THAT THE GUY WHO SCREAMED AT ME TO NOT HOLD BACK...
...WAS HIDING THIS ALL ALONG.
IT'S NOT LIKE THAT!
IT'S PROBABLY JUST DERIVED FROM THE ORIGINAL... IT'S STILL JUST A SINGLE QUIRK...
I WAS SHOCKED TOO! THIS HAS NEVER HAPPENED UNTIL TODAY.
RIGHT.
WELL, THAT SOUNDS ROUGH. SORRY FOR DOUBTING YOU.
BUT IT WAS PRETTY IMPRESSIVE.
HALF-AND-HALF IS SHARP BUT ALSO DULL AS A BRICK.
YOU TOO, TODOROKI.
YOUR FLAMES... YOU'RE REALLY GETTING THE HANG OF IT.
NO.
I STILL HAVE A LONG WAY TO GO, JUST LIKE YOU, I GUESS.
WHICH IS WHY...

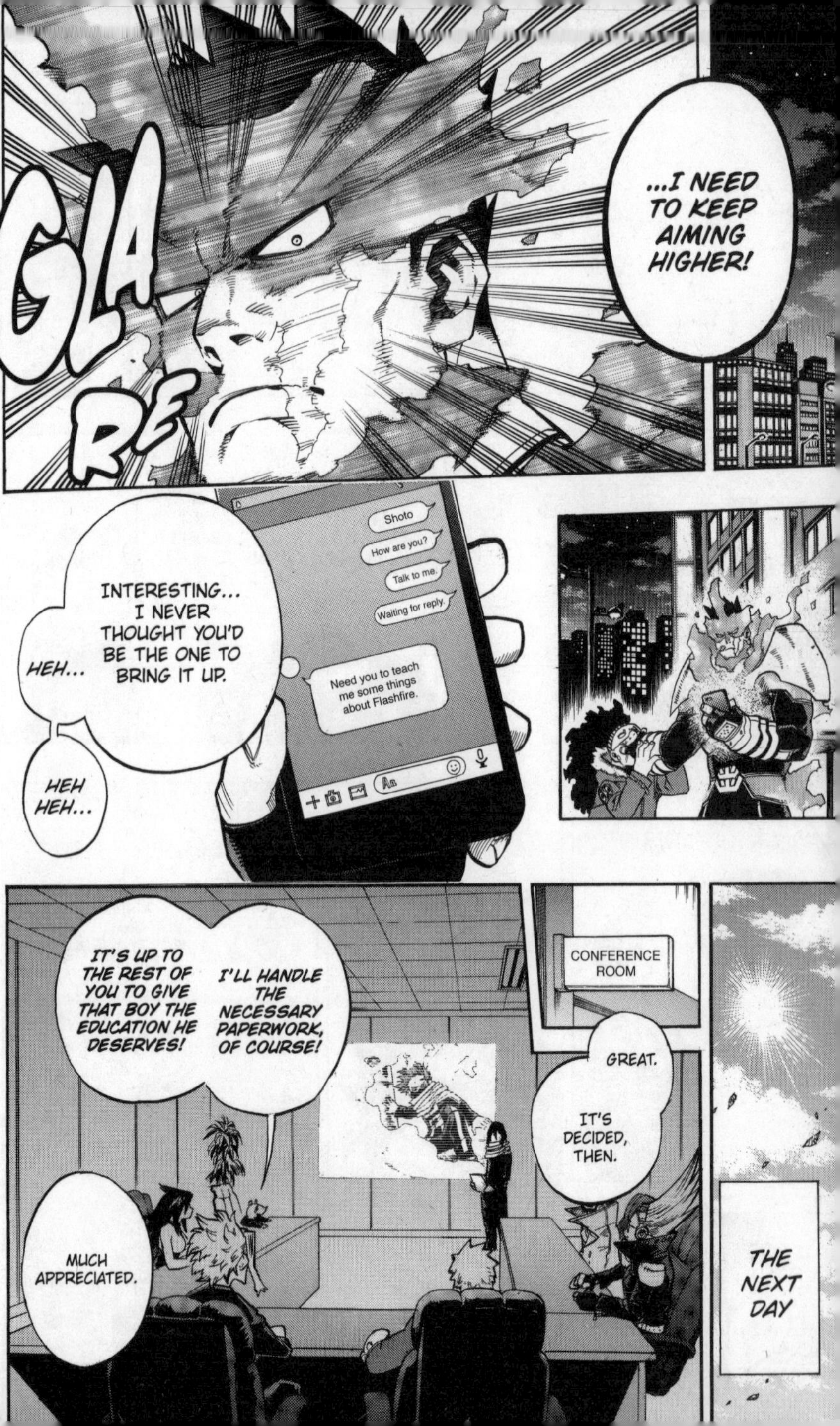

...I NEED TO KEEP AIMING HIGHER!
GLARE
Shoto
How are you?
Talk to me.
Waiting for reply.
Need you to teach me some things about Flashfire.
INTERESTING... I NEVER THOUGHT YOU'D BE THE ONE TO BRING IT UP.
HEH...
HEH HEH...
THE NEXT DAY
CONFERENCE ROOM
GREAT.
IT'S DECIDED, THEN.
I'LL HANDLE THE NECESSARY PAPERWORK, OF COURSE!
IT'S UP TO THE REST OF YOU TO GIVE THAT BOY THE EDUCATION HE DESERVES!
MUCH APPRECIATED.

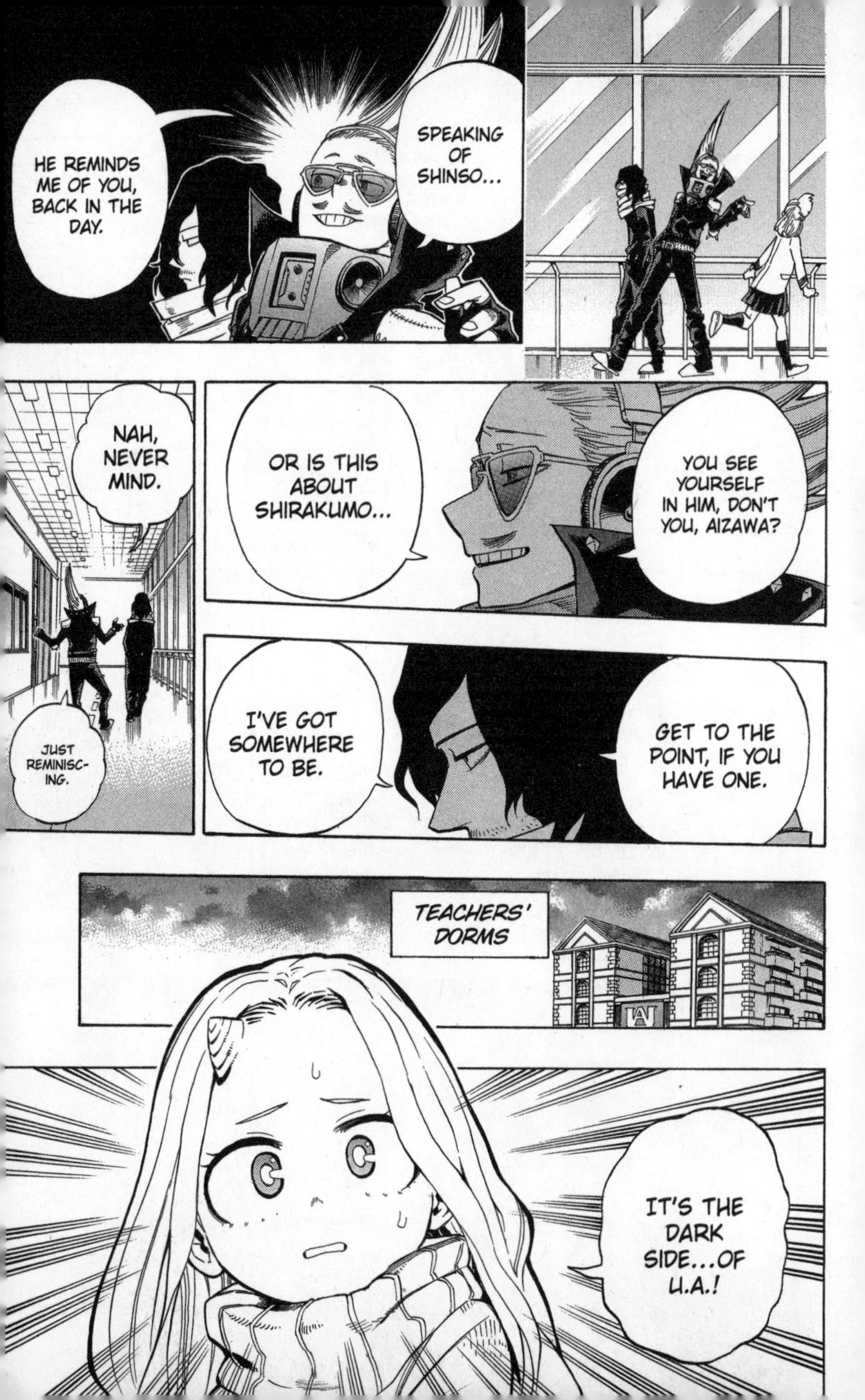
SPEAKING OF SHINSO...
HE REMINDS ME OF YOU, BACK IN THE DAY.
YOU SEE YOURSELF IN HIM, DON'T YOU, AIZAWA?
OR IS THIS ABOUT SHIRAKUMO...
GET TO THE POINT, IF YOU HAVE ONE.
I'VE GOT SOMEWHERE TO BE.
NAH, NEVER MIND.
JUST REMINISC-ING.
TEACHERS' DORMS
IT'S THE DARK SIDE...OF U.A.!

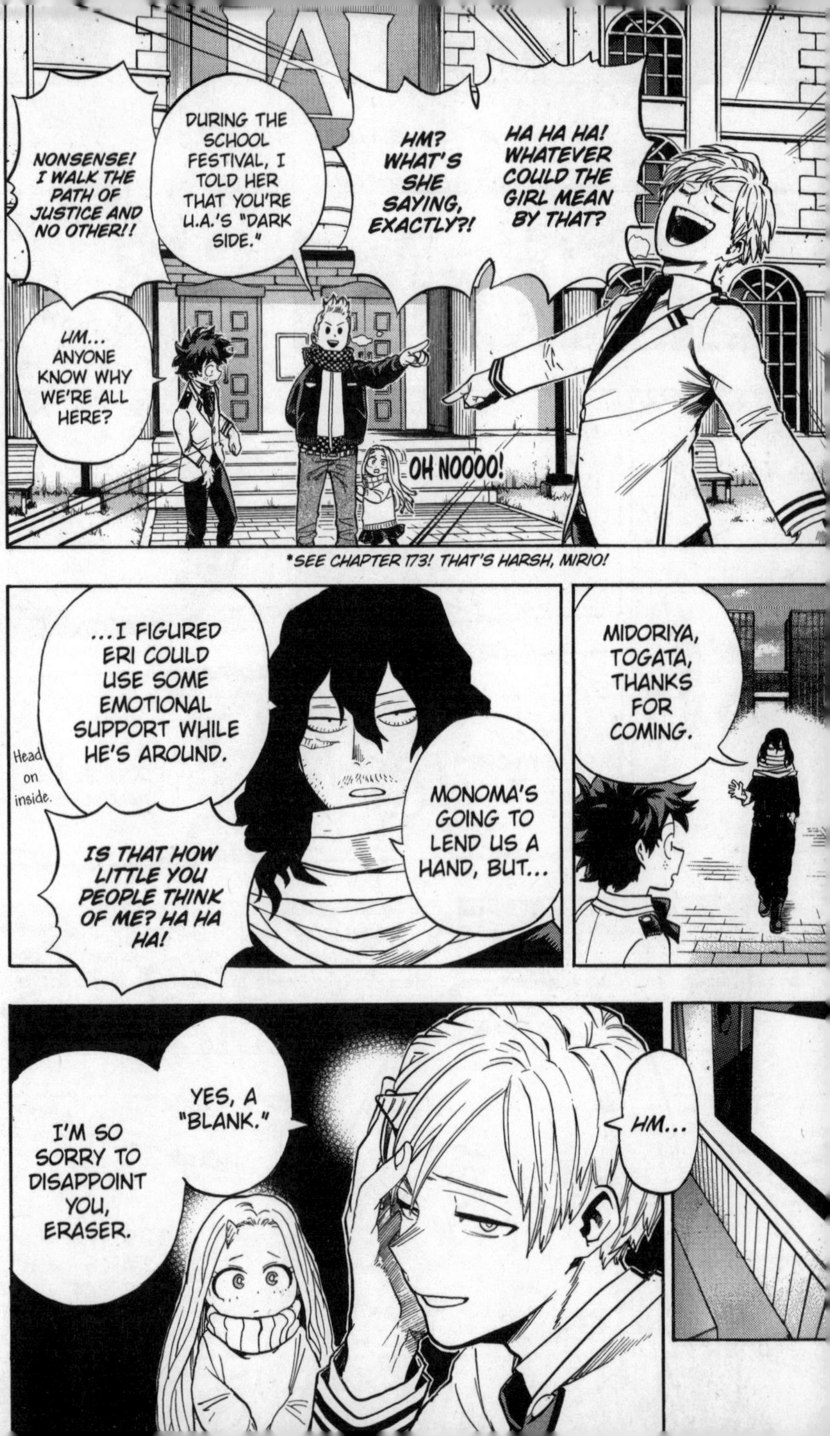
HA HA HA! WHATEVER COULD THE GIRL MEAN BY THAT?
HM? WHAT'S SHE SAYING, EXACTLY?!
DURING THE SCHOOL FESTIVAL, I TOLD HER THAT YOU'RE U.A.'S "DARK SIDE."
NONSENSE! I WALK THE PATH OF JUSTICE AND NO OTHER!!
UM... ANYONE KNOW WHY WE'RE ALL HERE?
OH NOOOO!
*SEE CHAPTER 173! THAT'S HARSH, MIRIO!
MIDORIYA, TOGATA, THANKS FOR COMING.
MONOMA'S GOING TO LEND US A HAND, BUT...
...I FIGURED ERI COULD USE SOME EMOTIONAL SUPPORT WHILE HE'S AROUND.
Head on inside.
IS THAT HOW LITTLE YOU PEOPLE THINK OF ME? HA HA HA!
HM...
YES, A "BLANK."
I'M SO SORRY TO DISAPPOINT YOU, ERASER.

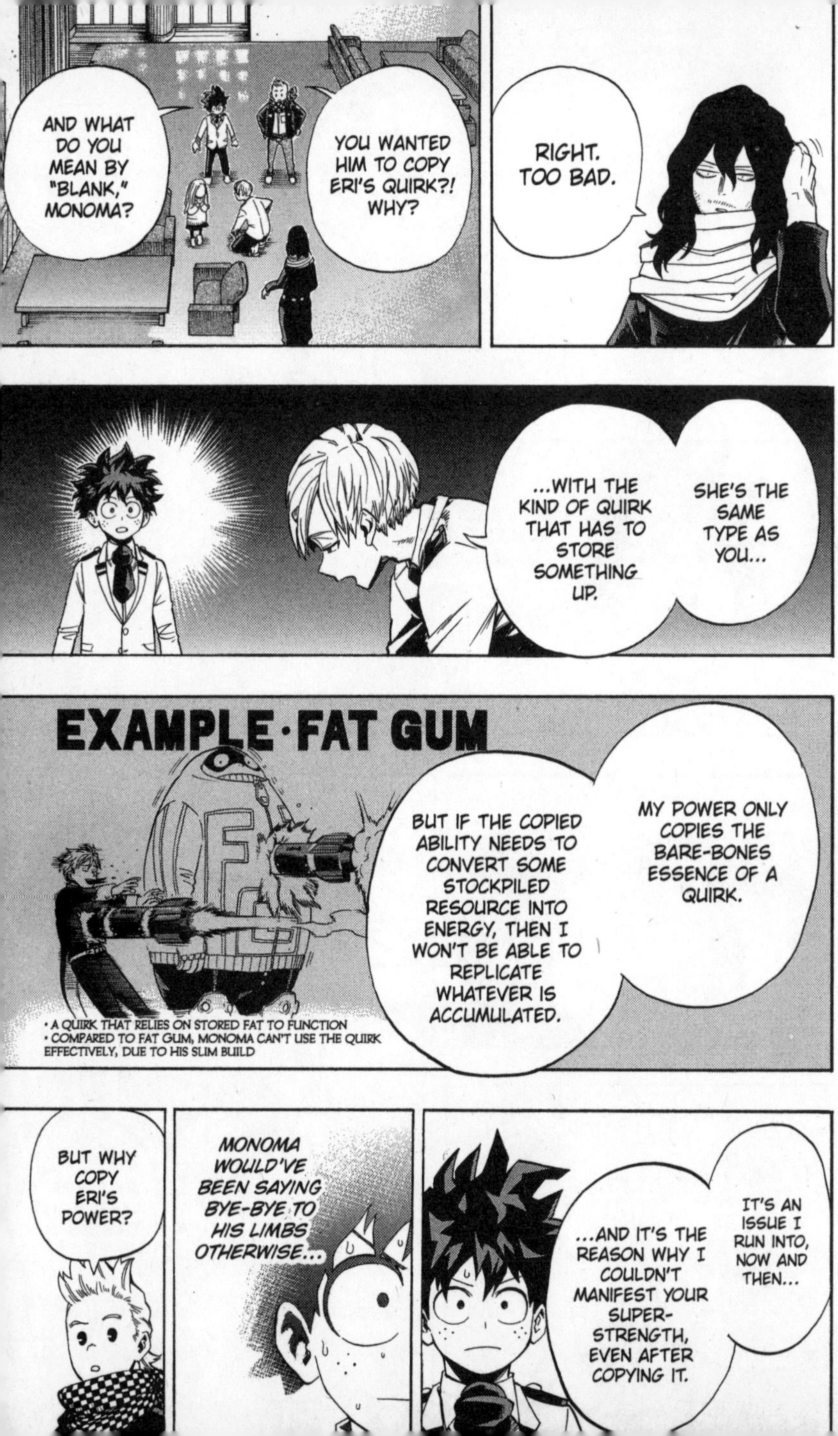
RIGHT. TOO BAD.
YOU WANTED HIM TO COPY ERI'S QUIRK?! WHY?
AND WHAT DO YOU MEAN BY "BLANK," MONOMA?
SHE'S THE SAME TYPE AS YOU...
...WITH THE KIND OF QUIRK THAT HAS TO STORE SOMETHING UP.
EXAMPLE·FAT GUM
MY POWER ONLY COPIES THE BARE-BONES ESSENCE OF A QUIRK.
BUT IF THE COPIED ABILITY NEEDS TO CONVERT SOME STOCKPILED RESOURCE INTO ENERGY, THEN I WON'T BE ABLE TO REPLICATE WHATEVER IS ACCUMULATED.
• A QUIRK THAT RELIES ON STORED FAT TO FUNCTION
• COMPARED TO FAT GUM, MONOMA CAN'T USE THE QUIRK EFFECTIVELY, DUE TO HIS SLIM BUILD
IT'S AN ISSUE I RUN INTO, NOW AND THEN...
...AND IT'S THE REASON WHY I COULDN'T MANIFEST YOUR SUPER-STRENGTH, EVEN AFTER COPYING IT.
MONOMA WOULD'VE BEEN SAYING BYE-BYE TO HIS LIMBS OTHERWISE...
BUT WHY COPY ERI'S POWER?

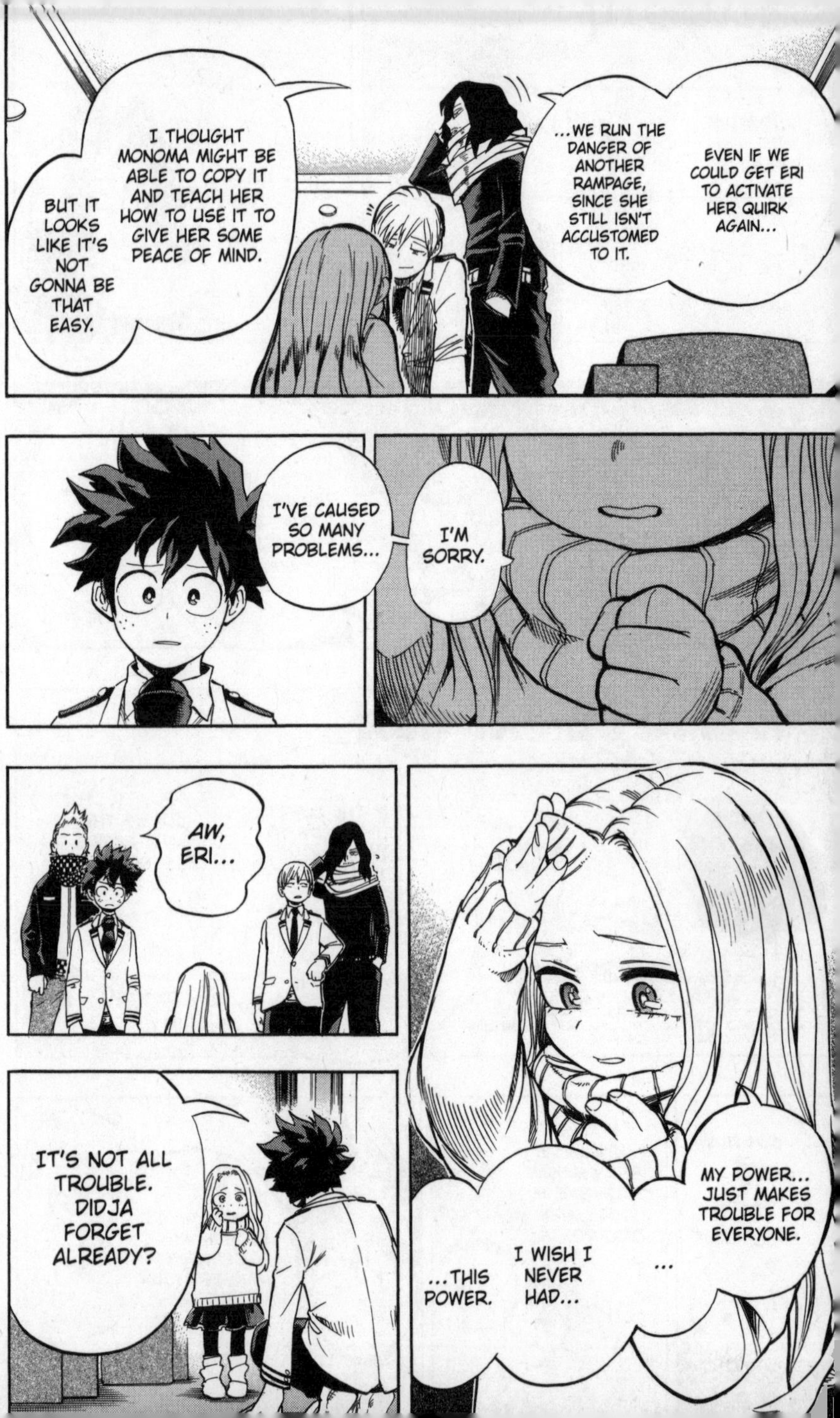
EVEN IF WE COULD GET ERI TO ACTIVATE HER QUIRK AGAIN...
...WE RUN THE DANGER OF ANOTHER RAMPAGE, SINCE SHE STILL ISN'T ACCUSTOMED TO IT.
I THOUGHT MONOMA MIGHT BE ABLE TO COPY IT AND TEACH HER HOW TO USE IT TO GIVE HER SOME PEACE OF MIND.
BUT IT LOOKS LIKE IT'S NOT GONNA BE THAT EASY.
I'M SORRY.
I'VE CAUSED SO MANY PROBLEMS...
MY POWER... JUST MAKES TROUBLE FOR EVERYONE.
...
I WISH I NEVER HAD...
...THIS POWER.
AW, ERI...
IT'S NOT ALL TROUBLE. DIDJA FORGET ALREADY?

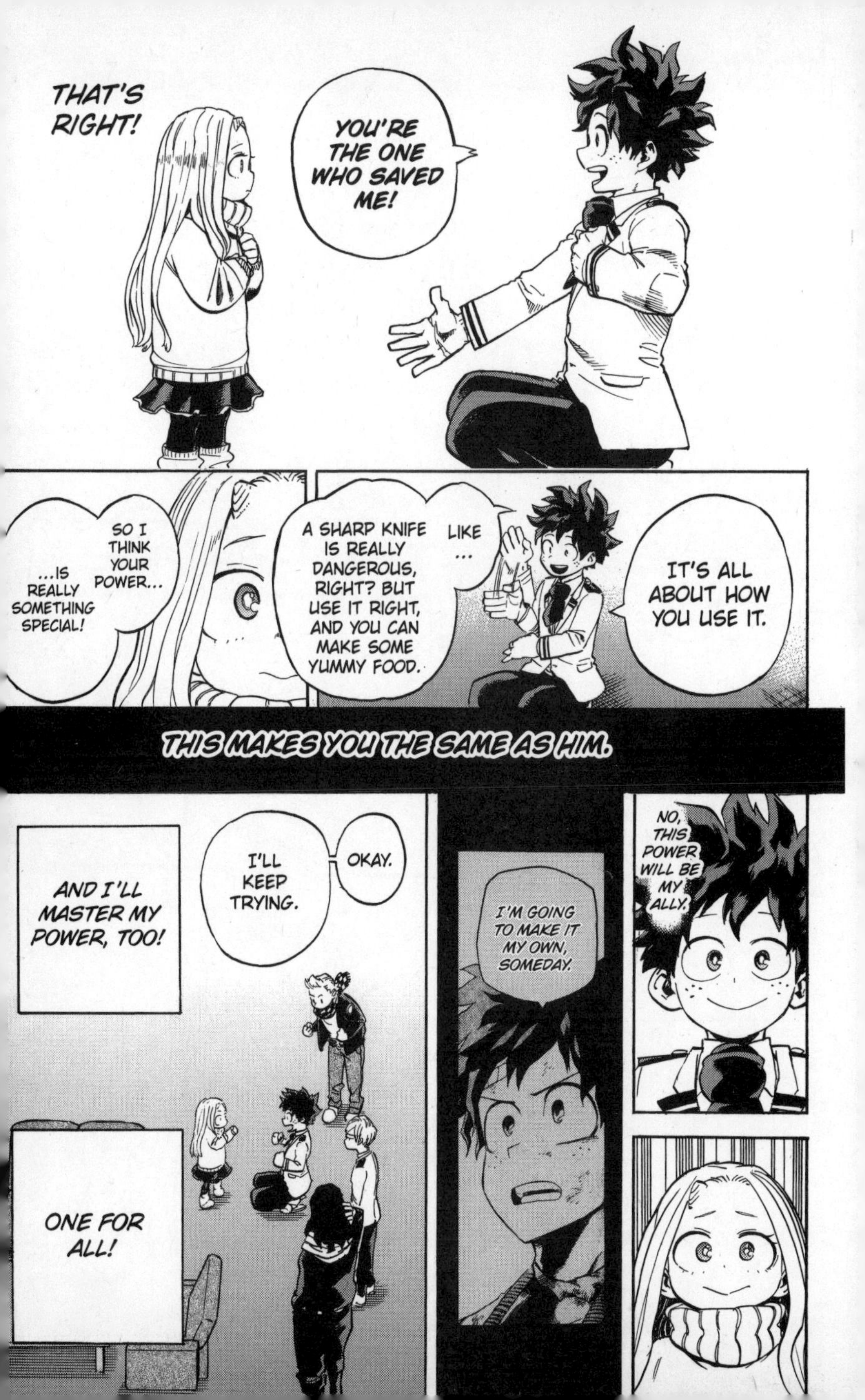
YOU'RE THE ONE WHO SAVED ME!
THAT'S RIGHT!
IT'S ALL ABOUT HOW YOU USE IT.
LIKE ...
A SHARP KNIFE IS REALLY DANGEROUS, RIGHT? BUT USE IT RIGHT, AND YOU CAN MAKE SOME YUMMY FOOD.
SO I THINK YOUR POWER...
...IS REALLY SOMETHING SPECIAL!
THIS MAKES YOU THE SAME AS HIM.
NO, THIS POWER WILL BE MY ALLY.
I'M GOING TO MAKE IT MY OWN, SOMEDAY.
OKAY.
I'LL KEEP TRYING.
AND I'LL MASTER MY POWER, TOO!
ONE FOR ALL!

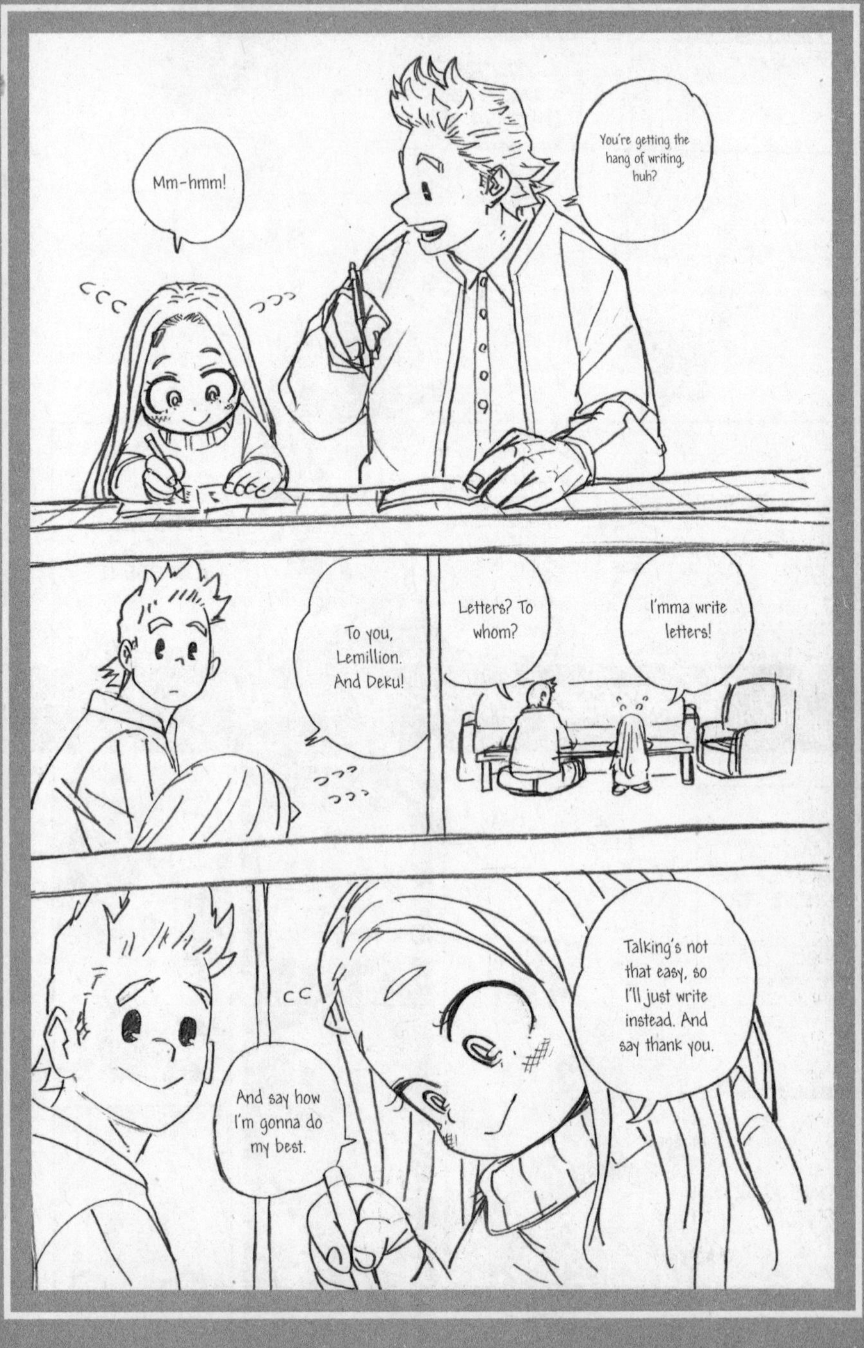
You're getting the hang of writing, huh?
Mm-hmm!
I'mma write letters!
Letters? To whom?
To you, Lemillion. And Deku!
Talking's not that easy, so I'll just write instead. And say thank you.
And say how I'm gonna do my best.

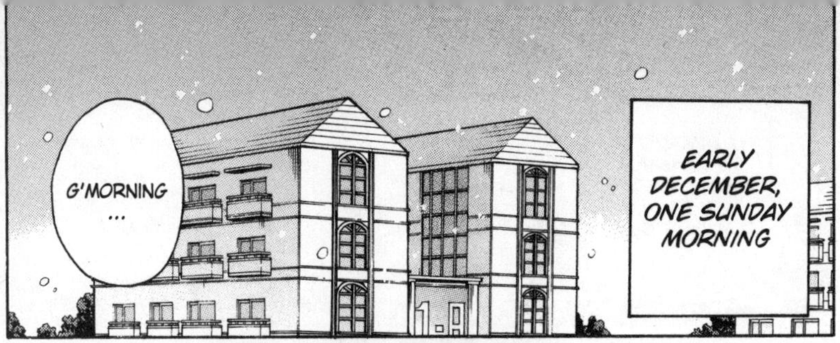
EARLY DECEMBER, ONE SUNDAY MORNING
G'MORNING ...

NO. 218 - THE META LIBERATION ARMY

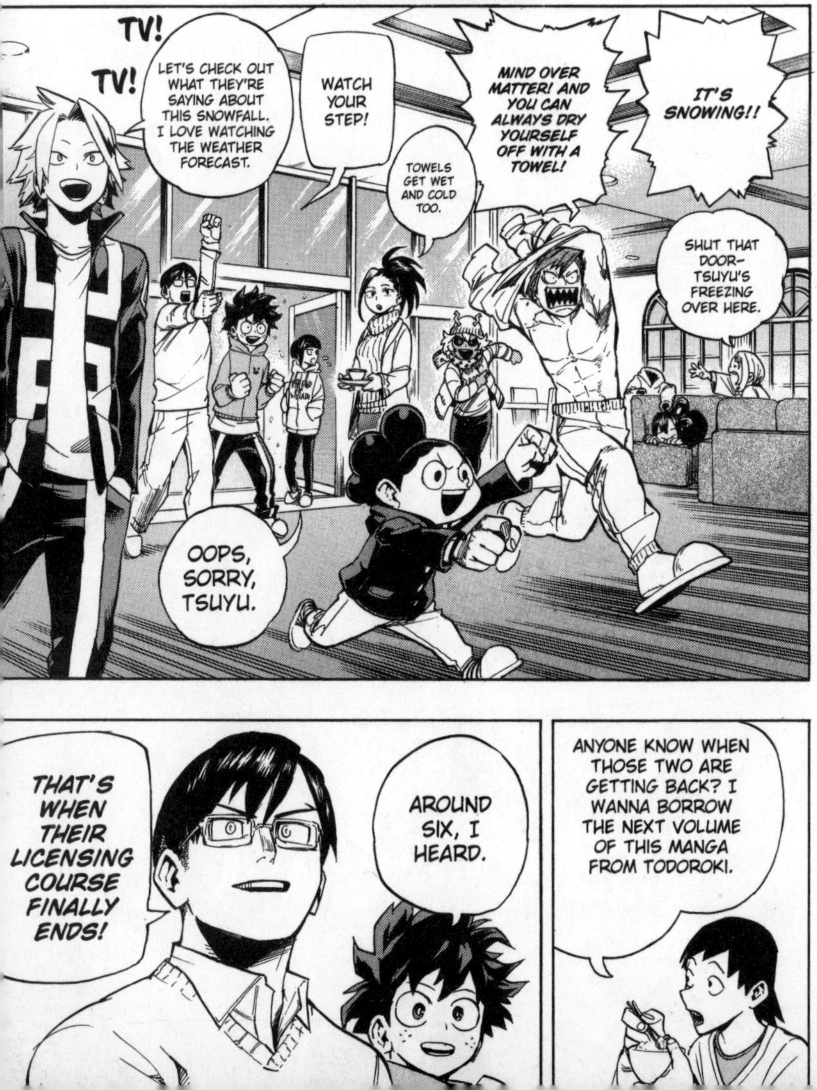
IT'S SNOWING!!
MIND OVER MATTER! AND YOU CAN ALWAYS DRY YOURSELF OFF WITH A TOWEL!
SHUT THAT DOOR- TSUYU'S FREEZING OVER HERE.
TOWELS GET WET AND COLD TOO.
WATCH YOUR STEP!
LET'S CHECK OUT WHAT THEY'RE SAYING ABOUT THIS SNOWFALL. I LOVE WATCHING THE WEATHER FORECAST.
TV!
TV!
OOPS, SORRY, TSUYU.
ANYONE KNOW WHEN THOSE TWO ARE GETTING BACK? I WANNA BORROW THE NEXT VOLUME OF THIS MANGA FROM TODOROKI.
AROUND SIX, I HEARD.
THAT'S WHEN THEIR LICENSING COURSE FINALLY ENDS!

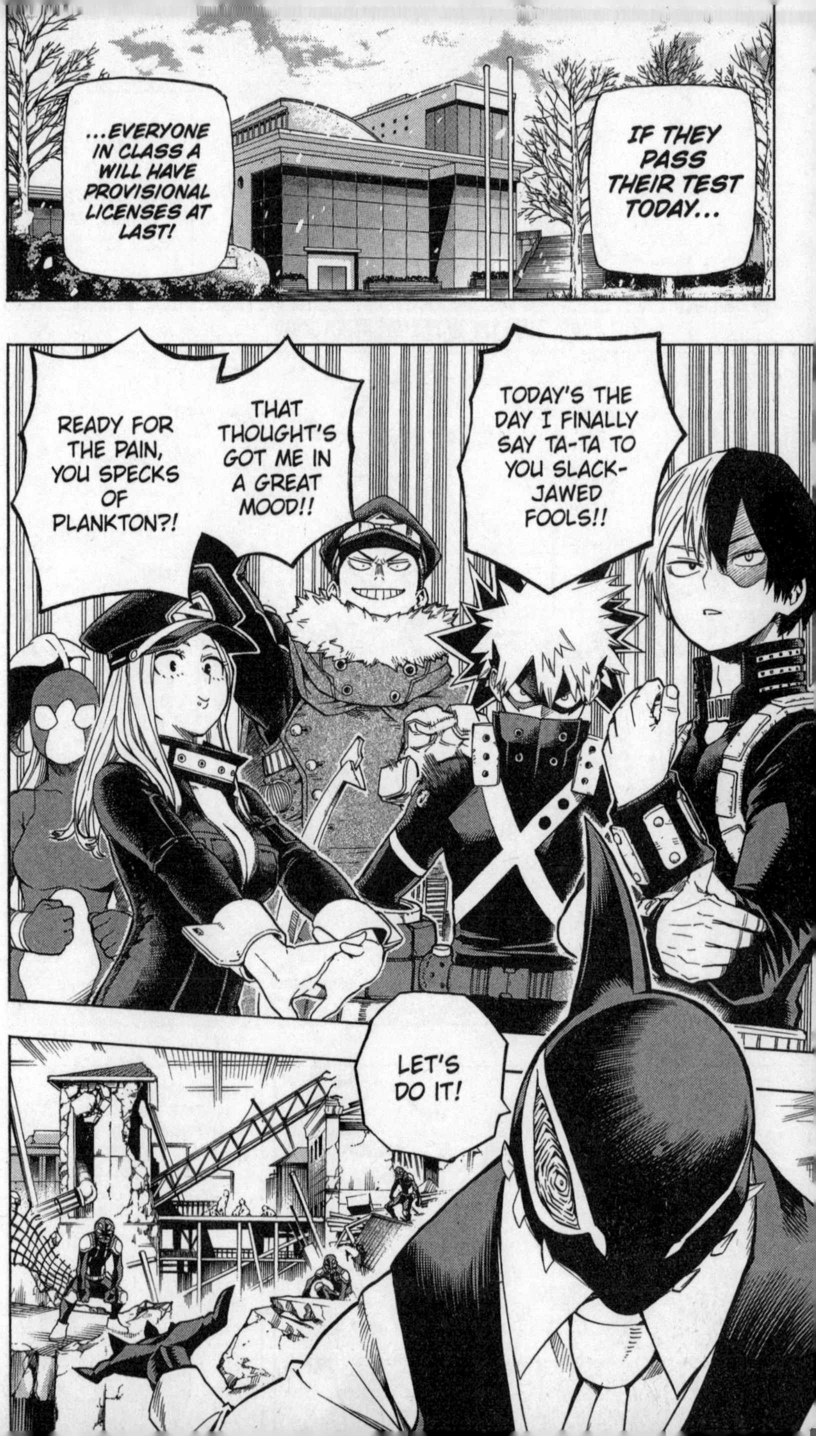
IF THEY PASS THEIR TEST TODAY...
...EVERYONE IN CLASS A WILL HAVE PROVISIONAL LICENSES AT LAST!
TODAY'S THE DAY I FINALLY SAY TA-TA TO YOU SLACK-JAWED FOOLS!!
THAT THOUGHT'S GOT ME IN A GREAT MOOD!!
READY FOR THE PAIN, YOU SPECKS OF PLANKTON?!
LET'S DO IT!

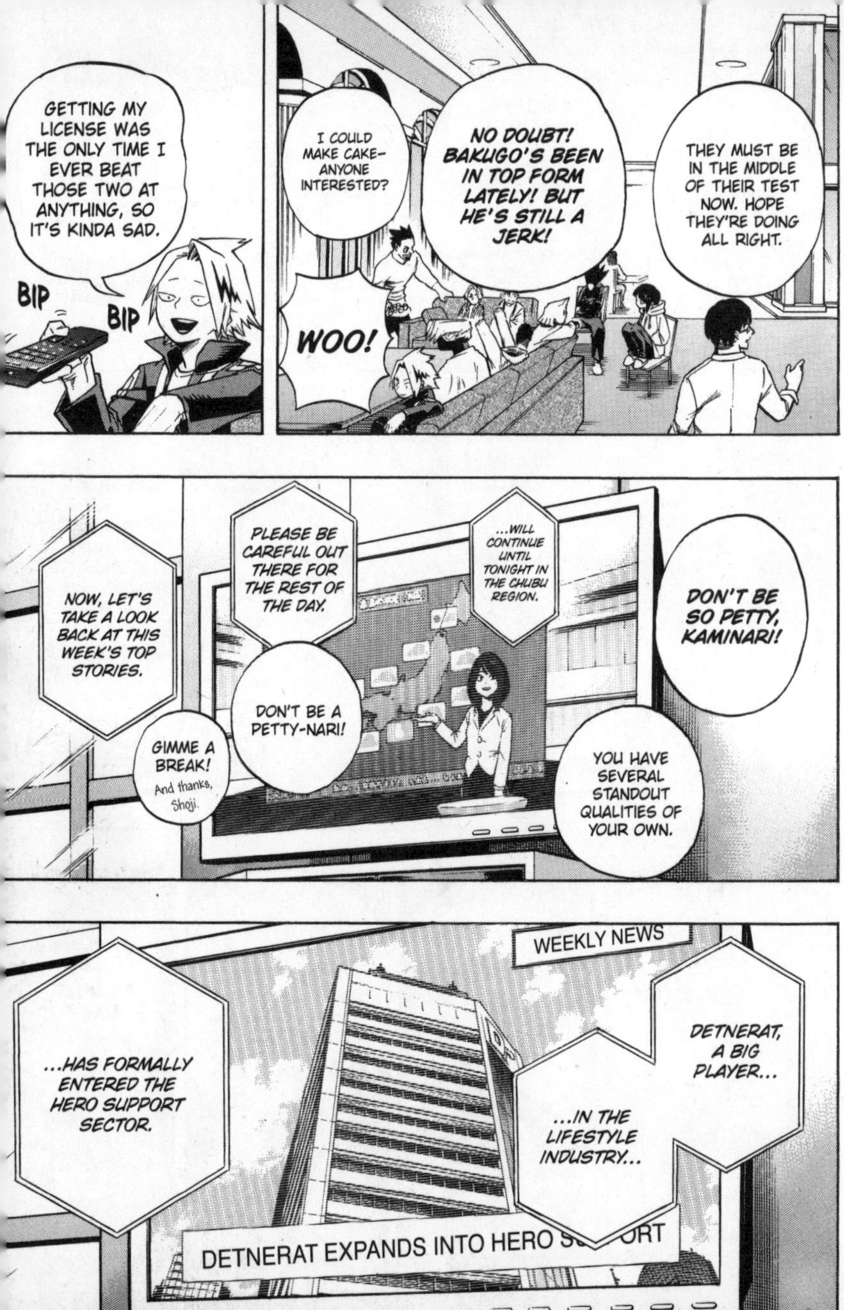
THEY MUST BE IN THE MIDDLE OF THEIR TEST NOW. HOPE THEY'RE DOING ALL RIGHT.
NO DOUBT! BAKUGO'S BEEN IN TOP FORM LATELY! BUT HE'S STILL A JERK!
I COULD MAKE CAKE-ANYONE INTERESTED?
WOO!
GETTING MY LICENSE WAS THE ONLY TIME I EVER BEAT THOSE TWO AT ANYTHING, SO IT'S KINDA SAD.
BIP
BIP
DON'T BE SO PETTY, KAMINARI!
...WILL CONTINUE UNTIL TONIGHT IN THE CHUBU REGION.
YOU HAVE SEVERAL STANDOUT QUALITIES OF YOUR OWN.
PLEASE BE CAREFUL OUT THERE FOR THE REST OF THE DAY.
DON'T BE A PETTY-NARI!
NOW, LET'S TAKE A LOOK BACK AT THIS WEEK'S TOP STORIES.
GIMME A BREAK! And thanks, Shoji.
WEEKLY NEWS
DETNERAT, A BIG PLAYER...
...IN THE LIFESTYLE INDUSTRY...
...HAS FORMALLY ENTERED THE HERO SUPPORT SECTOR.
DETNERAT EXPANDS INTO HERO SUPPORT

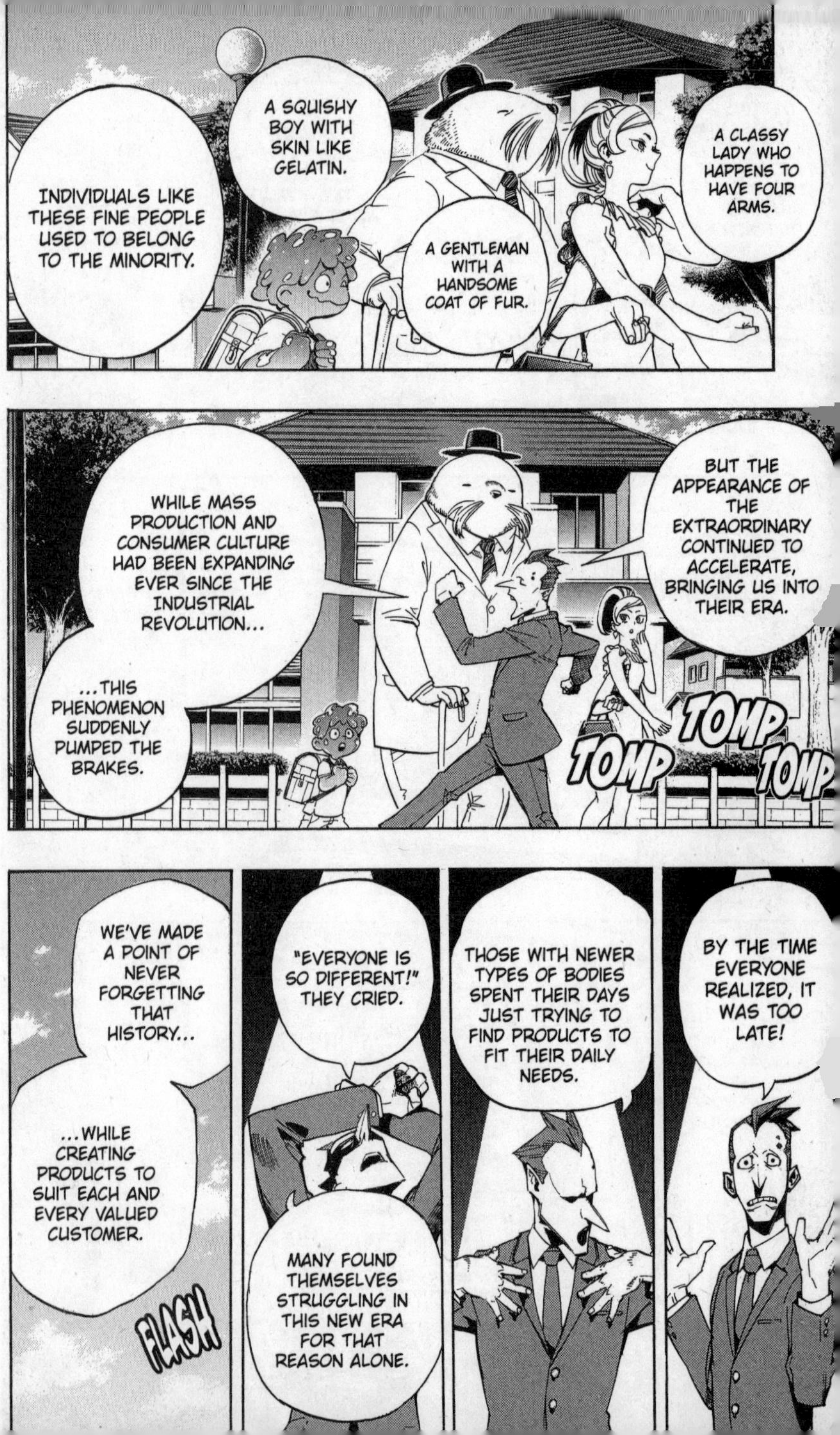
A CLASSY LADY WHO HAPPENS TO HAVE FOUR ARMS.
A GENTLEMAN WITH A HANDSOME COAT OF FUR.
A SQUISHY BOY WITH SKIN LIKE GELATIN.
INDIVIDUALS LIKE THESE FINE PEOPLE USED TO BELONG TO THE MINORITY.
WHILE MASS PRODUCTION AND CONSUMER CULTURE HAD BEEN EXPANDING EVER SINCE THE INDUSTRIAL REVOLUTION...
...THIS PHENOMENON SUDDENLY PUMPED THE BRAKES.
BUT THE APPEARANCE OF THE EXTRAORDINARY CONTINUED TO ACCELERATE, BRINGING US INTO THEIR ERA.
TOMP
TOMP
TOMP
BY THE TIME EVERYONE REALIZED, IT WAS TOO LATE!
THOSE WITH NEWER TYPES OF BODIES SPENT THEIR DAYS JUST TRYING TO FIND PRODUCTS TO FIT THEIR DAILY NEEDS.
"EVERYONE IS SO DIFFERENT!" THEY CRIED.
MANY FOUND THEMSELVES STRUGGLING IN THIS NEW ERA FOR THAT REASON ALONE.
WE'VE MADE A POINT OF NEVER FORGETTING THAT HISTORY...
...WHILE CREATING PRODUCTS TO SUIT EACH AND EVERY VALUED CUSTOMER.
FLASH

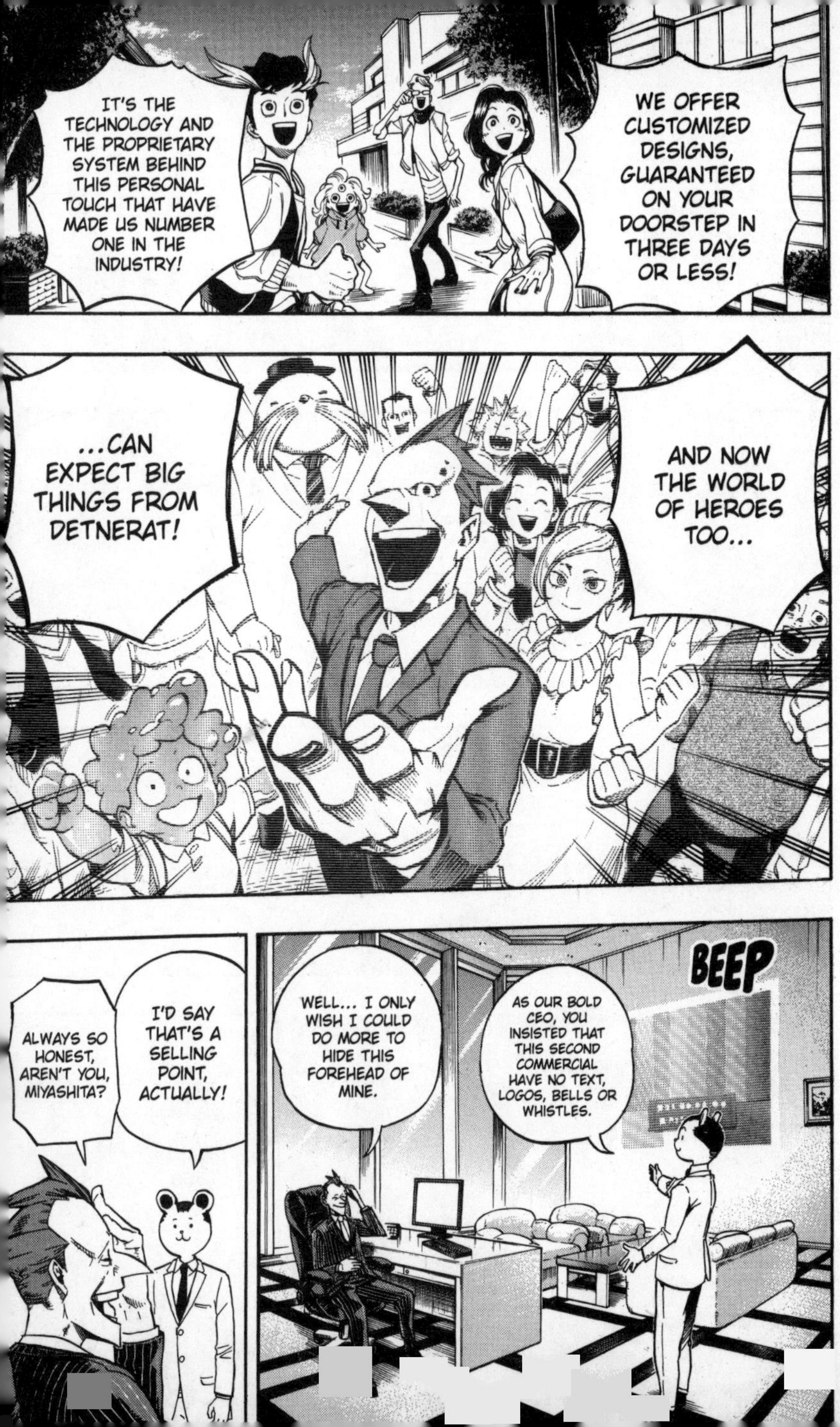
WE OFFER CUSTOMIZED DESIGNS, GUARANTEED ON YOUR DOORSTEP IN THREE DAYS OR LESS!
IT'S THE TECHNOLOGY AND THE PROPRIETARY SYSTEM BEHIND THIS PERSONAL TOUCH THAT HAVE MADE US NUMBER ONE IN THE INDUSTRY!
AND NOW THE WORLD OF HEROES TOO...
...CAN EXPECT BIG THINGS FROM DETNERAT!
BEEP
AS OUR BOLD CEO, YOU INSISTED THAT THIS SECOND COMMERCIAL HAVE NO TEXT, LOGOS, BELLS OR WHISTLES.
WELL... I ONLY WISH I COULD DO MORE TO HIDE THIS FOREHEAD OF MINE.
I'D SAY THAT'S A SELLING POINT, ACTUALLY!
ALWAYS SO HONEST, AREN'T YOU, MIYASHITA?

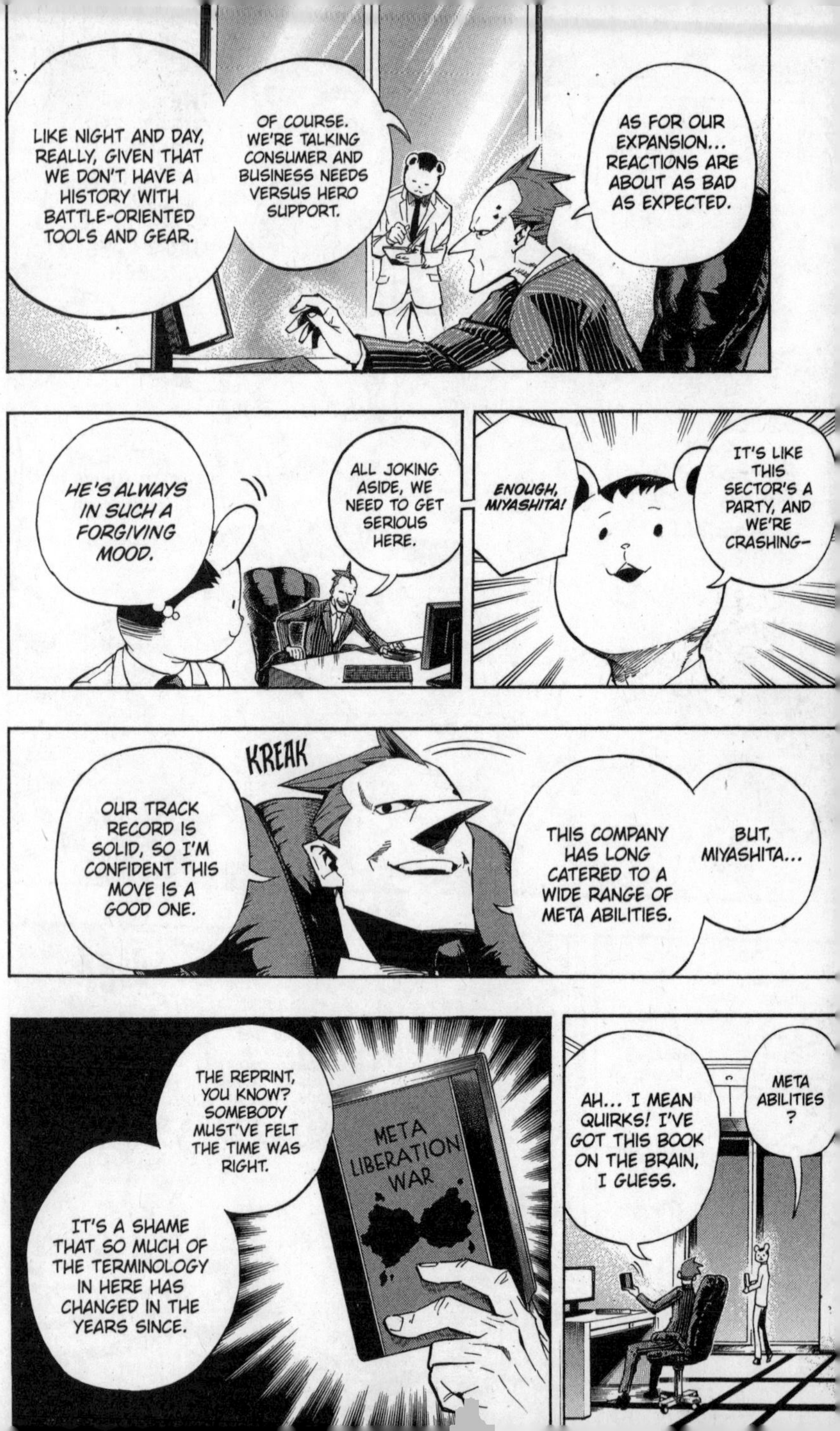
AS FOR OUR EXPANSION... REACTIONS ARE ABOUT AS BAD AS EXPECTED.
OF COURSE. WE'RE TALKING CONSUMER AND BUSINESS NEEDS VERSUS HERO SUPPORT.
LIKE NIGHT AND DAY, REALLY, GIVEN THAT WE DON'T HAVE A HISTORY WITH BATTLE-ORIENTED TOOLS AND GEAR.
IT'S LIKE THIS SECTOR'S A PARTY, AND WE'RE CRASHING—
ENOUGH, MIYASHITA!
ALL JOKING ASIDE, WE NEED TO GET SERIOUS HERE.
HE'S ALWAYS IN SUCH A FORGIVING MOOD.
BUT, MIYASHITA...
THIS COMPANY HAS LONG CATERED TO A WIDE RANGE OF META ABILITIES.
KREAK
OUR TRACK RECORD IS SOLID, SO I'M CONFIDENT THIS MOVE IS A GOOD ONE.
META ABILITIES?
AH... I MEAN QUIRKS! I'VE GOT THIS BOOK ON THE BRAIN, I GUESS.
THE REPRINT, YOU KNOW? SOMEBODY MUST'VE FELT THE TIME WAS RIGHT.
META LIBERATION WAR
IT'S A SHAME THAT SO MUCH OF THE TERMINOLOGY IN HERE HAS CHANGED IN THE YEARS SINCE.

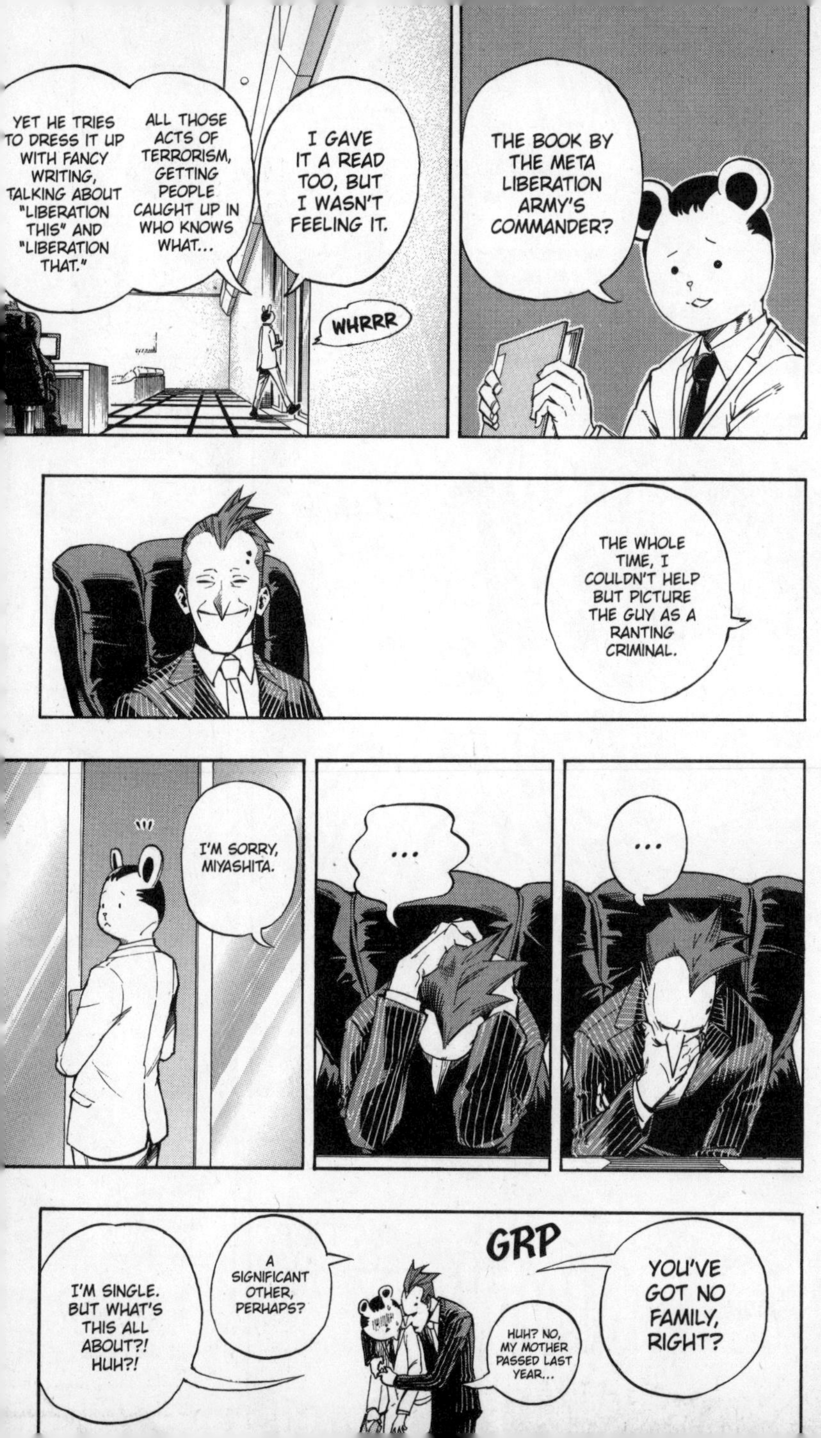
THE BOOK BY THE META LIBERATION ARMY'S COMMANDER?
I GAVE IT A READ TOO, BUT I WASN'T FEELING IT.
WHRRR
ALL THOSE ACTS OF TERRORISM, GETTING PEOPLE CAUGHT UP IN WHO KNOWS WHAT...
YET HE TRIES TO DRESS IT UP WITH FANCY WRITING, TALKING ABOUT "LIBERATION THIS" AND "LIBERATION THAT."
THE WHOLE TIME, I COULDN'T HELP BUT PICTURE THE GUY AS A RANTING CRIMINAL.
...
...
I'M SORRY, MIYASHITA.
GRP
YOU'VE GOT NO FAMILY, RIGHT?
HUH? NO, MY MOTHER PASSED LAST YEAR...
A SIGNIFICANT OTHER, PERHAPS?
I'M SINGLE. BUT WHAT'S THIS ALL ABOUT?! HUH?!

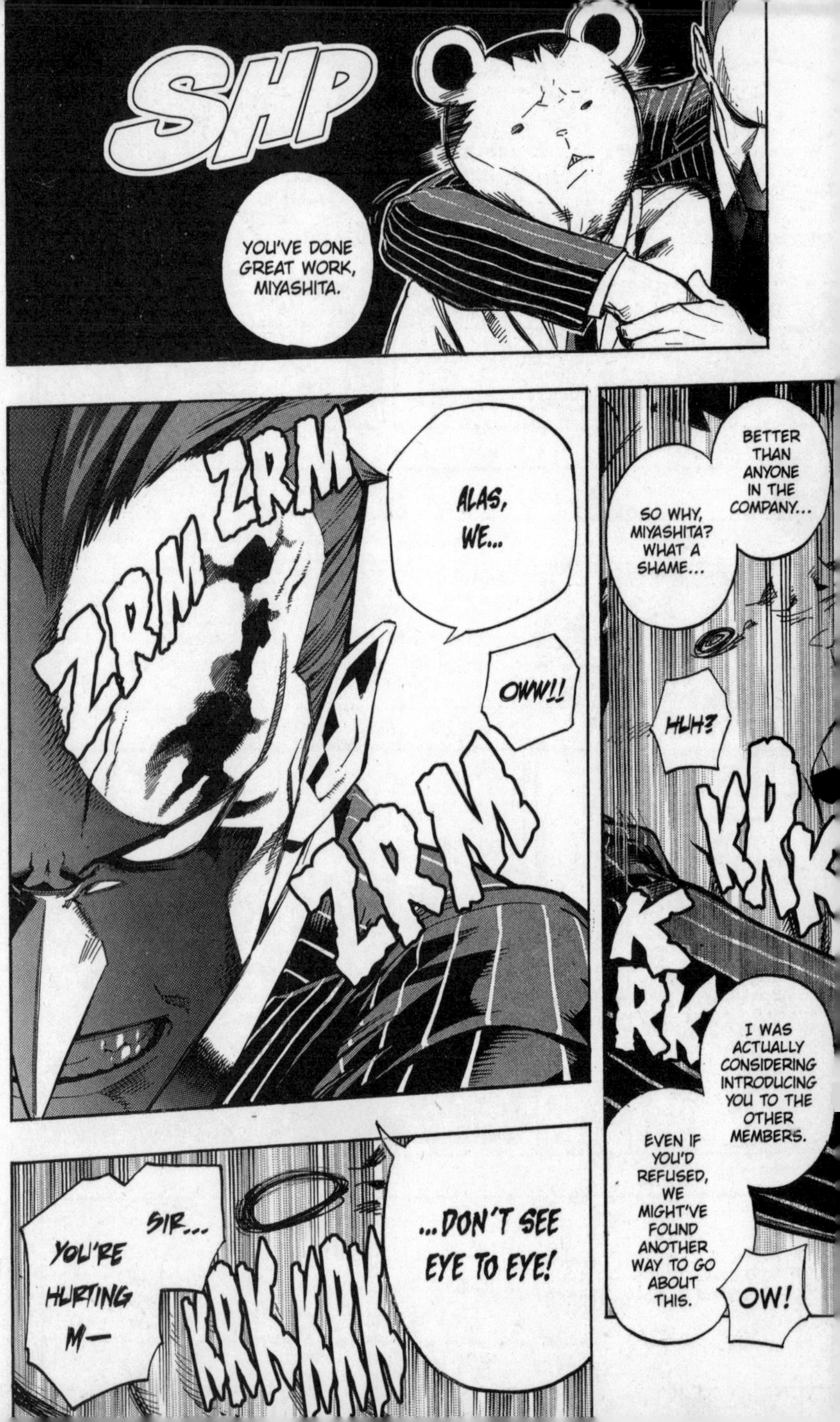
SHP
YOU'VE DONE GREAT WORK, MIYASHITA.
BETTER THAN ANYONE IN THE COMPANY...
SO WHY, MIYASHITA? WHAT A SHAME...
HUH?
KRK
KRK
I WAS ACTUALLY CONSIDERING INTRODUCING YOU TO THE OTHER MEMBERS.
EVEN IF YOU'D REFUSED, WE MIGHT'VE FOUND ANOTHER WAY TO GO ABOUT THIS.
OW!
ALAS, WE...
ZRM ZRM
ZRM
OWW!!
ZRM
...DON'T SEE EYE TO EYE!
KRK KRK
SIR...
YOU'RE HURTING M—

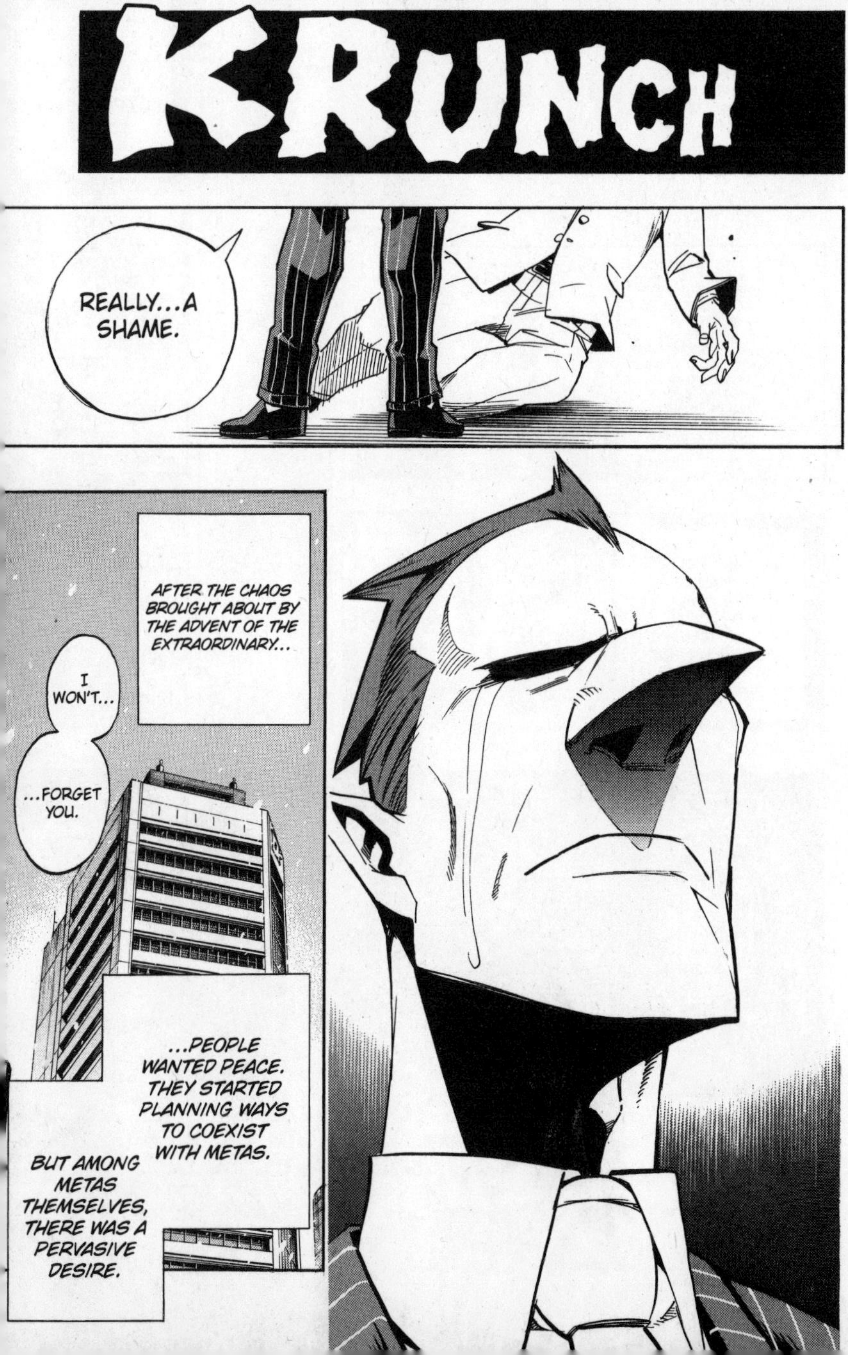
KRUNCH
REALLY...A SHAME.
AFTER THE CHAOS BROUGHT ABOUT BY THE ADVENT OF THE EXTRAORDINARY...
I WON'T...
...FORGET YOU.
...PEOPLE WANTED PEACE. THEY STARTED PLANNING WAYS TO COEXIST WITH METAS.
BUT AMONG METAS THEMSELVES, THERE WAS A PERVASIVE DESIRE.

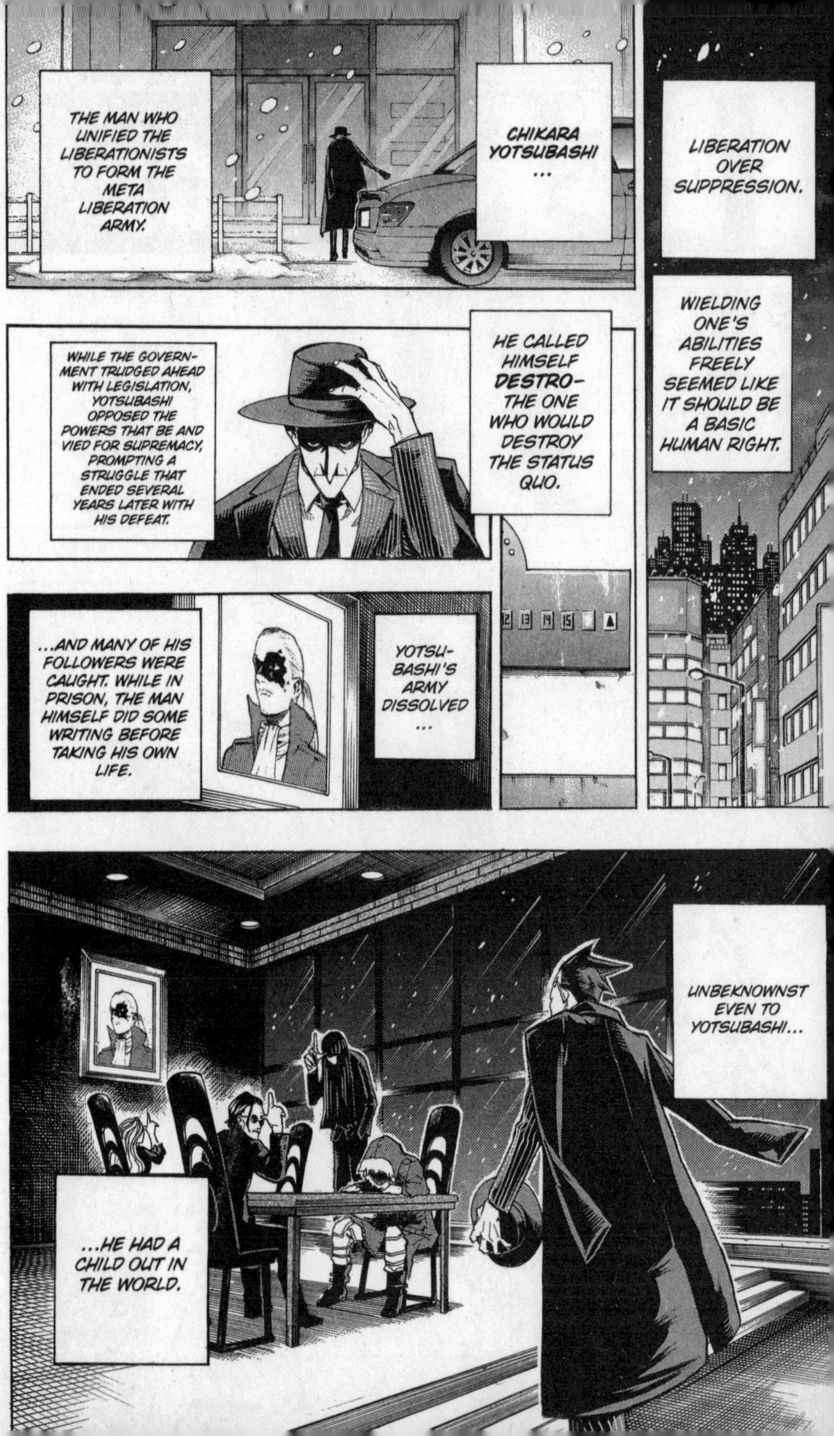
LIBERATION OVER SUPPRESSION.
WIELDING ONE'S ABILITIES FREELY SEEMED LIKE IT SHOULD BE A BASIC HUMAN RIGHT.
CHIKARA YOTSUBASHI ...
THE MAN WHO UNIFIED THE LIBERATIONISTS TO FORM THE META LIBERATION ARMY.
HE CALLED HIMSELF DESTRO-THE ONE WHO WOULD DESTROY THE STATUS QUO.
WHILE THE GOVERNMENT TRUDGED AHEAD WITH LEGISLATION, YOTSUBASHI OPPOSED THE POWERS THAT BE AND VIED FOR SUPREMACY, PROMPTING A STRUGGLE THAT ENDED SEVERAL YEARS LATER WITH HIS DEFEAT.
YOTSU-BASHI'S ARMY DISSOLVED ...
...AND MANY OF HIS FOLLOWERS WERE CAUGHT. WHILE IN PRISON, THE MAN HIMSELF DID SOME WRITING BEFORE TAKING HIS OWN LIFE.
UNBEKNOWNST EVEN TO YOTSUBASHI...
...HE HAD A CHILD OUT IN THE WORLD.

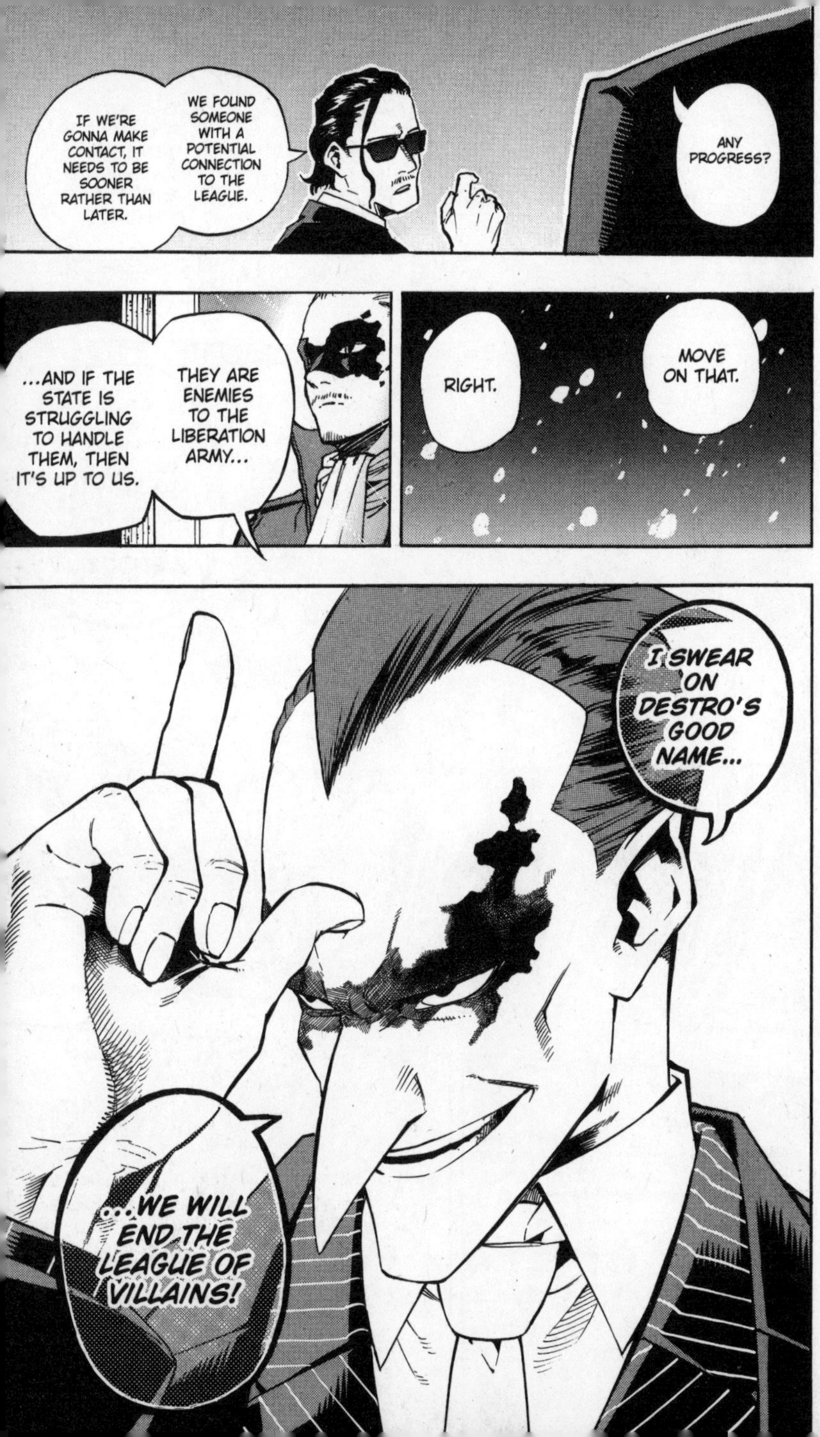
ANY PROGRESS?
WE FOUND SOMEONE WITH A POTENTIAL CONNECTION TO THE LEAGUE.
IF WE'RE GONNA MAKE CONTACT, IT NEEDS TO BE SOONER RATHER THAN LATER.
MOVE ON THAT.
RIGHT.
THEY ARE ENEMIES TO THE LIBERATION ARMY...
...AND IF THE STATE IS STRUGGLING TO HANDLE THEM, THEN IT'S UP TO US.
I SWEAR ON DESTRO'S GOOD NAME...
...WE WILL END THE LEAGUE OF VILLAINS!

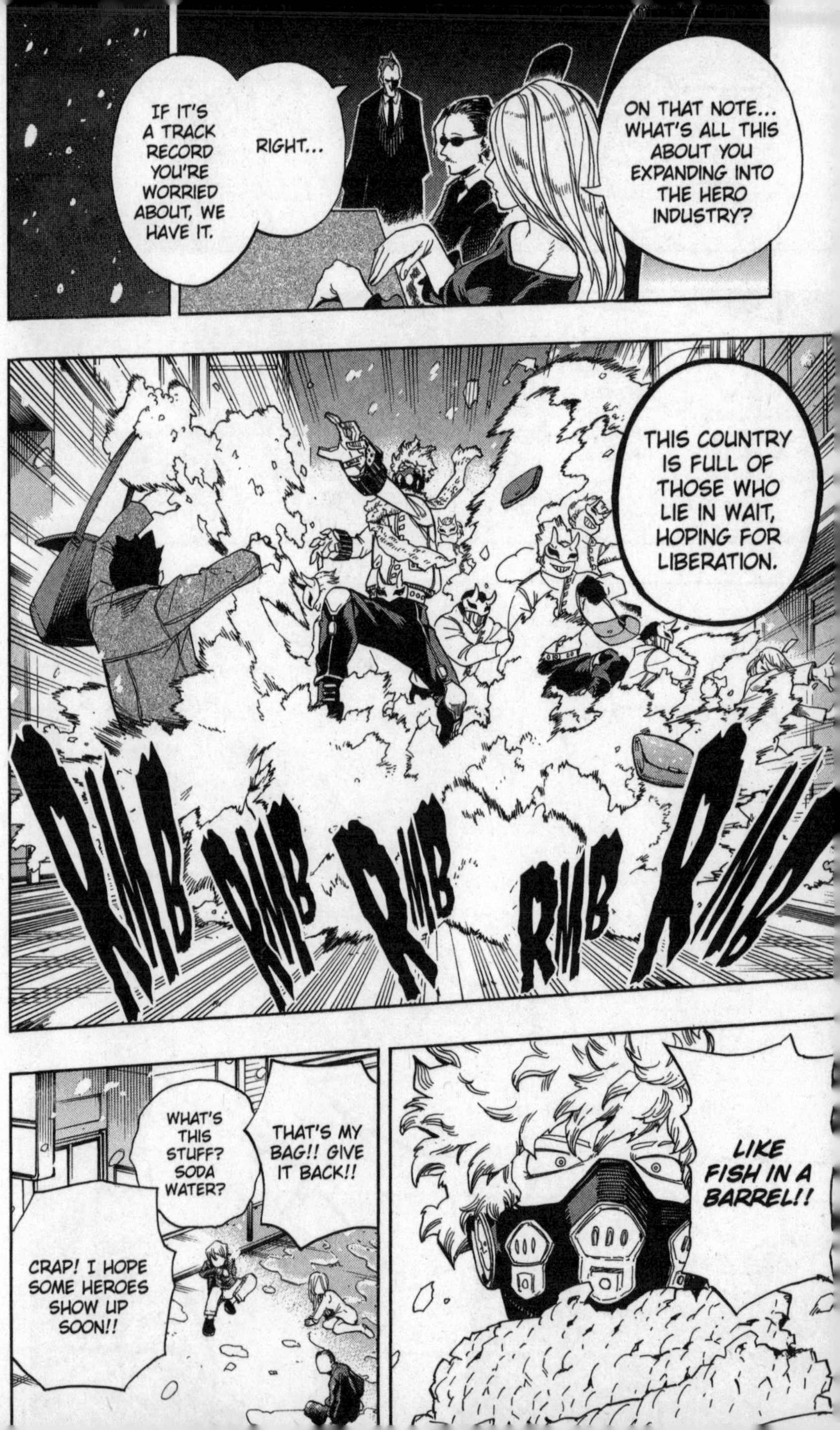
ON THAT NOTE... WHAT'S ALL THIS ABOUT YOU EXPANDING INTO THE HERO INDUSTRY?
RIGHT...
IF IT'S A TRACK RECORD YOU'RE WORRIED ABOUT, WE HAVE IT.
THIS COUNTRY IS FULL OF THOSE WHO LIE IN WAIT, HOPING FOR LIBERATION.
RMB
RMB
RMB
RMB
RMB
LIKE FISH IN A BARREL!!
THAT'S MY BAG!! GIVE IT BACK!!
WHAT'S THIS STUFF? SODA WATER?
CRAP! I HOPE SOME HEROES SHOW UP SOON!!

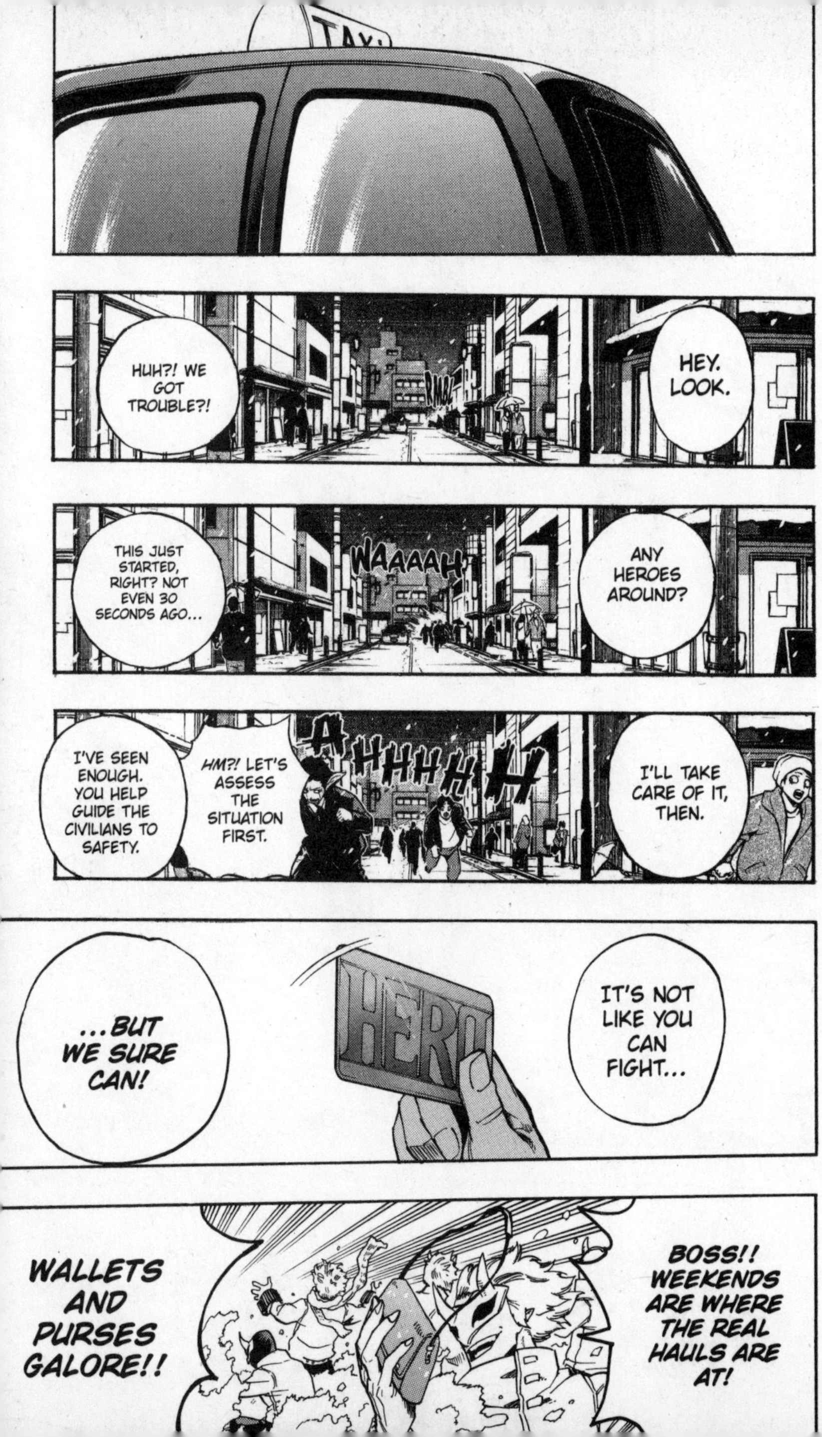
HEY. LOOK.
RMBL
HUH?! WE GOT TROUBLE?!
ANY HEROES AROUND?
WAAAAH
THIS JUST STARTED, RIGHT? NOT EVEN 30 SECONDS AGO...
I'LL TAKE CARE OF IT, THEN.
AHHHHHH
HM?! LET'S ASSESS THE SITUATION FIRST.
I'VE SEEN ENOUGH. YOU HELP GUIDE THE CIVILIANS TO SAFETY.
IT'S NOT LIKE YOU CAN FIGHT...
HERO
...BUT WE SURE CAN!
BOSS!! WEEKENDS ARE WHERE THE REAL HAULS ARE AT!
WALLETS AND PURSES GALORE!!

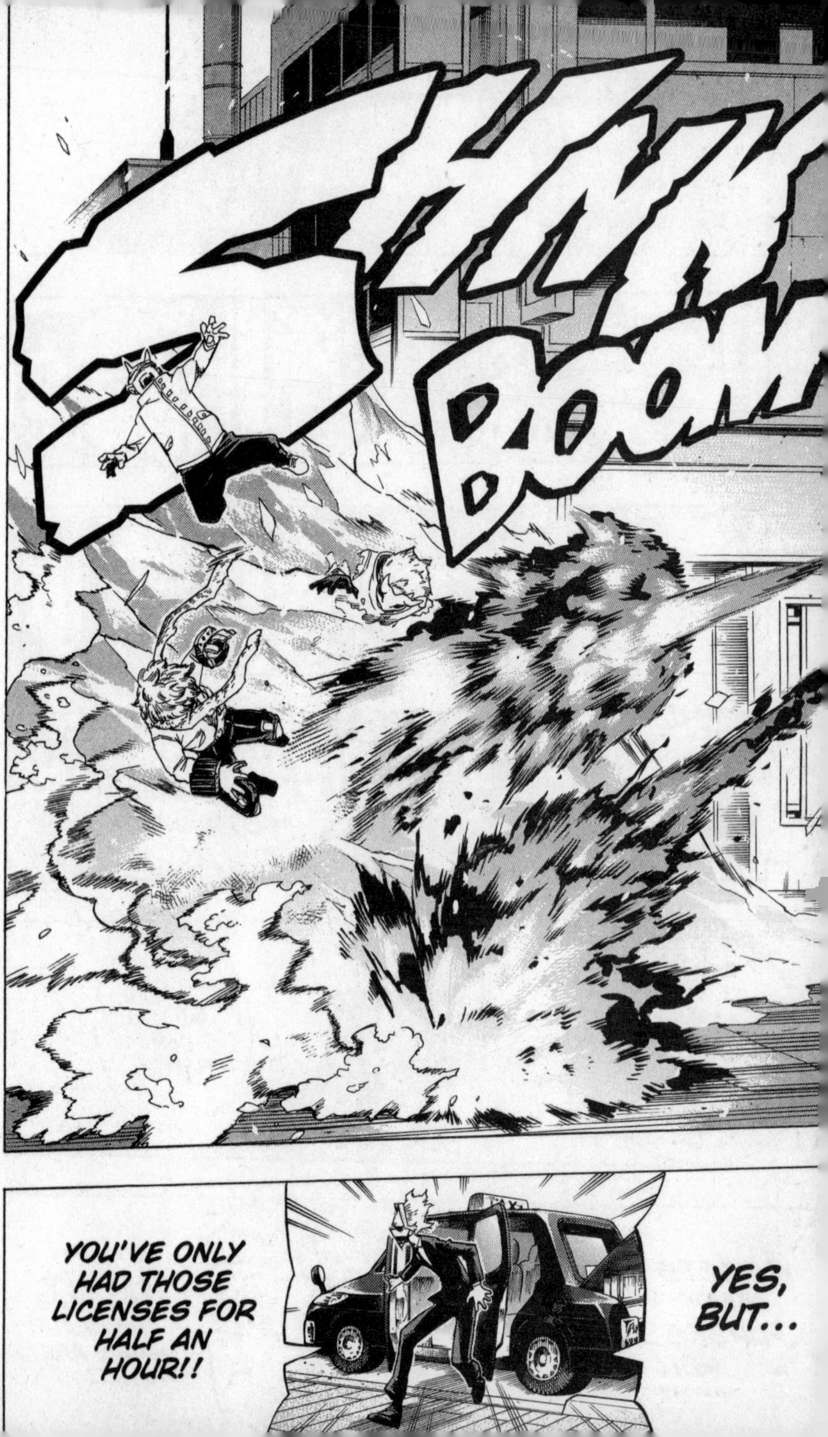

YES, BUT...
YOU'VE ONLY HAD THOSE LICENSES FOR HALF AN HOUR!!

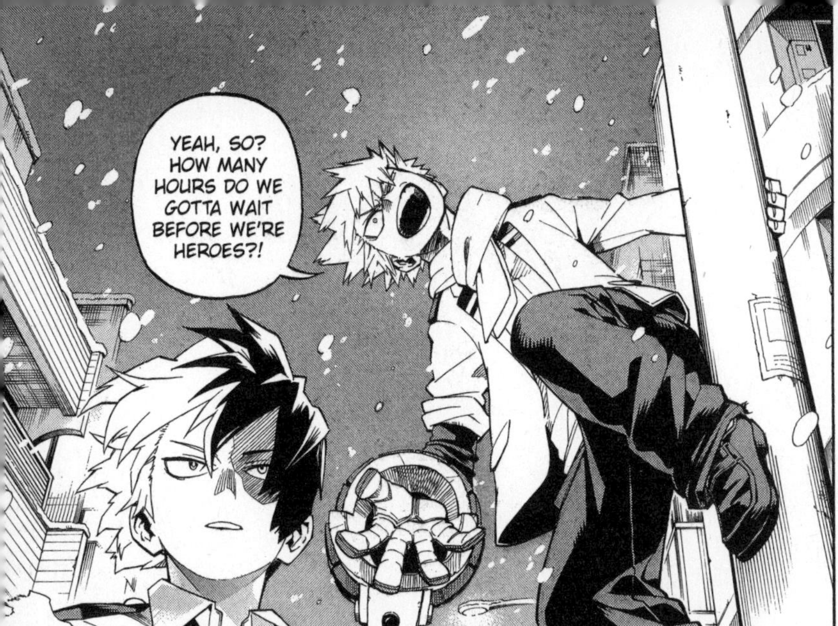
YEAH, SO? HOW MANY HOURS DO WE GOTTA WAIT BEFORE WE'RE HEROES?!

No. 218 - The Meta Liberation Army

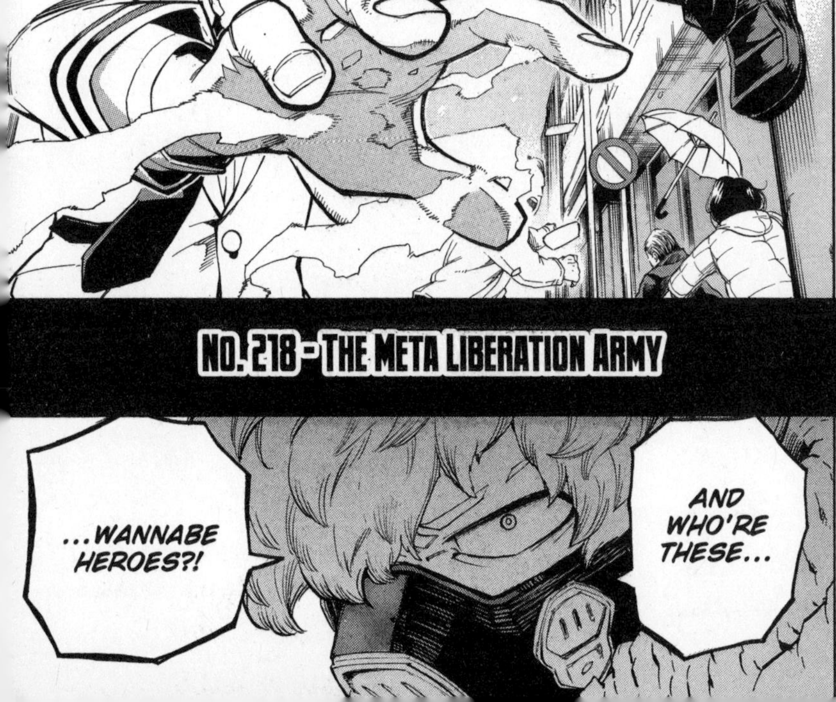
AND WHO'RE THESE...
...WANNABE HEROES?!

Bakugo jumped up and used his Armor-Piercing Shot from above, so as not to catch any civilians in the cross fire.

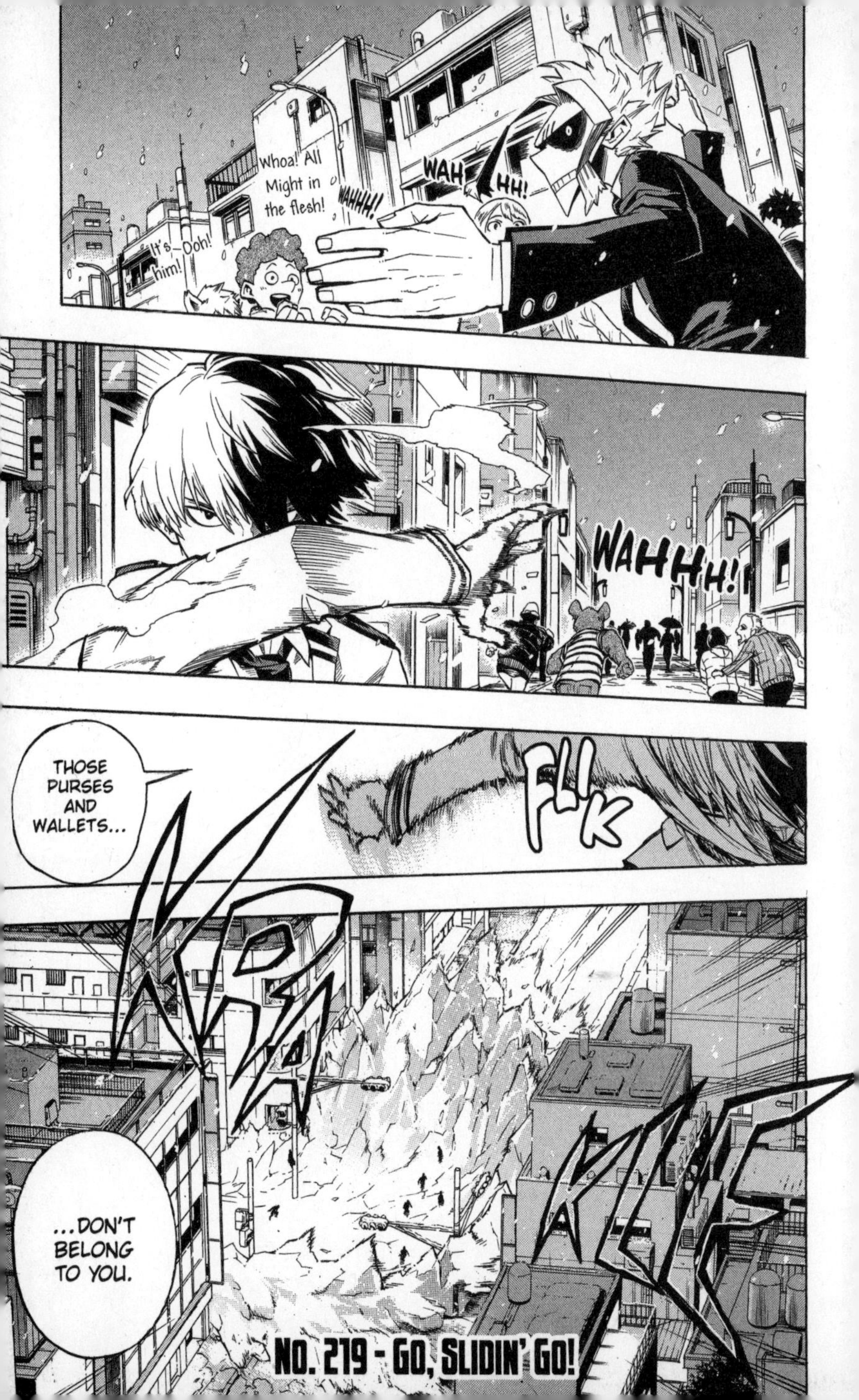
WAH HH!
WAHHH!
Whoa! All Might in the flesh!
Ooh!
It's him!
WAHHHH!
FLIK
THOSE PURSES AND WALLETS...
...DON'T BELONG TO YOU.
NO. 219 - GO, SLIDIN' GO!

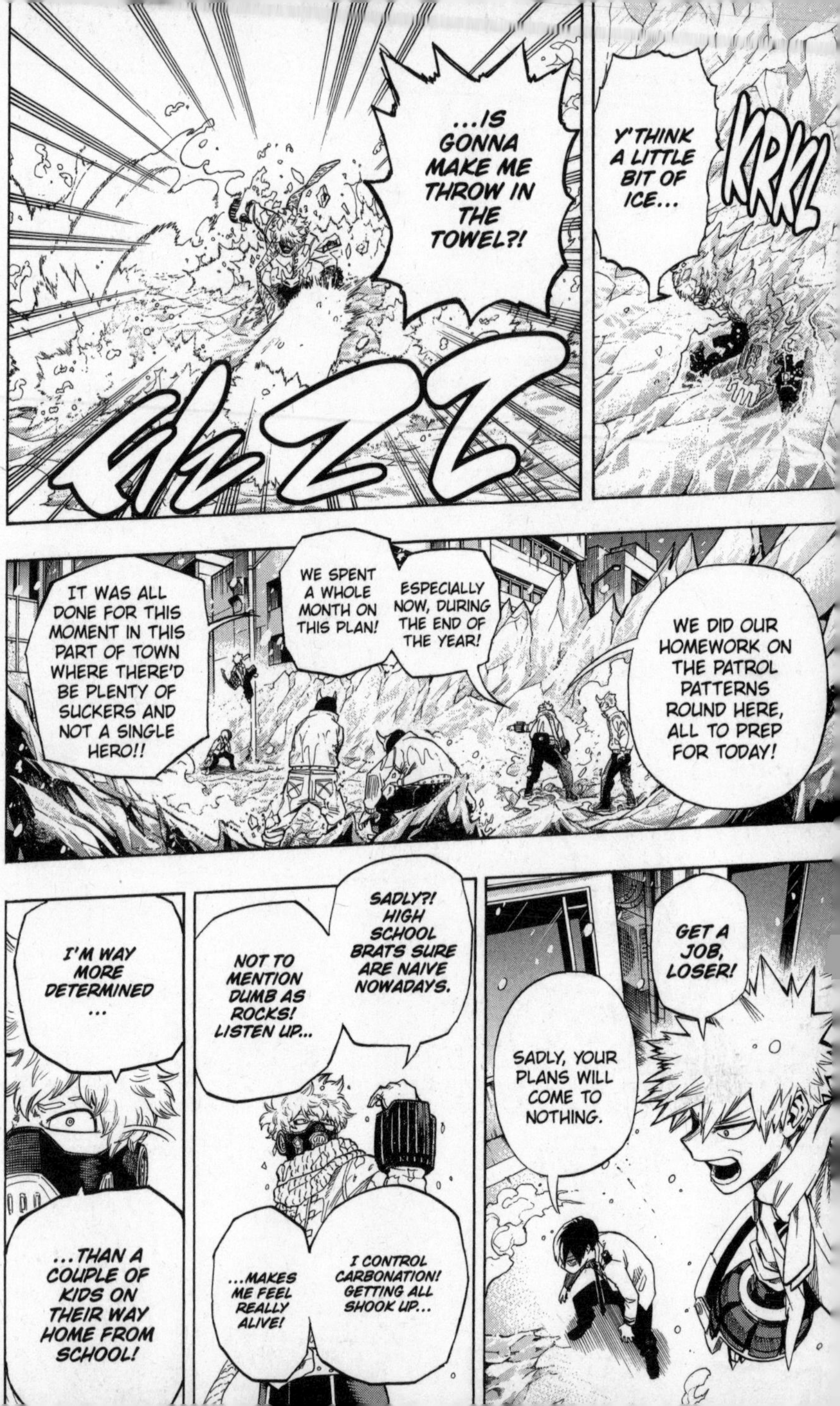
Y'THINK A LITTLE BIT OF ICE...
KRKL
...IS GONNA MAKE ME THROW IN THE TOWEL?!
WE DID OUR HOMEWORK ON THE PATROL PATTERNS ROUND HERE, ALL TO PREP FOR TODAY!
ESPECIALLY NOW, DURING THE END OF THE YEAR!
WE SPENT A WHOLE MONTH ON THIS PLAN!
IT WAS ALL DONE FOR THIS MOMENT IN THIS PART OF TOWN WHERE THERE'D BE PLENTY OF SUCKERS AND NOT A SINGLE HERO!!
GET A JOB, LOSER!
SADLY, YOUR PLANS WILL COME TO NOTHING.
SADLY?! HIGH SCHOOL BRATS SURE ARE NAIVE NOWADAYS.
NOT TO MENTION DUMB AS ROCKS! LISTEN UP...
I CONTROL CARBONATION! GETTING ALL SHOOK UP...
...MAKES ME FEEL REALLY ALIVE!
I'M WAY MORE DETERMINED...
...THAN A COUPLE OF KIDS ON THEIR WAY HOME FROM SCHOOL!

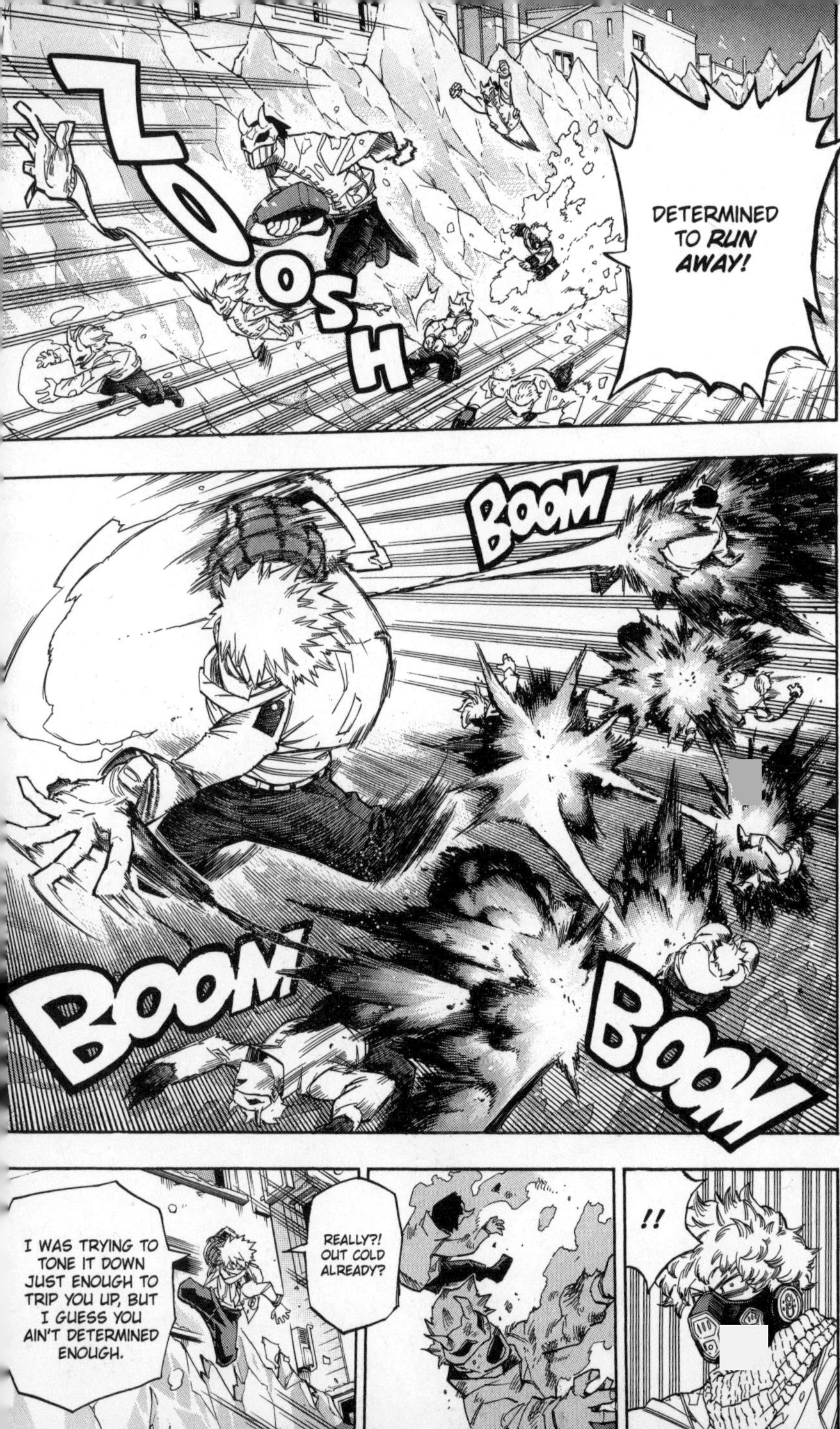
DETERMINED TO *RUN AWAY!*
ZOOSH
BOOM
BOOM
BOOM
!!
REALLY?! OUT COLD ALREADY?
I WAS TRYING TO TONE IT DOWN JUST ENOUGH TO TRIP YOU UP, BUT I GUESS YOU AIN'T DETERMINED ENOUGH.

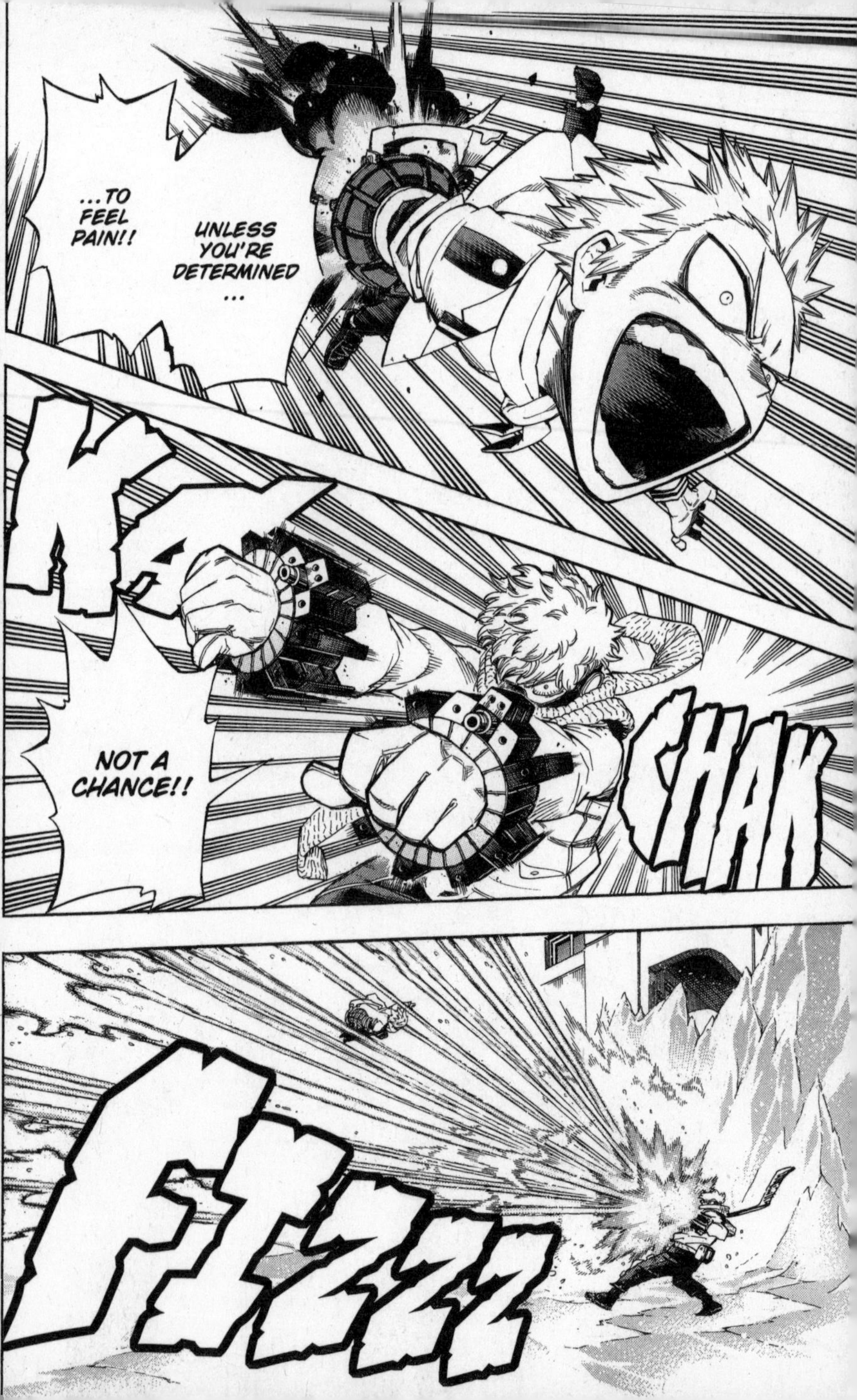
UNLESS YOU'RE DETERMINED ...
...TO FEEL PAIN!!
CHAK
NOT A CHANCE!!
FIZZZ

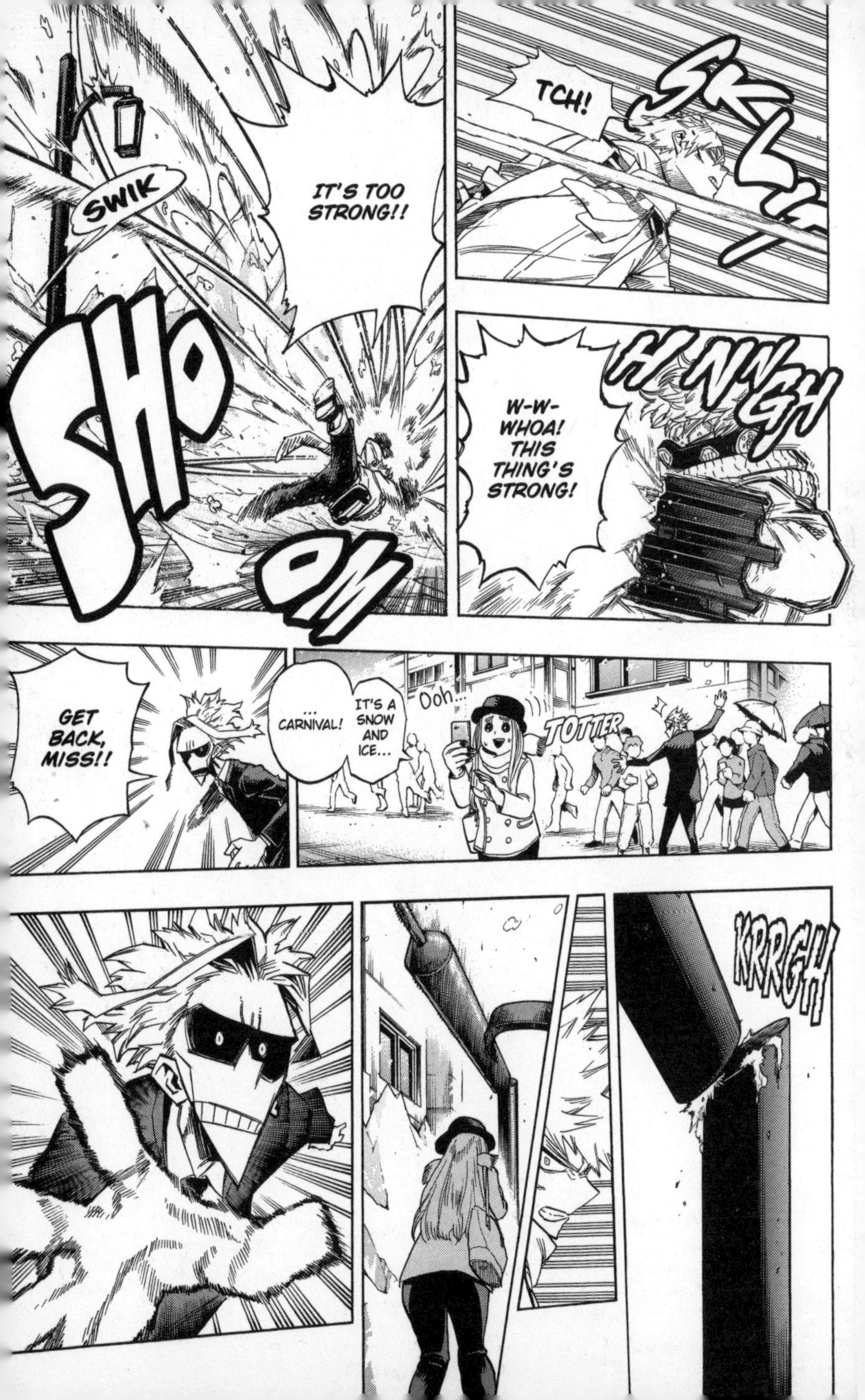
TCH!
W-W-WHOA! THIS THING'S STRONG!
HNNGH
SWIK
IT'S TOO STRONG!!
SHOOM
IT'S A SNOW AND ICE...
... CARNIVAL!
Ooh...
TOTTER
GET BACK, MISS!!
KRRGH

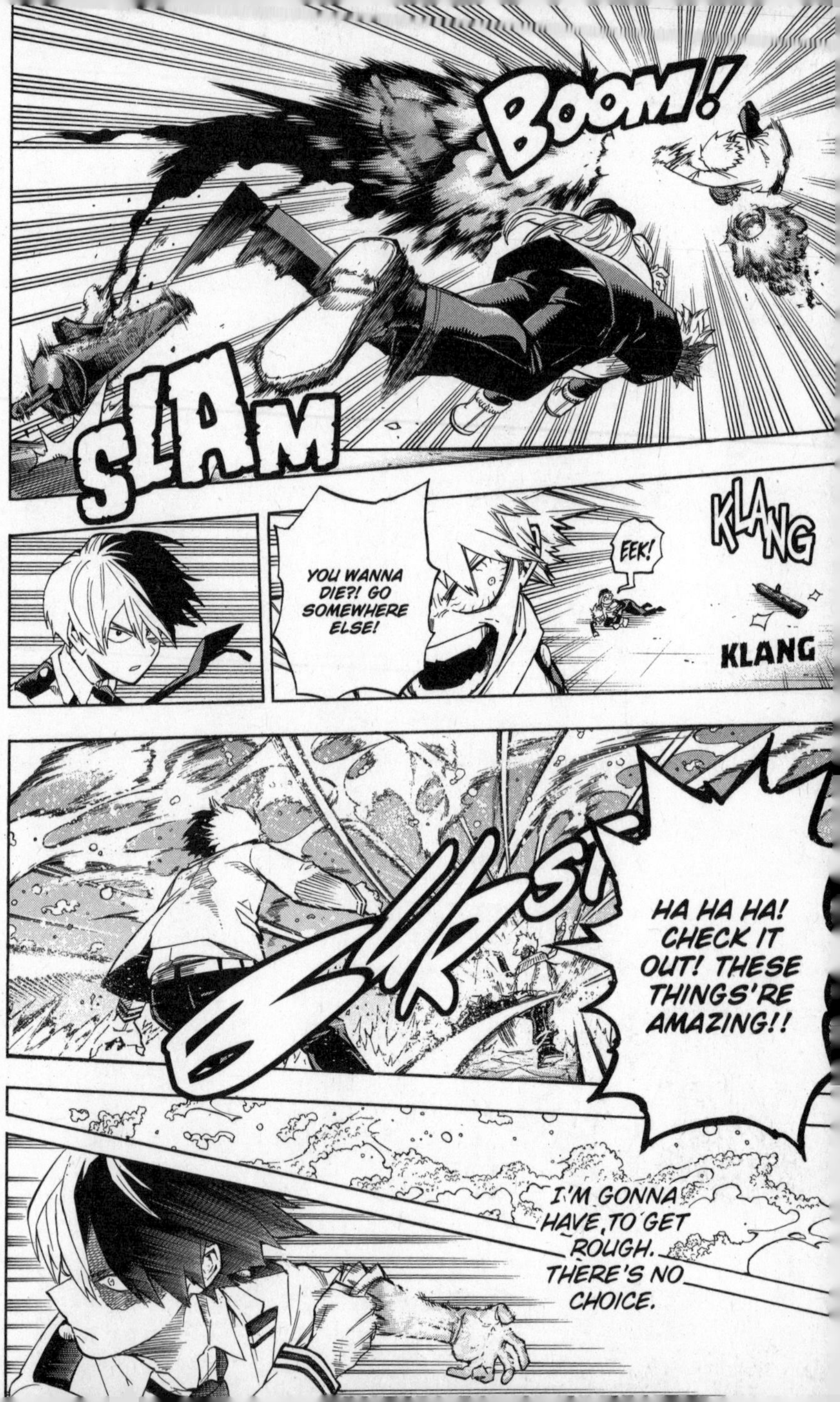
BOOM!
SLAM
KLANG
EEK!
YOU WANNA DIE?! GO SOMEWHERE ELSE!
KLANG
HA HA HA! CHECK IT OUT! THESE THINGS'RE AMAZING!!
I'M GONNA HAVE TO GET ROUGH. THERE'S NO CHOICE.

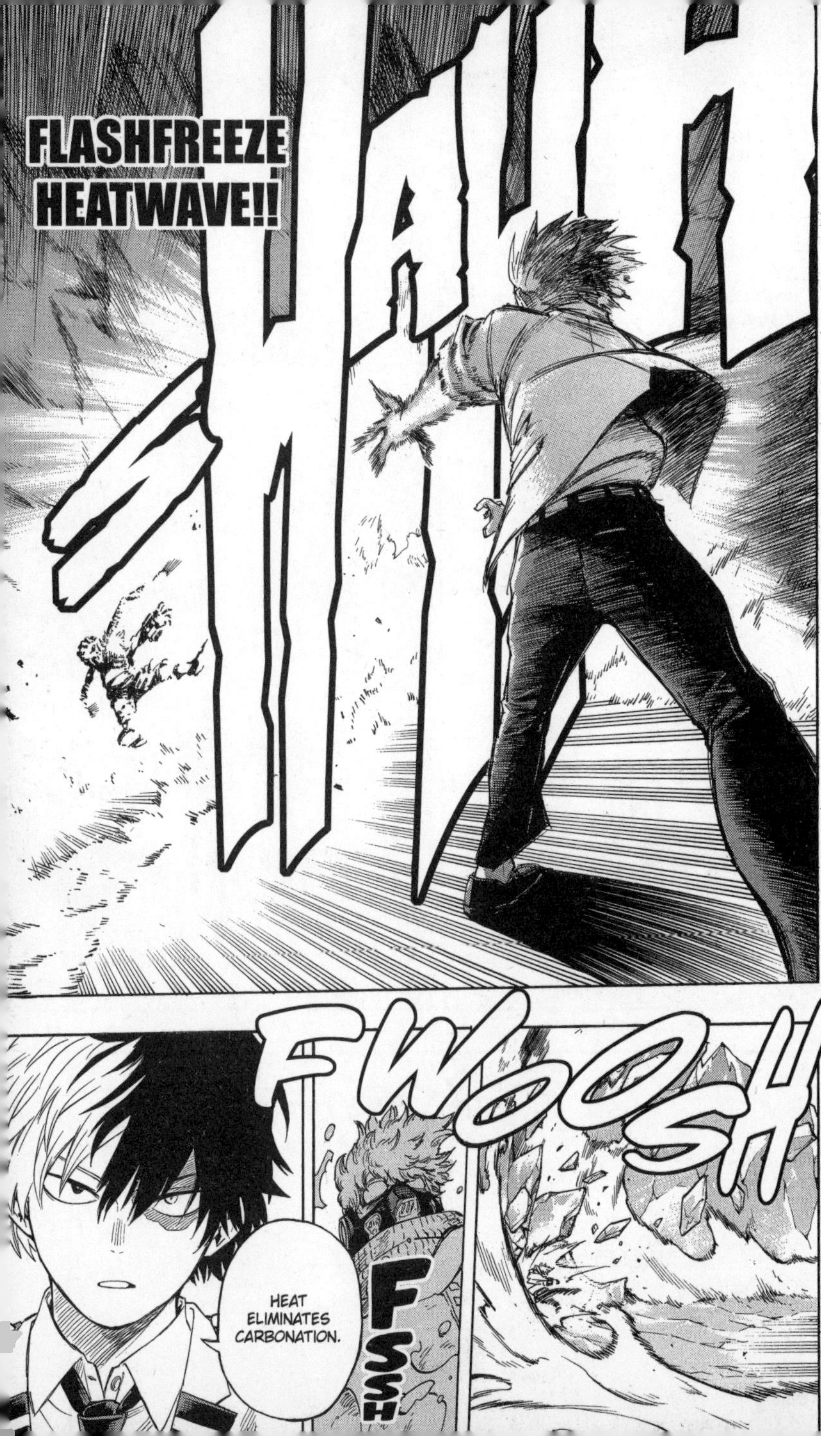
FLASHFREEZE HEATWAVE!!
FWOOSH
FSSH
HEAT ELIMINATES CARBONATION.

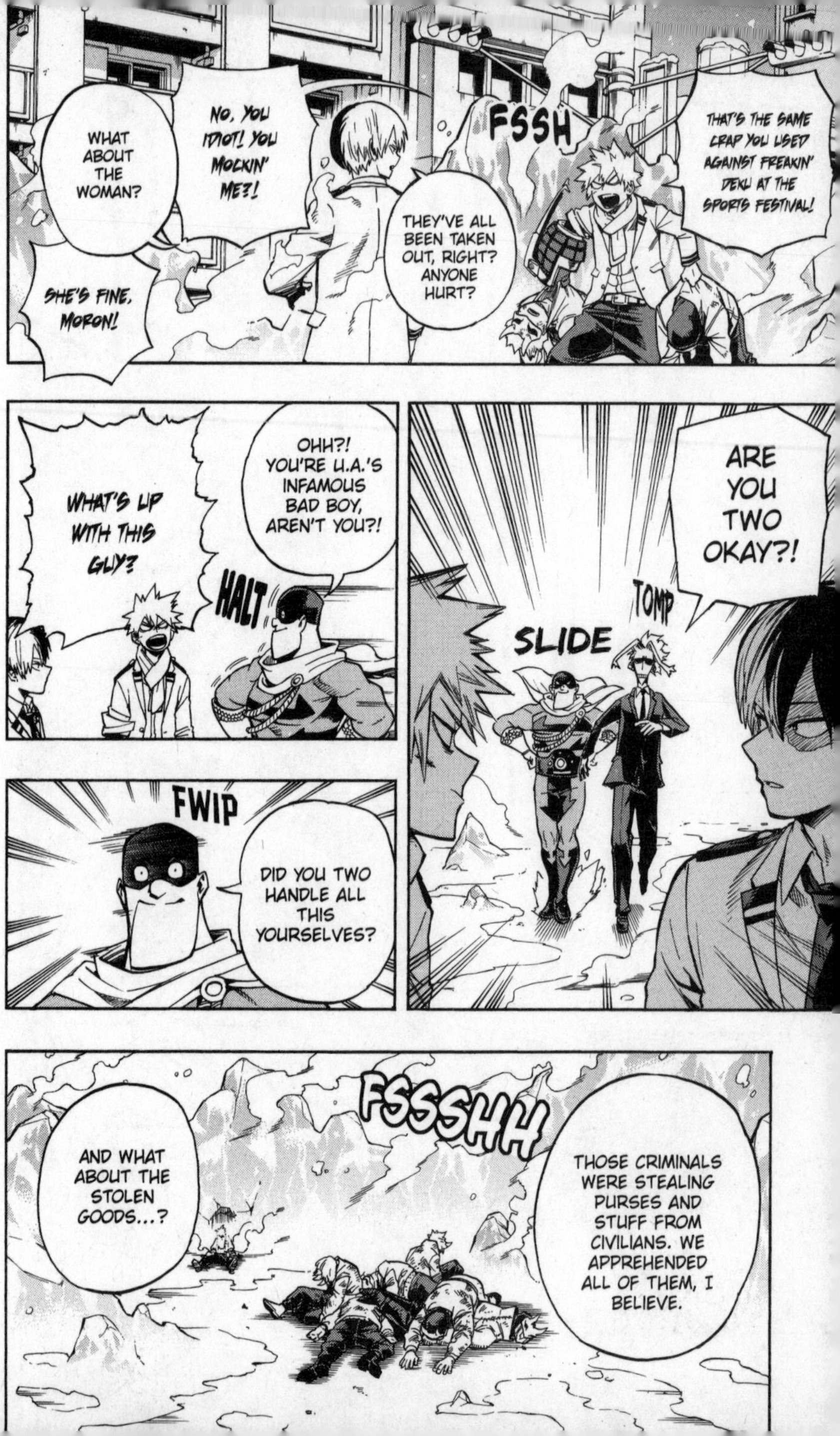
THAT'S THE SAME CRAP YOU USED AGAINST FREAKIN' DEKU AT THE SPORTS FESTIVAL!
FSSH
THEY'VE ALL BEEN TAKEN OUT, RIGHT? ANYONE HURT?
NO, YOU IDIOT! YOU MOCKIN' ME?!
WHAT ABOUT THE WOMAN?
SHE'S FINE, MORON!
ARE YOU TWO OKAY?!
TOMP
SLIDE
OHH?! YOU'RE U.A.'S INFAMOUS BAD BOY, AREN'T YOU?!
HALT
WHAT'S UP WITH THIS GUY?
FWIP
DID YOU TWO HANDLE ALL THIS YOURSELVES?
FSSSHH
THOSE CRIMINALS WERE STEALING PURSES AND STUFF FROM CIVILIANS. WE APPREHENDED ALL OF THEM, I BELIEVE.
AND WHAT ABOUT THE STOLEN GOODS...?

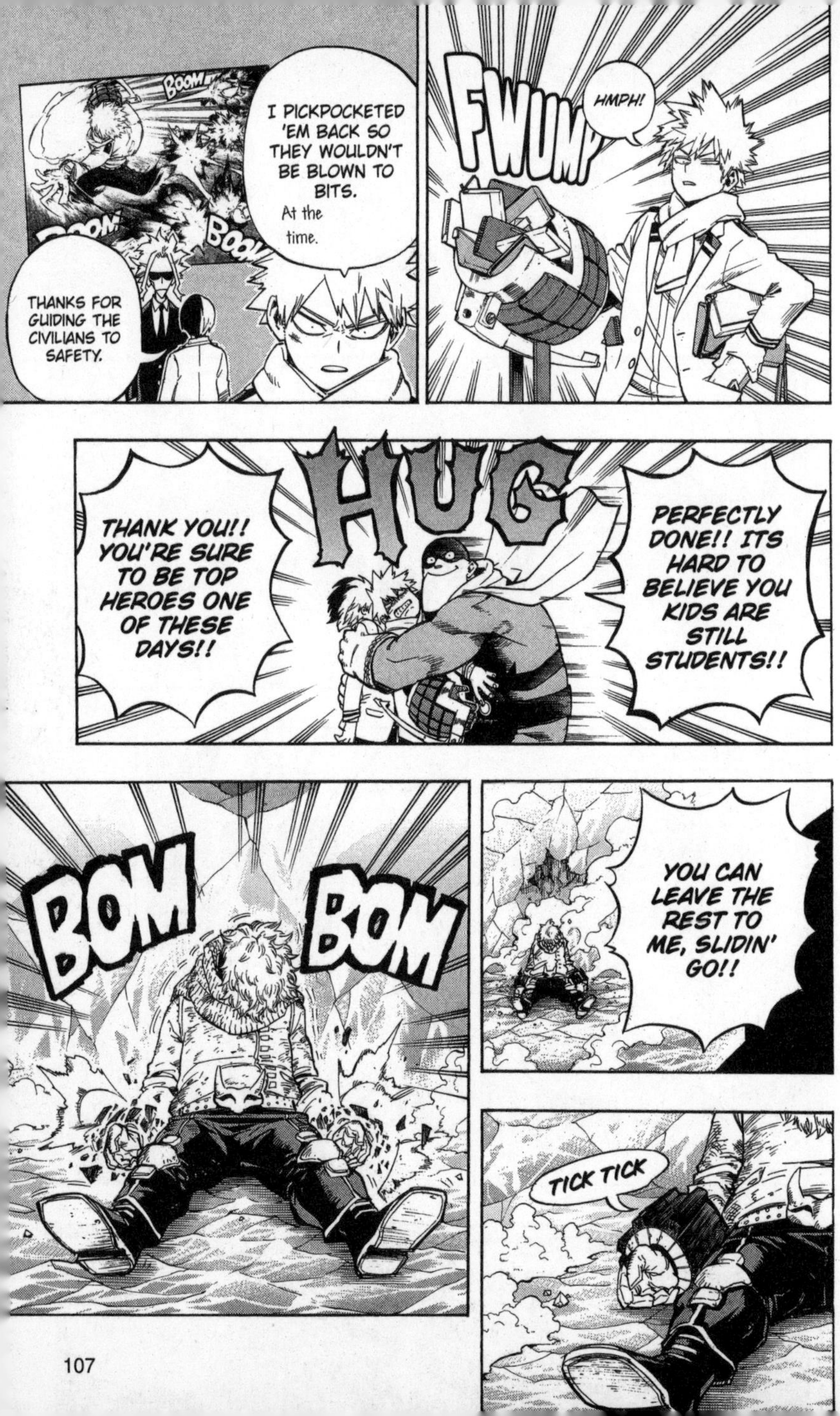
HMPH!
FWUMP
I PICKPOCKETED 'EM BACK SO THEY WOULDN'T BE BLOWN TO BITS.
At the time.
BOOM
BOOM
THANKS FOR GUIDING THE CIVILIANS TO SAFETY.
PERFECTLY DONE!! ITS HARD TO BELIEVE YOU KIDS ARE STILL STUDENTS!!
HUG
THANK YOU!! YOU'RE SURE TO BE TOP HEROES ONE OF THESE DAYS!!
YOU CAN LEAVE THE REST TO ME, SLIDIN' GO!!
TICK TICK
BOM
BOM

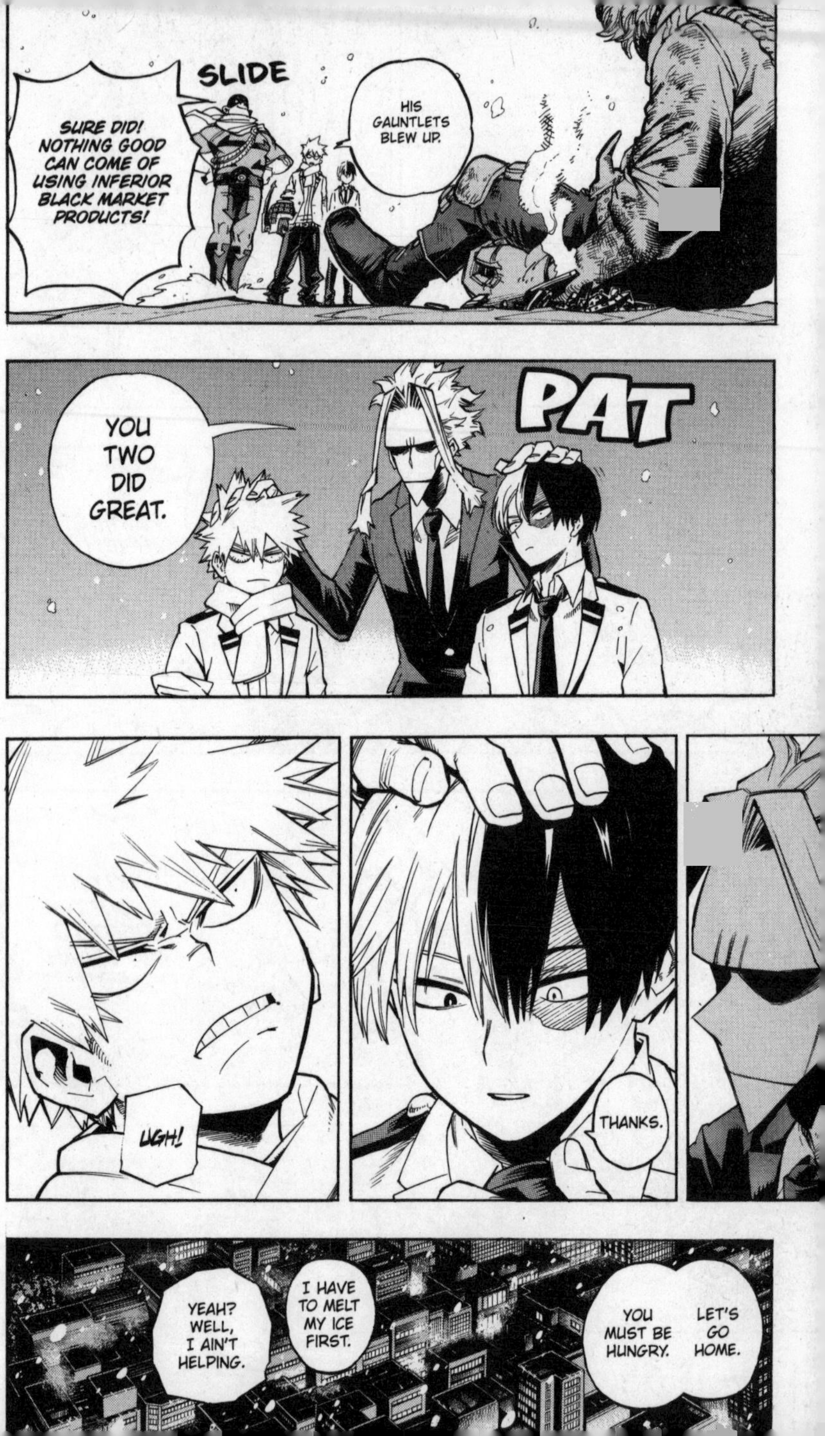
HIS GAUNTLETS BLEW UP.
SLIDE
SURE DID! NOTHING GOOD CAN COME OF USING INFERIOR BLACK MARKET PRODUCTS!
PAT
YOU TWO DID GREAT.
THANKS.
UGH!
LET'S GO HOME.
YOU MUST BE HUNGRY.
I HAVE TO MELT MY ICE FIRST.
YEAH? WELL, I AIN'T HELPING.

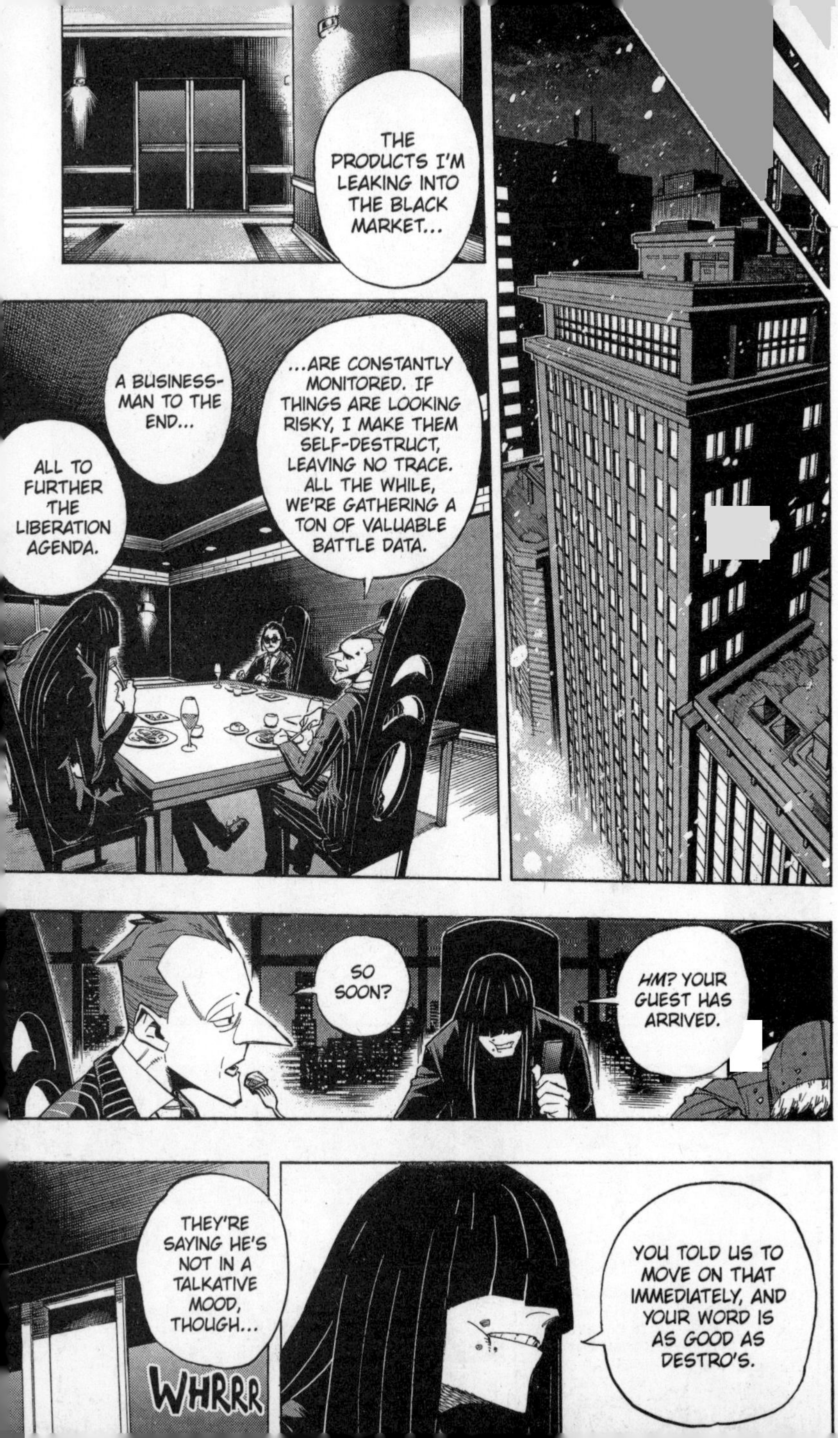
THE PRODUCTS I'M LEAKING INTO THE BLACK MARKET...
...ARE CONSTANTLY MONITORED. IF THINGS ARE LOOKING RISKY, I MAKE THEM SELF-DESTRUCT, LEAVING NO TRACE. ALL THE WHILE, WE'RE GATHERING A TON OF VALUABLE BATTLE DATA.
A BUSINESS-MAN TO THE END...
ALL TO FURTHER THE LIBERATION AGENDA.
HM? YOUR GUEST HAS ARRIVED.
SO SOON?
YOU TOLD US TO MOVE ON THAT IMMEDIATELY, AND YOUR WORD IS AS GOOD AS DESTRO'S.
THEY'RE SAYING HE'S NOT IN A TALKATIVE MOOD, THOUGH...
WHRRR

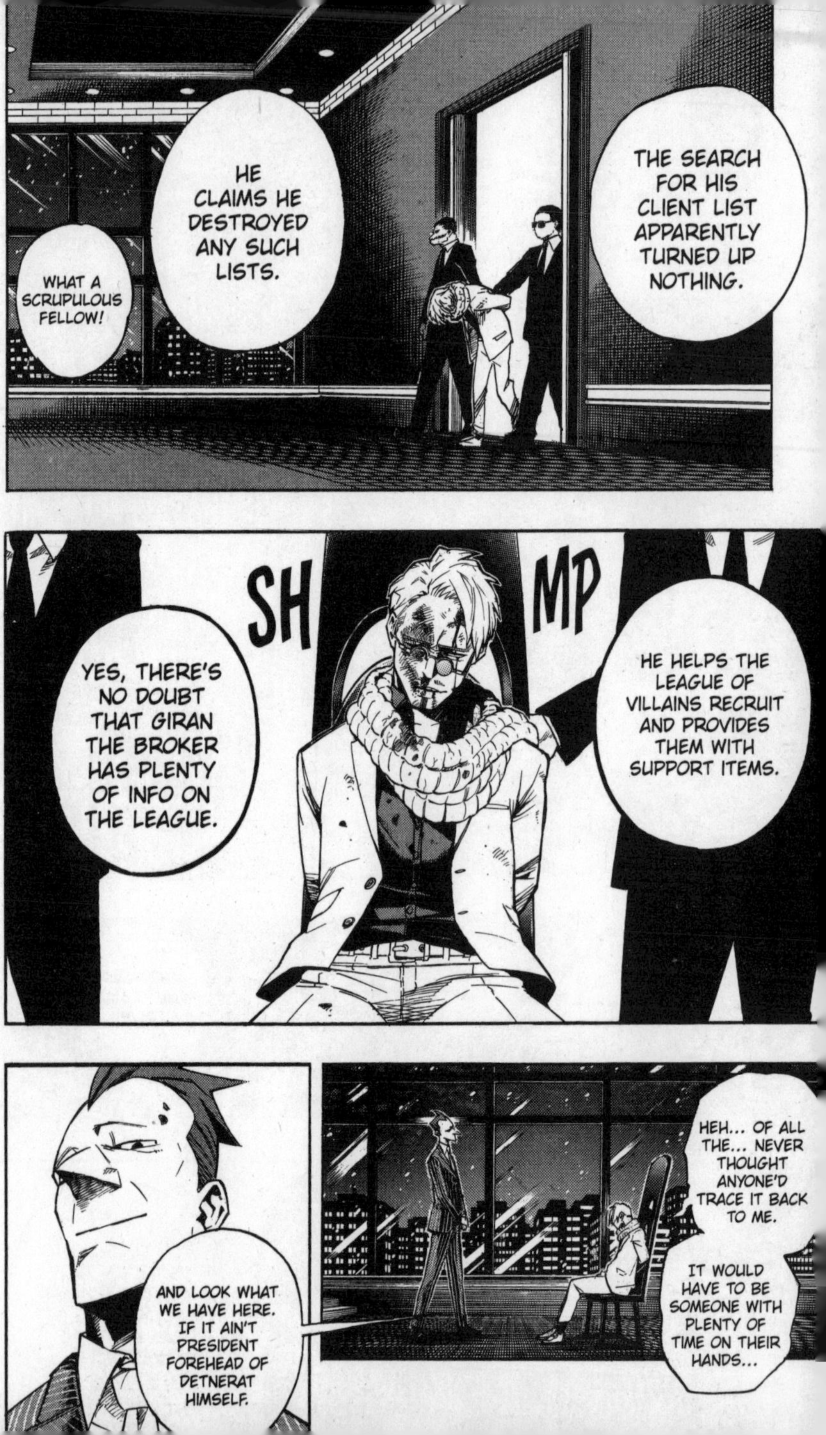
THE SEARCH FOR HIS CLIENT LIST APPARENTLY TURNED UP NOTHING.
HE CLAIMS HE DESTROYED ANY SUCH LISTS.
WHAT A SCRUPULOUS FELLOW!
SHMP
HE HELPS THE LEAGUE OF VILLAINS RECRUIT AND PROVIDES THEM WITH SUPPORT ITEMS.
YES, THERE'S NO DOUBT THAT GIRAN THE BROKER HAS PLENTY OF INFO ON THE LEAGUE.
HEH... OF ALL THE... NEVER THOUGHT ANYONE'D TRACE IT BACK TO ME.
IT WOULD HAVE TO BE SOMEONE WITH PLENTY OF TIME ON THEIR HANDS...
AND LOOK WHAT WE HAVE HERE. IF IT AIN'T PRESIDENT FOREHEAD OF DETNERAT HIMSELF.

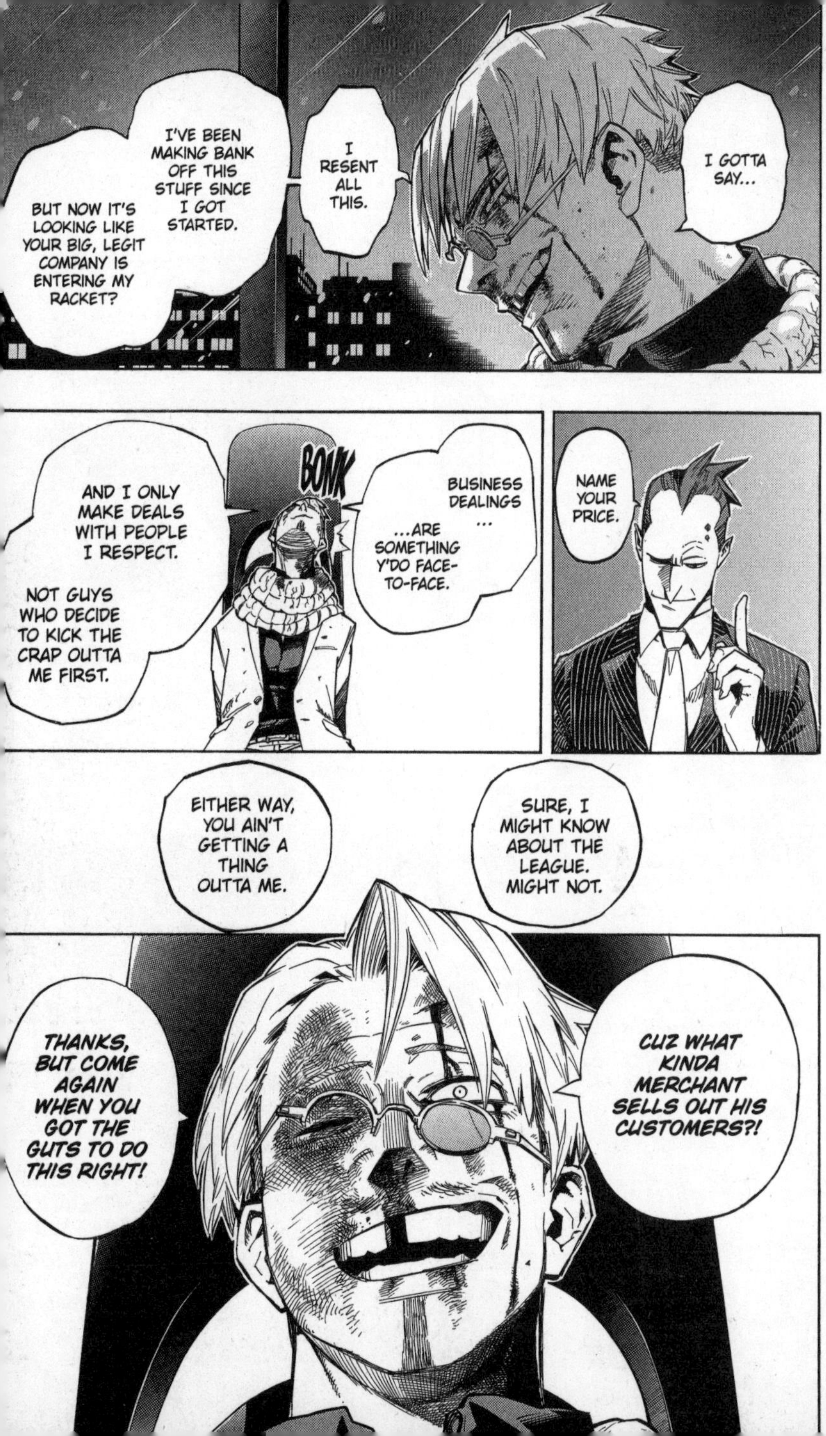
I GOTTA SAY...
I RESENT ALL THIS.
I'VE BEEN MAKING BANK OFF THIS STUFF SINCE I GOT STARTED.
BUT NOW IT'S LOOKING LIKE YOUR BIG, LEGIT COMPANY IS ENTERING MY RACKET?
NAME YOUR PRICE.
BONK
BUSINESS DEALINGS ...
...ARE SOMETHING Y'DO FACE-TO-FACE.
AND I ONLY MAKE DEALS WITH PEOPLE I RESPECT.
NOT GUYS WHO DECIDE TO KICK THE CRAP OUTTA ME FIRST.
SURE, I MIGHT KNOW ABOUT THE LEAGUE. MIGHT NOT.
EITHER WAY, YOU AIN'T GETTING A THING OUTTA ME.
CUZ WHAT KINDA MERCHANT SELLS OUT HIS CUSTOMERS?!
THANKS, BUT COME AGAIN WHEN YOU GOT THE GUTS TO DO THIS RIGHT!

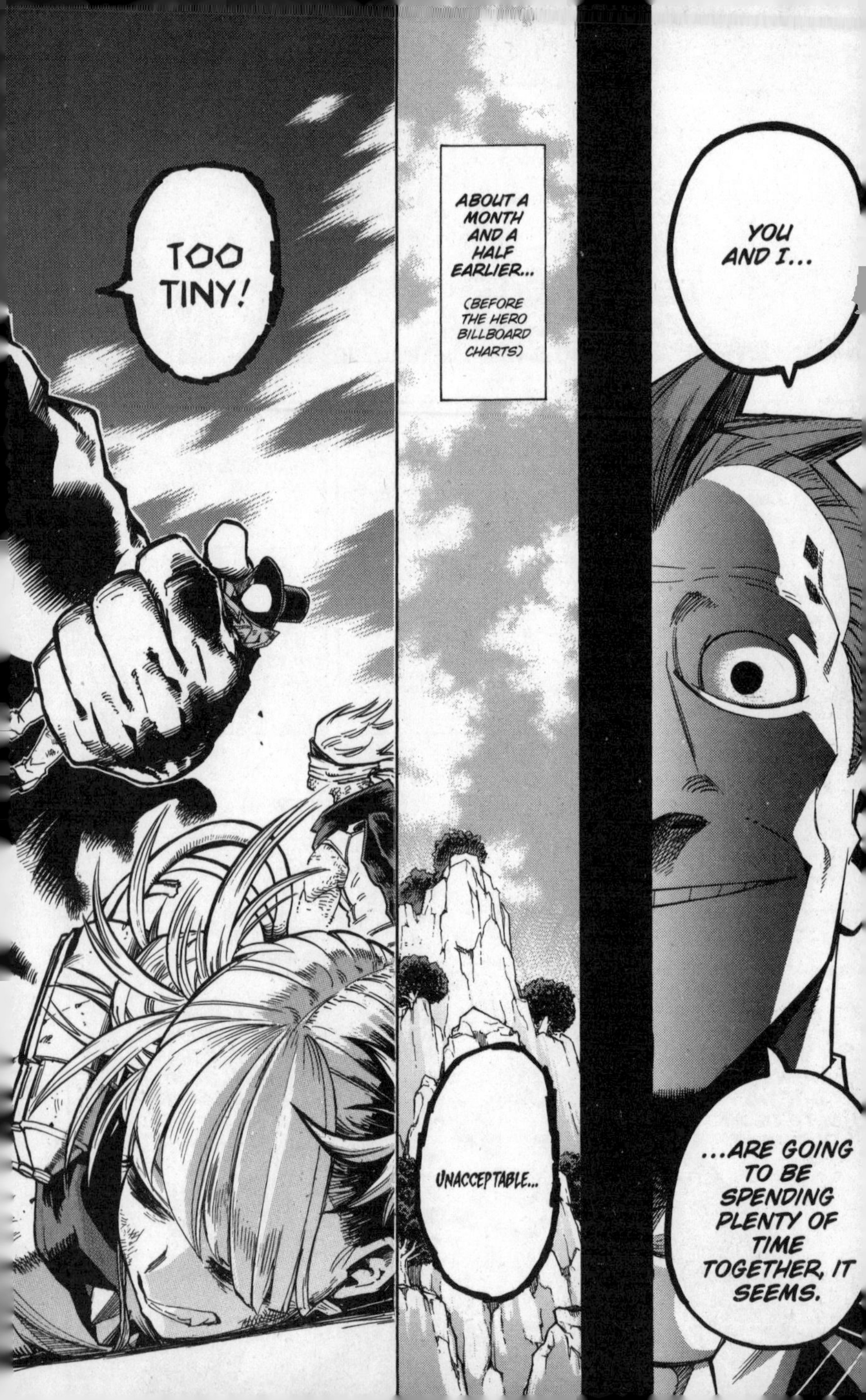
YOU AND I...
...ARE GOING TO BE SPENDING PLENTY OF TIME TOGETHER, IT SEEMS.
ABOUT A MONTH AND A HALF EARLIER...
(BEFORE THE HERO BILLBOARD CHARTS)
UNACCEPTABLE...
TOO TINY!

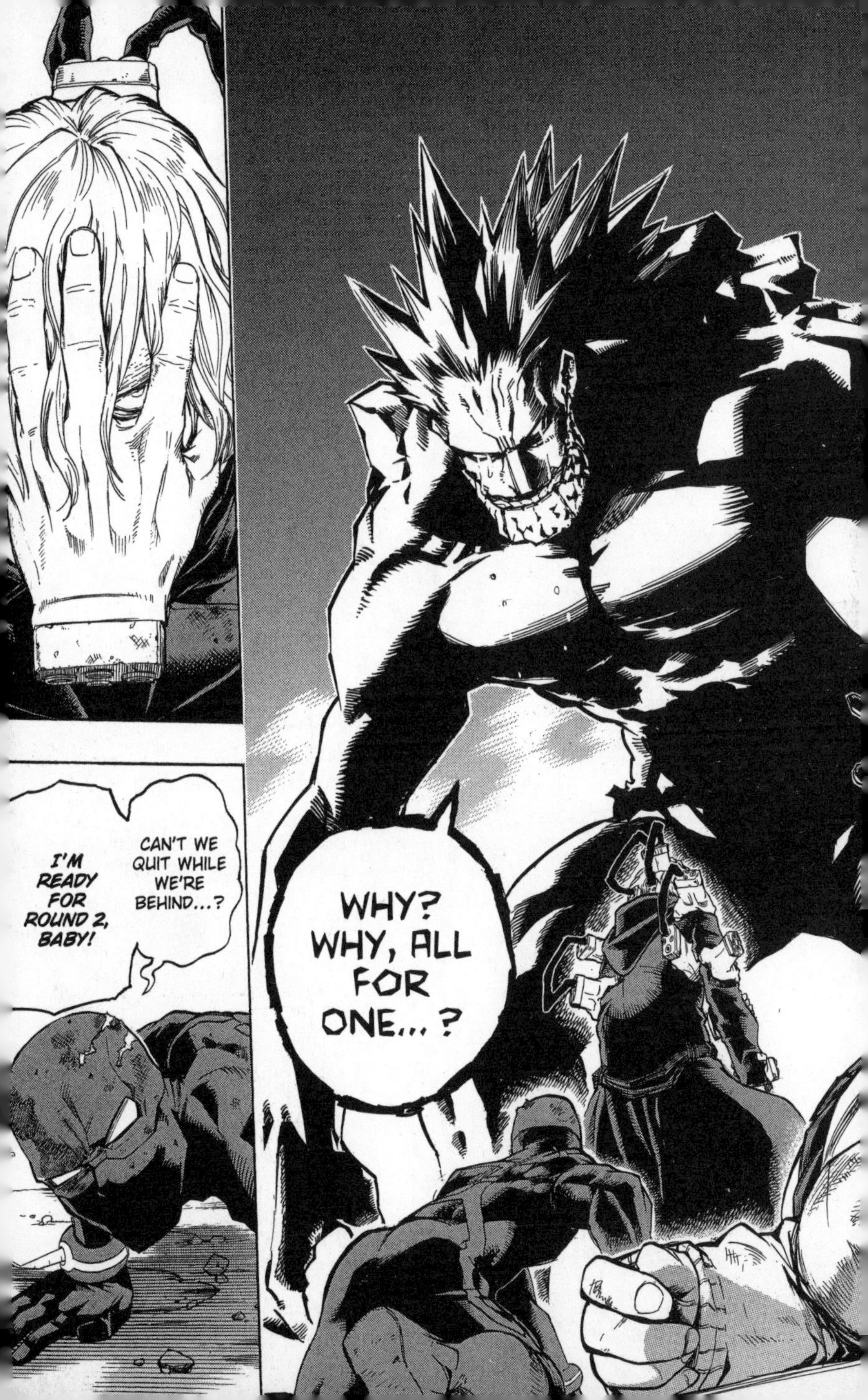
WHY? WHY, ALL FOR ONE...?
CAN'T WE QUIT WHILE WE'RE BEHIND...?
I'M READY FOR ROUND 2, BABY!

HERO

SLIDIN' GO [36] [TATSUYUKI TOKONAME]

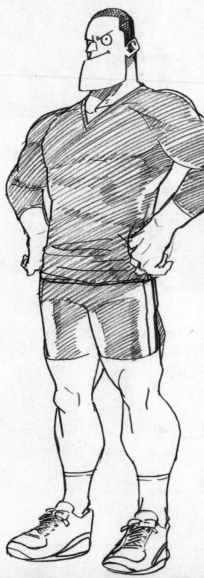

STREET CLOTHES

Birthday: 3/1
Height: 187 cm
Favorite Thing: Reading

THE SLIDIN' GO!!
Drawing this kind of character just makes me wicked happy!

So fun.

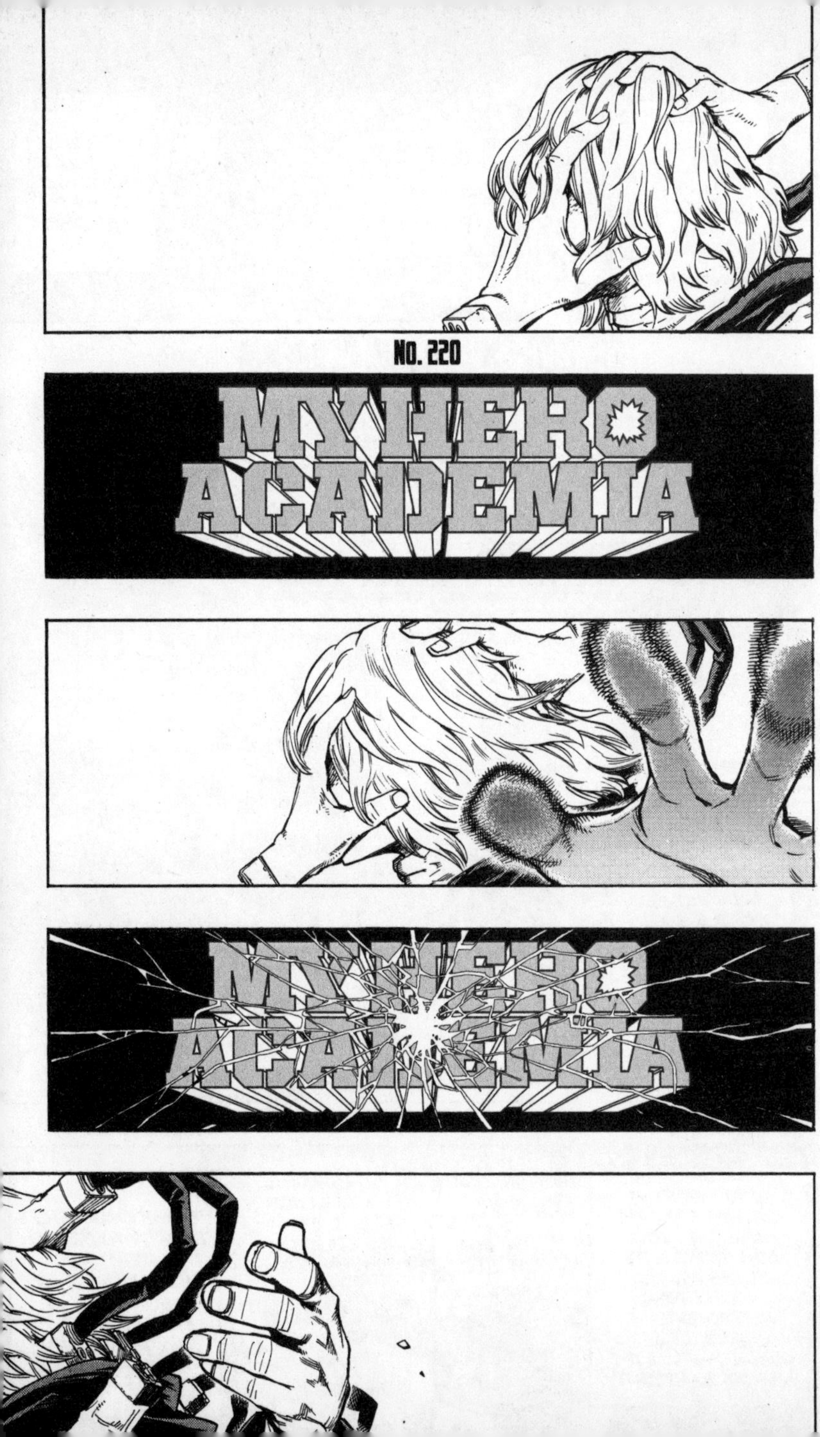
NO. 220
MY HERO ACADEMIA
MY HERO ACADEMIA

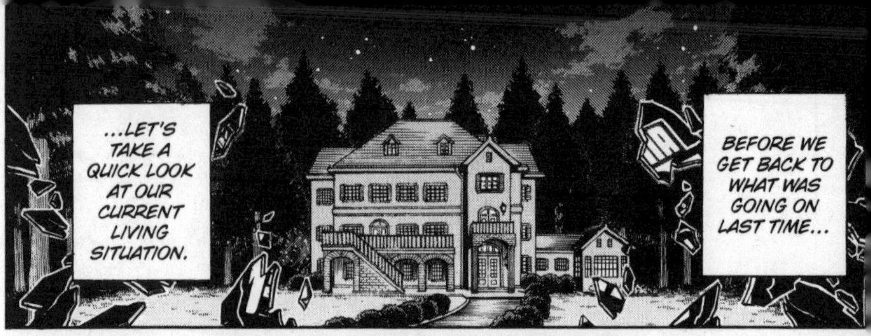
BEFORE WE GET BACK TO WHAT WAS GOING ON LAST TIME...
...LET'S TAKE A QUICK LOOK AT OUR CURRENT LIVING SITUATION.

No. 220 - My Villain Academia

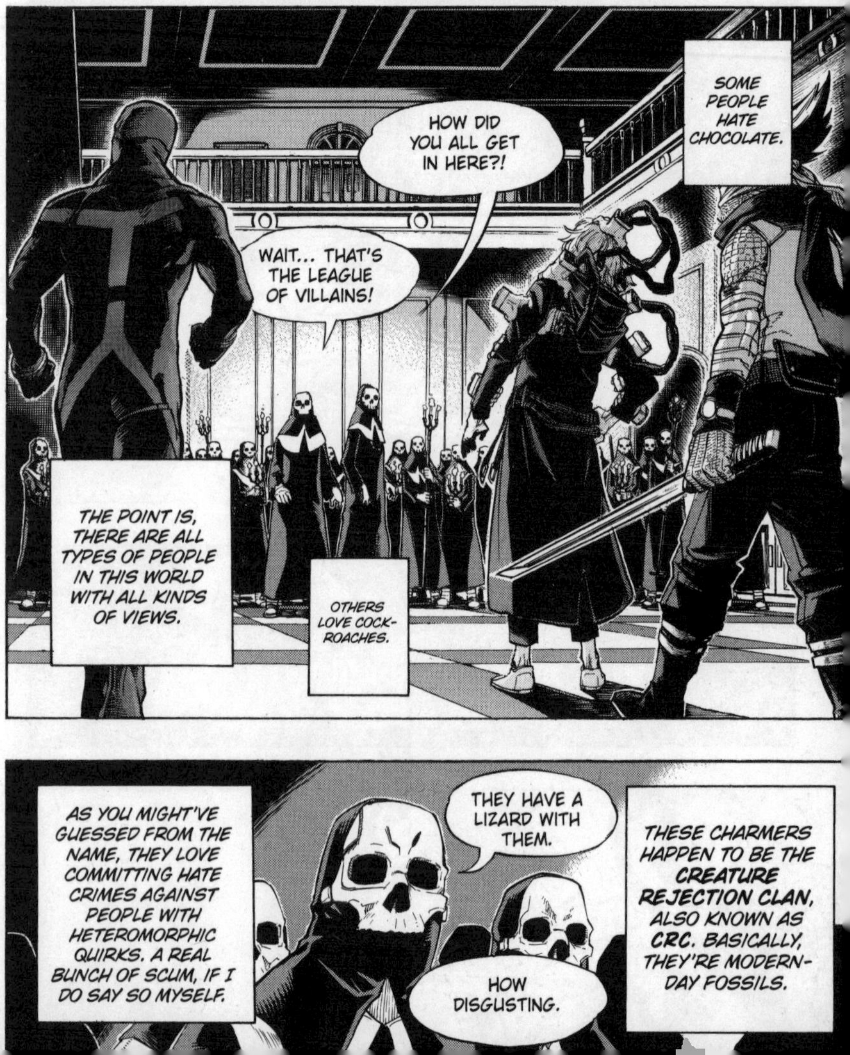
SOME PEOPLE HATE CHOCOLATE.
HOW DID YOU ALL GET IN HERE?!
WAIT... THAT'S THE LEAGUE OF VILLAINS!
OTHERS LOVE COCK-ROACHES.
THE POINT IS, THERE ARE ALL TYPES OF PEOPLE IN THIS WORLD WITH ALL KINDS OF VIEWS.
THESE CHARMERS HAPPEN TO BE THE **CREATURE REJECTION CLAN**, ALSO KNOWN AS **CRC**. BASICALLY, THEY'RE MODERN-DAY FOSSILS.
THEY HAVE A LIZARD WITH THEM.
HOW DISGUSTING.
AS YOU MIGHT'VE GUESSED FROM THE NAME, THEY LOVE COMMITTING HATE CRIMES AGAINST PEOPLE WITH HETEROMORPHIC QUIRKS. A REAL BUNCH OF SCUM, IF I DO SAY SO MYSELF.

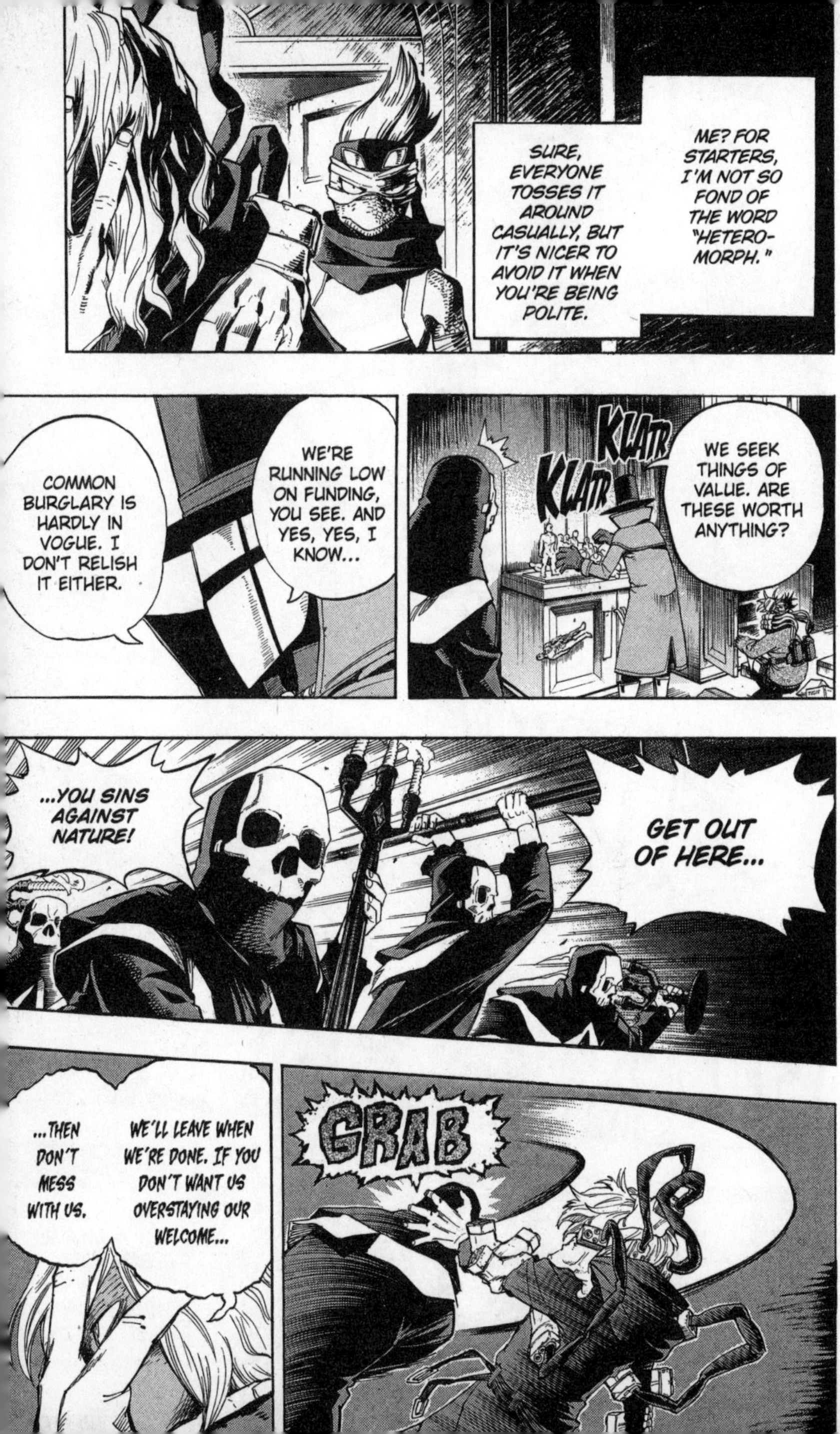
ME? FOR STARTERS, I'M NOT SO FOND OF THE WORD "HETERO-MORPH."
SURE, EVERYONE TOSSES IT AROUND CASUALLY, BUT IT'S NICER TO AVOID IT WHEN YOU'RE BEING POLITE.
KLATR KLATR
WE SEEK THINGS OF VALUE. ARE THESE WORTH ANYTHING?
WE'RE RUNNING LOW ON FUNDING, YOU SEE. AND YES, YES, I KNOW...
COMMON BURGLARY IS HARDLY IN VOGUE. I DON'T RELISH IT EITHER.
GET OUT OF HERE...
...YOU SINS AGAINST NATURE!
GRAB
WE'LL LEAVE WHEN WE'RE DONE. IF YOU DON'T WANT US OVERSTAYING OUR WELCOME...
...THEN DON'T MESS WITH US.

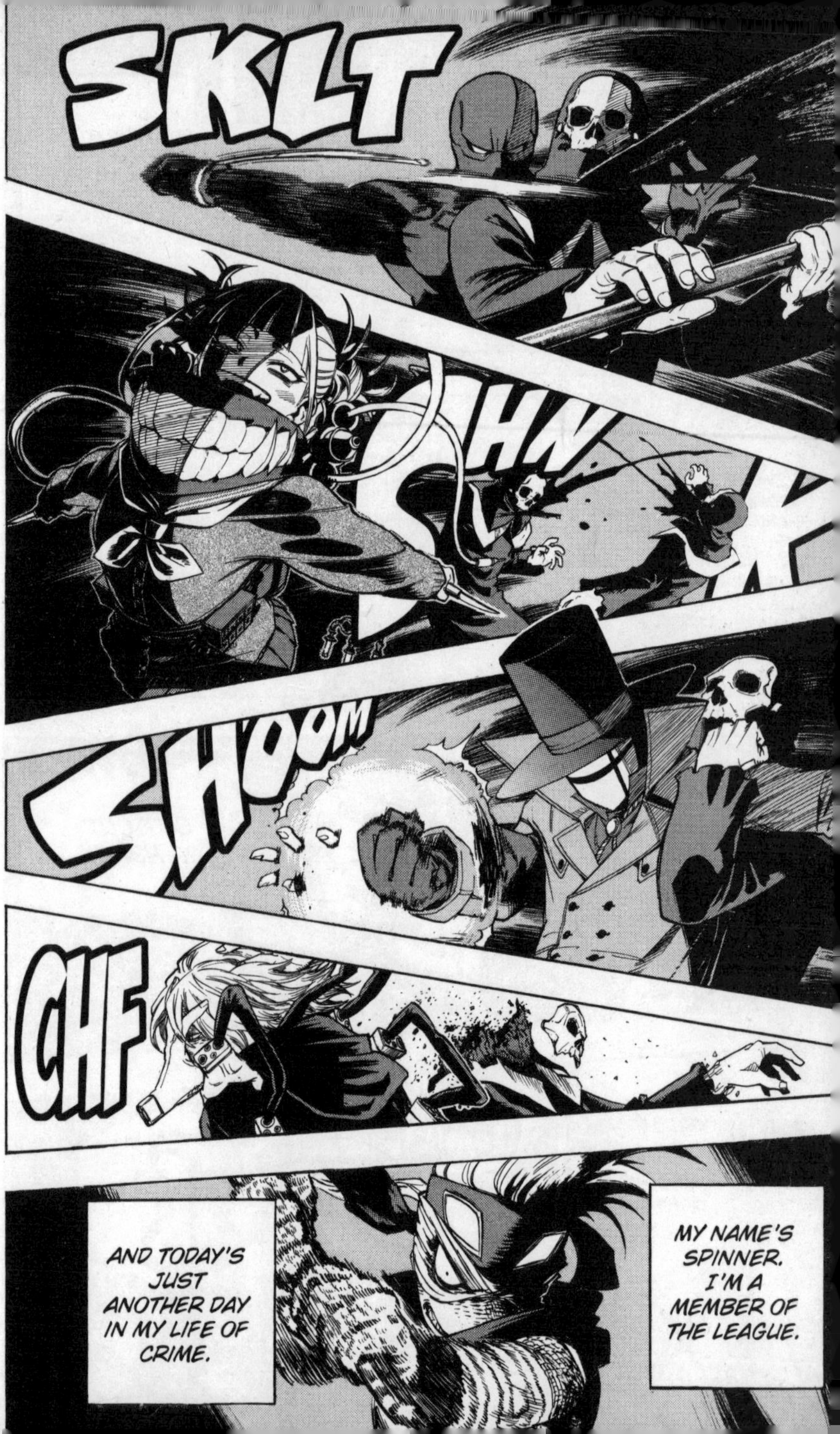
SKLT
SHNK
SHOOM
CHF
MY NAME'S SPINNER. I'M A MEMBER OF THE LEAGUE.
AND TODAY'S JUST ANOTHER DAY IN MY LIFE OF CRIME.

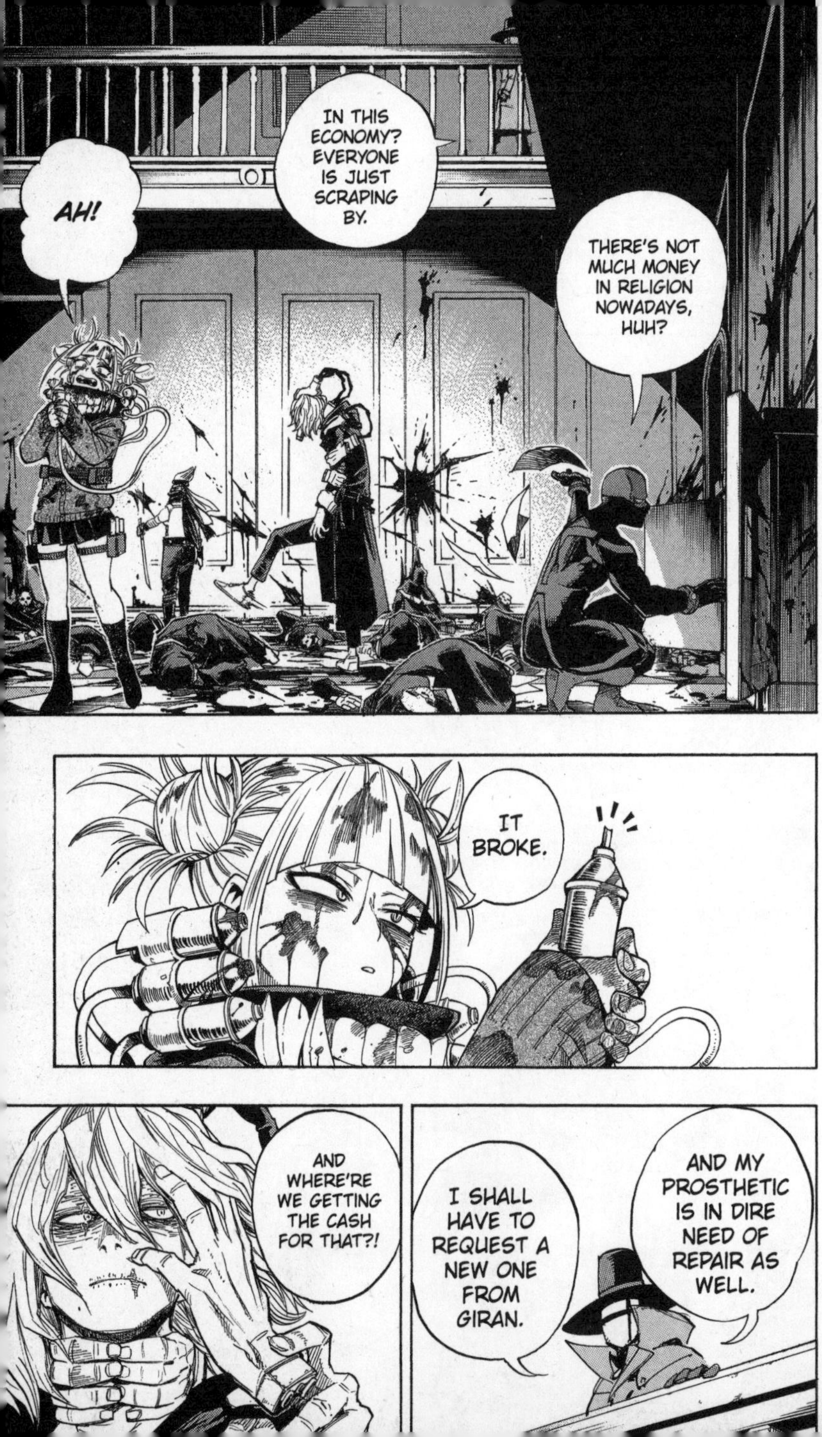
THERE'S NOT MUCH MONEY IN RELIGION NOWADAYS, HUH?
IN THIS ECONOMY? EVERYONE IS JUST SCRAPING BY.
AH!
IT BROKE.
AND MY PROSTHETIC IS IN DIRE NEED OF REPAIR AS WELL.
I SHALL HAVE TO REQUEST A NEW ONE FROM GIRAN.
AND WHERE'RE WE GETTING THE CASH FOR THAT?!

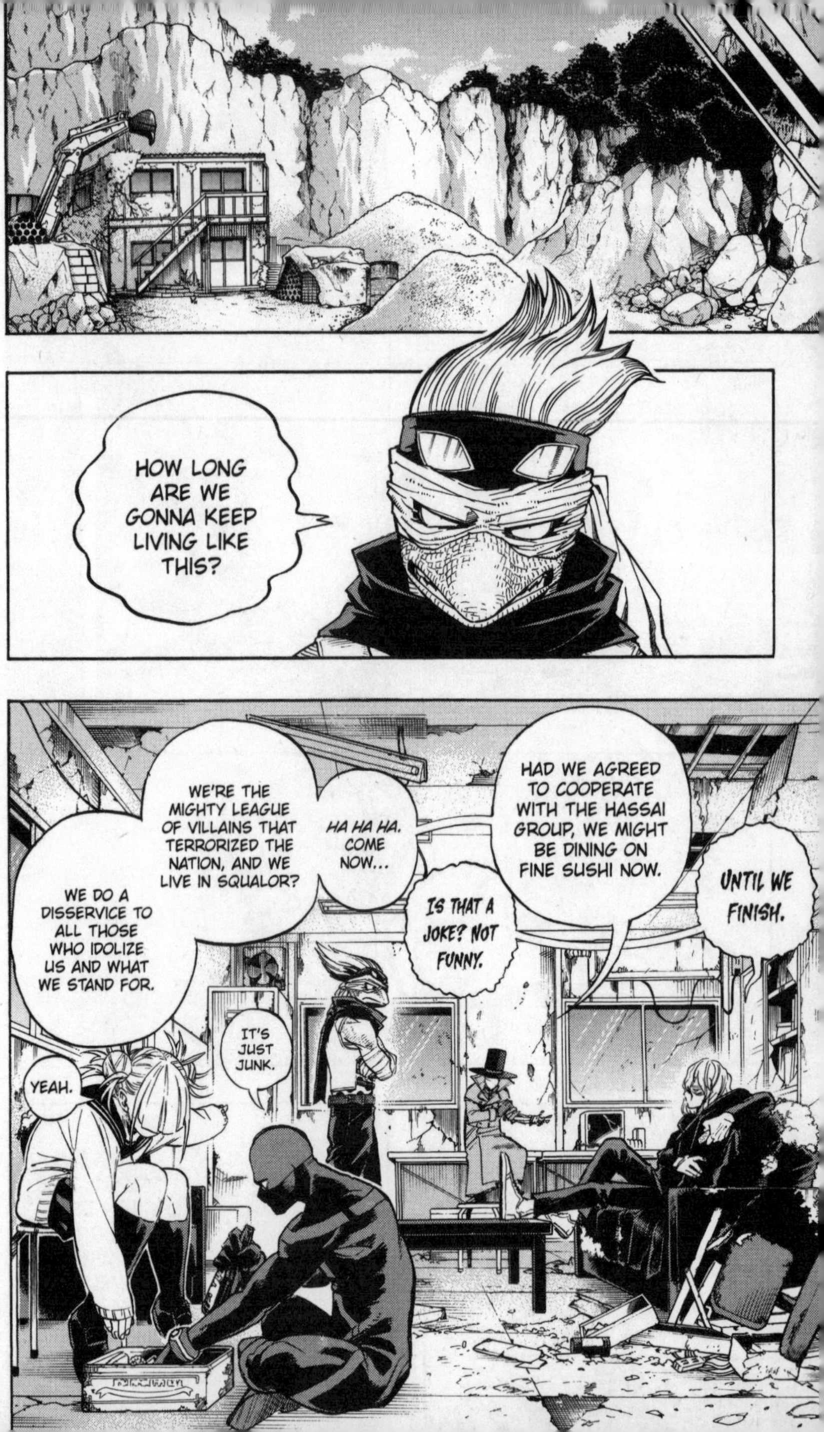
HOW LONG ARE WE GONNA KEEP LIVING LIKE THIS?
HAD WE AGREED TO COOPERATE WITH THE HASSAI GROUP, WE MIGHT BE DINING ON FINE SUSHI NOW.
UNTIL WE FINISH.
IS THAT A JOKE? NOT FUNNY.
HA HA HA. COME NOW...
WE'RE THE MIGHTY LEAGUE OF VILLAINS THAT TERRORIZED THE NATION, AND WE LIVE IN SQUALOR?
WE DO A DISSERVICE TO ALL THOSE WHO IDOLIZE US AND WHAT WE STAND FOR.
IT'S JUST JUNK.
YEAH.

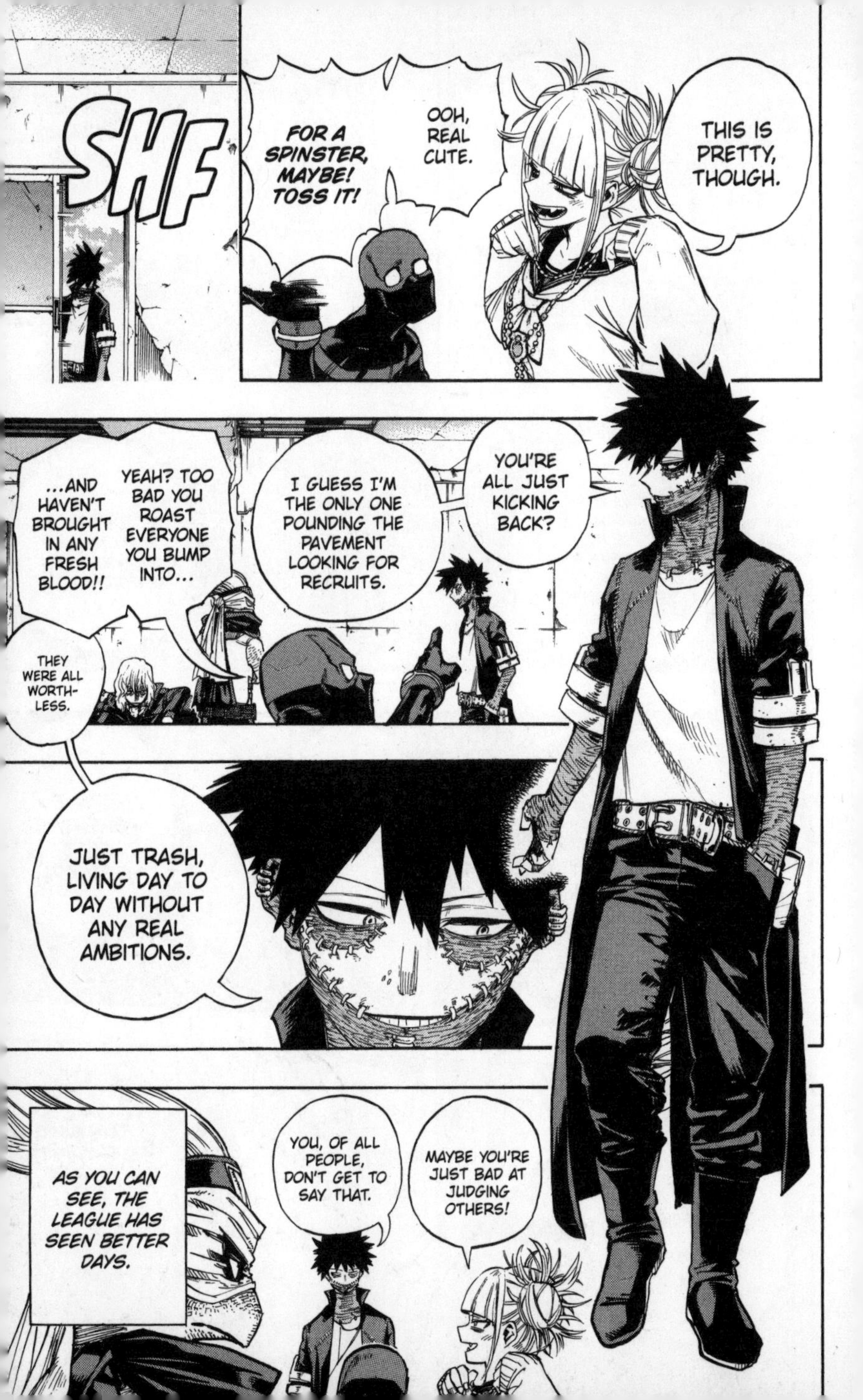
THIS IS PRETTY, THOUGH.
OOH, REAL CUTE.
FOR A SPINSTER, MAYBE! TOSS IT!
SHF
YOU'RE ALL JUST KICKING BACK?
I GUESS I'M THE ONLY ONE POUNDING THE PAVEMENT LOOKING FOR RECRUITS.
YEAH? TOO BAD YOU ROAST EVERYONE YOU BUMP INTO...
...AND HAVEN'T BROUGHT IN ANY FRESH BLOOD!!
THEY WERE ALL WORTHLESS.
JUST TRASH, LIVING DAY TO DAY WITHOUT ANY REAL AMBITIONS.
MAYBE YOU'RE JUST BAD AT JUDGING OTHERS!
YOU, OF ALL PEOPLE, DON'T GET TO SAY THAT.
AS YOU CAN SEE, THE LEAGUE HAS SEEN BETTER DAYS.

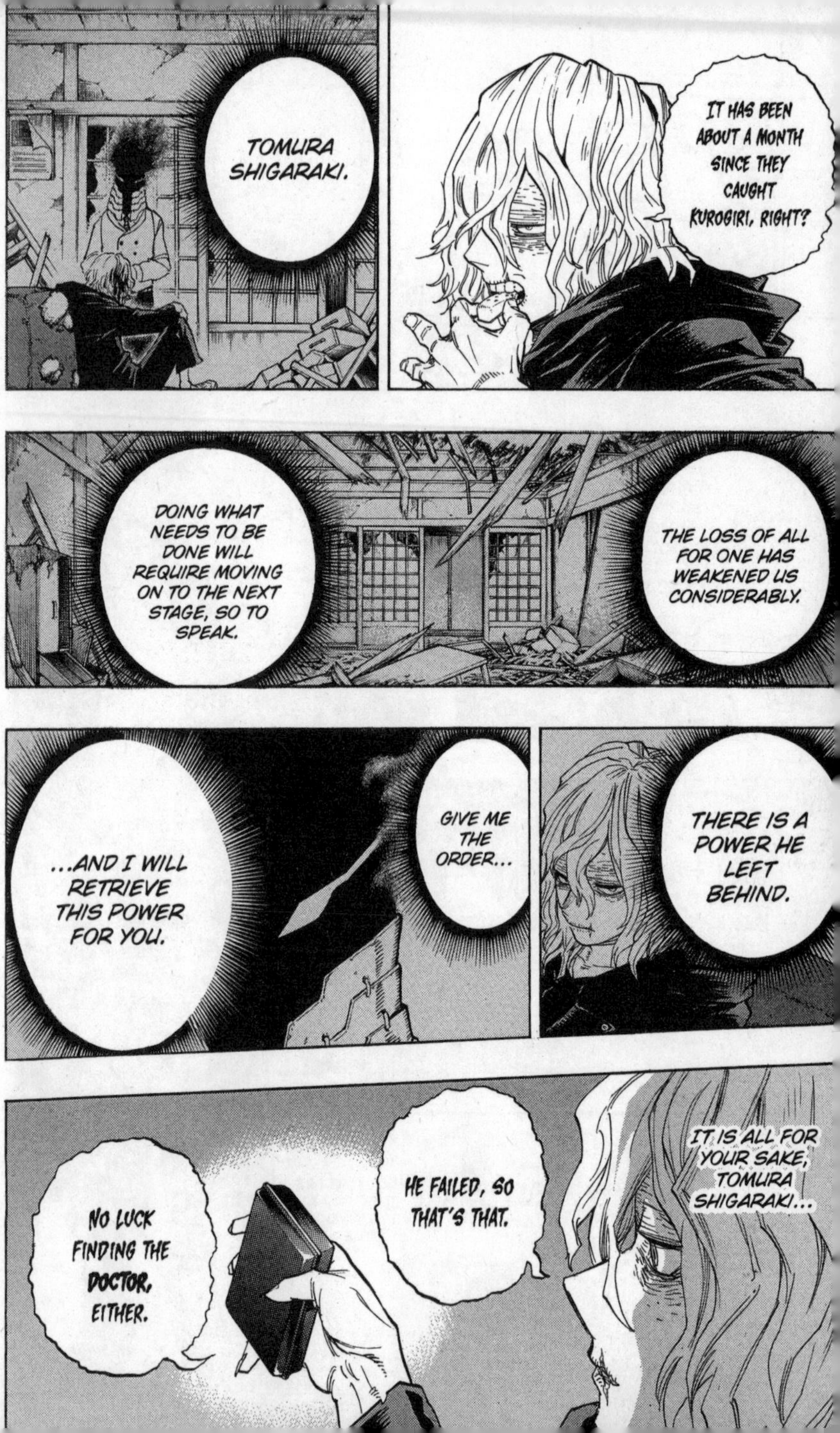
IT HAS BEEN ABOUT A MONTH SINCE THEY CAUGHT KUROGIRI, RIGHT?
TOMURA SHIGARAKI.
THE LOSS OF ALL FOR ONE HAS WEAKENED US CONSIDERABLY.
DOING WHAT NEEDS TO BE DONE WILL REQUIRE MOVING ON TO THE NEXT STAGE, SO TO SPEAK.
THERE IS A POWER HE LEFT BEHIND.
GIVE ME THE ORDER...
...AND I WILL RETRIEVE THIS POWER FOR YOU.
IT IS ALL FOR YOUR SAKE, TOMURA SHIGARAKI...
HE FAILED, SO THAT'S THAT.
NO LUCK FINDING THE DOCTOR, EITHER.

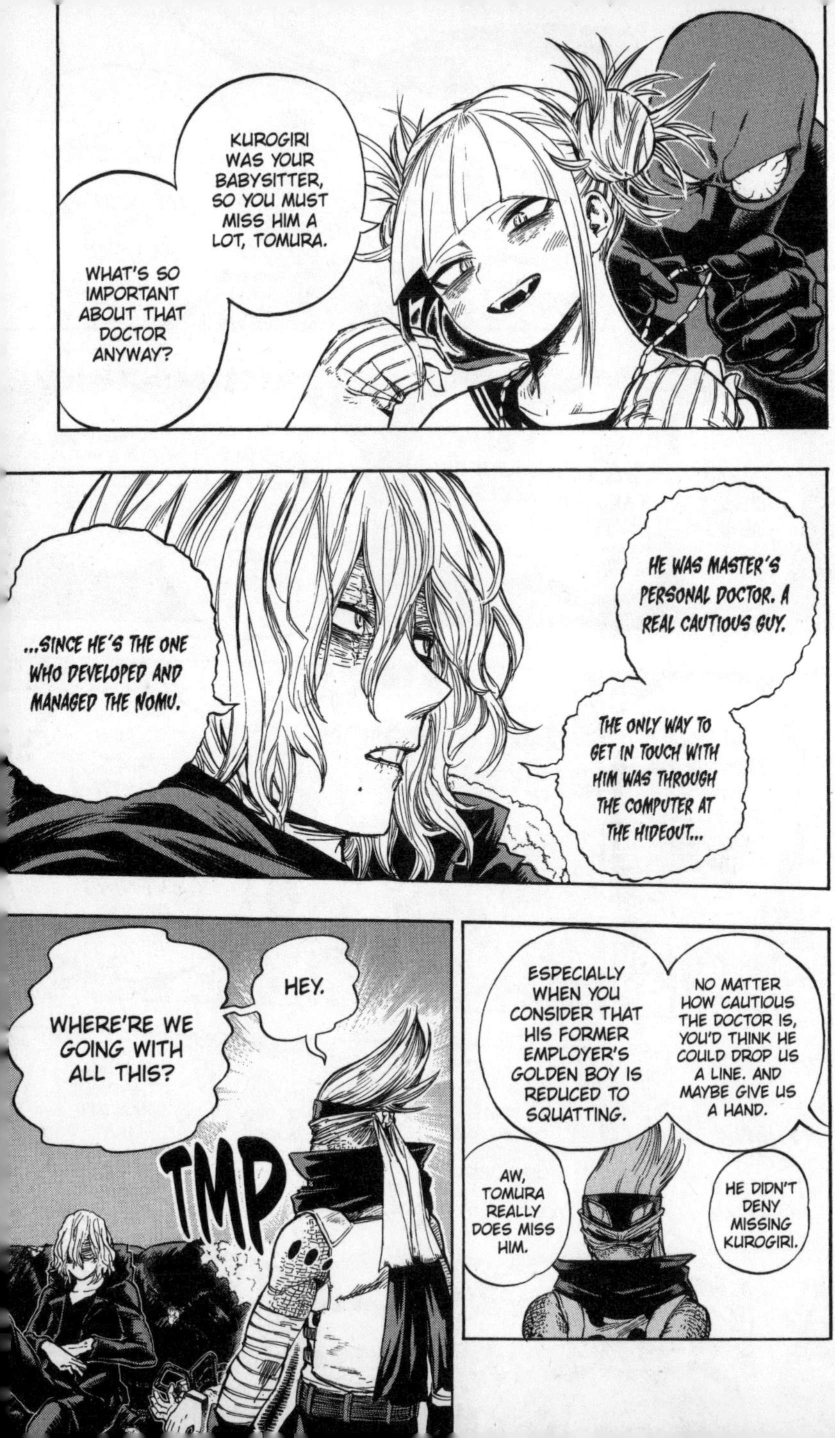
KUROGIRI WAS YOUR BABYSITTER, SO YOU MUST MISS HIM A LOT, TOMURA.
WHAT'S SO IMPORTANT ABOUT THAT DOCTOR ANYWAY?
HE WAS MASTER'S PERSONAL DOCTOR. A REAL CAUTIOUS GUY.
THE ONLY WAY TO GET IN TOUCH WITH HIM WAS THROUGH THE COMPUTER AT THE HIDEOUT...
...SINCE HE'S THE ONE WHO DEVELOPED AND MANAGED THE NOMU.
NO MATTER HOW CAUTIOUS THE DOCTOR IS, YOU'D THINK HE COULD DROP US A LINE. AND MAYBE GIVE US A HAND.
ESPECIALLY WHEN YOU CONSIDER THAT HIS FORMER EMPLOYER'S GOLDEN BOY IS REDUCED TO SQUATTING.
HE DIDN'T DENY MISSING KUROGIRI.
AW, TOMURA REALLY DOES MISS HIM.
HEY.
WHERE'RE WE GOING WITH ALL THIS?
TMP

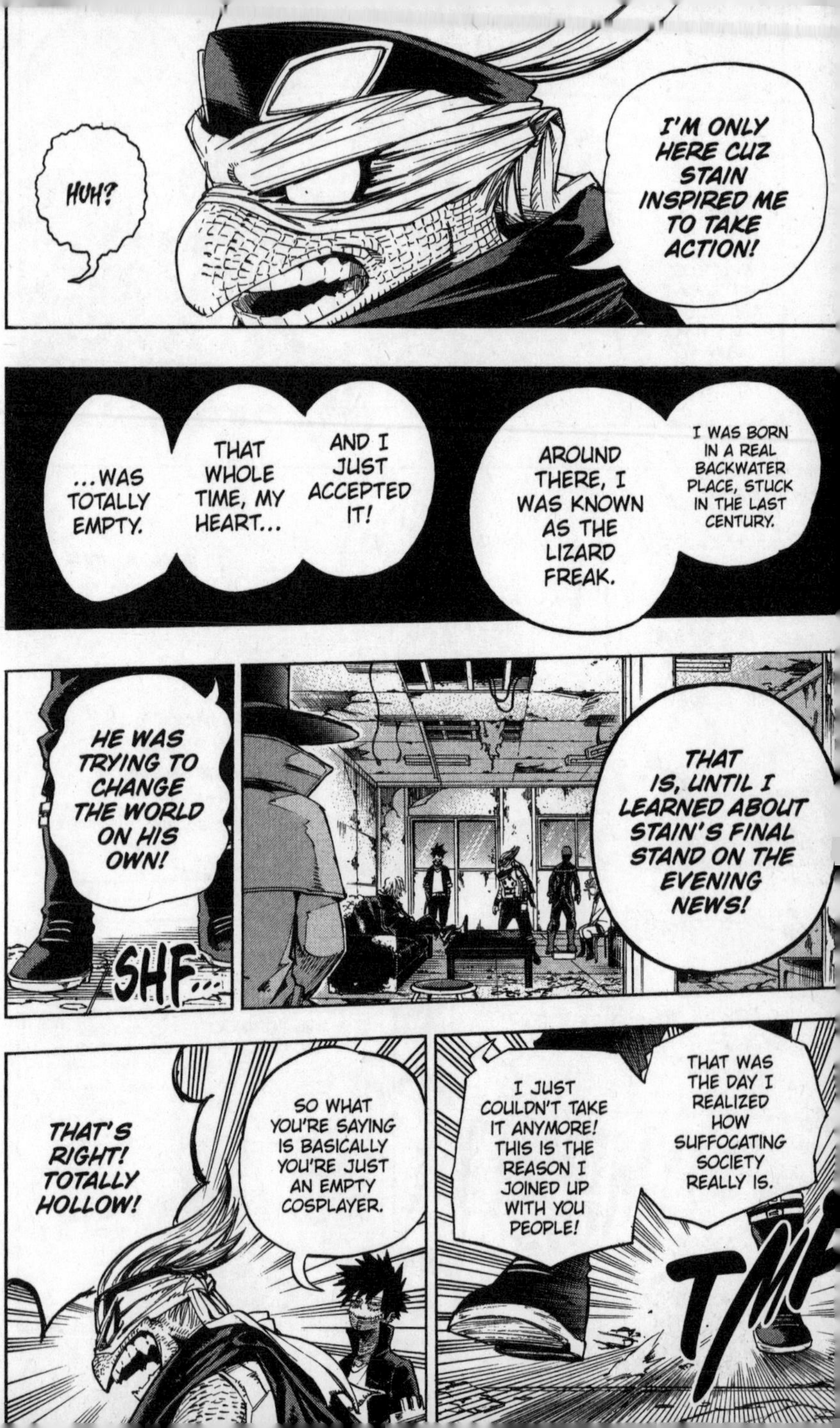
I'M ONLY HERE CUZ STAIN INSPIRED ME TO TAKE ACTION!
HUH?
I WAS BORN IN A REAL BACKWATER PLACE, STUCK IN THE LAST CENTURY.
AROUND THERE, I WAS KNOWN AS THE LIZARD FREAK.
AND I JUST ACCEPTED IT!
THAT WHOLE TIME, MY HEART...
...WAS TOTALLY EMPTY.
THAT IS, UNTIL I LEARNED ABOUT STAIN'S FINAL STAND ON THE EVENING NEWS!
HE WAS TRYING TO CHANGE THE WORLD ON HIS OWN!
SHF...
THAT WAS THE DAY I REALIZED HOW SUFFOCATING SOCIETY REALLY IS.
I JUST COULDN'T TAKE IT ANYMORE! THIS IS THE REASON I JOINED UP WITH YOU PEOPLE!
SO WHAT YOU'RE SAYING IS BASICALLY YOU'RE JUST AN EMPTY COSPLAYER.
THAT'S RIGHT! TOTALLY HOLLOW!

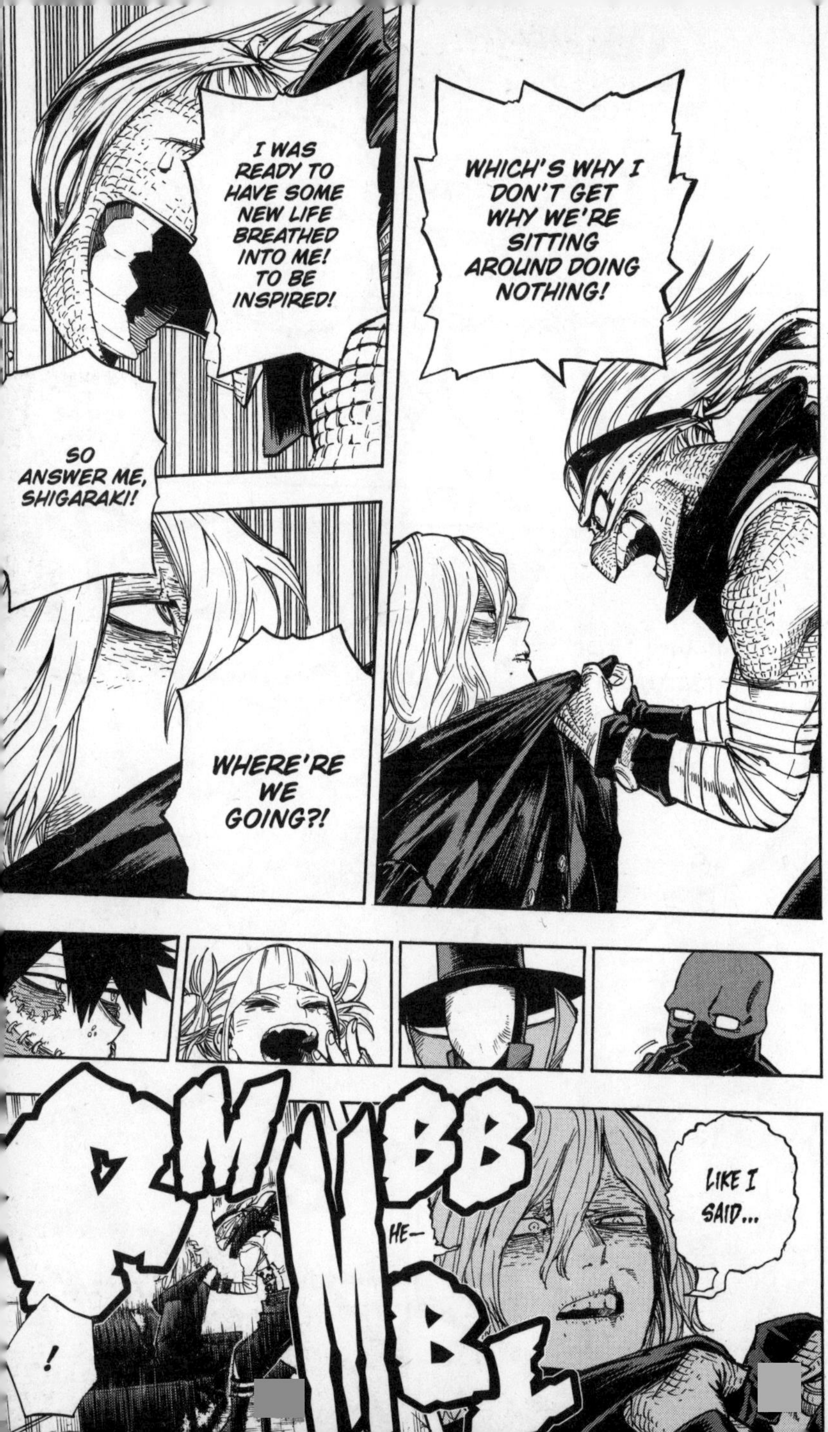
WHICH'S WHY I DON'T GET WHY WE'RE SITTING AROUND DOING NOTHING!
I WAS READY TO HAVE SOME NEW LIFE BREATHED INTO ME! TO BE INSPIRED!
SO ANSWER ME, SHIGARAKI!
WHERE'RE WE GOING?!
LIKE I SAID...
HE—
!

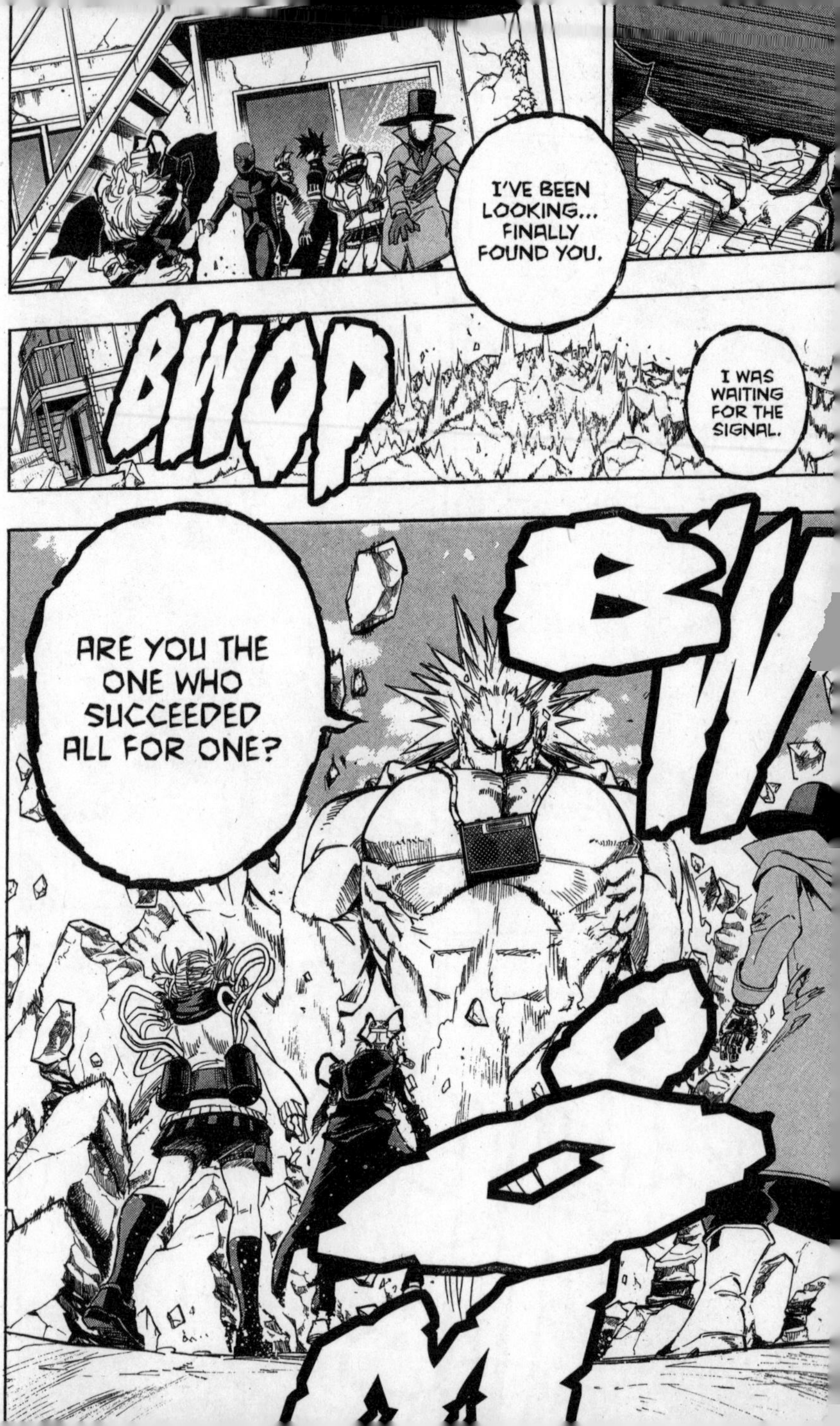
I'VE BEEN LOOKING... FINALLY FOUND YOU.
I WAS WAITING FOR THE SIGNAL.
BWOP
ARE YOU THE ONE WHO SUCCEEDED ALL FOR ONE?

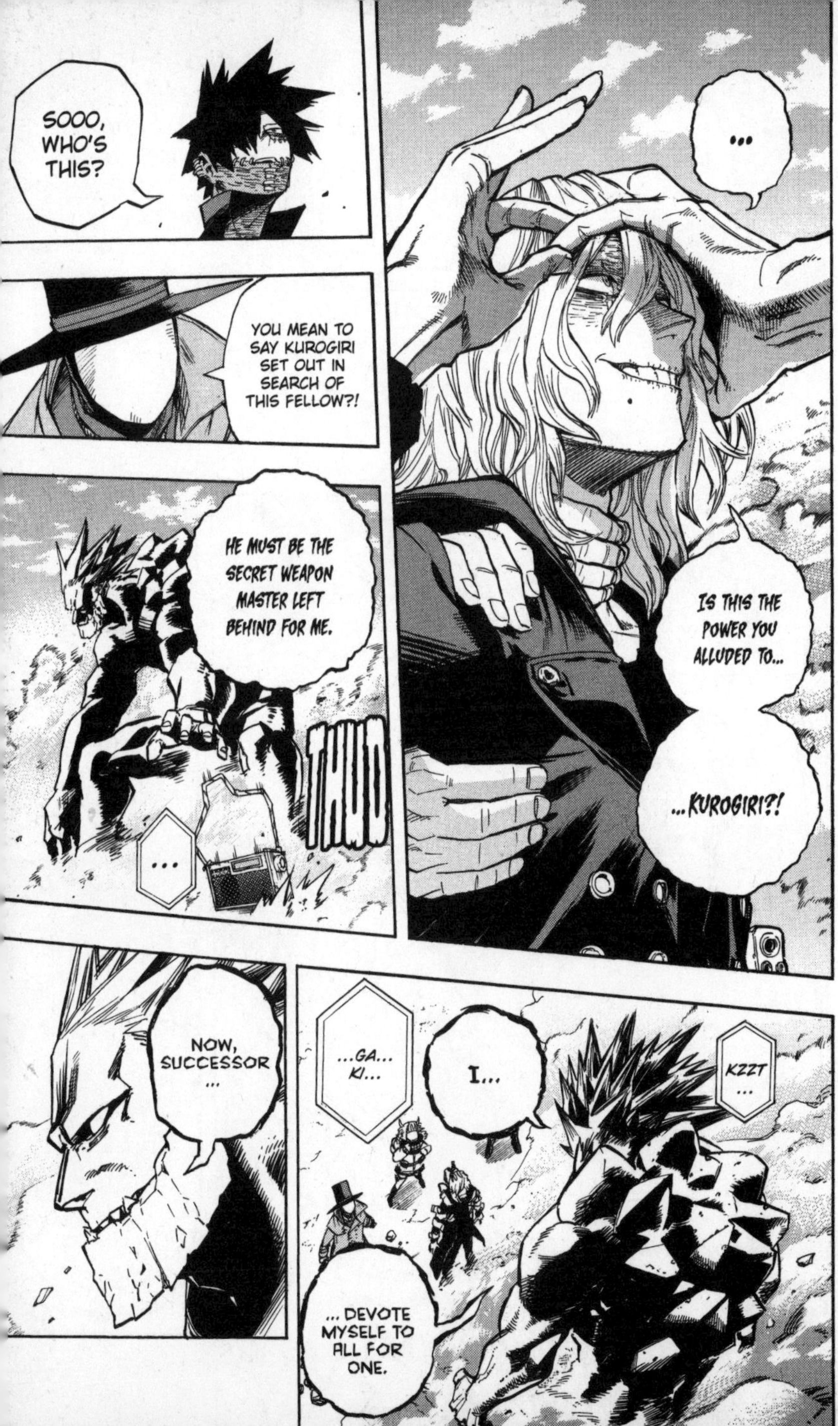
...
IS THIS THE POWER YOU ALLUDED TO...
...KUROGIRI?!
SOOO, WHO'S THIS?
YOU MEAN TO SAY KUROGIRI SET OUT IN SEARCH OF THIS FELLOW?!
HE MUST BE THE SECRET WEAPON MASTER LEFT BEHIND FOR ME.
THUD
...
KZZT ...
I...
...GA... KI...
... DEVOTE MYSELF TO ALL FOR ONE.
NOW, SUCCESSOR ...

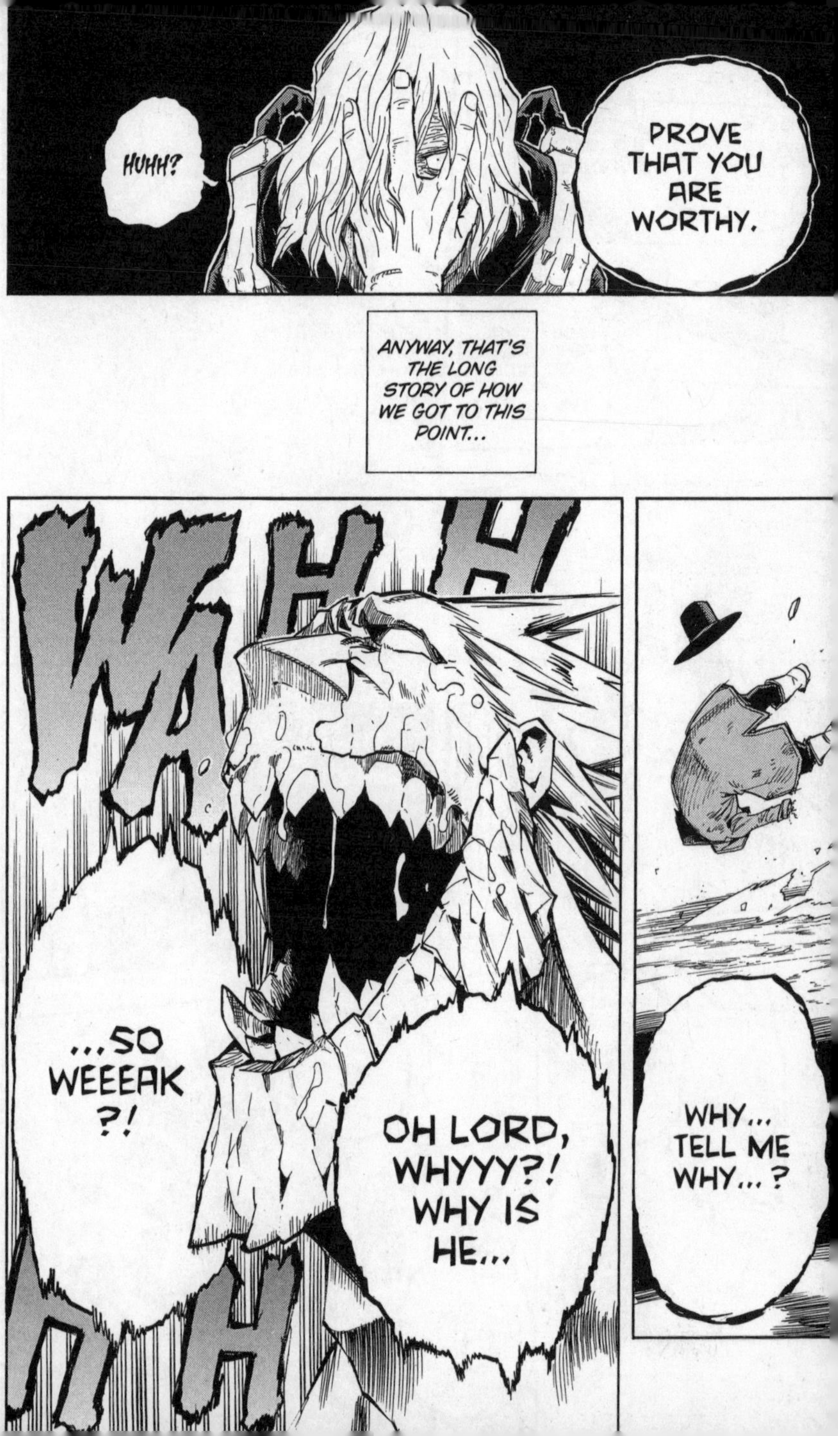
PROVE THAT YOU ARE WORTHY.
HUHH?
ANYWAY, THAT'S THE LONG STORY OF HOW WE GOT TO THIS POINT...
WHY... TELL ME WHY...?
WAHH
OH LORD, WHYYY?! WHY IS HE...
...SO WEEEAK?!

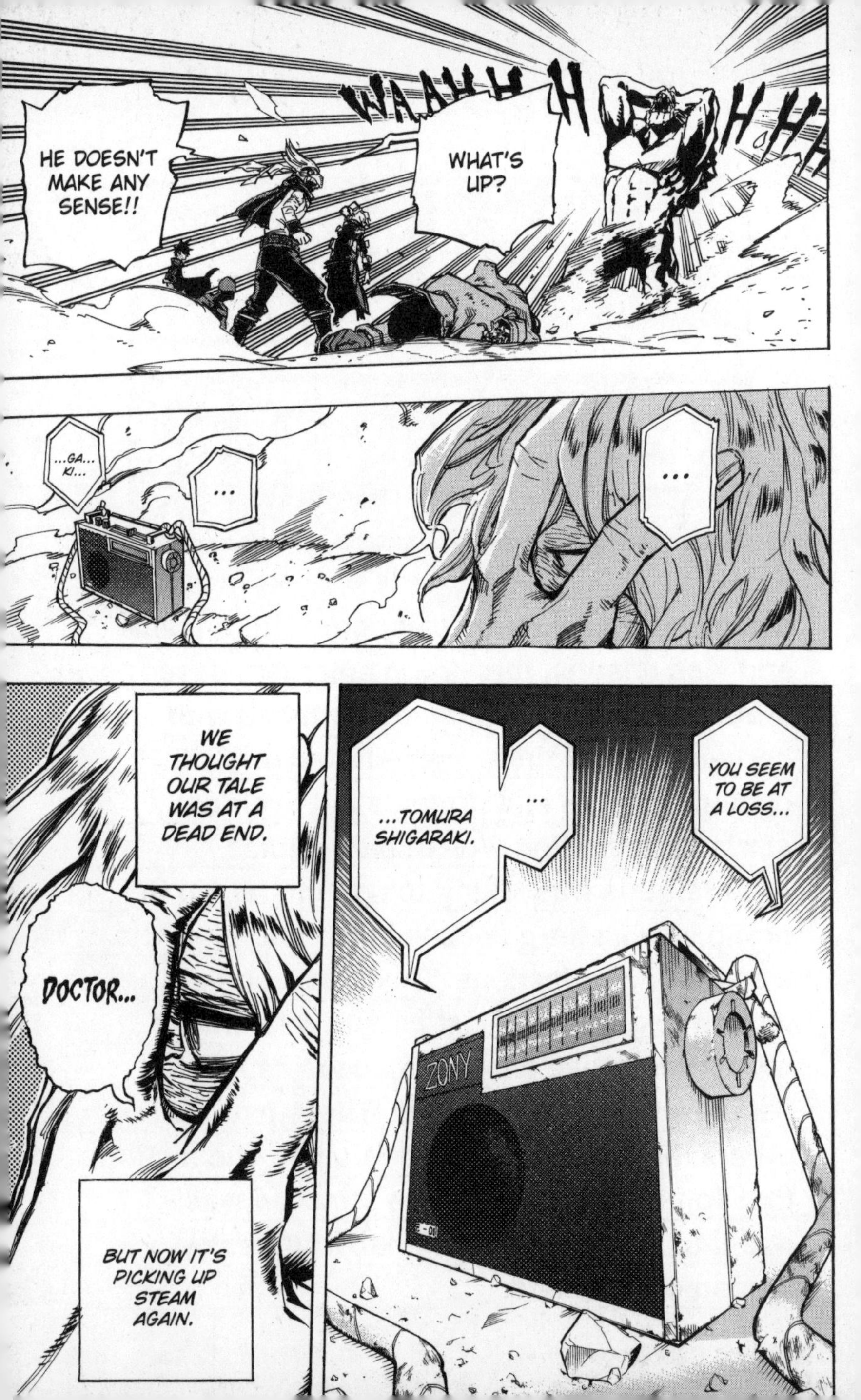
WAAHH H H HH
WHAT'S UP?
HE DOESN'T MAKE ANY SENSE!!
...
...
...GA... KI...
YOU SEEM TO BE AT A LOSS...
...
...TOMURA SHIGARAKI.
ZONY
WE THOUGHT OUR TALE WAS AT A DEAD END.
DOCTOR...
BUT NOW IT'S PICKING UP STEAM AGAIN.

CREATURE REJECTION CLAN

Once superpowered society grew more stable and less chaotic, this group emerged, based around a lack of acceptance for those with body-altering Quirks. They started out with demonstrations and protests but eventually started committing violent hate crimes. Most felt this was taking things too far, so the group saw a sharp decline in membership and a scattering of factions. These days, one faction might only reject people with animal properties, while another focuses its hate on people with irregular heads. These two, among others, have very few members left. The faction that Tomura and the villains attacked was one that stood by the original group's fundamental tenets.

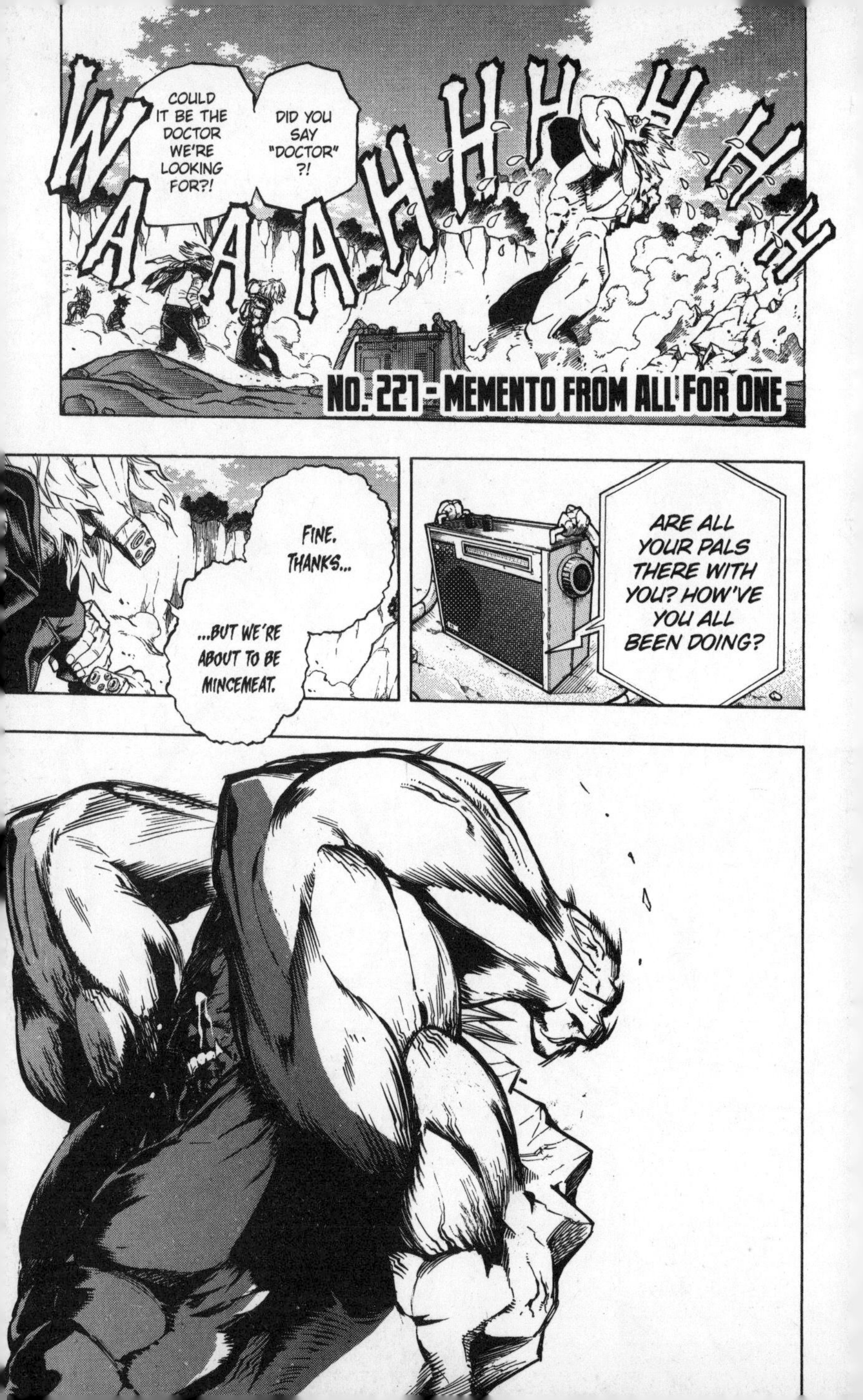
WAAAHHHHHH
DID YOU SAY "DOCTOR"?!
COULD IT BE THE DOCTOR WE'RE LOOKING FOR?!
NO. 221 - MEMENTO FROM ALL FOR ONE
ARE ALL YOUR PALS THERE WITH YOU? HOW'VE YOU ALL BEEN DOING?
FINE. THANKS...
...BUT WE'RE ABOUT TO BE MINCEMEAT.

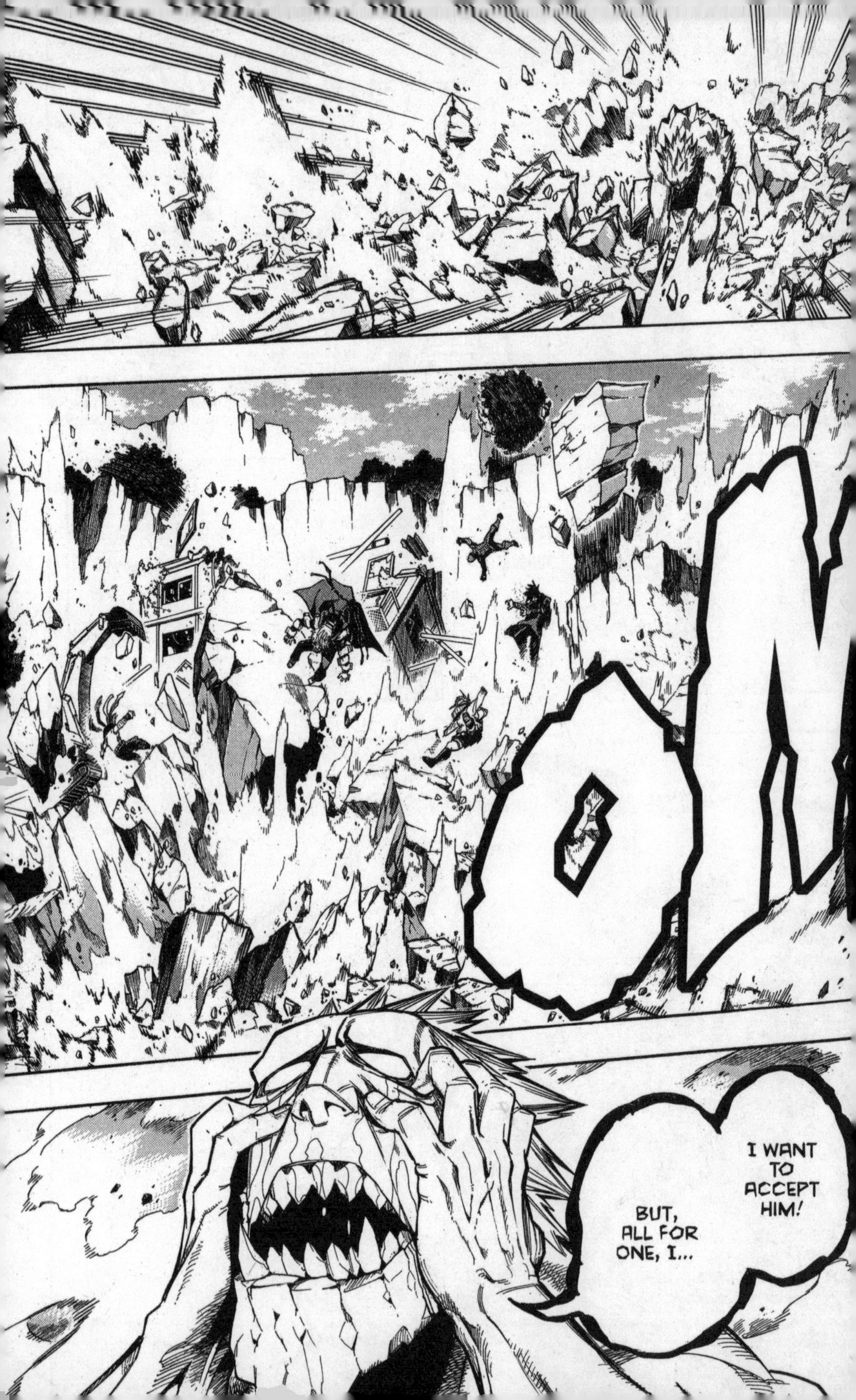
I WANT TO ACCEPT HIM!
BUT, ALL FOR ONE, I...

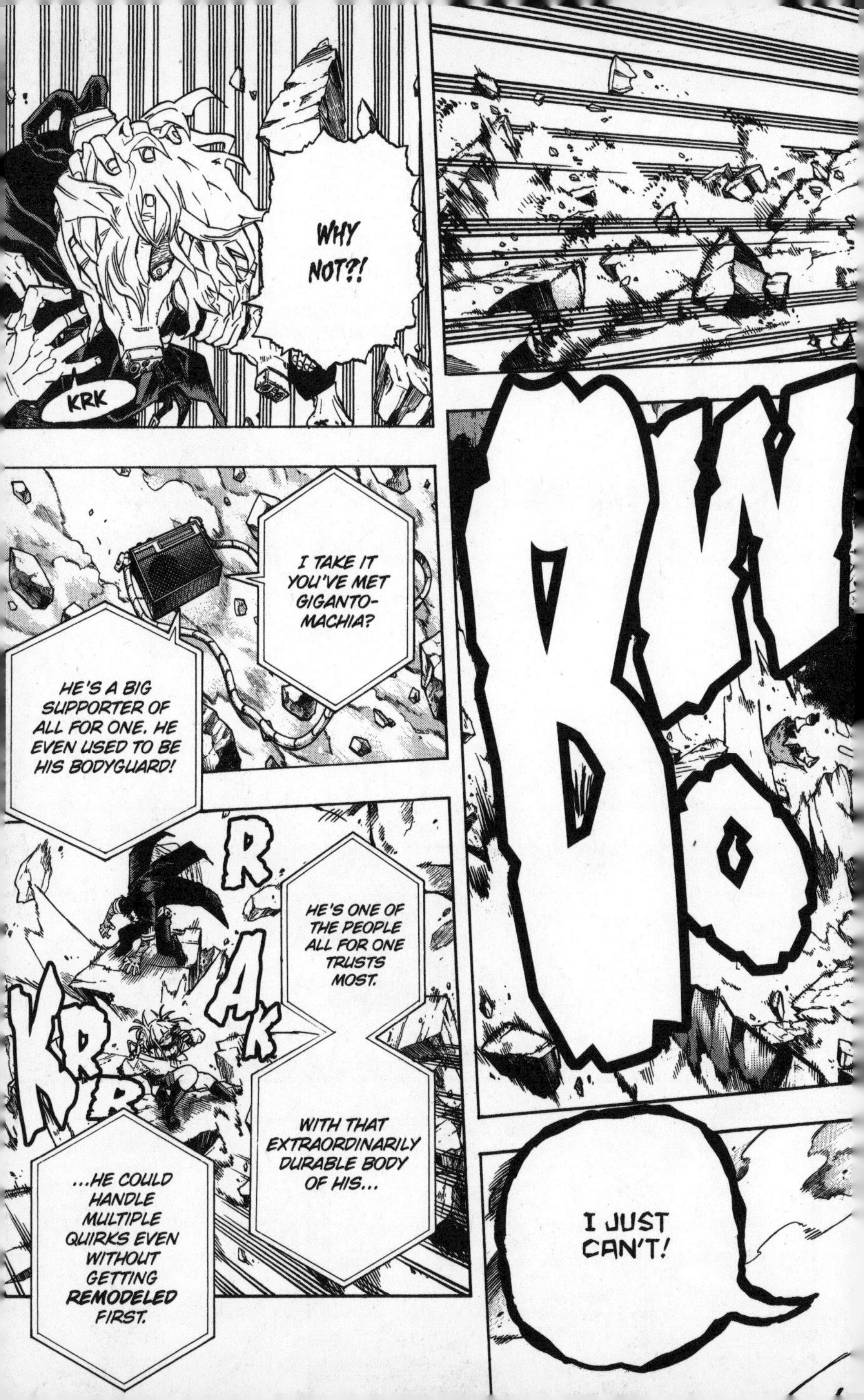
WHY NOT?!
KRK
I JUST CAN'T!
I TAKE IT YOU'VE MET GIGANTO-MACHIA?
HE'S A BIG SUPPORTER OF ALL FOR ONE. HE EVEN USED TO BE HIS BODYGUARD!
HE'S ONE OF THE PEOPLE ALL FOR ONE TRUSTS MOST.
KRRRAK
WITH THAT EXTRAORDINARILY DURABLE BODY OF HIS...
...HE COULD HANDLE MULTIPLE QUIRKS EVEN WITHOUT GETTING REMODELED FIRST.

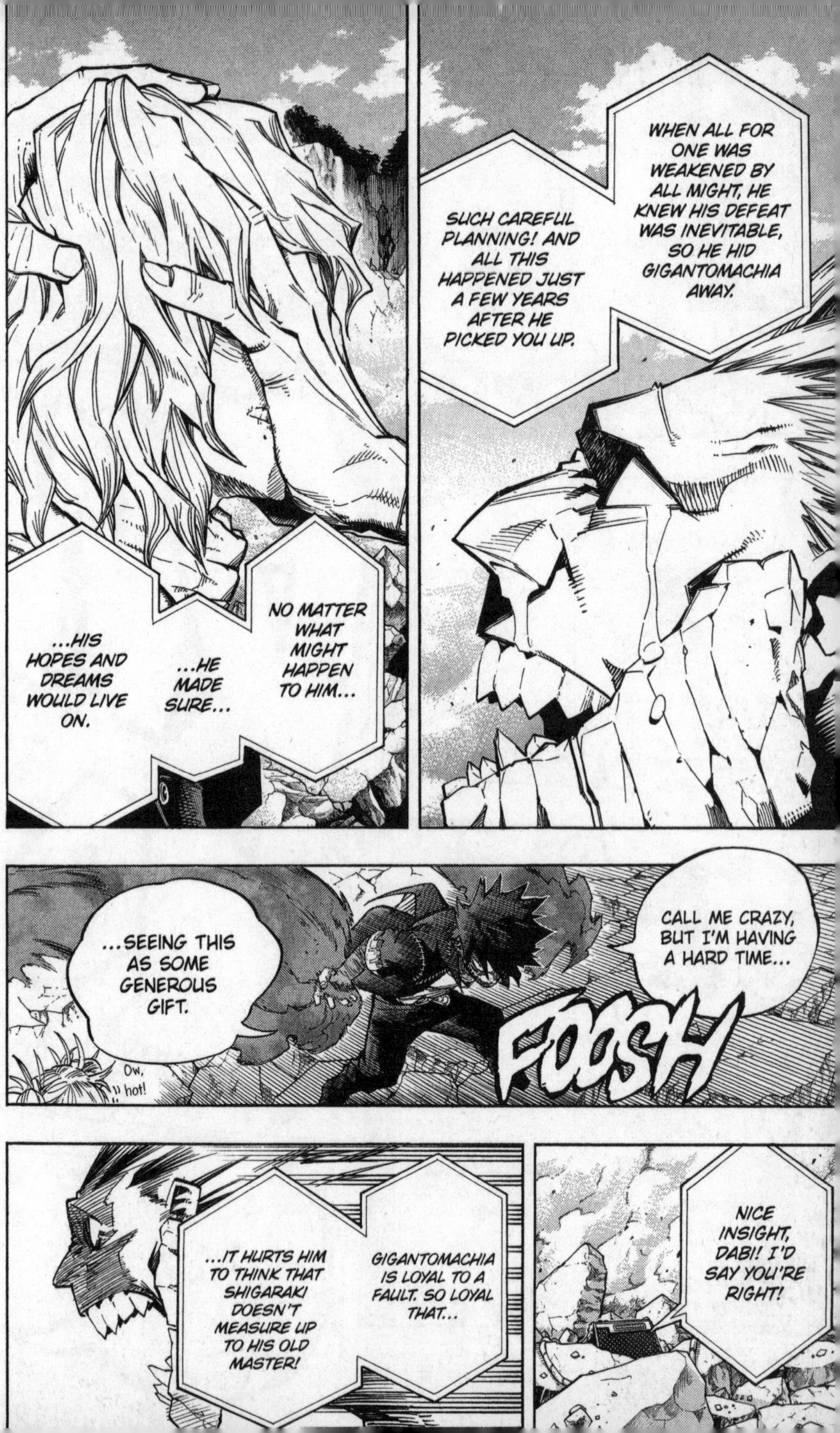
WHEN ALL FOR ONE WAS WEAKENED BY ALL MIGHT, HE KNEW HIS DEFEAT WAS INEVITABLE, SO HE HID GIGANTOMACHIA AWAY.
SUCH CAREFUL PLANNING! AND ALL THIS HAPPENED JUST A FEW YEARS AFTER HE PICKED YOU UP.
NO MATTER WHAT MIGHT HAPPEN TO HIM...
...HE MADE SURE...
...HIS HOPES AND DREAMS WOULD LIVE ON.
CALL ME CRAZY, BUT I'M HAVING A HARD TIME...
FOOSH
...SEEING THIS AS SOME GENEROUS GIFT.
Ow, hot!
NICE INSIGHT, DABI! I'D SAY YOU'RE RIGHT!
GIGANTOMACHIA IS LOYAL TO A FAULT. SO LOYAL THAT...
...IT HURTS HIM TO THINK THAT SHIGARAKI DOESN'T MEASURE UP TO HIS OLD MASTER!

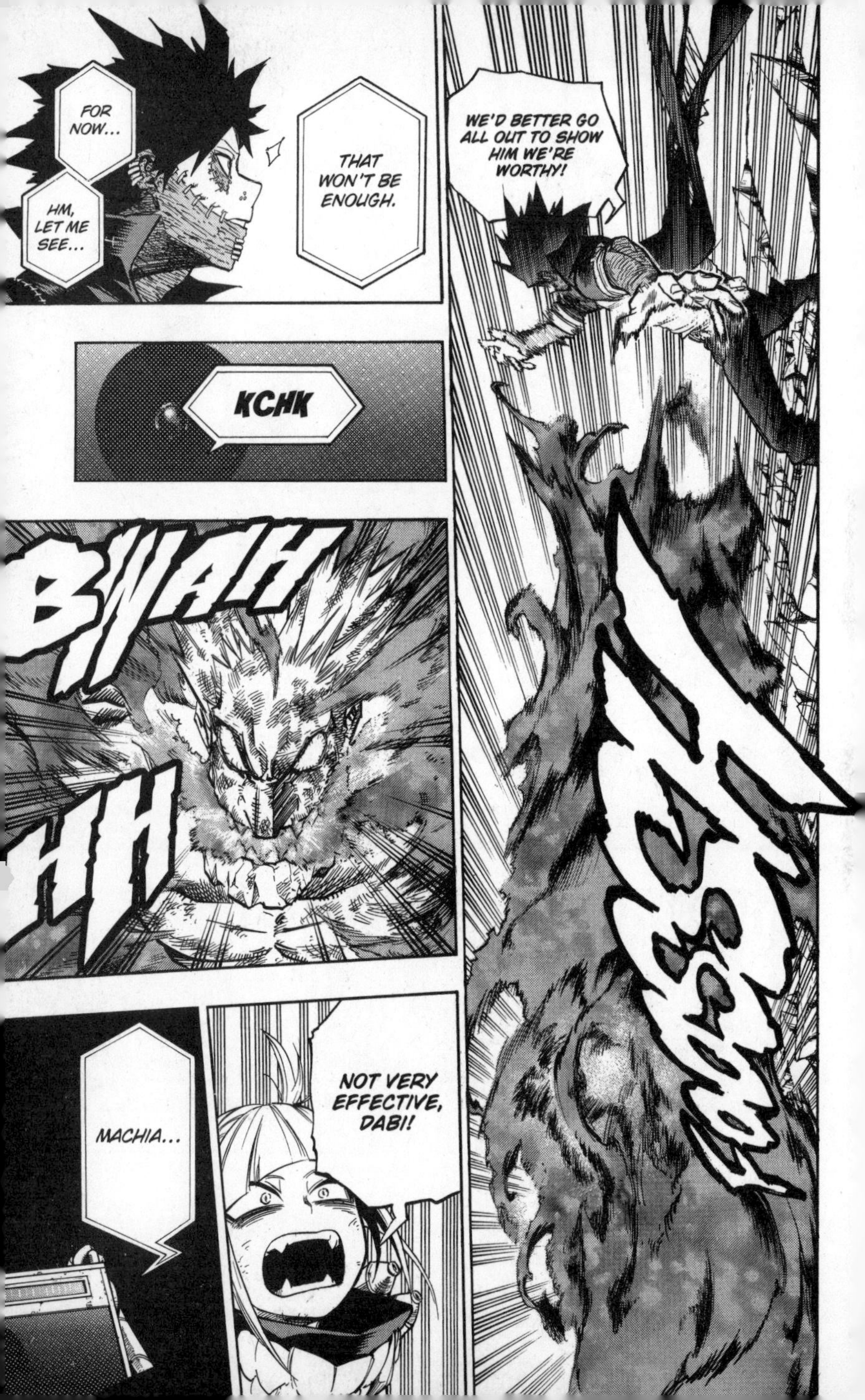

WE'D BETTER GO ALL OUT TO SHOW HIM WE'RE WORTHY!
THAT WON'T BE ENOUGH.
FOR NOW...
HM, LET ME SEE...
KCHK
BWAH
NOT VERY EFFECTIVE, DABI!
MACHIA...

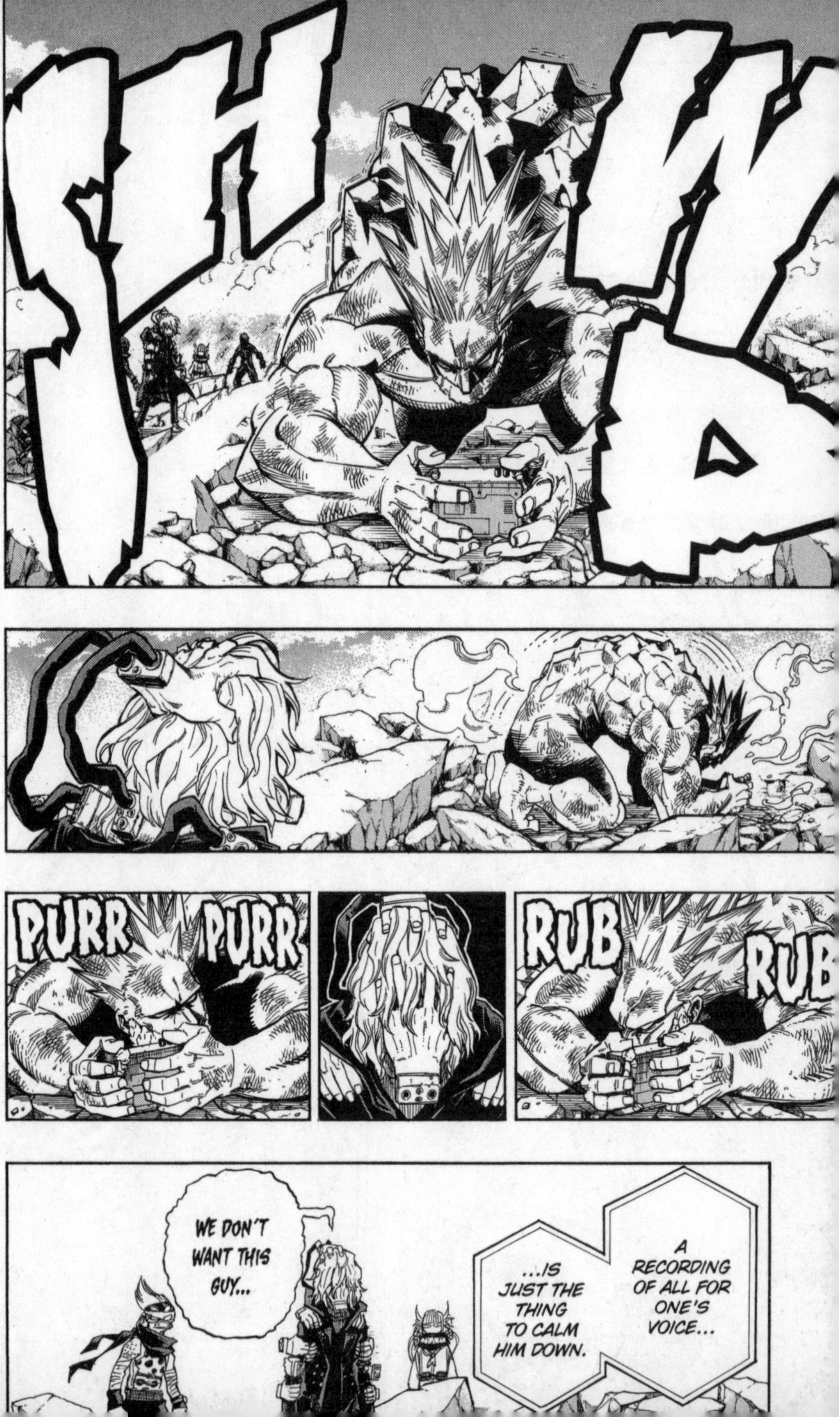
RUB
RUB
PURR
PURR
A RECORDING OF ALL FOR ONE'S VOICE...
...IS JUST THE THING TO CALM HIM DOWN.
WE DON'T WANT THIS GUY...

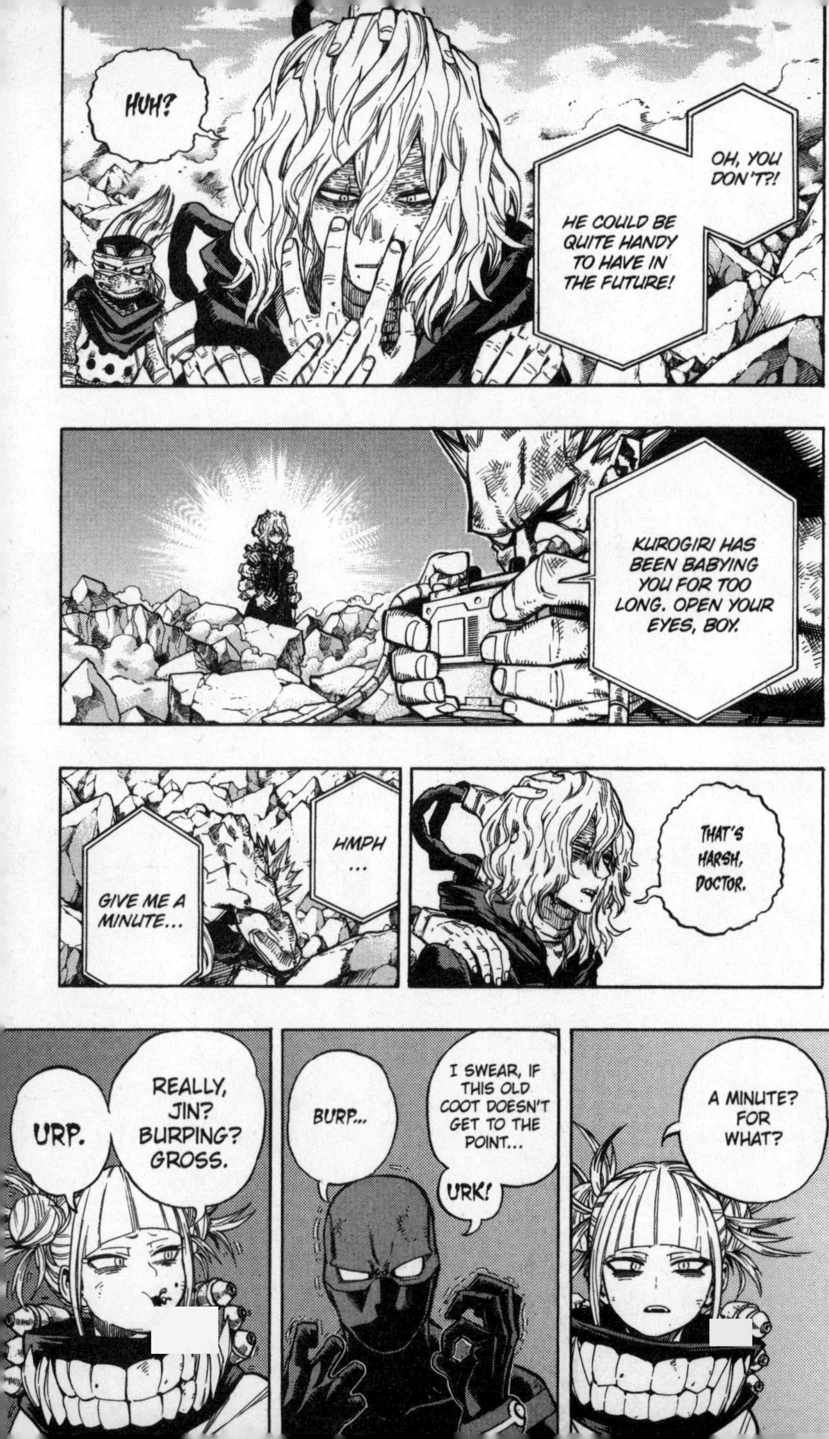
OH, YOU DON'T?!
HE COULD BE QUITE HANDY TO HAVE IN THE FUTURE!
HUH?
KUROGIRI HAS BEEN BABYING YOU FOR TOO LONG. OPEN YOUR EYES, BOY.
THAT'S HARSH, DOCTOR.
HMPH ...
GIVE ME A MINUTE...
A MINUTE? FOR WHAT?
I SWEAR, IF THIS OLD COOT DOESN'T GET TO THE POINT...
URK!
BURP...
REALLY, JIN? BURPING? GROSS.
URP.

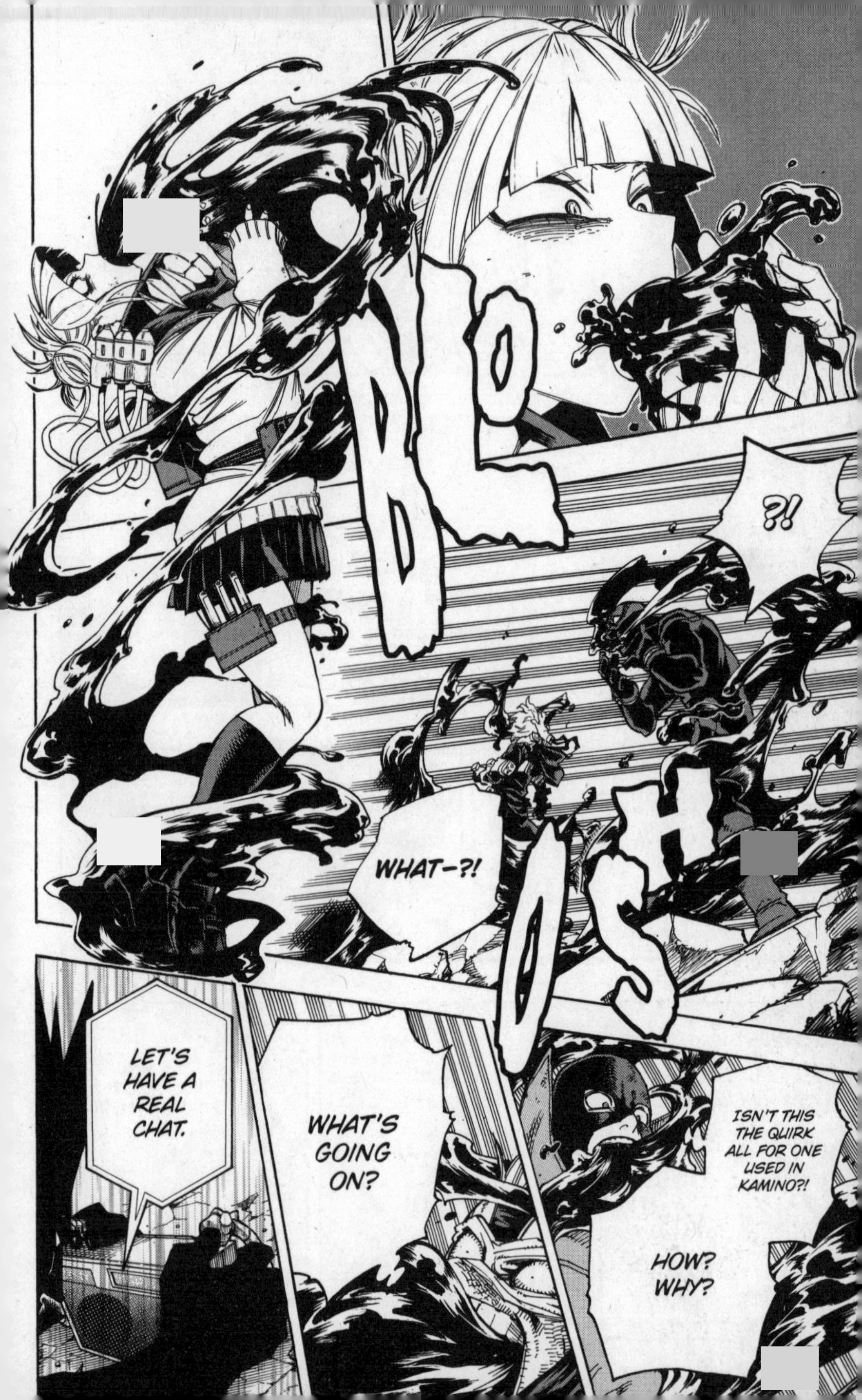
?!
WHAT-?!
ISN'T THIS THE QUIRK ALL FOR ONE USED IN KAMINO?!
HOW? WHY?
WHAT'S GOING ON?
LET'S HAVE A REAL CHAT.

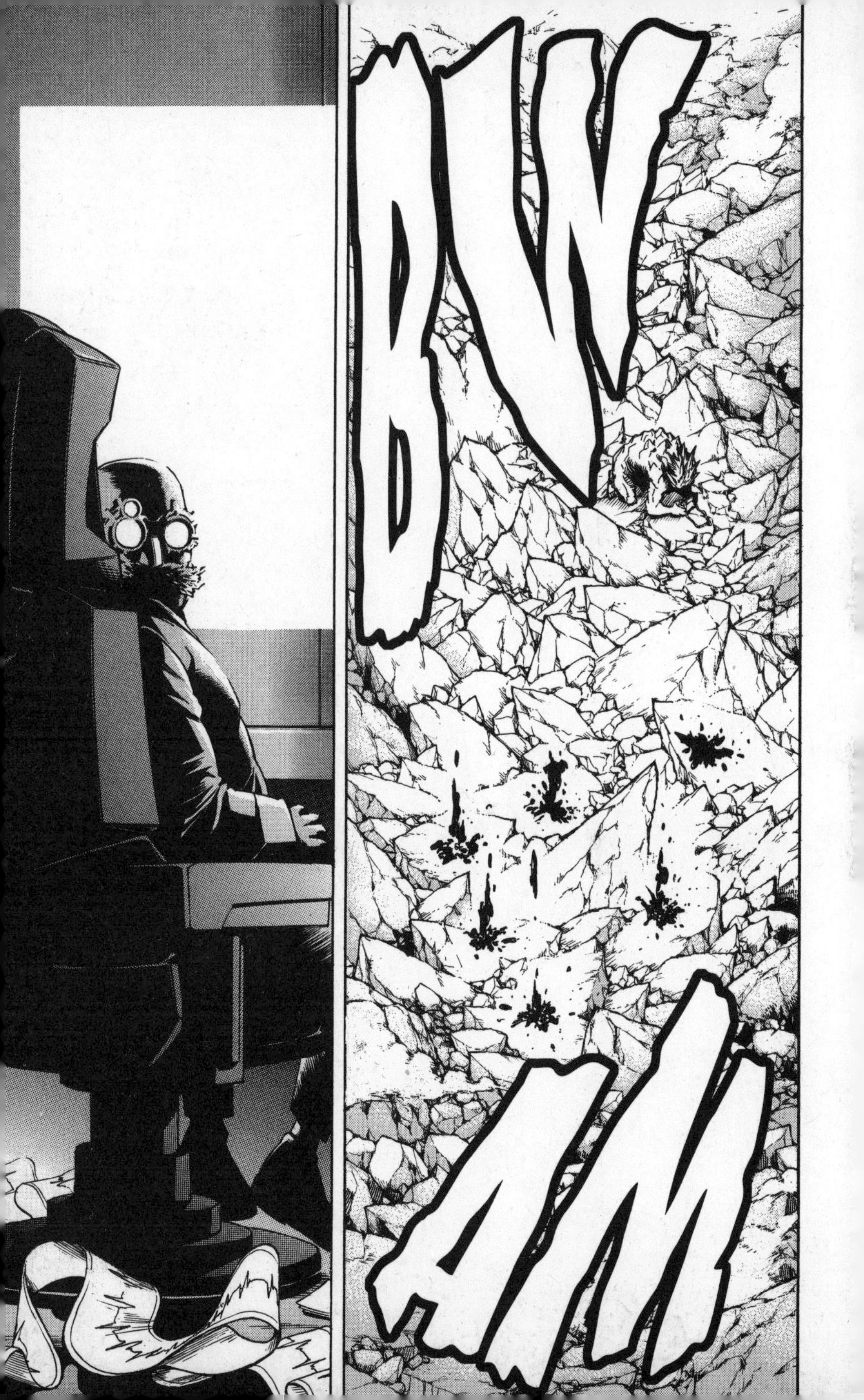
BAM

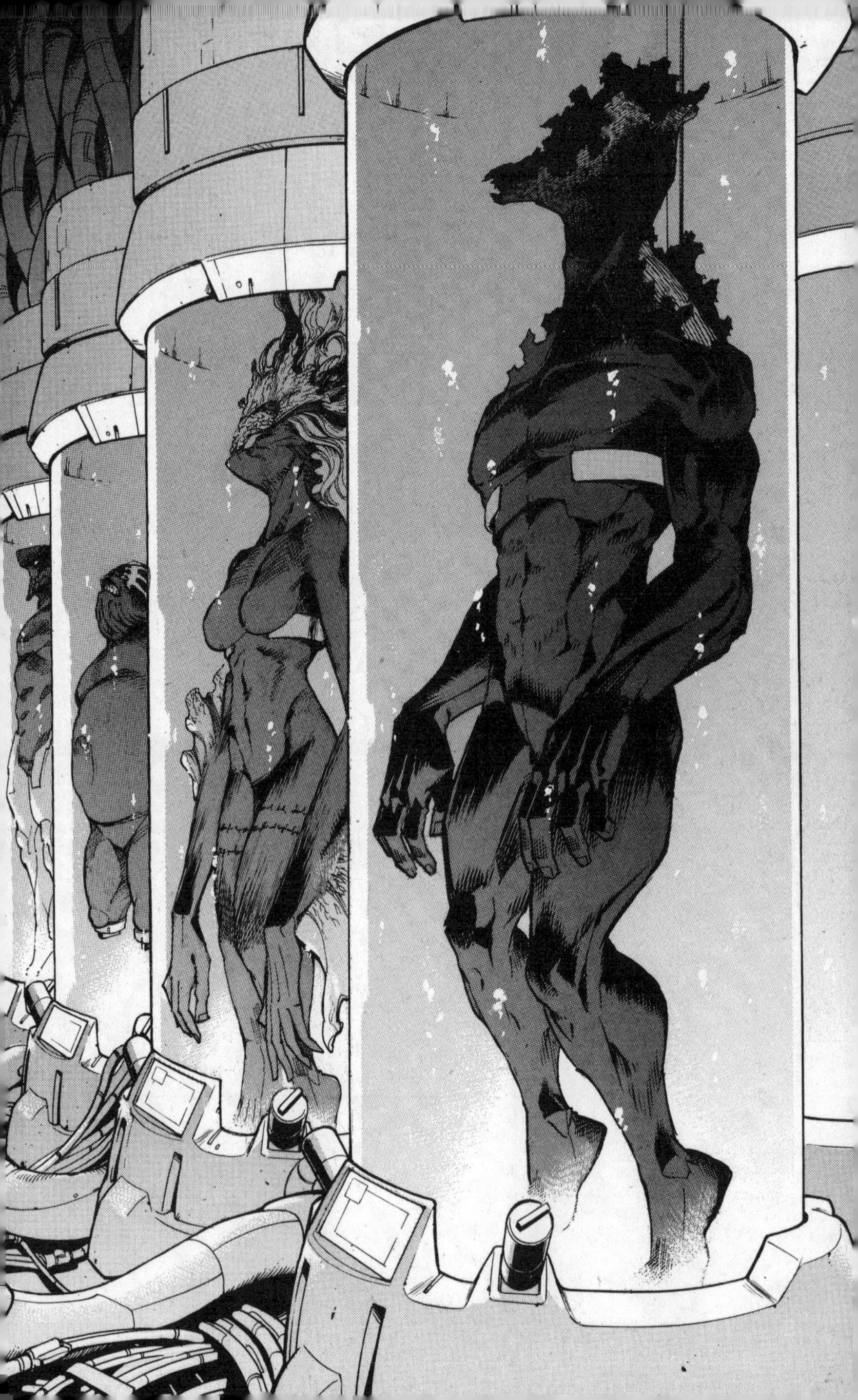

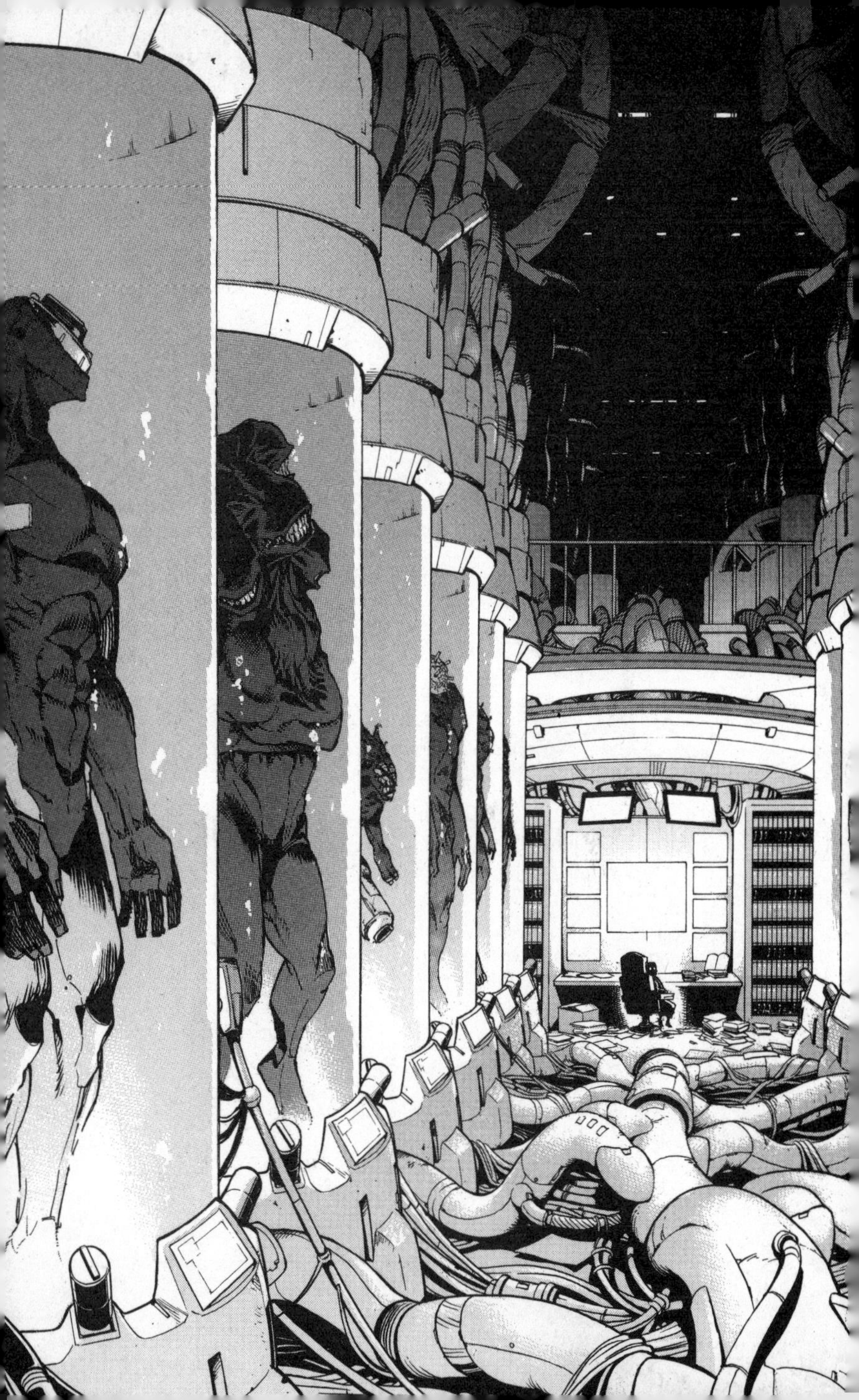

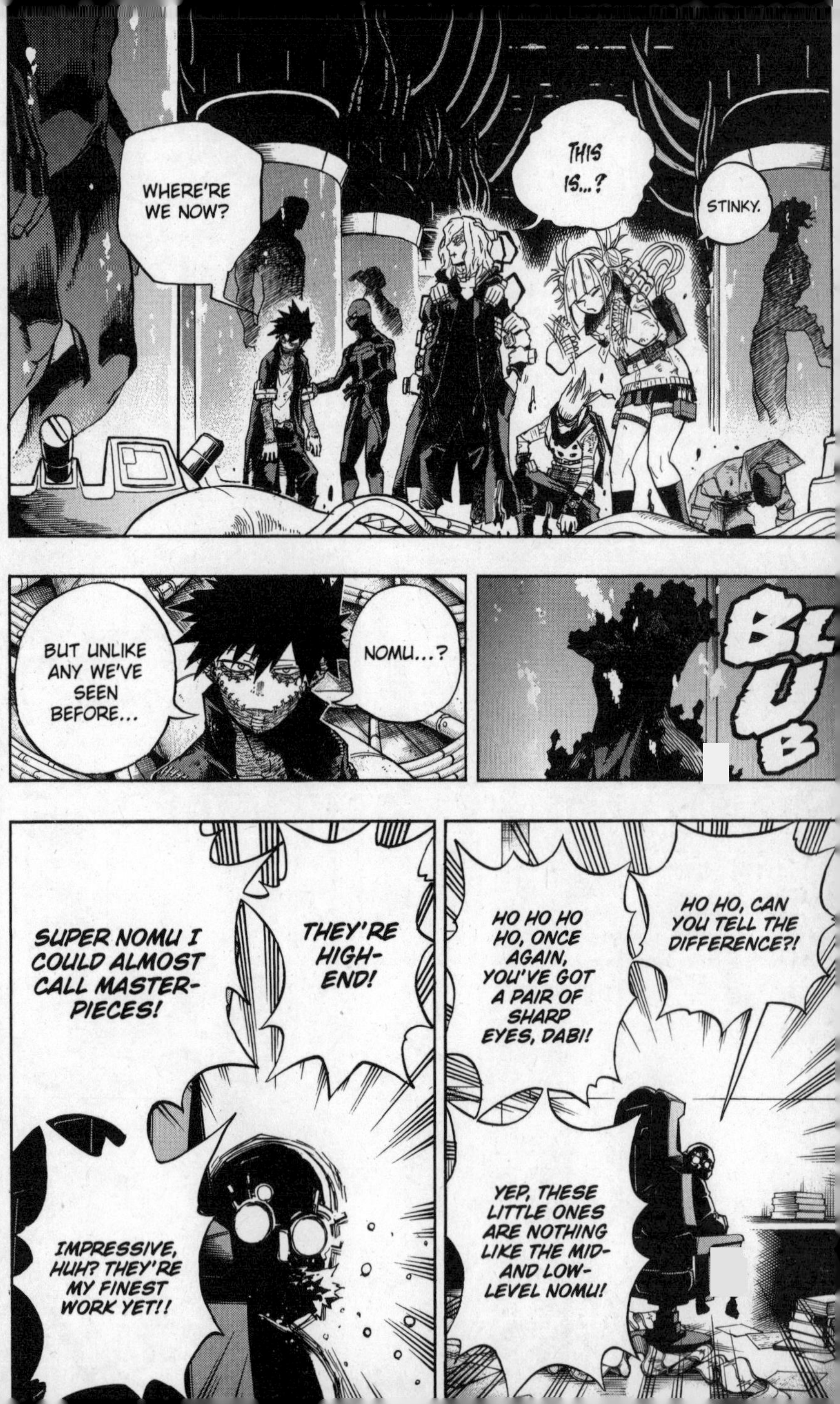
STINKY.
THIS IS...?
WHERE'RE WE NOW?
BLUB
NOMU...?
BUT UNLIKE ANY WE'VE SEEN BEFORE...
HO HO, CAN YOU TELL THE DIFFERENCE?!
HO HO HO HO, ONCE AGAIN, YOU'VE GOT A PAIR OF SHARP EYES, DABI!
YEP, THESE LITTLE ONES ARE NOTHING LIKE THE MID- AND LOW-LEVEL NOMU!
THEY'RE HIGH-END!
SUPER NOMU I COULD ALMOST CALL MASTER-PIECES!
IMPRESSIVE, HUH? THEY'RE MY FINEST WORK YET!!

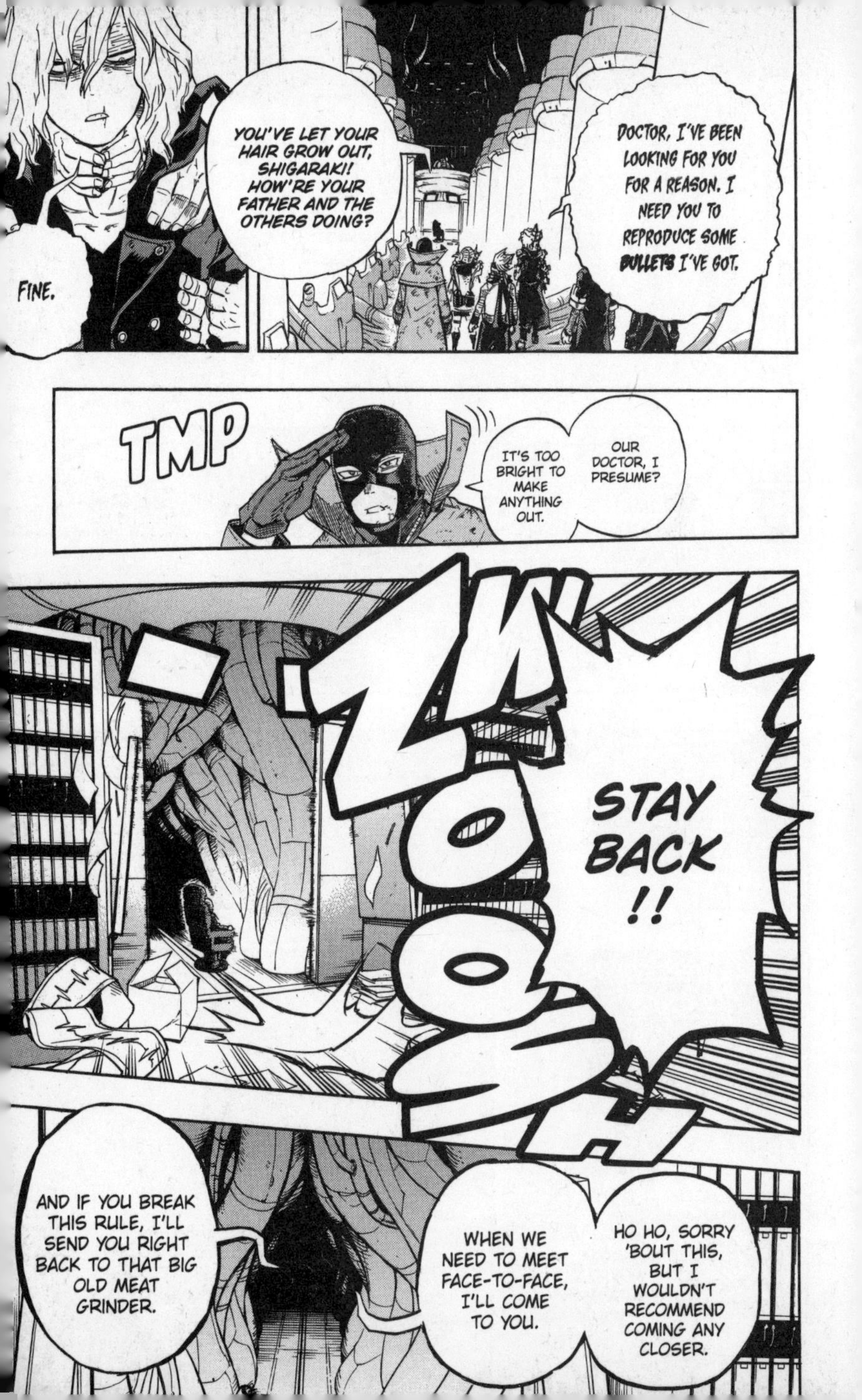

DOCTOR, I'VE BEEN LOOKING FOR YOU FOR A REASON. I NEED YOU TO REPRODUCE SOME BULLETS I'VE GOT.
YOU'VE LET YOUR HAIR GROW OUT, SHIGARAKI!! HOW'RE YOUR FATHER AND THE OTHERS DOING?
FINE.
OUR DOCTOR, I PRESUME?
IT'S TOO BRIGHT TO MAKE ANYTHING OUT.
TMP
STAY BACK!!
HO HO, SORRY 'BOUT THIS, BUT I WOULDN'T RECOMMEND COMING ANY CLOSER.
WHEN WE NEED TO MEET FACE-TO-FACE, I'LL COME TO YOU.
AND IF YOU BREAK THIS RULE, I'LL SEND YOU RIGHT BACK TO THAT BIG OLD MEAT GRINDER.

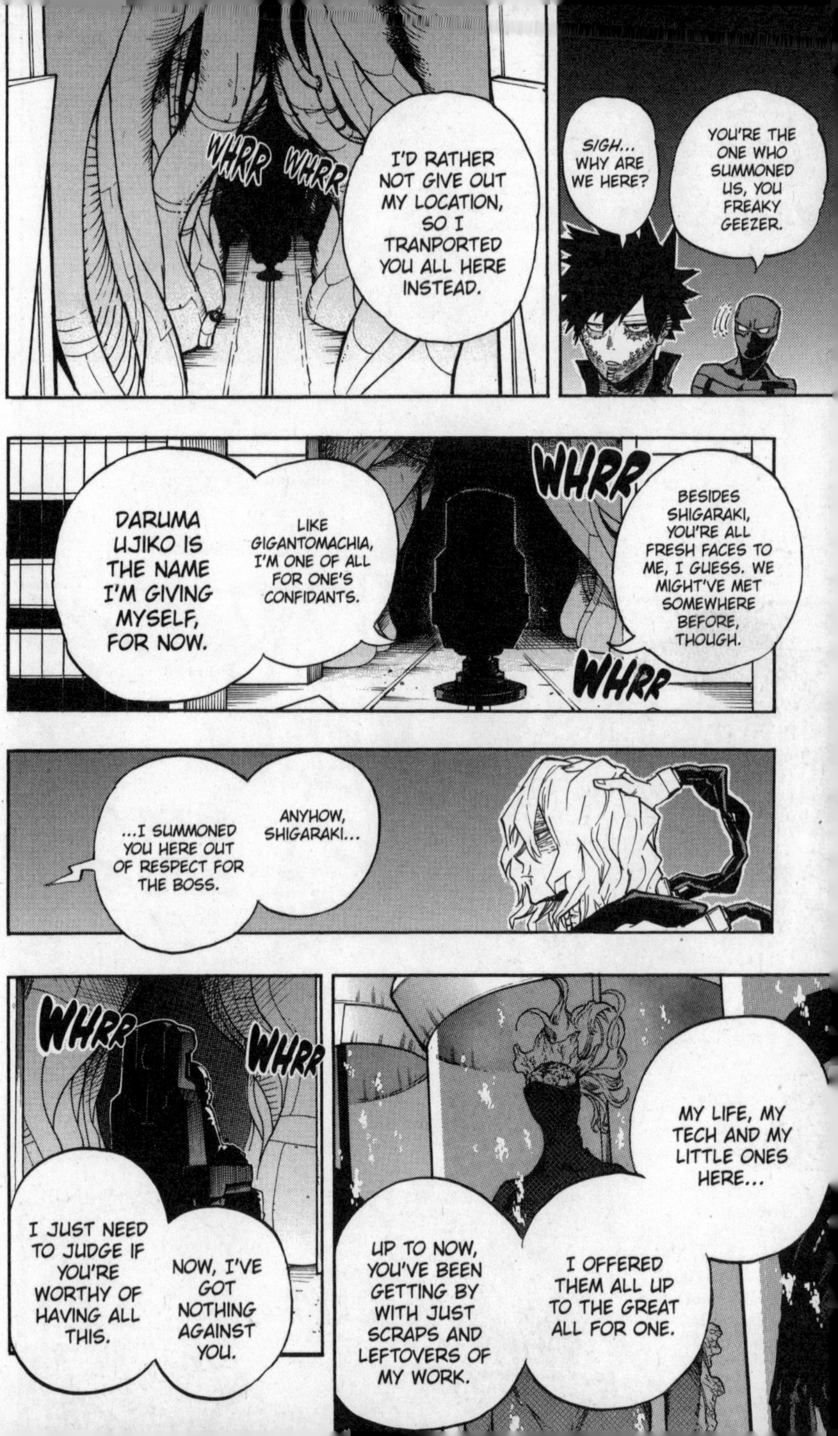
YOU'RE THE ONE WHO SUMMONED US, YOU FREAKY GEEZER.
SIGH... WHY ARE WE HERE?
WHRR WHRR
I'D RATHER NOT GIVE OUT MY LOCATION, SO I TRANPORTED YOU ALL HERE INSTEAD.
WHRR
BESIDES SHIGARAKI, YOU'RE ALL FRESH FACES TO ME, I GUESS. WE MIGHT'VE MET SOMEWHERE BEFORE, THOUGH.
WHRR
LIKE GIGANTOMACHIA, I'M ONE OF ALL FOR ONE'S CONFIDANTS.
DARUMA UJIKO IS THE NAME I'M GIVING MYSELF, FOR NOW.
ANYHOW, SHIGARAKI...
...I SUMMONED YOU HERE OUT OF RESPECT FOR THE BOSS.
MY LIFE, MY TECH AND MY LITTLE ONES HERE...
I OFFERED THEM ALL UP TO THE GREAT ALL FOR ONE.
UP TO NOW, YOU'VE BEEN GETTING BY WITH JUST SCRAPS AND LEFTOVERS OF MY WORK.
WHRR
WHRR
NOW, I'VE GOT NOTHING AGAINST YOU.
I JUST NEED TO JUDGE IF YOU'RE WORTHY OF HAVING ALL THIS.

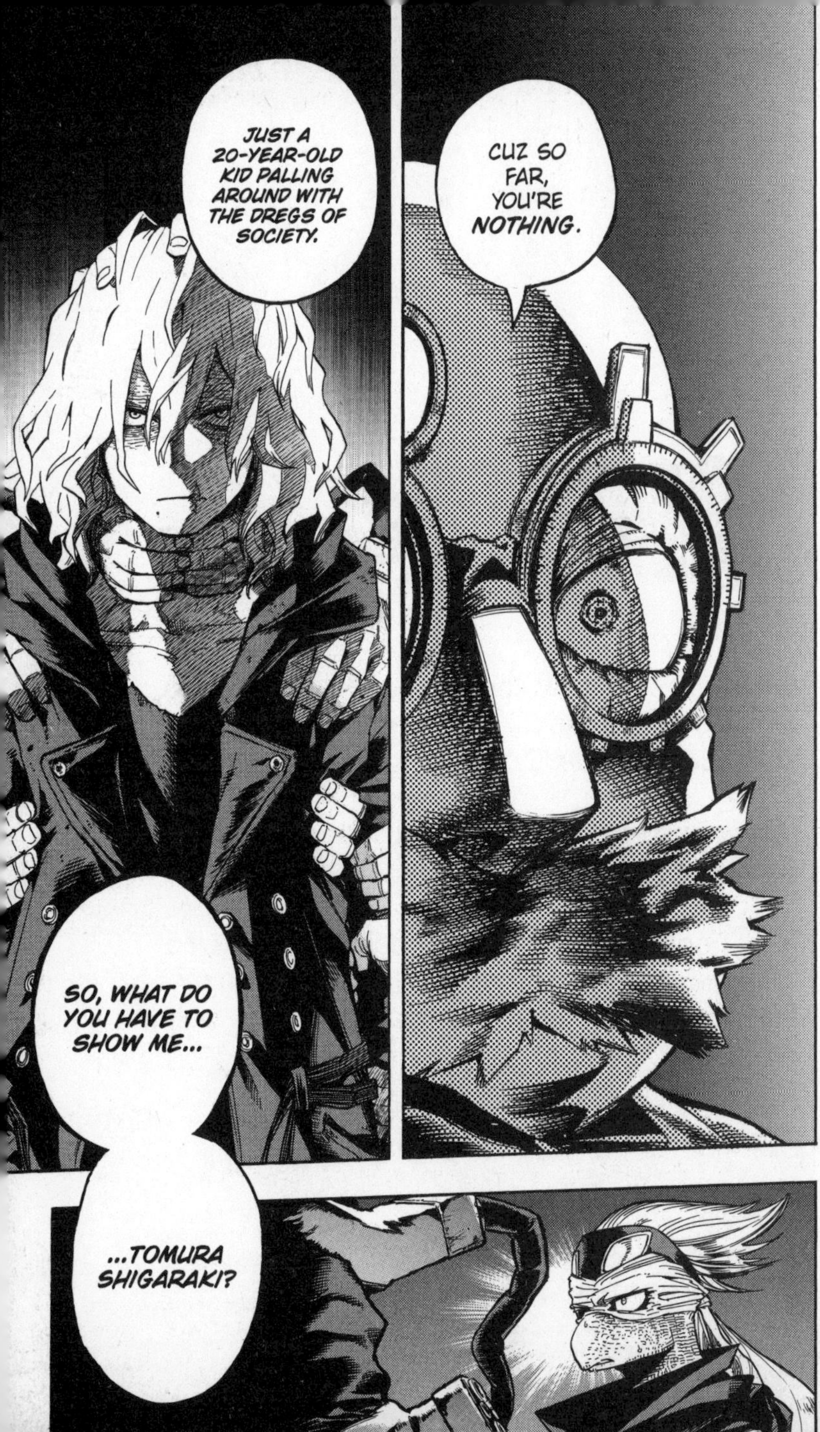
CUZ SO FAR, YOU'RE NOTHING.
JUST A 20-YEAR-OLD KID PALLING AROUND WITH THE DREGS OF SOCIETY.
SO, WHAT DO YOU HAVE TO SHOW ME...
...TOMURA SHIGARAKI?

On April Fool's Day, the title page to the
left was framed as a key visual reveal for
the second movie.

The anime staff had their own corresponding
version too.

April Fool's jokes are kind of pointless once it's
not April Fool's anymore, but I hope you enjoy
this one anyway, even if it's past its sell-by date.

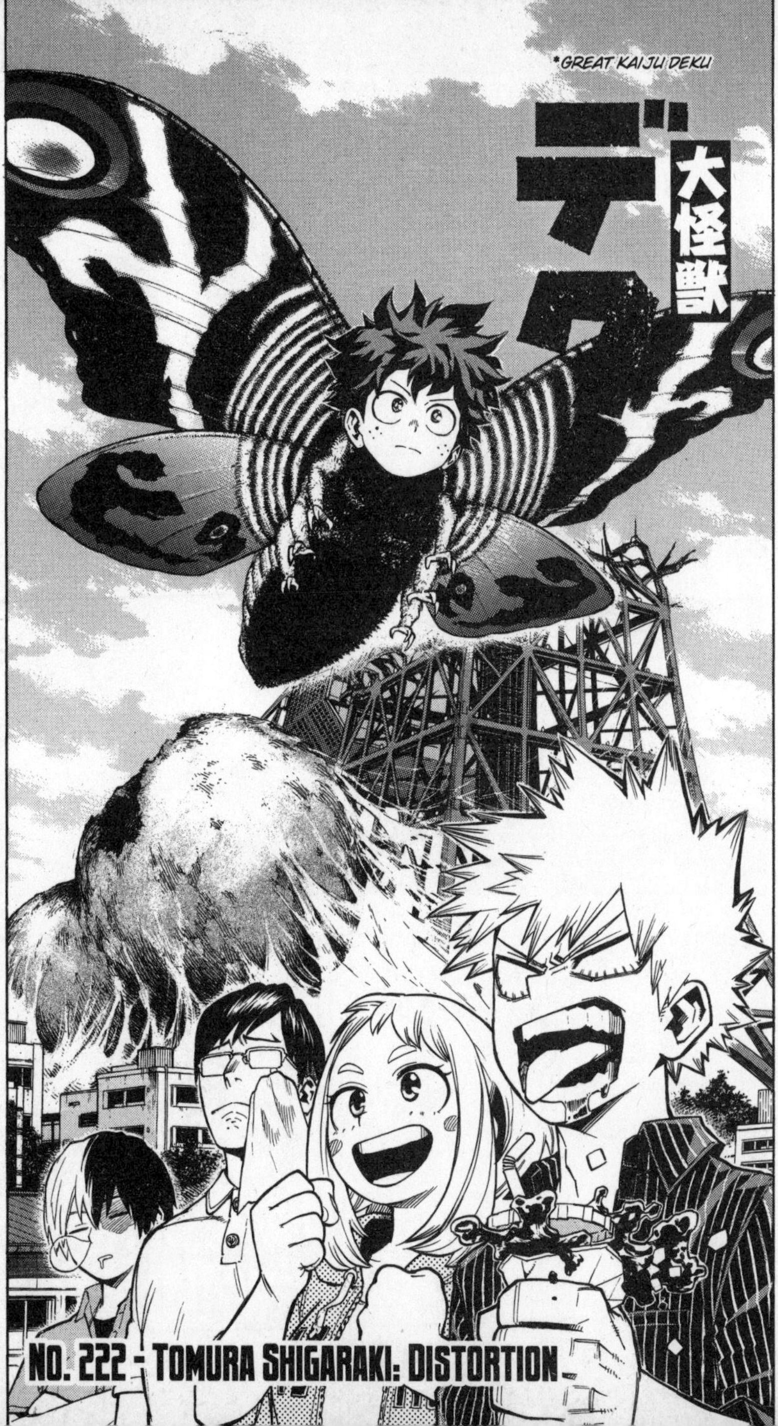
大怪獣デク
*GREAT KAIJU DEKU
NO. 222 - TOMURA SHIGARAKI: DISTORTION

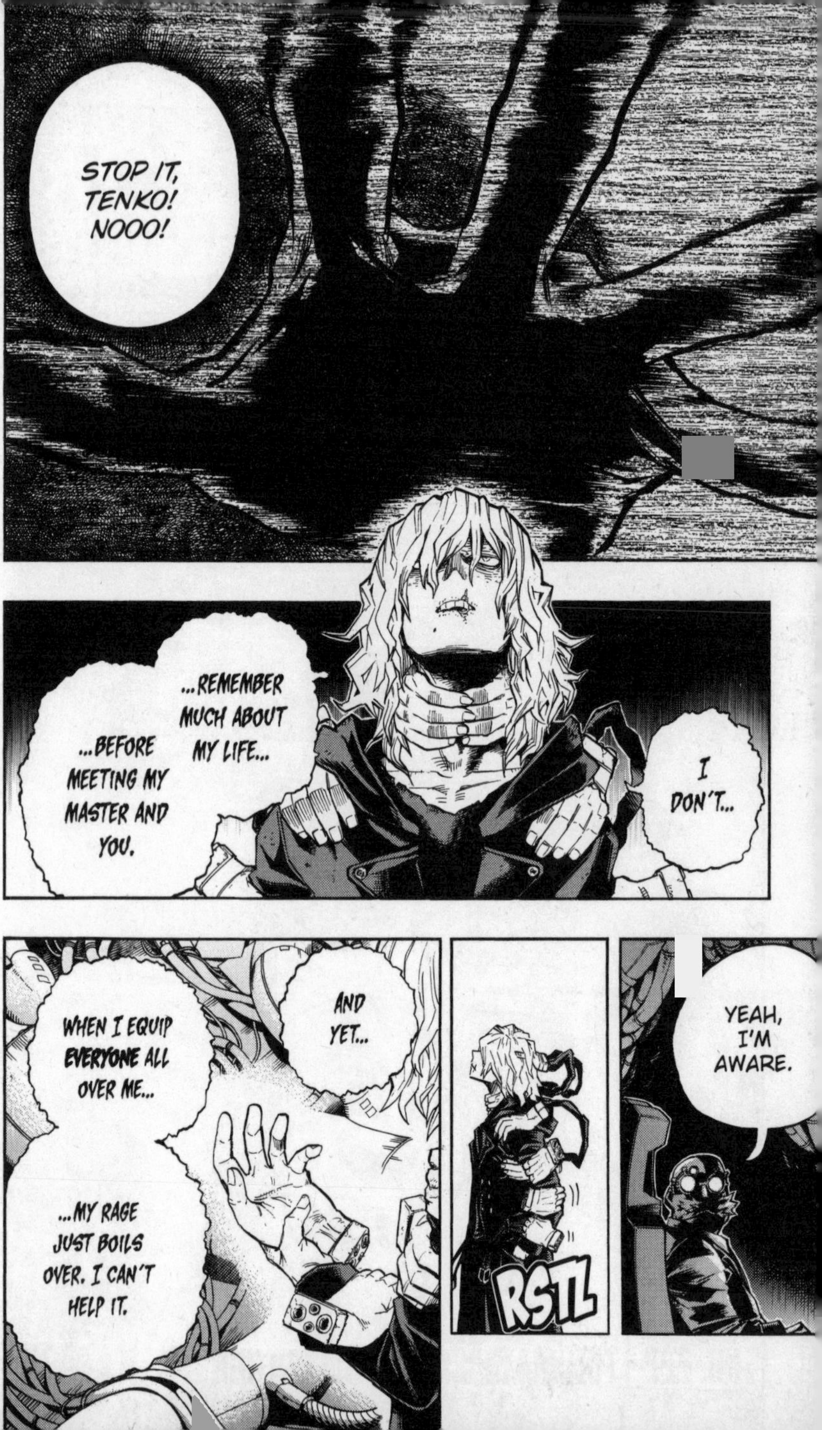
STOP IT, TENKO! NOOO!
I DON'T...
...REMEMBER MUCH ABOUT MY LIFE...
...BEFORE MEETING MY MASTER AND YOU.
YEAH, I'M AWARE.
RSTL
AND YET...
WHEN I EQUIP EVERYONE ALL OVER ME...
...MY RAGE JUST BOILS OVER. I CAN'T HELP IT.

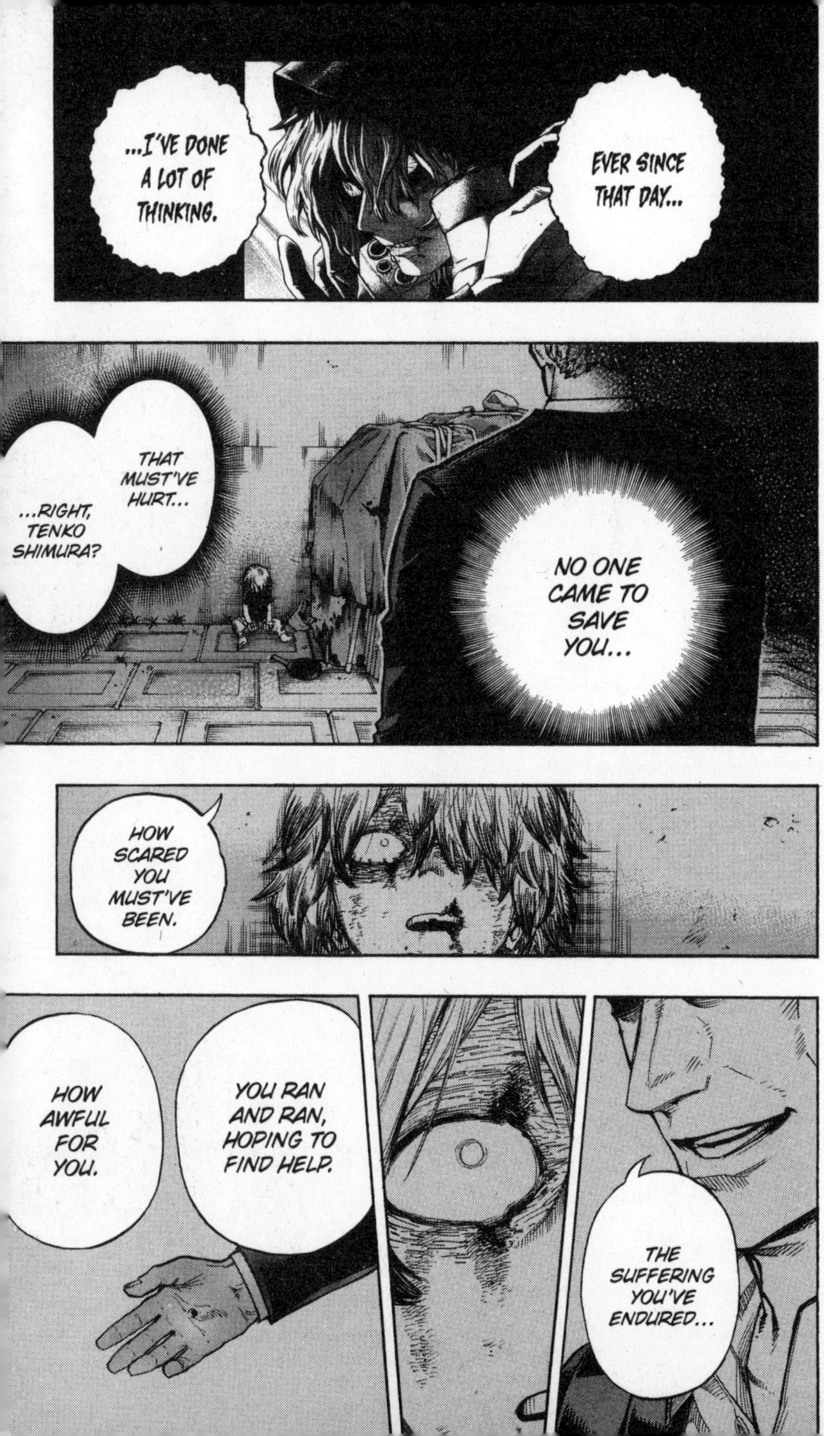
EVER SINCE THAT DAY...
...I'VE DONE A LOT OF THINKING.
NO ONE CAME TO SAVE YOU...
THAT MUST'VE HURT...
...RIGHT, TENKO SHIMURA?
HOW SCARED YOU MUST'VE BEEN.
THE SUFFERING YOU'VE ENDURED...
YOU RAN AND RAN, HOPING TO FIND HELP.
HOW AWFUL FOR YOU.

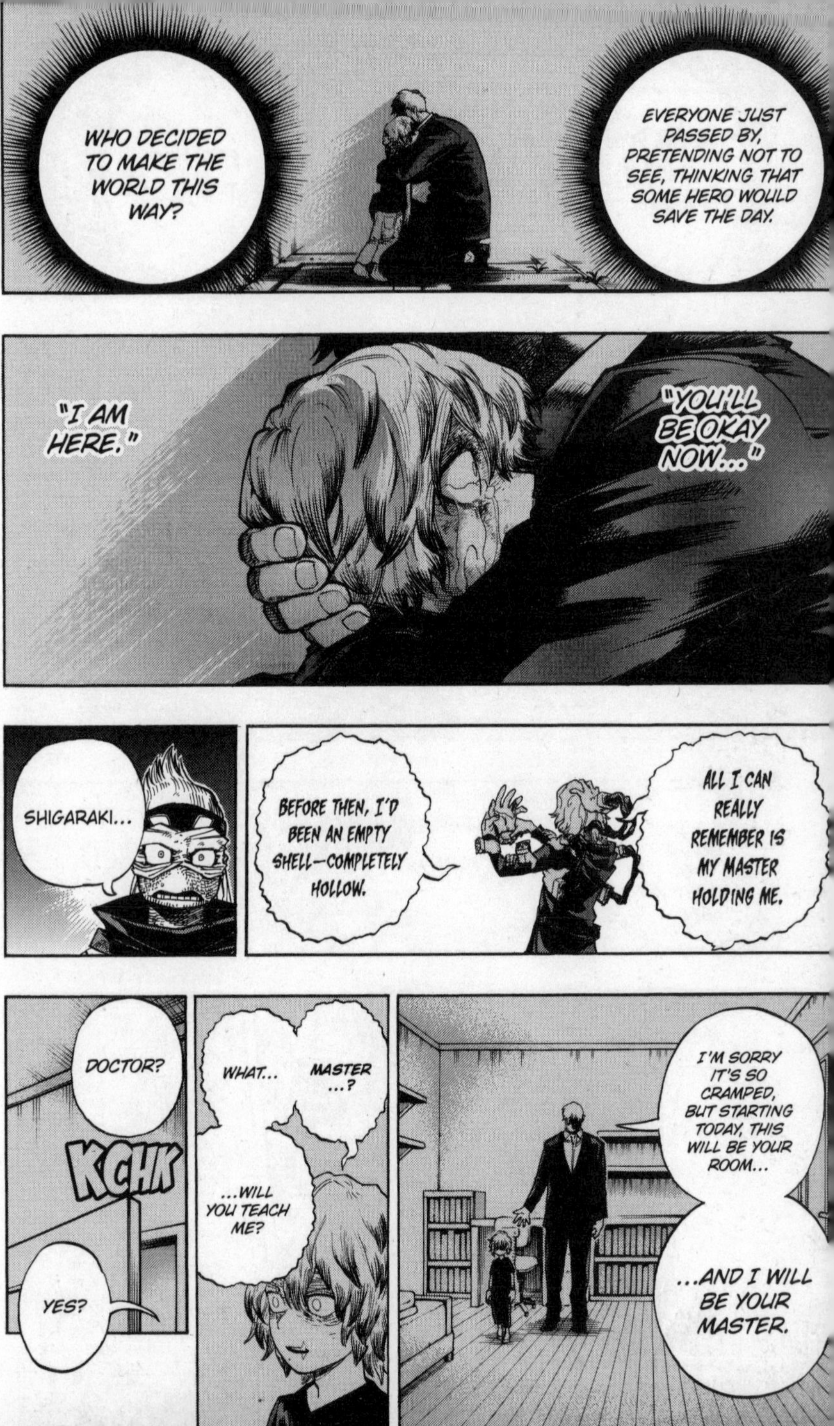
EVERYONE JUST PASSED BY, PRETENDING NOT TO SEE, THINKING THAT SOME HERO WOULD SAVE THE DAY.
WHO DECIDED TO MAKE THE WORLD THIS WAY?
"YOU'LL BE OKAY NOW..."
"I AM HERE."
ALL I CAN REALLY REMEMBER IS MY MASTER HOLDING ME.
BEFORE THEN, I'D BEEN AN EMPTY SHELL—COMPLETELY HOLLOW.
SHIGARAKI...
I'M SORRY IT'S SO CRAMPED, BUT STARTING TODAY, THIS WILL BE YOUR ROOM...
...AND I WILL BE YOUR MASTER.
WHAT... MASTER ...?
...WILL YOU TEACH ME?
DOCTOR?
KCHK
YES?

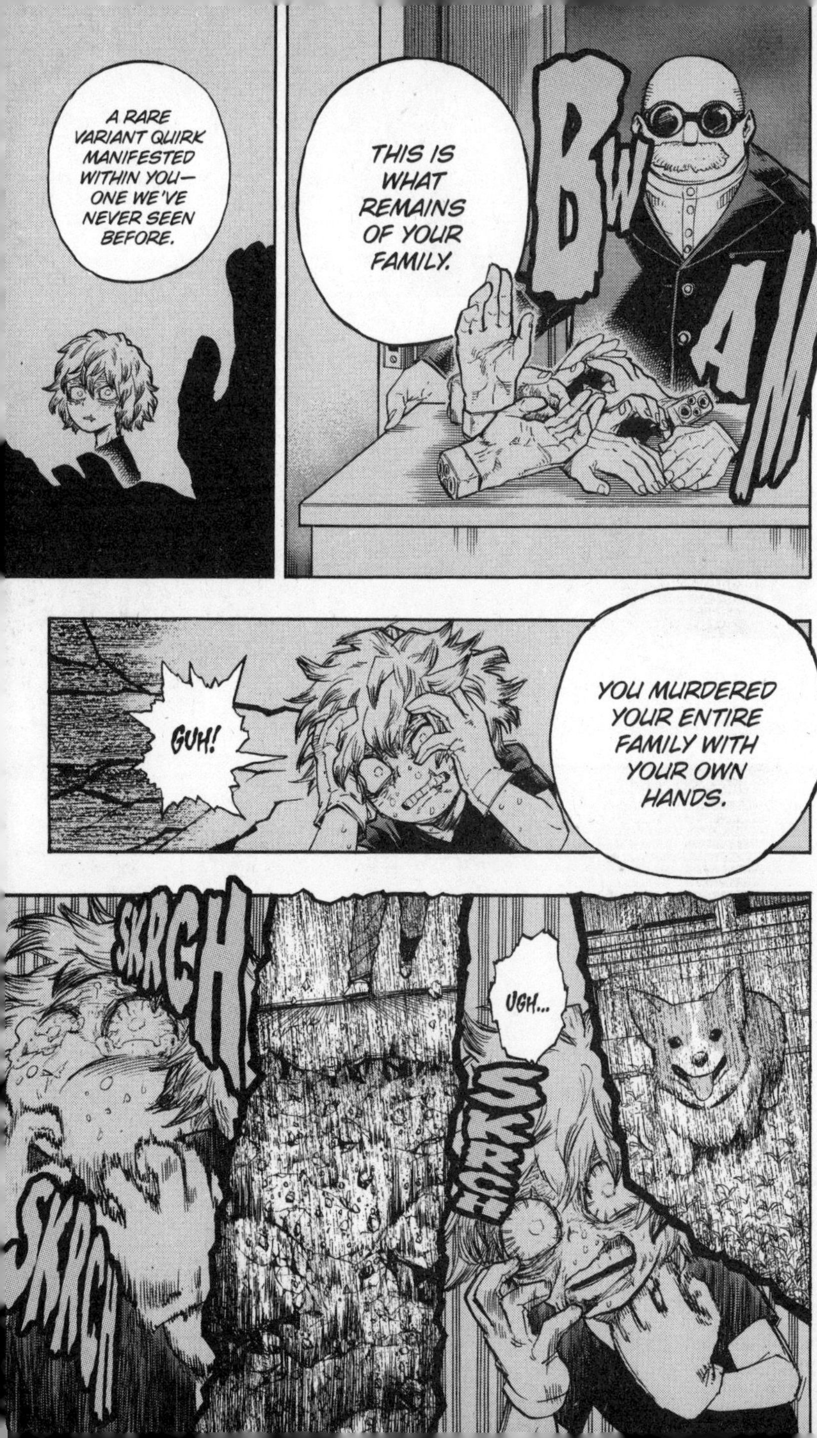
BWAM
THIS IS WHAT REMAINS OF YOUR FAMILY.
A RARE VARIANT QUIRK MANIFESTED WITHIN YOU—ONE WE'VE NEVER SEEN BEFORE.
YOU MURDERED YOUR ENTIRE FAMILY WITH YOUR OWN HANDS.
GUH!
UGH...
SKRCH
SKRCH
SKRCH

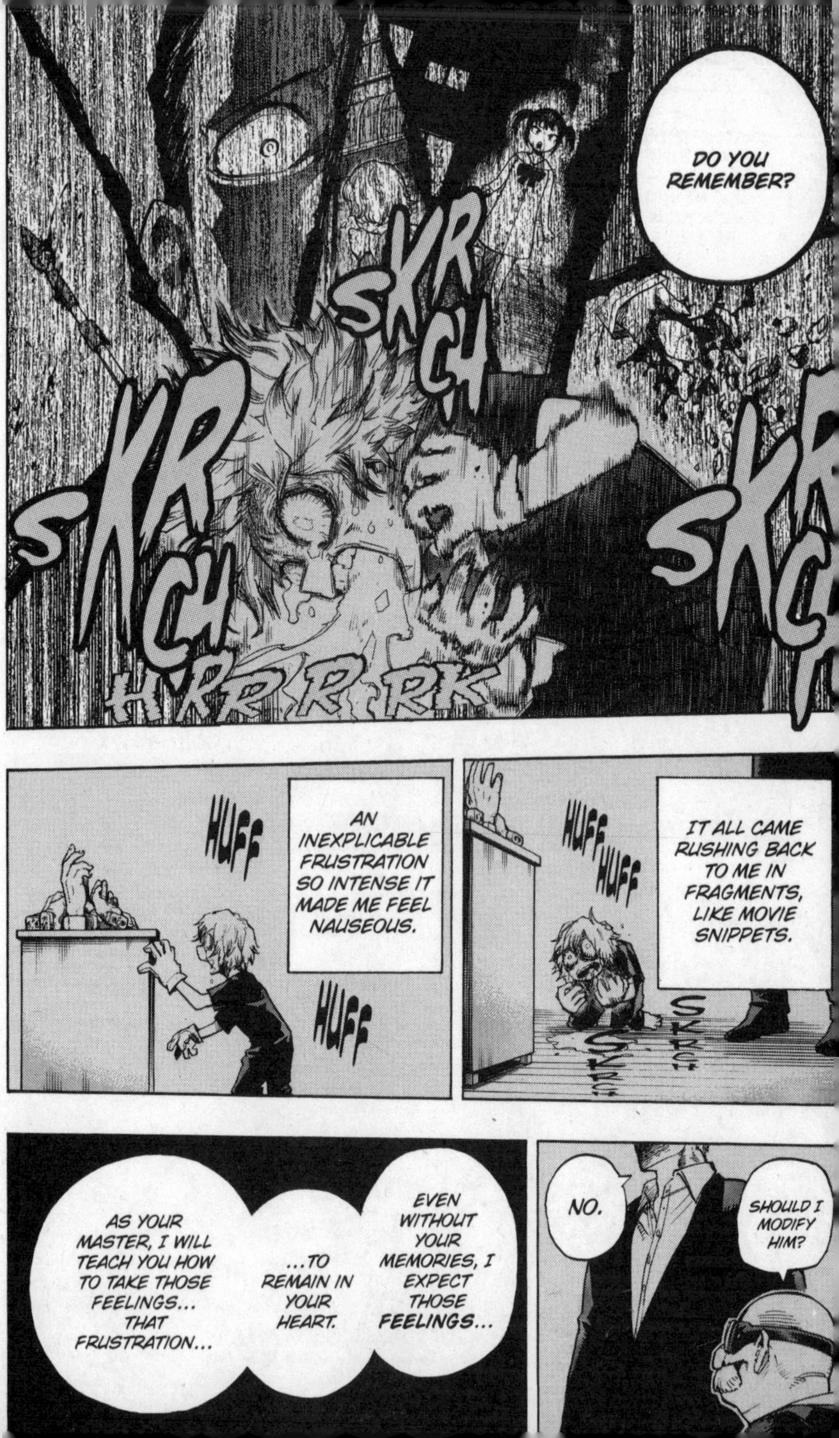

SKRCH
DO YOU REMEMBER?
SKRCH
SKRCH
HRRRRRK
IT ALL CAME RUSHING BACK TO ME IN FRAGMENTS, LIKE MOVIE SNIPPETS.
HUFF HUFF
SKRCH
SKRCH
AN INEXPLICABLE FRUSTRATION SO INTENSE IT MADE ME FEEL NAUSEOUS.
HUFF
HUFF
SHOULD I MODIFY HIM?
NO.
EVEN WITHOUT YOUR MEMORIES, I EXPECT THOSE FEELINGS...
...TO REMAIN IN YOUR HEART.
AS YOUR MASTER, I WILL TEACH YOU HOW TO TAKE THOSE FEELINGS... THAT FRUSTRATION...

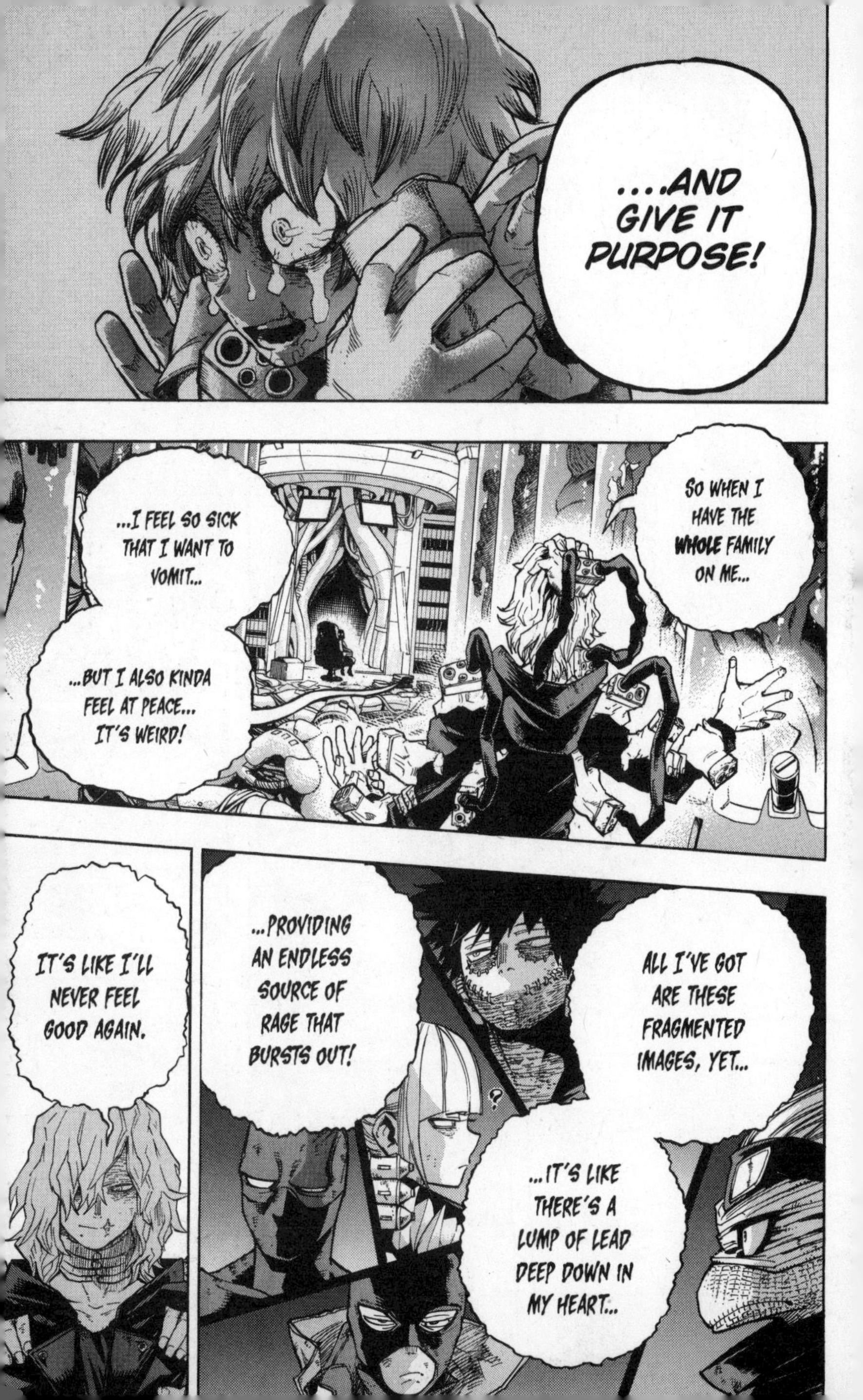
....AND GIVE IT PURPOSE!
SO WHEN I HAVE THE WHOLE FAMILY ON ME...
...I FEEL SO SICK THAT I WANT TO VOMIT...
...BUT I ALSO KINDA FEEL AT PEACE... IT'S WEIRD!
ALL I'VE GOT ARE THESE FRAGMENTED IMAGES, YET...
...IT'S LIKE THERE'S A LUMP OF LEAD DEEP DOWN IN MY HEART...
...PROVIDING AN ENDLESS SOURCE OF RAGE THAT BURSTS OUT!
IT'S LIKE I'LL NEVER FEEL GOOD AGAIN.

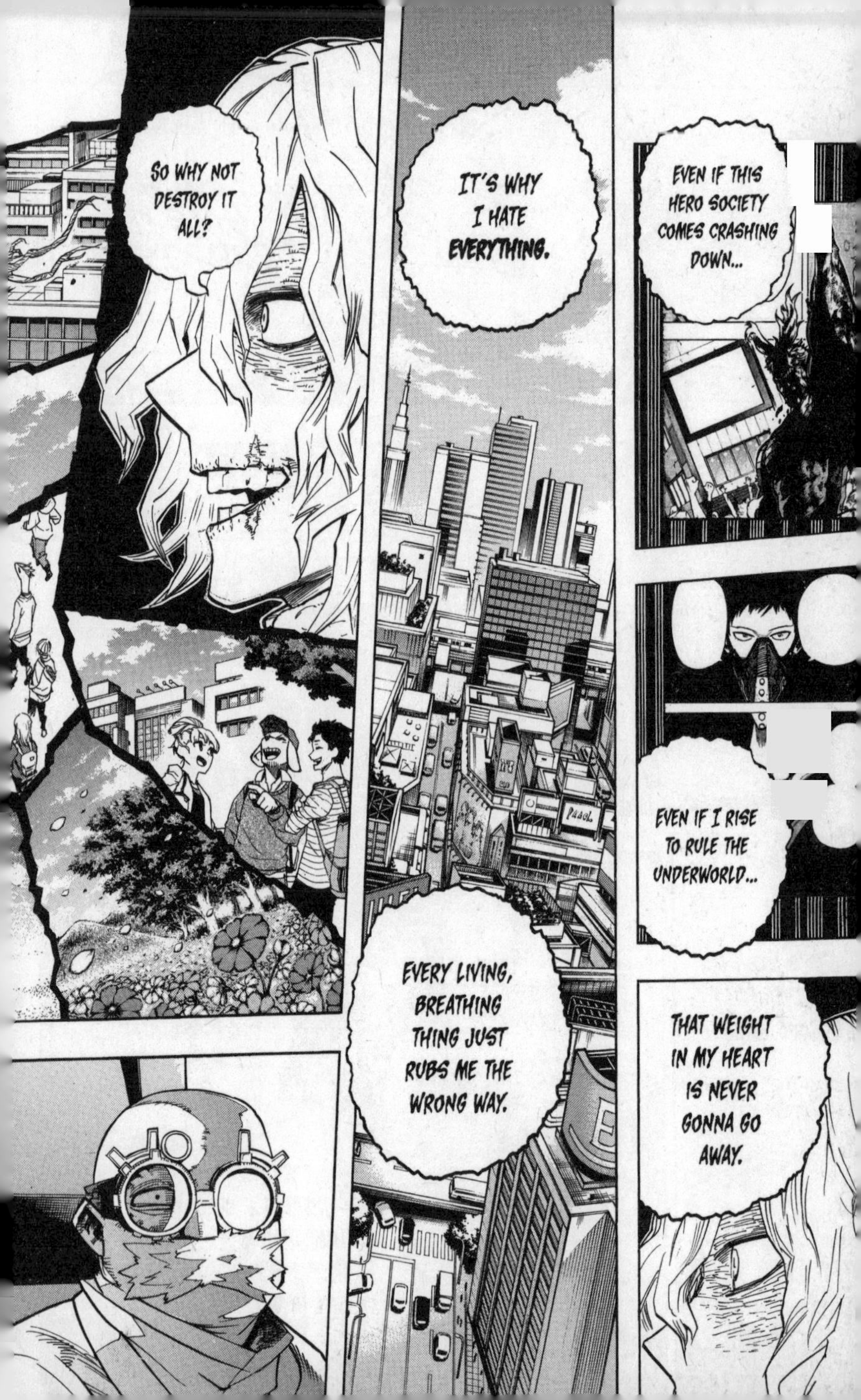
EVEN IF THIS HERO SOCIETY COMES CRASHING DOWN...
EVEN IF I RISE TO RULE THE UNDERWORLD...
THAT WEIGHT IN MY HEART IS NEVER GONNA GO AWAY.
IT'S WHY I HATE EVERYTHING.
EVERY LIVING, BREATHING THING JUST RUBS ME THE WRONG WAY.
SO WHY NOT DESTROY IT ALL?

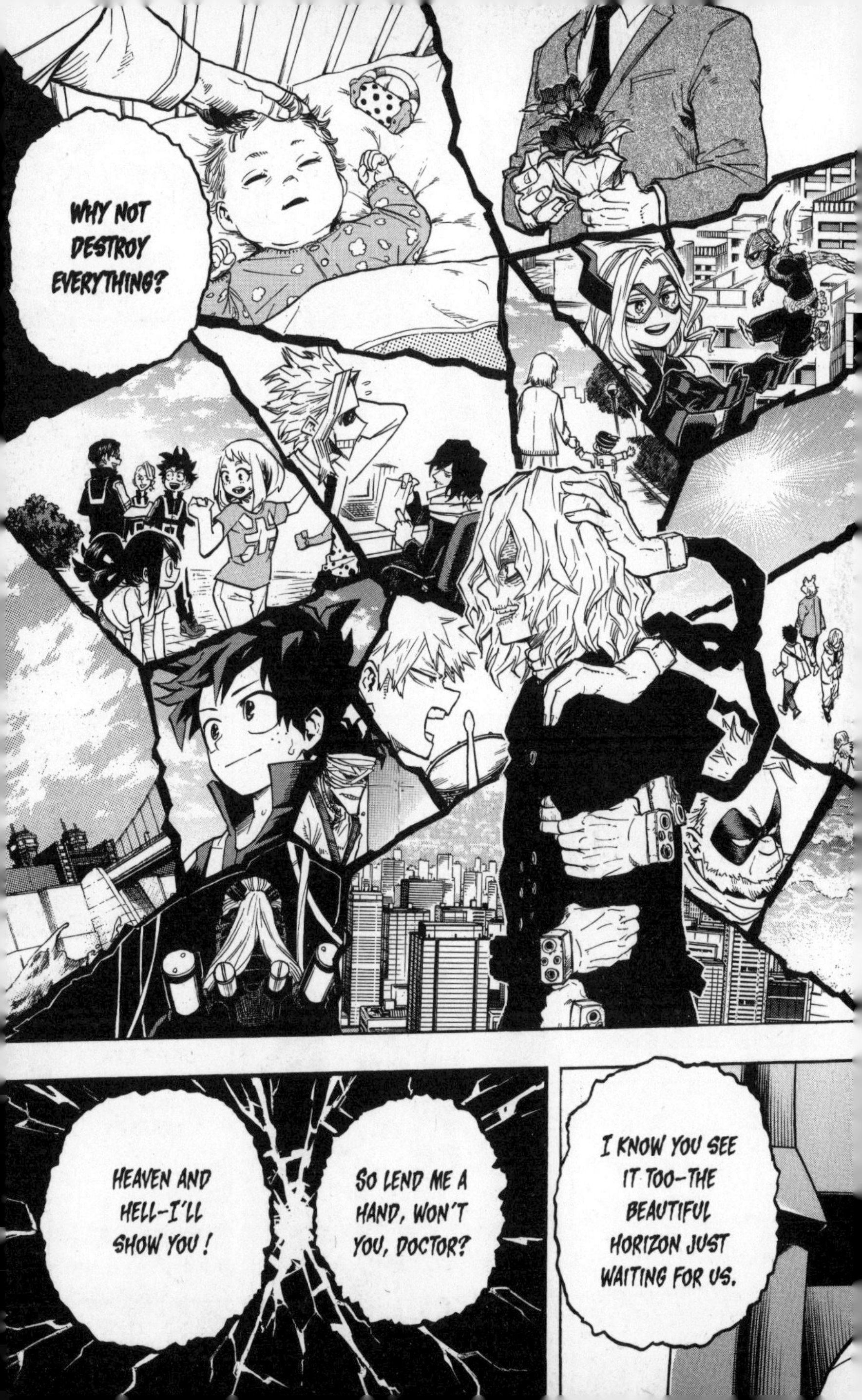
WHY NOT DESTROY EVERYTHING?
I KNOW YOU SEE IT TOO—THE BEAUTIFUL HORIZON JUST WAITING FOR US.
SO LEND ME A HAND, WON'T YOU, DOCTOR?
HEAVEN AND HELL—I'LL SHOW YOU!

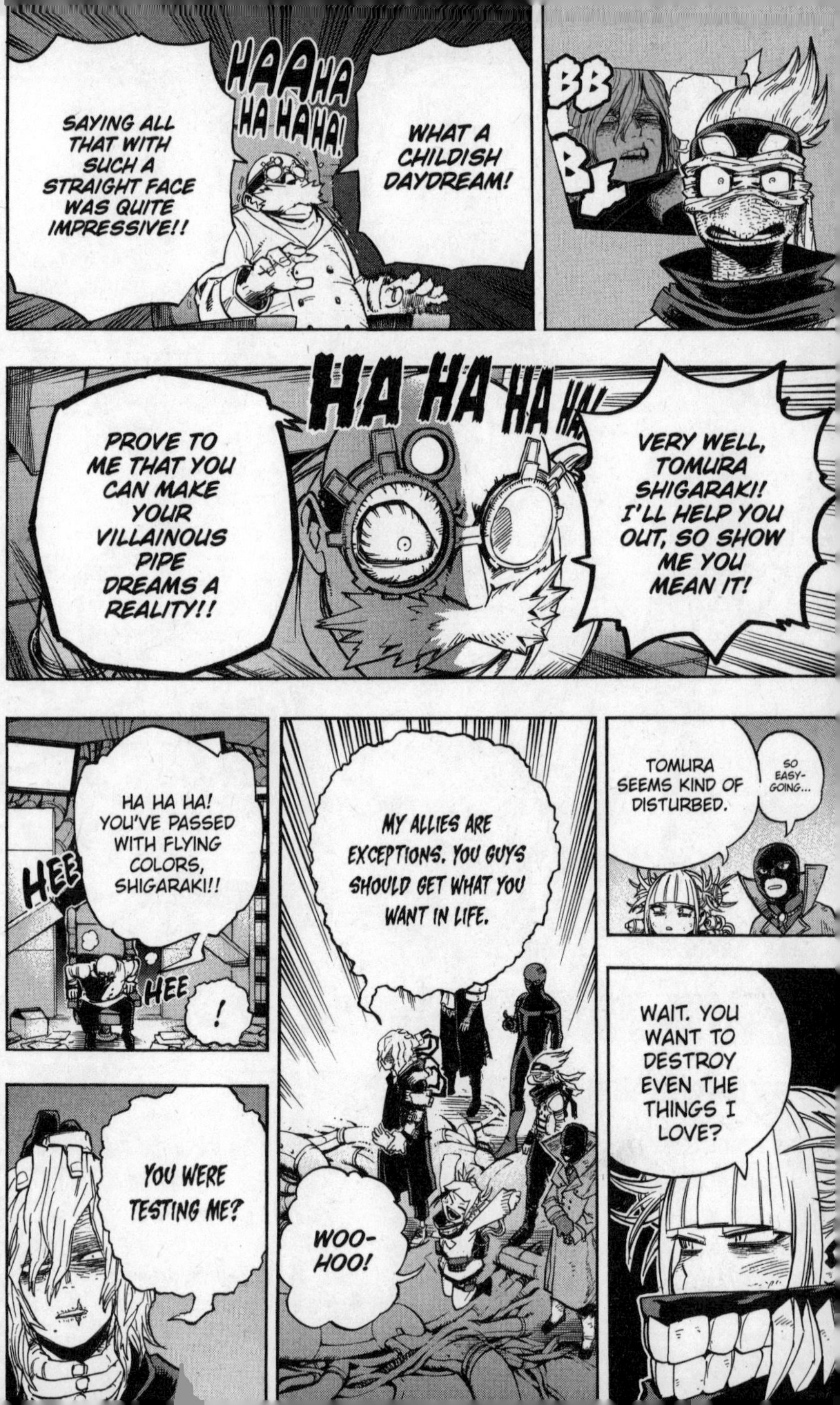

HAAHA HA HAHA!
WHAT A CHILDISH DAYDREAM!
SAYING ALL THAT WITH SUCH A STRAIGHT FACE WAS QUITE IMPRESSIVE!!
HA HA HA HA
VERY WELL, TOMURA SHIGARAKI! I'LL HELP YOU OUT, SO SHOW ME YOU MEAN IT!
PROVE TO ME THAT YOU CAN MAKE YOUR VILLAINOUS PIPE DREAMS A REALITY!!
SO EASY-GOING...
TOMURA SEEMS KIND OF DISTURBED.
WAIT. YOU WANT TO DESTROY EVEN THE THINGS I LOVE?
MY ALLIES ARE EXCEPTIONS. YOU GUYS SHOULD GET WHAT YOU WANT IN LIFE.
WOO-HOO!
HA HA HA! YOU'VE PASSED WITH FLYING COLORS, SHIGARAKI!!
HEE
HEE
!
YOU WERE TESTING ME?

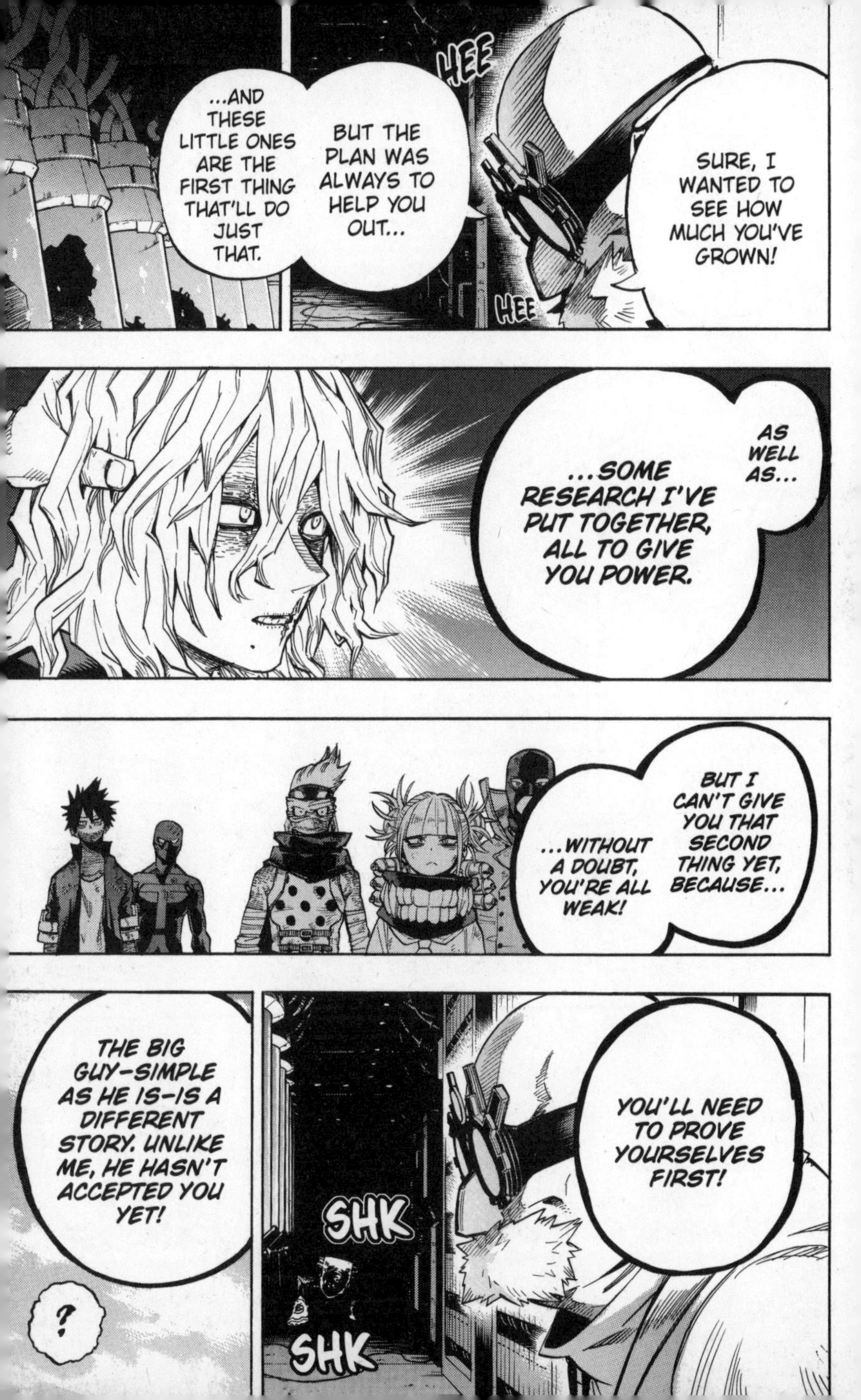
HEE
SURE, I WANTED TO SEE HOW MUCH YOU'VE GROWN!
HEE
BUT THE PLAN WAS ALWAYS TO HELP YOU OUT...
...AND THESE LITTLE ONES ARE THE FIRST THING THAT'LL DO JUST THAT.
AS WELL AS...
...SOME RESEARCH I'VE PUT TOGETHER, ALL TO GIVE YOU POWER.
BUT I CAN'T GIVE YOU THAT SECOND THING YET, BECAUSE...
...WITHOUT A DOUBT, YOU'RE ALL WEAK!
YOU'LL NEED TO PROVE YOURSELVES FIRST!
SHK
SHK
THE BIG GUY—SIMPLE AS HE IS—IS A DIFFERENT STORY. UNLIKE ME, HE HASN'T ACCEPTED YOU YET!
?

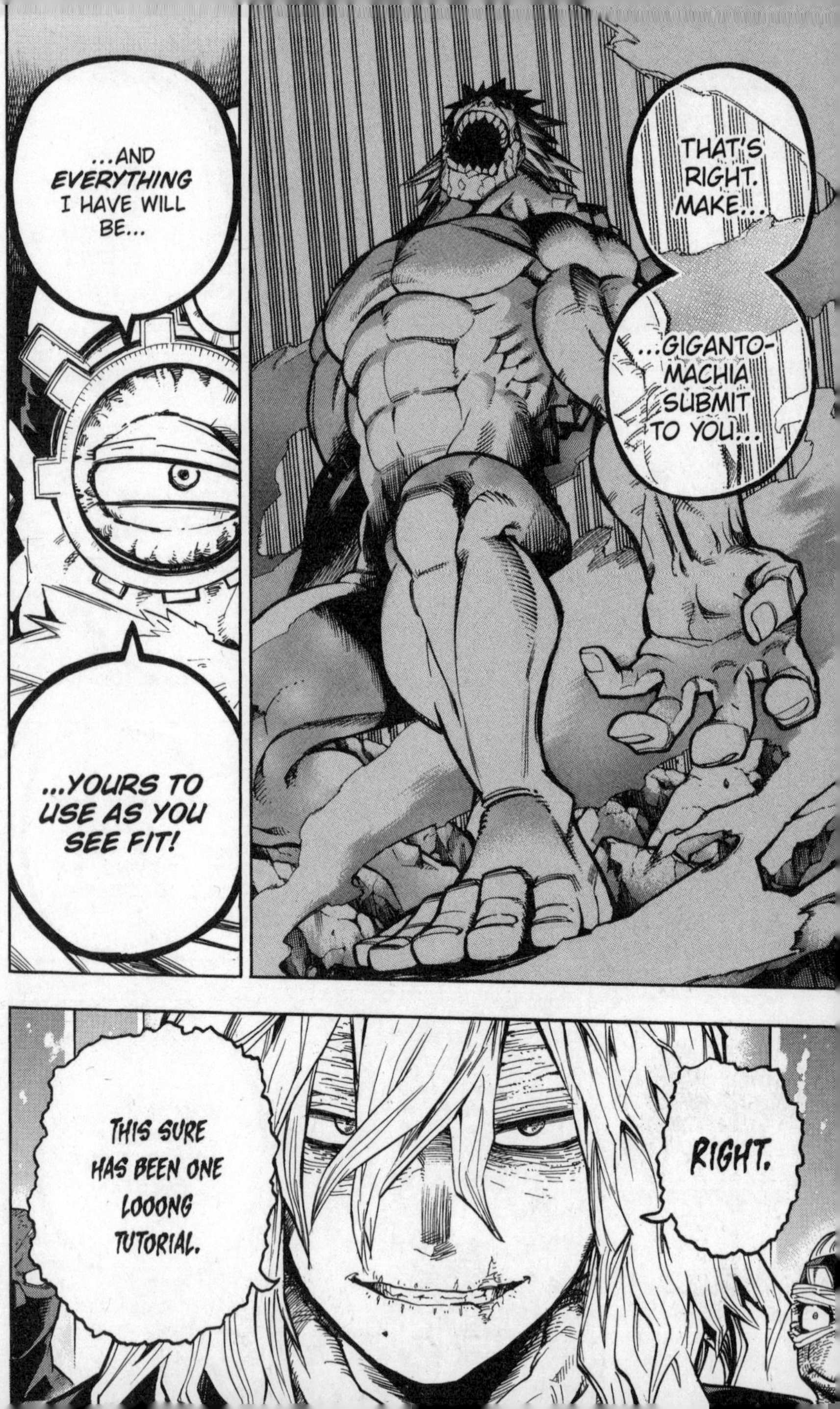
THAT'S RIGHT. MAKE...
...GIGANTO-MACHIA SUBMIT TO YOU...
...AND EVERYTHING I HAVE WILL BE...
...YOURS TO USE AS YOU SEE FIT!
RIGHT.
THIS SURE HAS BEEN ONE LOOONG TUTORIAL.

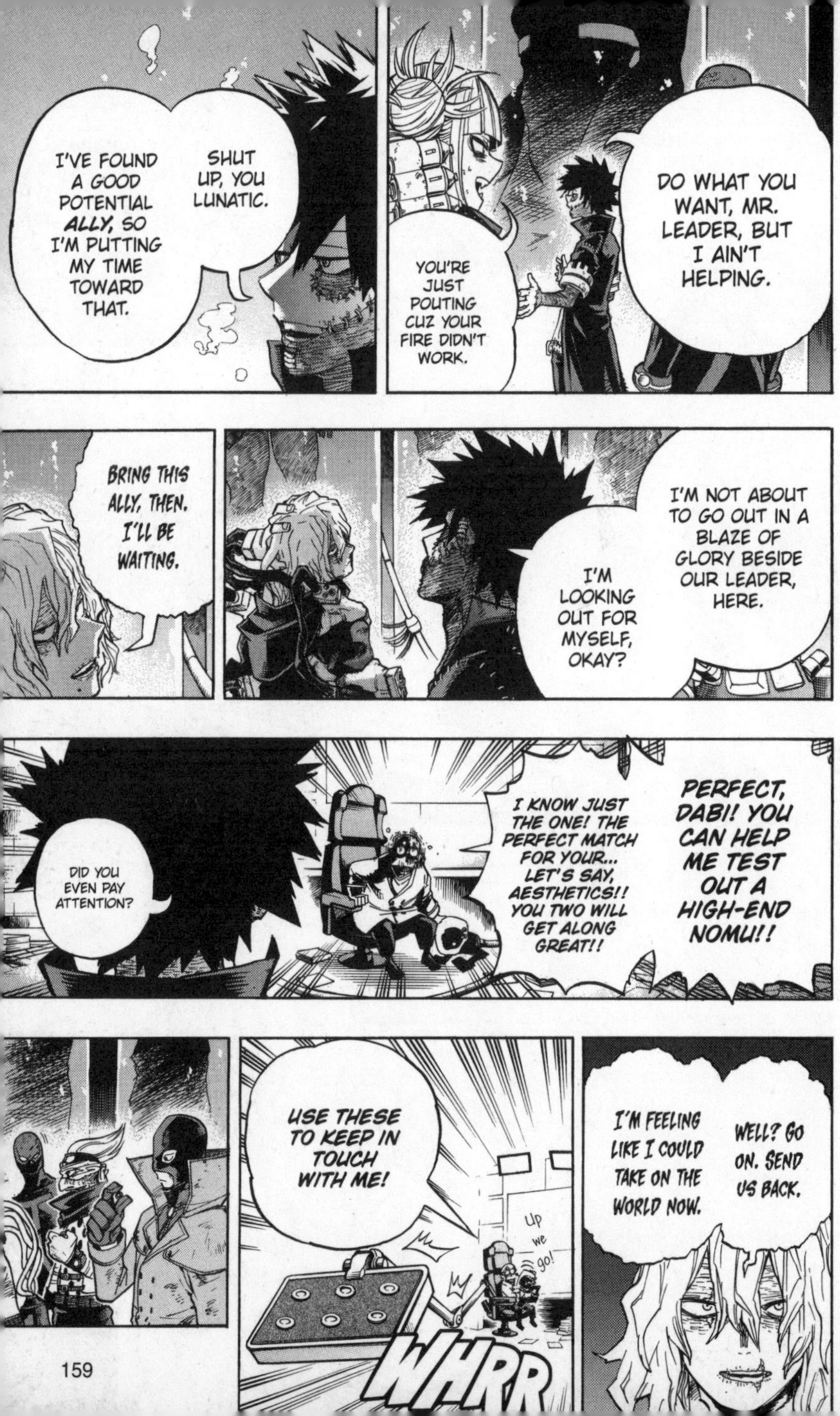
DO WHAT YOU WANT, MR. LEADER, BUT I AIN'T HELPING.
YOU'RE JUST POUTING CUZ YOUR FIRE DIDN'T WORK.
SHUT UP, YOU LUNATIC.
I'VE FOUND A GOOD POTENTIAL *ALLY,* SO I'M PUTTING MY TIME TOWARD THAT.
I'M NOT ABOUT TO GO OUT IN A BLAZE OF GLORY BESIDE OUR LEADER, HERE.
I'M LOOKING OUT FOR MYSELF, OKAY?
BRING THIS ALLY, THEN. I'LL BE WAITING.
PERFECT, DABI! YOU CAN HELP ME TEST OUT A HIGH-END NOMU!!
I KNOW JUST THE ONE! THE PERFECT MATCH FOR YOUR... LET'S SAY, AESTHETICS!! YOU TWO WILL GET ALONG GREAT!!
DID YOU EVEN PAY ATTENTION?
WELL? GO ON. SEND US BACK.
I'M FEELING LIKE I COULD TAKE ON THE WORLD NOW.
USE THESE TO KEEP IN TOUCH WITH ME!
Up we go!
WHRR

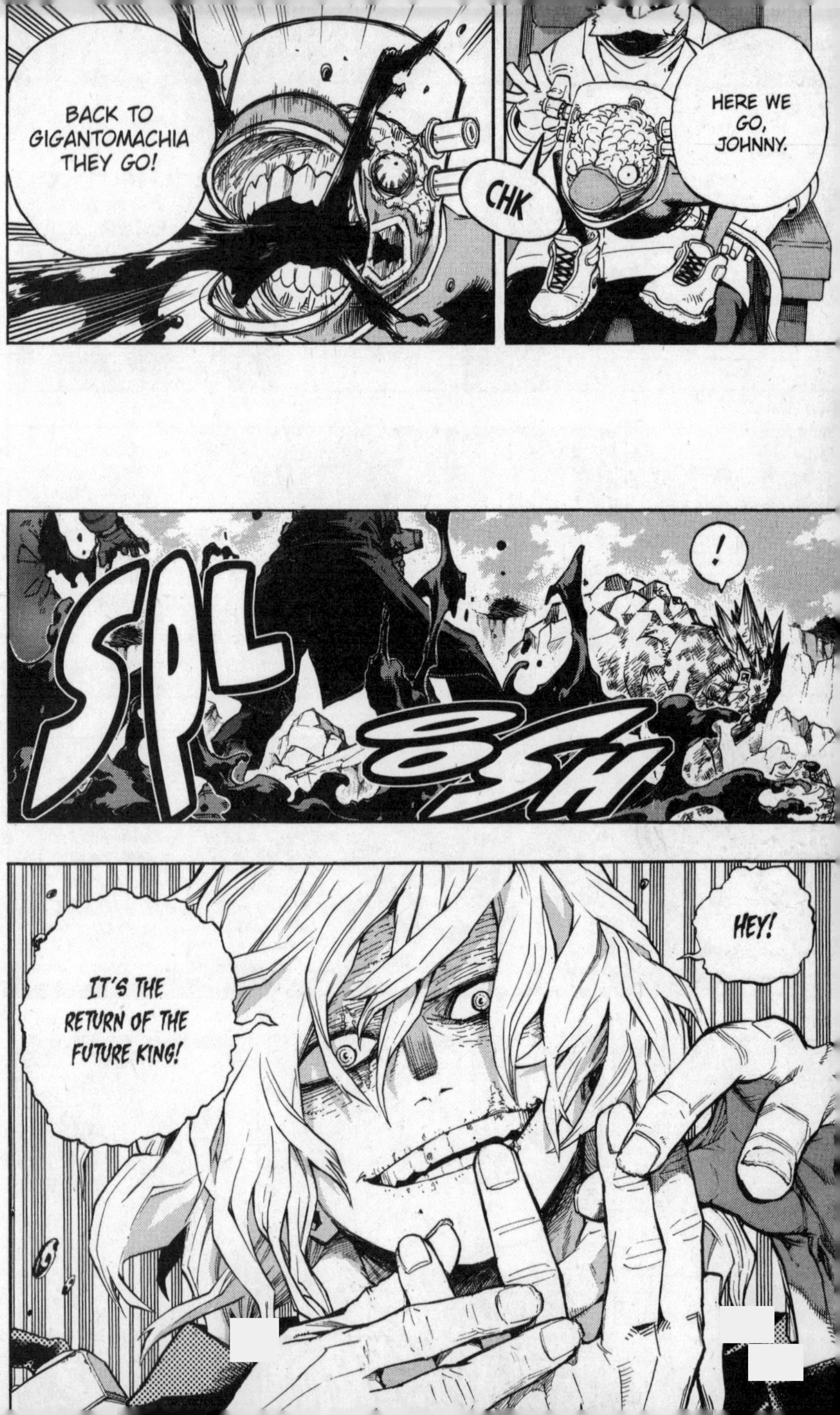
HERE WE GO, JOHNNY.
CHK
BACK TO GIGANTOMACHIA THEY GO!
!
SPLOOSH
HEY!
IT'S THE RETURN OF THE FUTURE KING!

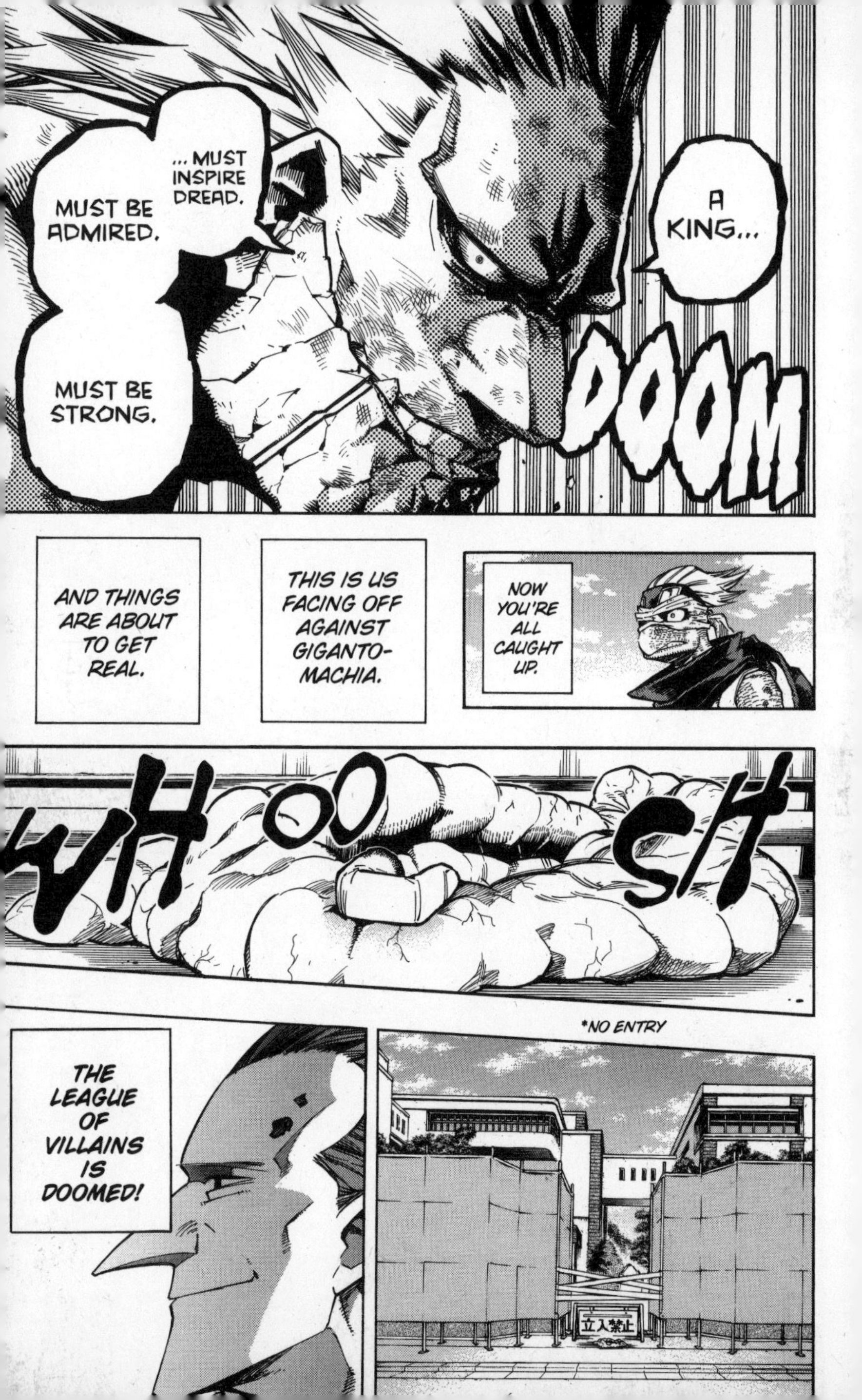
A KING...
DOOM
...MUST INSPIRE DREAD.
MUST BE ADMIRED.
MUST BE STRONG.
NOW YOU'RE ALL CAUGHT UP.
THIS IS US FACING OFF AGAINST GIGANTO-MACHIA.
AND THINGS ARE ABOUT TO GET REAL.
WHOOSH
立入禁止
*NO ENTRY
THE LEAGUE OF VILLAINS IS DOOMED!

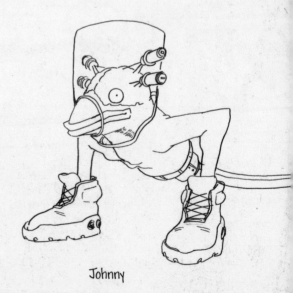

Johnny

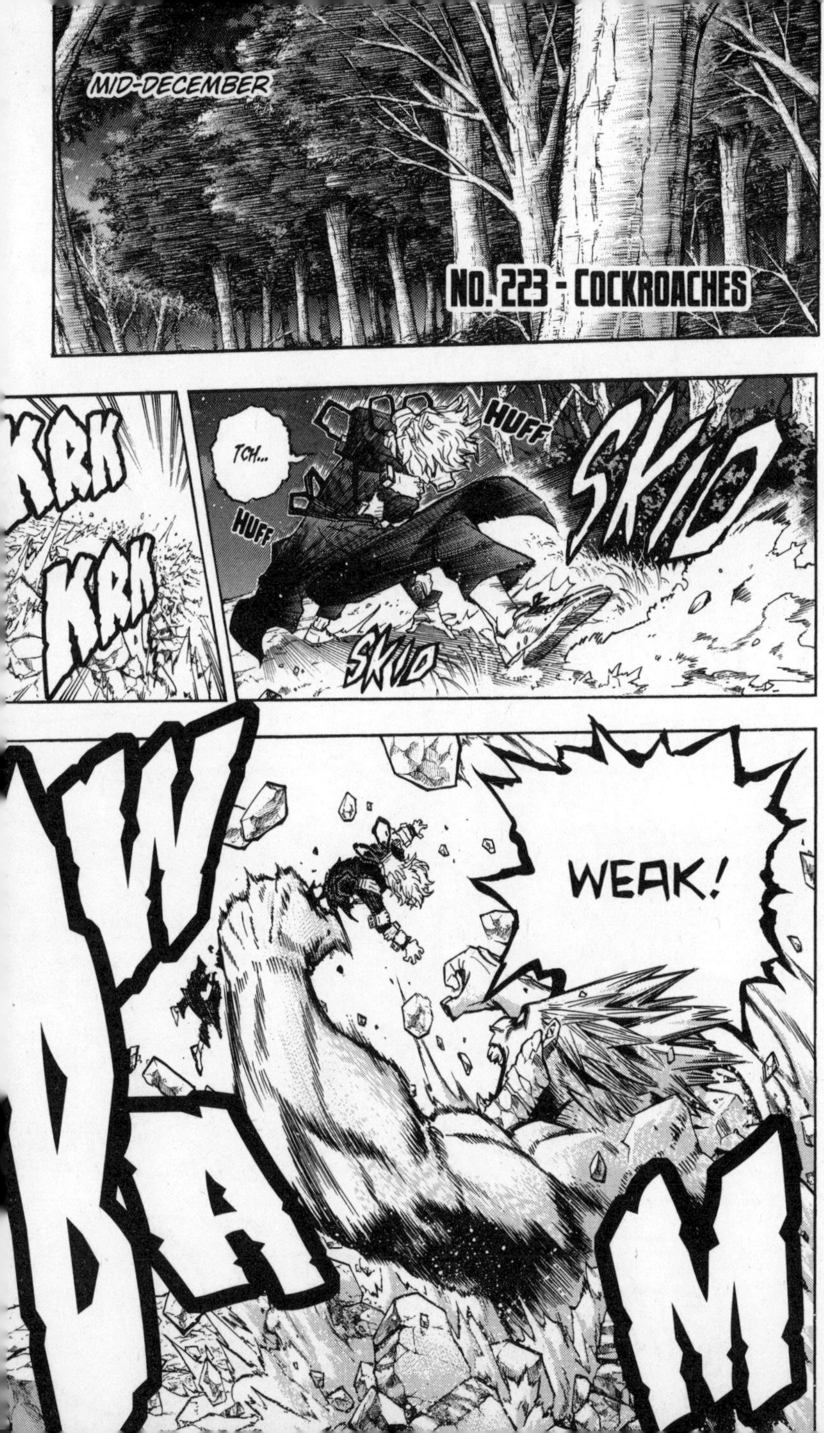
MID-DECEMBER
NO. 223 - COCKROACHES
TCH...
HUFF
HUFF
SKID
SKID
KRK
KRK
WEAK!

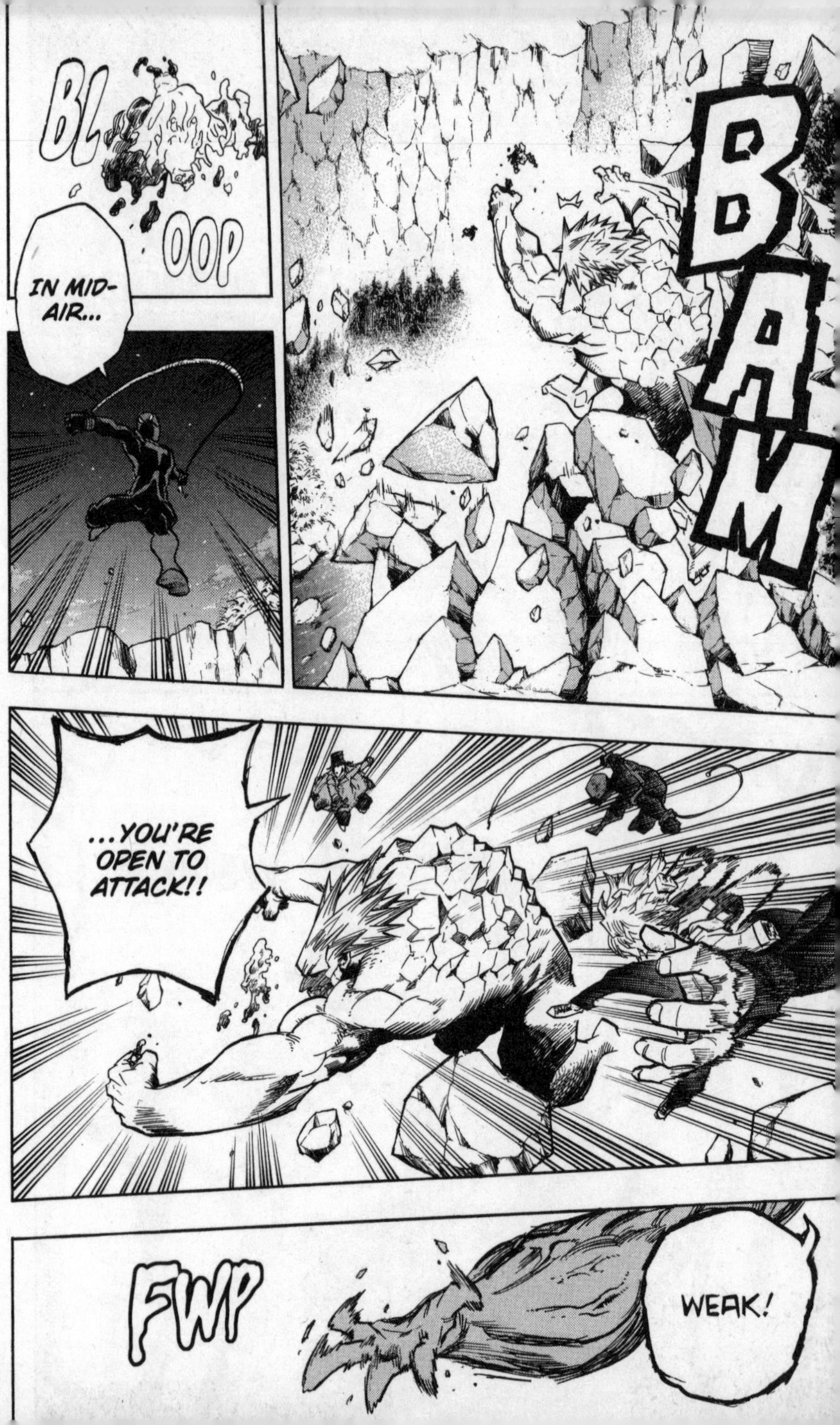
BAM
BLOOP
IN MID-AIR...
...YOU'RE OPEN TO ATTACK!!
WEAK!
FWP

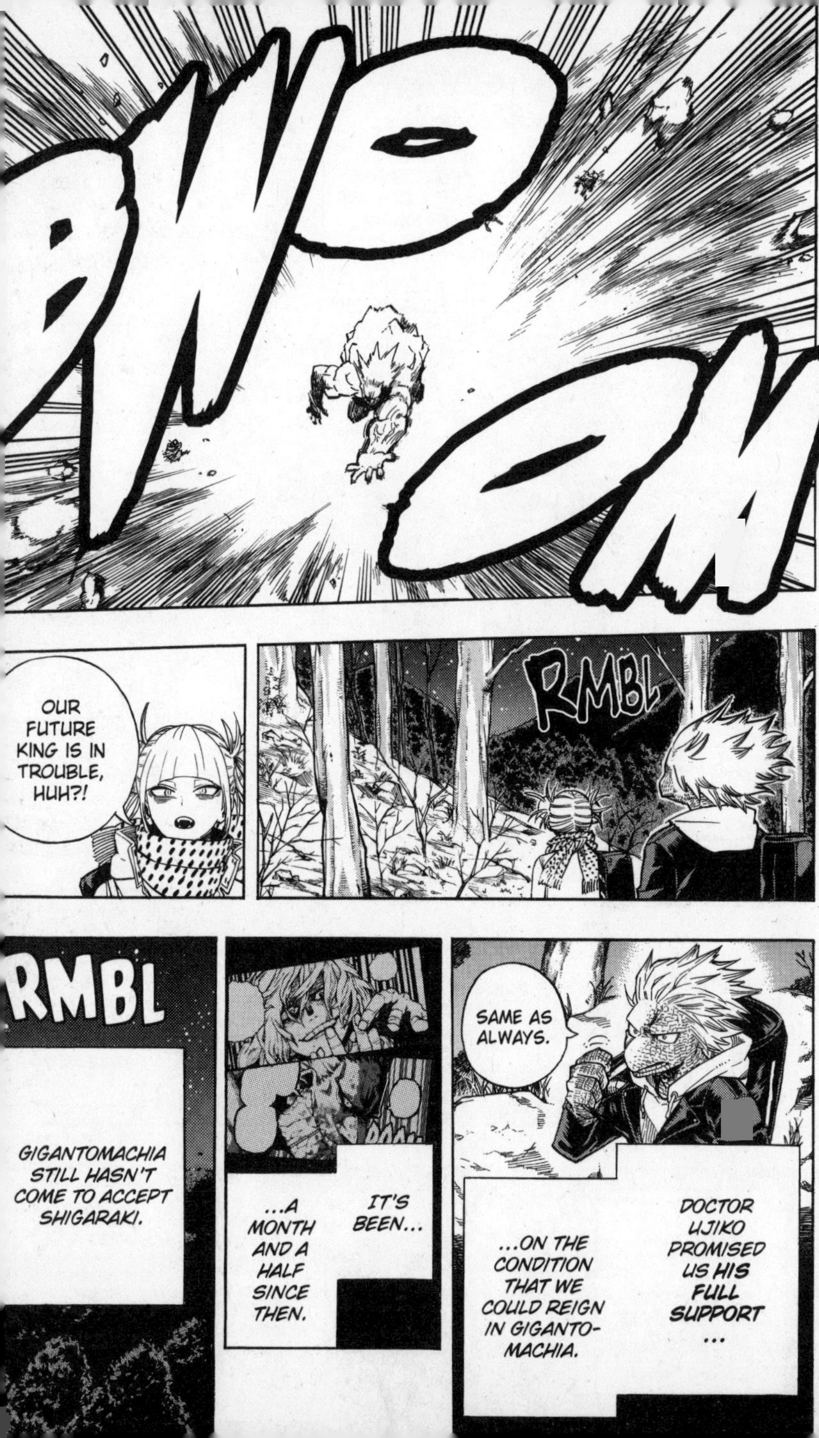
RMBL
OUR FUTURE KING IS IN TROUBLE, HUH?!
SAME AS ALWAYS.
DOCTOR UJIKO PROMISED US HIS FULL SUPPORT...
...ON THE CONDITION THAT WE COULD REIGN IN GIGANTO-MACHIA.
IT'S BEEN...
...A MONTH AND A HALF SINCE THEN.
RMBL
GIGANTOMACHIA STILL HASN'T COME TO ACCEPT SHIGARAKI.

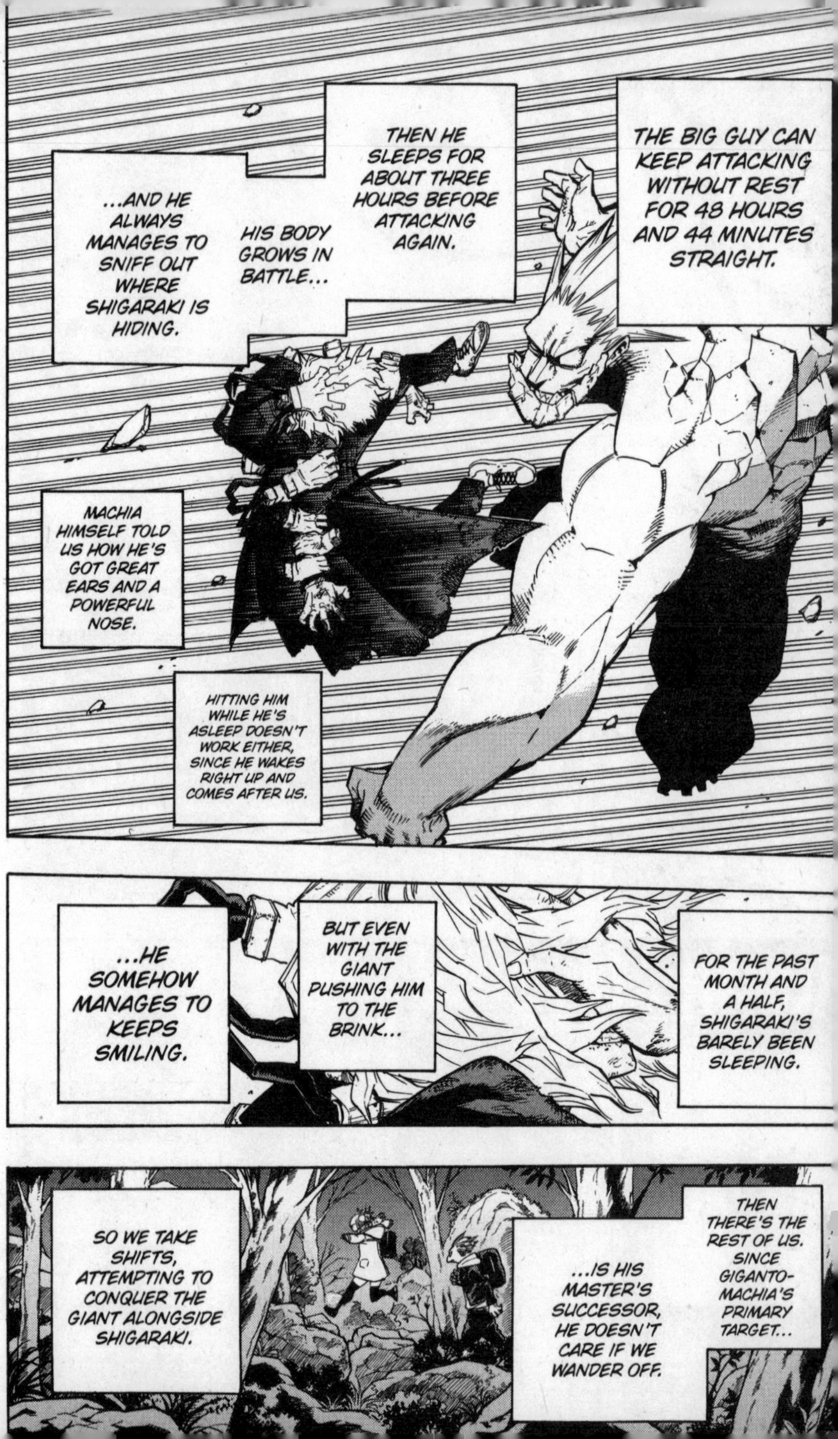
THE BIG GUY CAN KEEP ATTACKING WITHOUT REST FOR 48 HOURS AND 44 MINUTES STRAIGHT.
THEN HE SLEEPS FOR ABOUT THREE HOURS BEFORE ATTACKING AGAIN.
HIS BODY GROWS IN BATTLE...
...AND HE ALWAYS MANAGES TO SNIFF OUT WHERE SHIGARAKI IS HIDING.
MACHIA HIMSELF TOLD US HOW HE'S GOT GREAT EARS AND A POWERFUL NOSE.
HITTING HIM WHILE HE'S ASLEEP DOESN'T WORK EITHER, SINCE HE WAKES RIGHT UP AND COMES AFTER US.
FOR THE PAST MONTH AND A HALF, SHIGARAKI'S BARELY BEEN SLEEPING.
BUT EVEN WITH THE GIANT PUSHING HIM TO THE BRINK...
...HE SOMEHOW MANAGES TO KEEPS SMILING.
THEN THERE'S THE REST OF US. SINCE GIGANTO-MACHIA'S PRIMARY TARGET...
...IS HIS MASTER'S SUCCESSOR, HE DOESN'T CARE IF WE WANDER OFF.
SO WE TAKE SHIFTS, ATTEMPTING TO CONQUER THE GIANT ALONGSIDE SHIGARAKI.

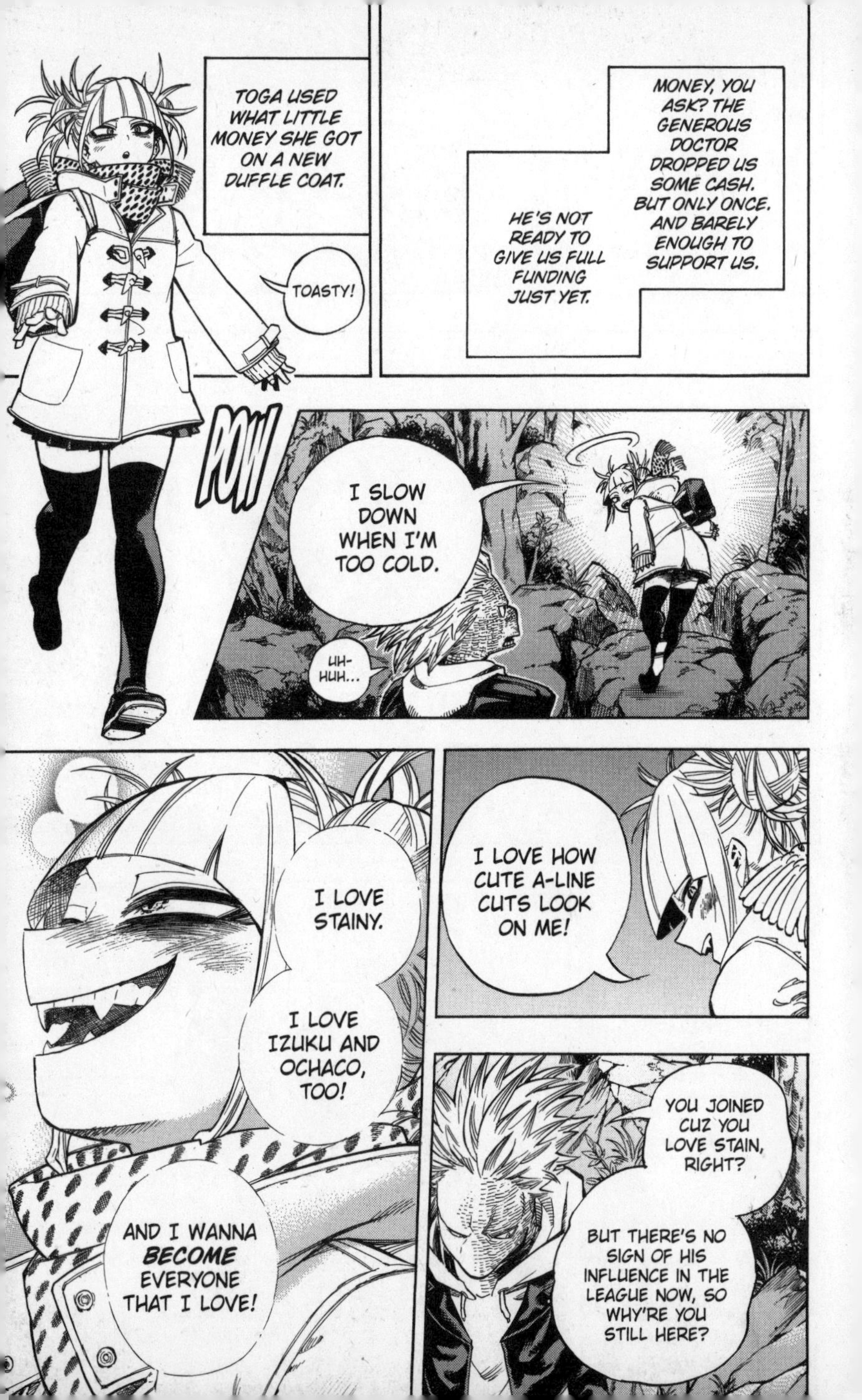
MONEY, YOU ASK? THE GENEROUS DOCTOR DROPPED US SOME CASH. BUT ONLY ONCE. AND BARELY ENOUGH TO SUPPORT US.
HE'S NOT READY TO GIVE US FULL FUNDING JUST YET.
TOGA USED WHAT LITTLE MONEY SHE GOT ON A NEW DUFFLE COAT.
TOASTY!
POW
I SLOW DOWN WHEN I'M TOO COLD.
UH-HUH...
I LOVE HOW CUTE A-LINE CUTS LOOK ON ME!
YOU JOINED CUZ YOU LOVE STAIN, RIGHT?
BUT THERE'S NO SIGN OF HIS INFLUENCE IN THE LEAGUE NOW, SO WHY'RE YOU STILL HERE?
I LOVE STAINY.
I LOVE IZUKU AND OCHACO, TOO!
AND I WANNA ***BECOME*** EVERYONE THAT I LOVE!

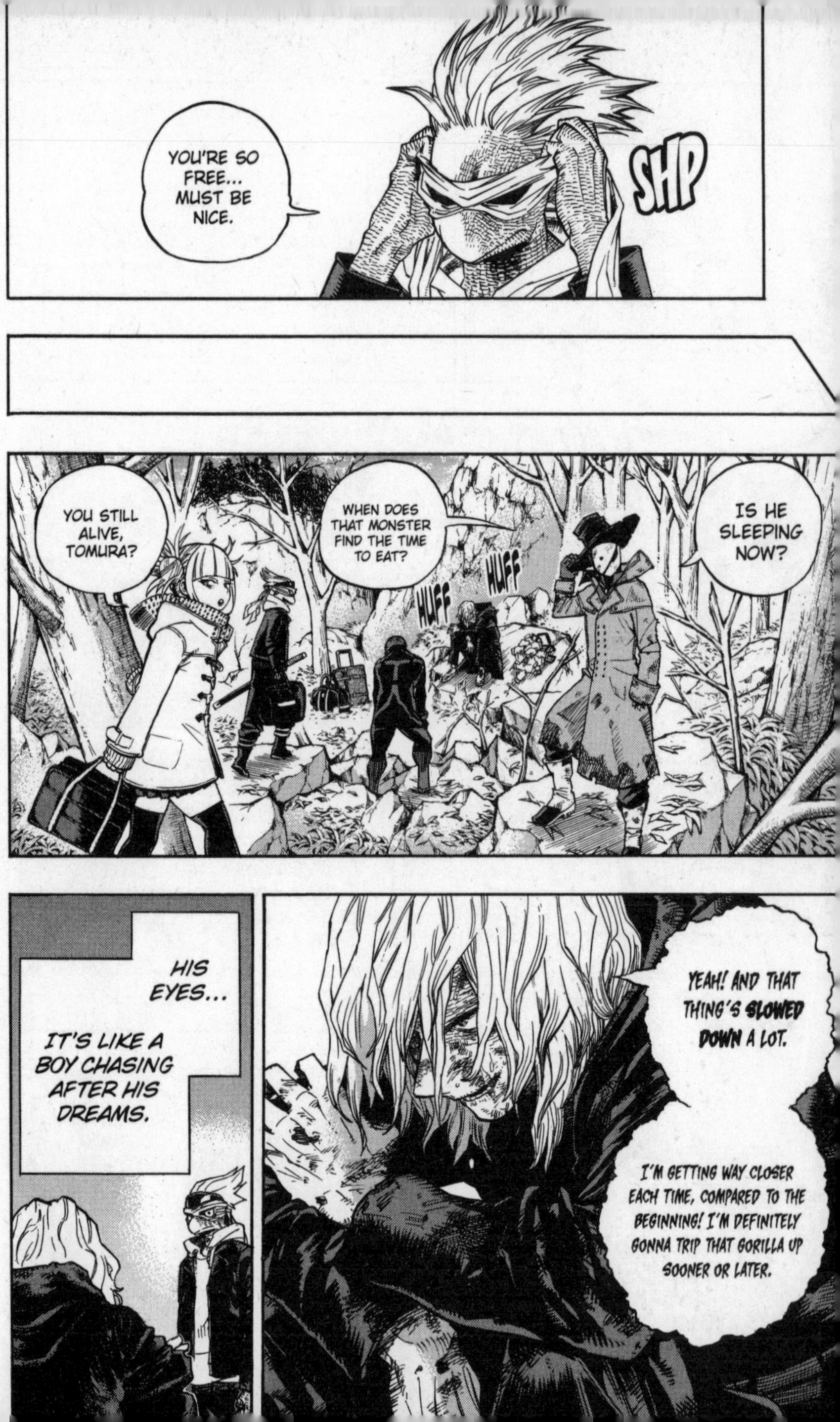
YOU'RE SO FREE... MUST BE NICE.
SHP
IS HE SLEEPING NOW?
HUFF
HUFF
WHEN DOES THAT MONSTER FIND THE TIME TO EAT?
YOU STILL ALIVE, TOMURA?
YEAH! AND THAT THING'S SLOWED DOWN A LOT.
I'M GETTING WAY CLOSER EACH TIME, COMPARED TO THE BEGINNING! I'M DEFINITELY GONNA TRIP THAT GORILLA UP SOONER OR LATER.
HIS EYES...
IT'S LIKE A BOY CHASING AFTER HIS DREAMS.

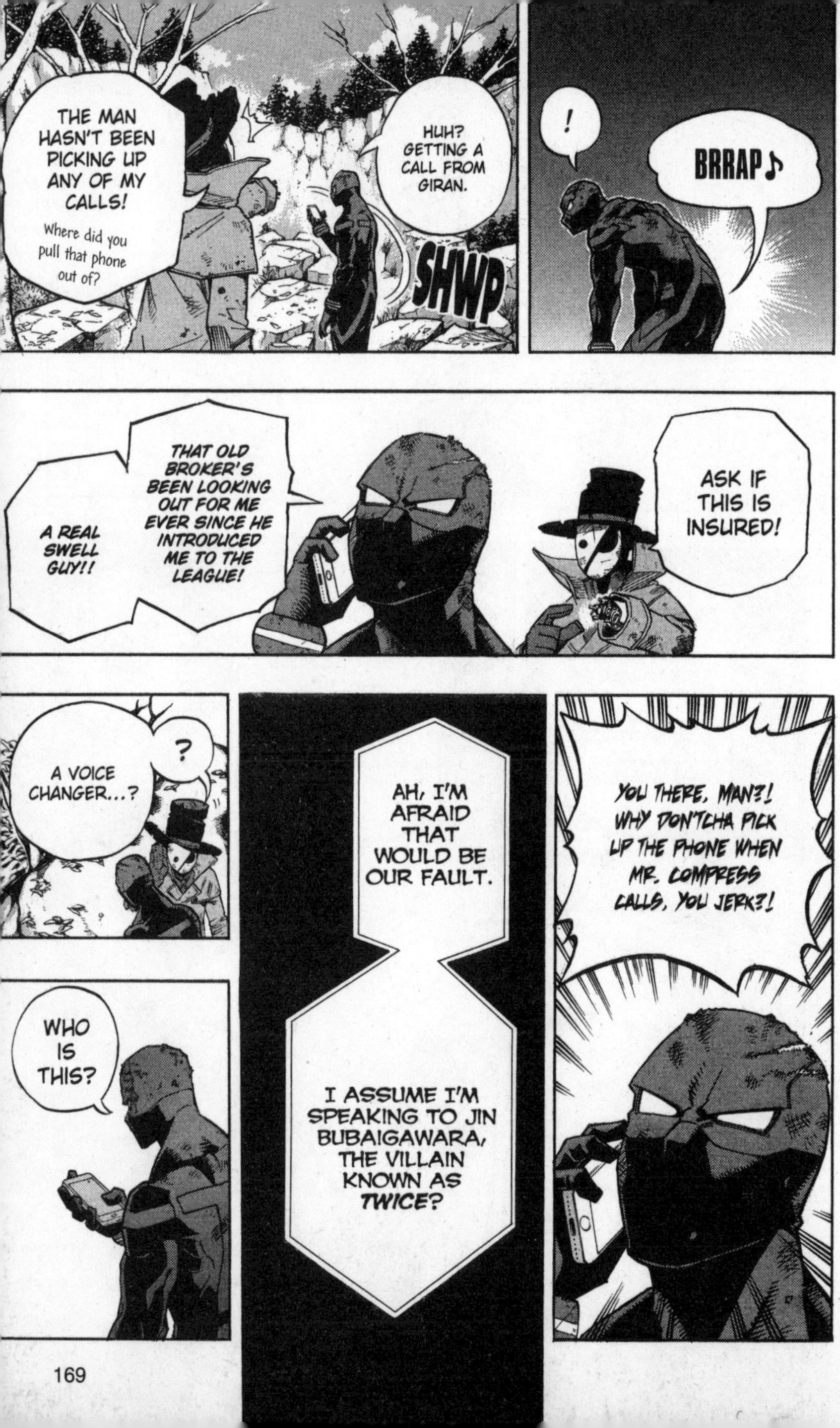
!
BRRAP♪
HUH? GETTING A CALL FROM GIRAN.
SHWP
THE MAN HASN'T BEEN PICKING UP ANY OF MY CALLS!
Where did you pull that phone out of?
ASK IF THIS IS INSURED!
THAT OLD BROKER'S BEEN LOOKING OUT FOR ME EVER SINCE HE INTRODUCED ME TO THE LEAGUE!
A REAL SWELL GUY!!
YOU THERE, MAN?! WHY DON'TCHA PICK UP THE PHONE WHEN MR. COMPRESS CALLS, YOU JERK?!
AH, I'M AFRAID THAT WOULD BE OUR FAULT.
I ASSUME I'M SPEAKING TO JIN BUBAIGAWARA, THE VILLAIN KNOWN AS *TWICE*?
?
A VOICE CHANGER...?
WHO IS THIS?

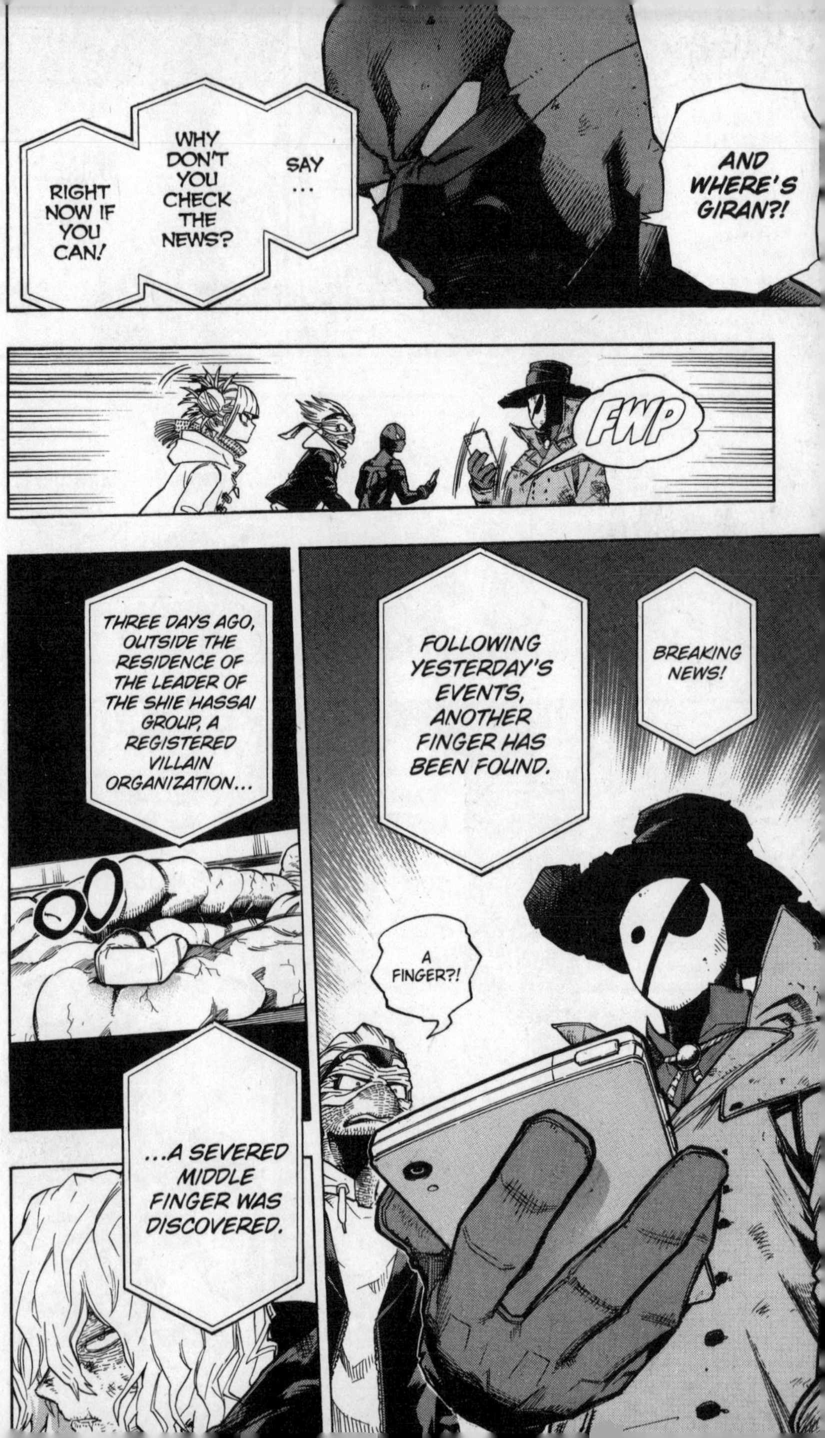
AND WHERE'S GIRAN?!
SAY ... WHY DON'T YOU CHECK THE NEWS? RIGHT NOW IF YOU CAN!
FWP
BREAKING NEWS!
FOLLOWING YESTERDAY'S EVENTS, ANOTHER FINGER HAS BEEN FOUND.
A FINGER?!
THREE DAYS AGO, OUTSIDE THE RESIDENCE OF THE LEADER OF THE SHIE HASSAI GROUP, A REGISTERED VILLAIN ORGANIZATION...
...A SEVERED MIDDLE FINGER WAS DISCOVERED.

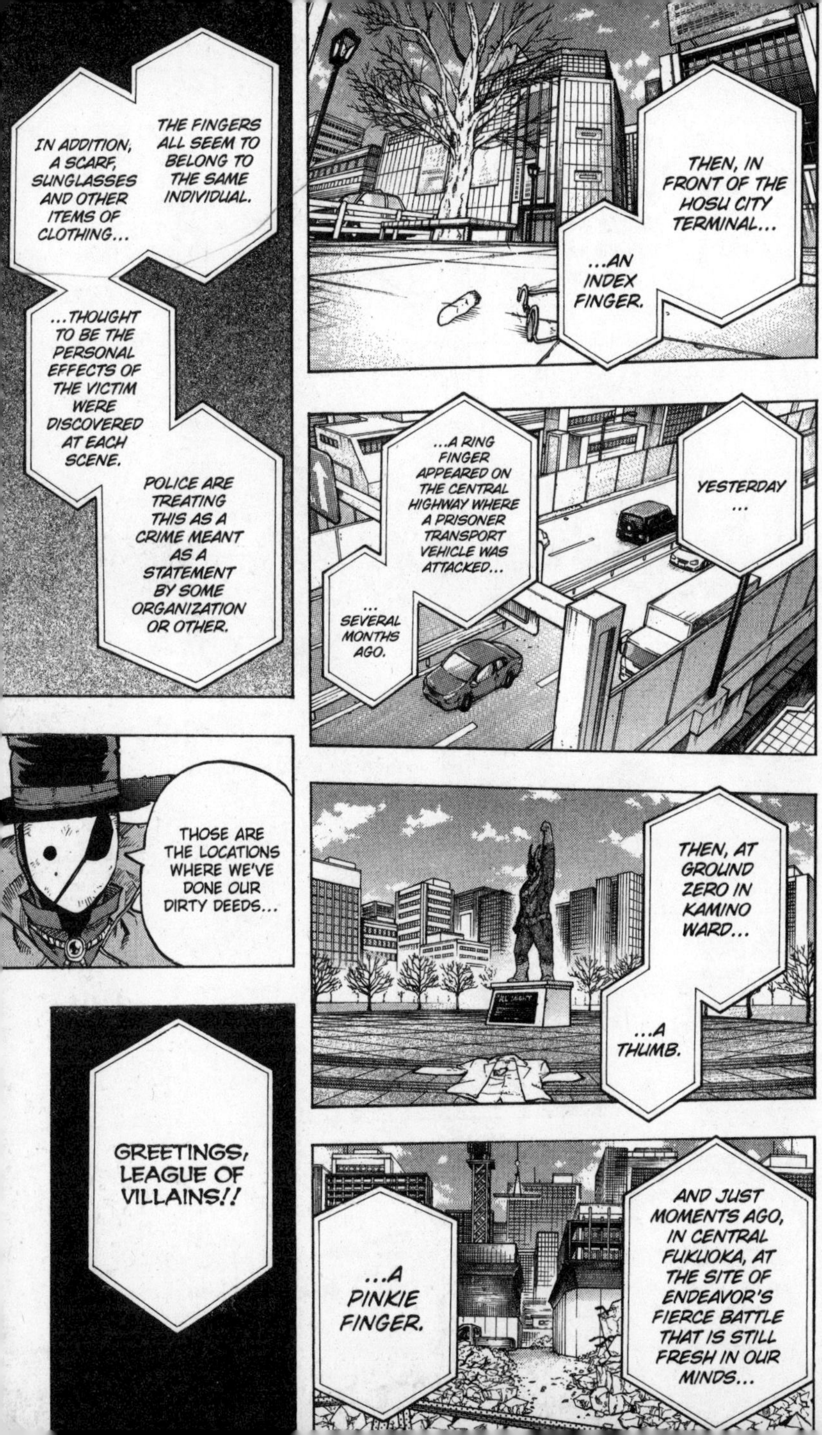
THEN, IN FRONT OF THE HOSU CITY TERMINAL...
...AN INDEX FINGER.
YESTERDAY...
...A RING FINGER APPEARED ON THE CENTRAL HIGHWAY WHERE A PRISONER TRANSPORT VEHICLE WAS ATTACKED...
...SEVERAL MONTHS AGO.
THE FINGERS ALL SEEM TO BELONG TO THE SAME INDIVIDUAL.
IN ADDITION, A SCARF, SUNGLASSES AND OTHER ITEMS OF CLOTHING...
...THOUGHT TO BE THE PERSONAL EFFECTS OF THE VICTIM WERE DISCOVERED AT EACH SCENE.
POLICE ARE TREATING THIS AS A CRIME MEANT AS A STATEMENT BY SOME ORGANIZATION OR OTHER.
THEN, AT GROUND ZERO IN KAMINO WARD...
...A THUMB.
THOSE ARE THE LOCATIONS WHERE WE'VE DONE OUR DIRTY DEEDS...
AND JUST MOMENTS AGO, IN CENTRAL FUKUOKA, AT THE SITE OF ENDEAVOR'S FIERCE BATTLE THAT IS STILL FRESH IN OUR MINDS...
...A PINKIE FINGER.
GREETINGS, LEAGUE OF VILLAINS!!

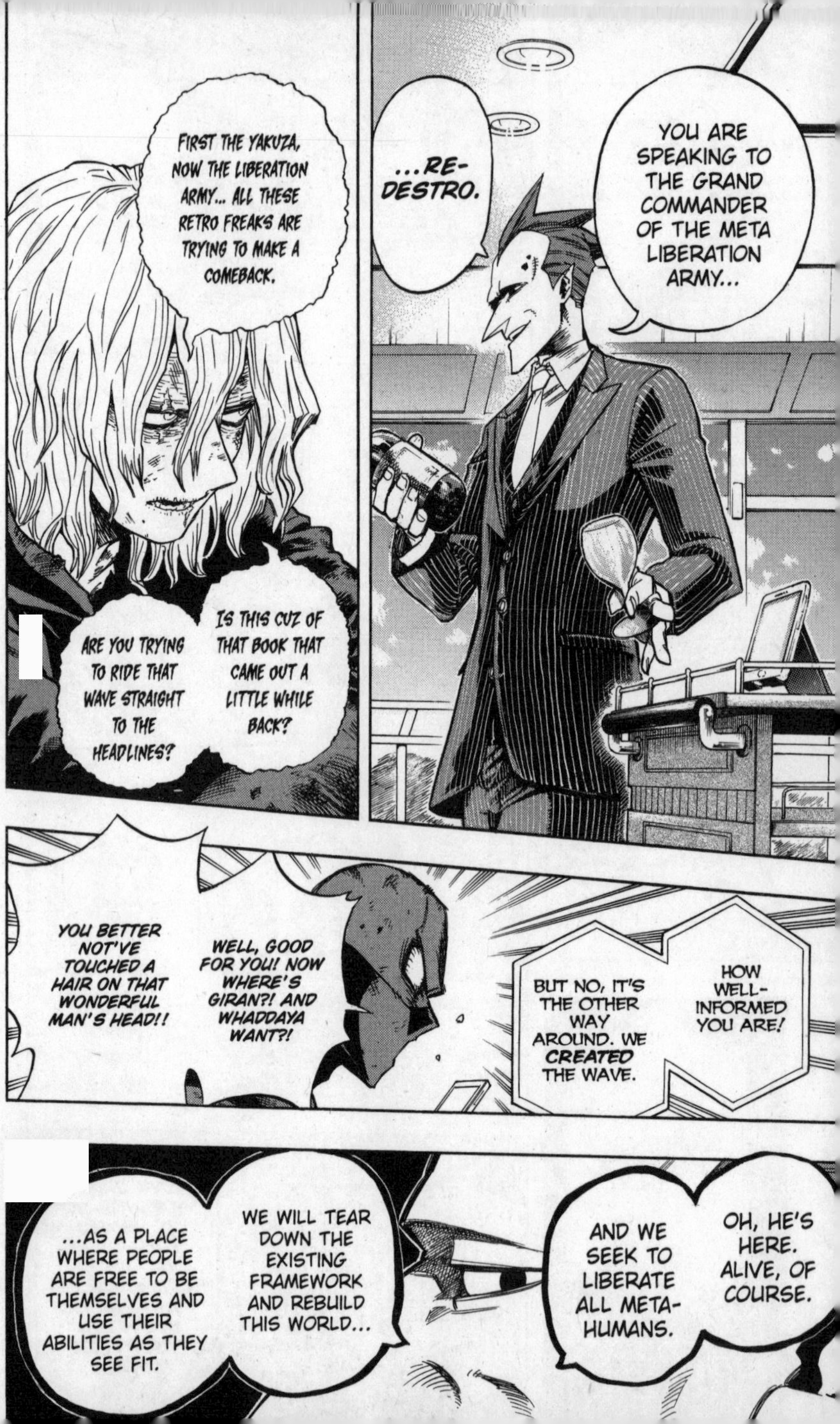

YOU ARE SPEAKING TO THE GRAND COMMANDER OF THE META LIBERATION ARMY...
...RE-DESTRO.
FIRST THE YAKUZA, NOW THE LIBERATION ARMY... ALL THESE RETRO FREAKS ARE TRYING TO MAKE A COMEBACK.
IS THIS CUZ OF THAT BOOK THAT CAME OUT A LITTLE WHILE BACK?
ARE YOU TRYING TO RIDE THAT WAVE STRAIGHT TO THE HEADLINES?
HOW WELL-INFORMED YOU ARE!
BUT NO, IT'S THE OTHER WAY AROUND. WE CREATED THE WAVE.
WELL, GOOD FOR YOU! NOW WHERE'S GIRAN?! AND WHADDAYA WANT?!
YOU BETTER NOT'VE TOUCHED A HAIR ON THAT WONDERFUL MAN'S HEAD!!
OH, HE'S HERE. ALIVE, OF COURSE.
AND WE SEEK TO LIBERATE ALL META-HUMANS.
WE WILL TEAR DOWN THE EXISTING FRAMEWORK AND REBUILD THIS WORLD...
...AS A PLACE WHERE PEOPLE ARE FREE TO BE THEMSELVES AND USE THEIR ABILITIES AS THEY SEE FIT.

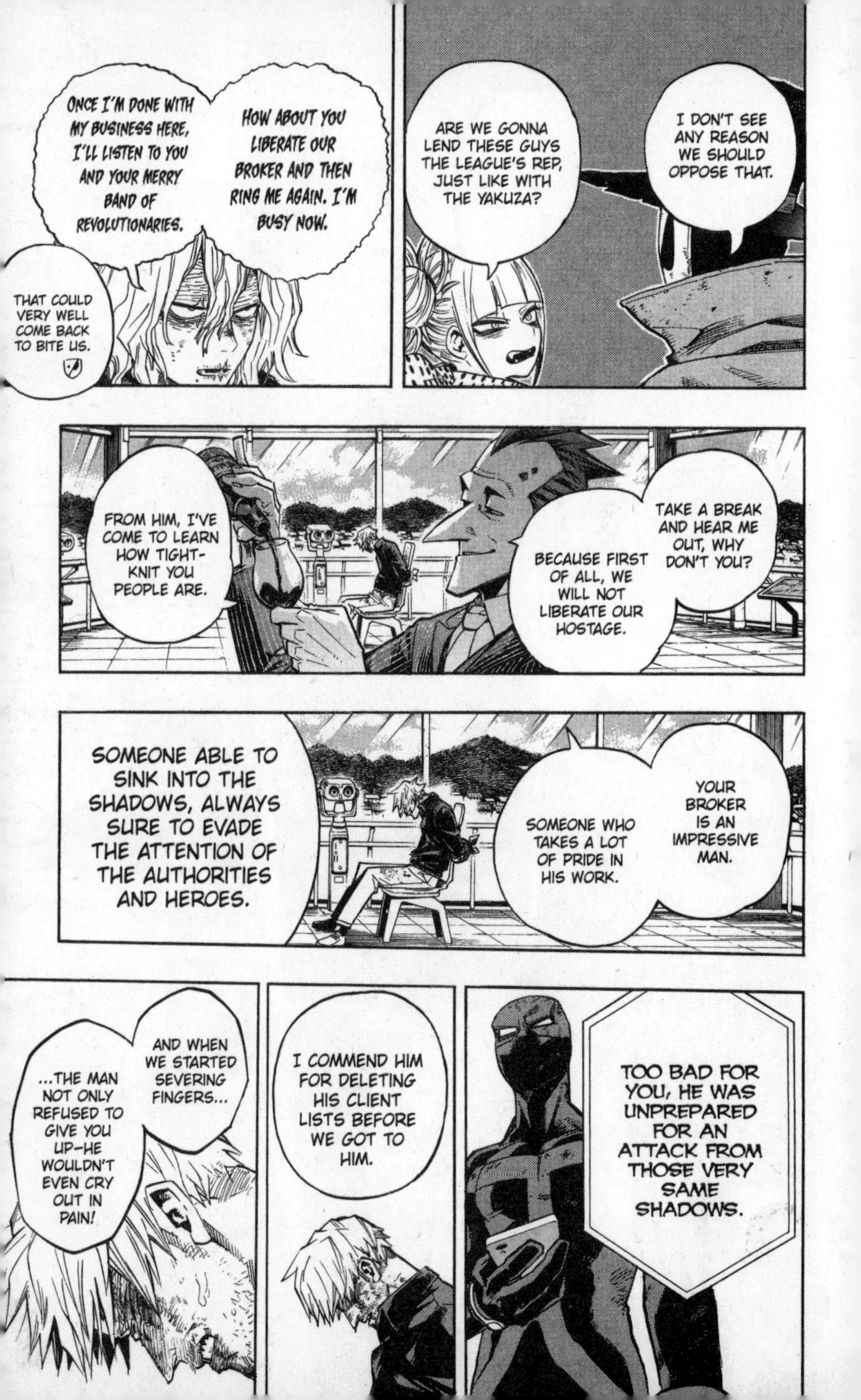
ARE WE GONNA LEND THESE GUYS THE LEAGUE'S REP, JUST LIKE WITH THE YAKUZA?
I DON'T SEE ANY REASON WE SHOULD OPPOSE THAT.
HOW ABOUT YOU LIBERATE OUR BROKER AND THEN RING ME AGAIN. I'M BUSY NOW.
ONCE I'M DONE WITH MY BUSINESS HERE, I'LL LISTEN TO YOU AND YOUR MERRY BAND OF REVOLUTIONARIES.
THAT COULD VERY WELL COME BACK TO BITE US.
TAKE A BREAK AND HEAR ME OUT, WHY DON'T YOU?
BECAUSE FIRST OF ALL, WE WILL NOT LIBERATE OUR HOSTAGE.
FROM HIM, I'VE COME TO LEARN HOW TIGHT-KNIT YOU PEOPLE ARE.
YOUR BROKER IS AN IMPRESSIVE MAN.
SOMEONE WHO TAKES A LOT OF PRIDE IN HIS WORK.
SOMEONE ABLE TO SINK INTO THE SHADOWS, ALWAYS SURE TO EVADE THE ATTENTION OF THE AUTHORITIES AND HEROES.
TOO BAD FOR YOU, HE WAS UNPREPARED FOR AN ATTACK FROM THOSE VERY SAME SHADOWS.
I COMMEND HIM FOR DELETING HIS CLIENT LISTS BEFORE WE GOT TO HIM.
AND WHEN WE STARTED SEVERING FINGERS...
...THE MAN NOT ONLY REFUSED TO GIVE YOU UP—HE WOULDN'T EVEN CRY OUT IN PAIN!

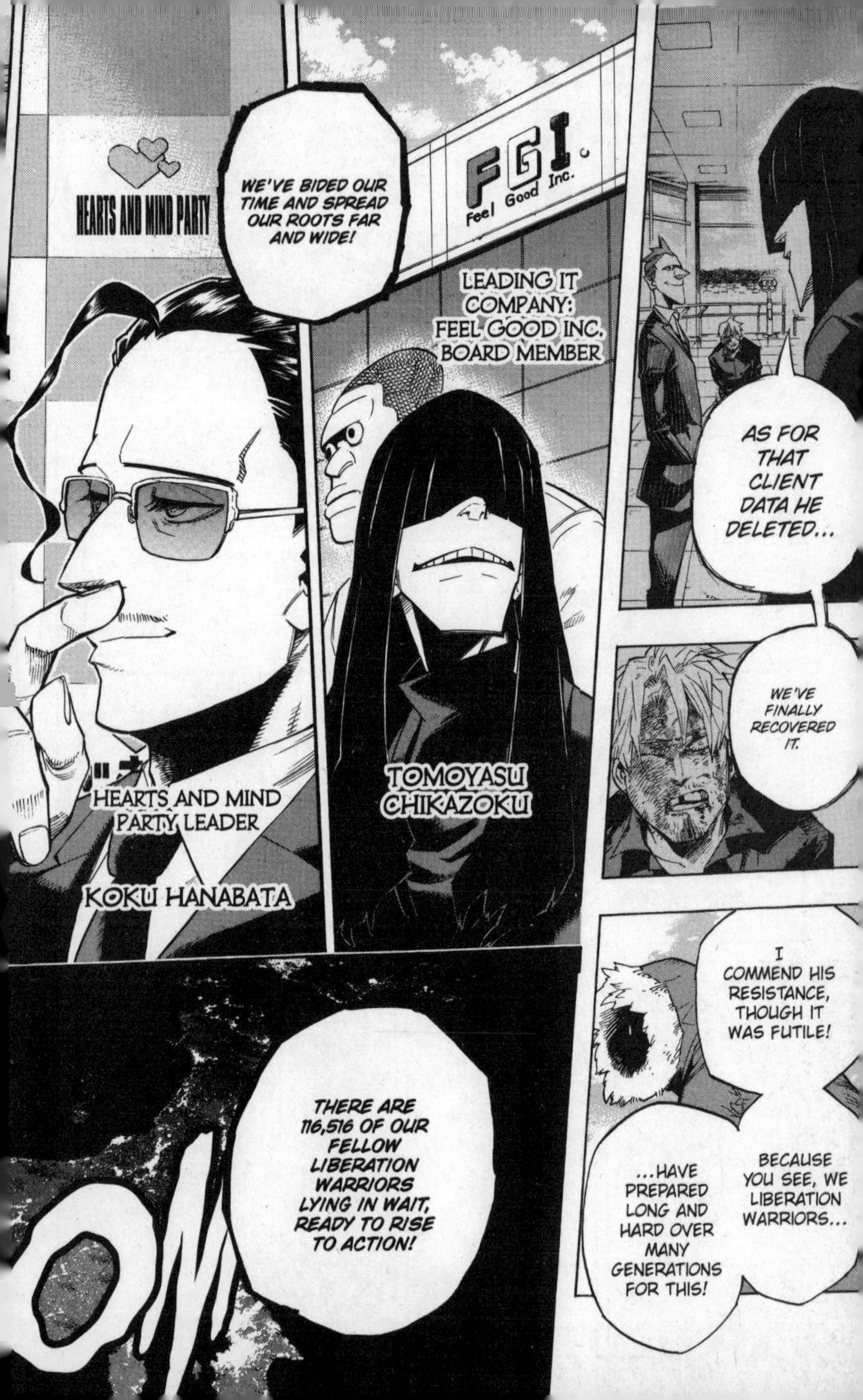

AS FOR THAT CLIENT DATA HE DELETED...
WE'VE FINALLY RECOVERED IT.
FGI. Feel Good Inc.
LEADING IT COMPANY: FEEL GOOD INC. BOARD MEMBER
TOMOYASU CHIKAZOKU
WE'VE BIDED OUR TIME AND SPREAD OUR ROOTS FAR AND WIDE!
HEARTS AND MIND PARTY
HEARTS AND MIND PARTY LEADER
KOKU HANABATA
I COMMEND HIS RESISTANCE, THOUGH IT WAS FUTILE!
BECAUSE YOU SEE, WE LIBERATION WARRIORS...
...HAVE PREPARED LONG AND HARD OVER MANY GENERATIONS FOR THIS!
THERE ARE 116,516 OF OUR FELLOW LIBERATION WARRIORS LYING IN WAIT, READY TO RISE TO ACTION!

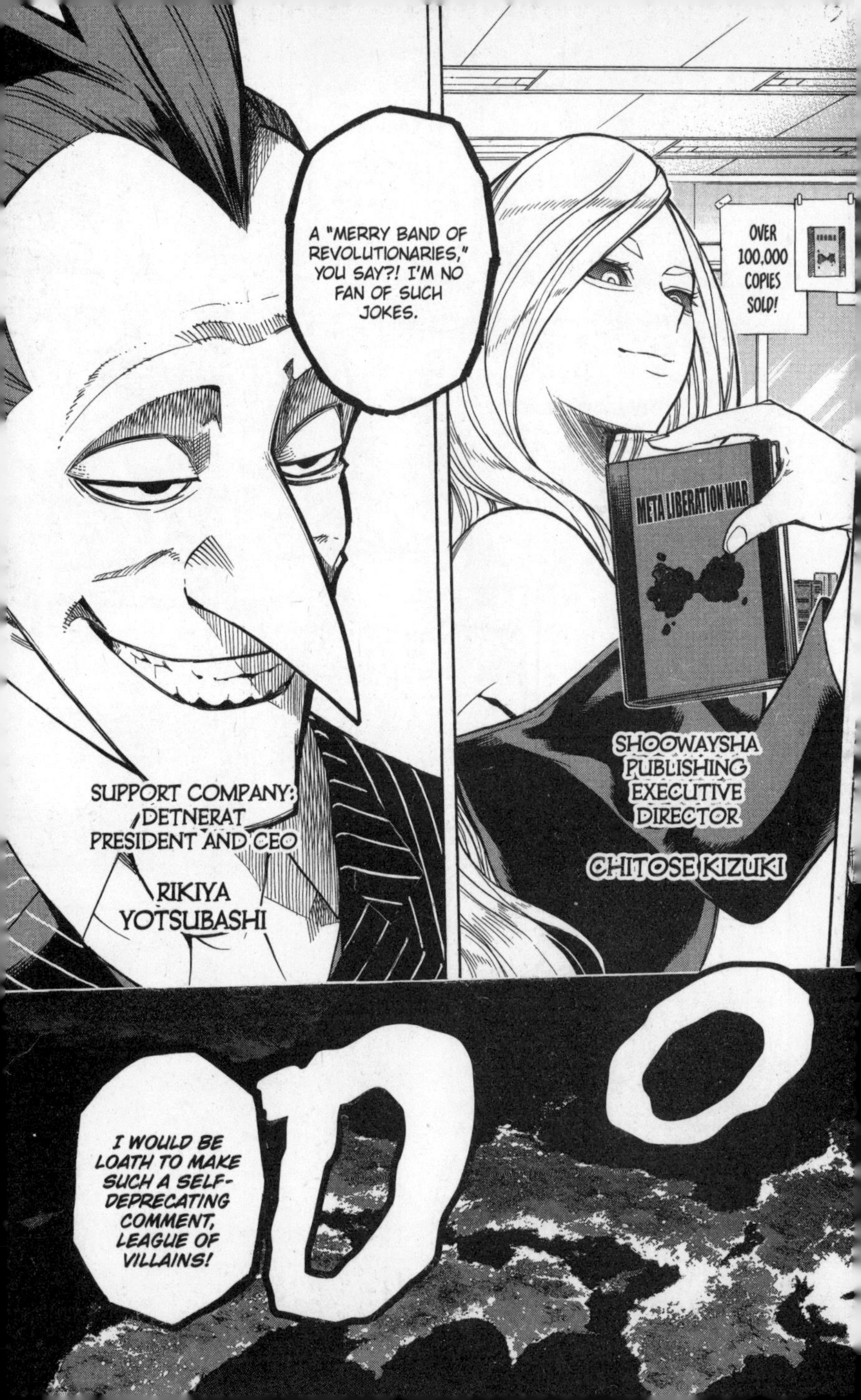
OVER 100,000 COPIES SOLD!
META LIBERATION WAR
SHOOWAYSHA PUBLISHING EXECUTIVE DIRECTOR
CHITOSE KIZUKI
A "MERRY BAND OF REVOLUTIONARIES," YOU SAY?! I'M NO FAN OF SUCH JOKES.
SUPPORT COMPANY: DETNERAT PRESIDENT AND CEO
RIKIYA YOTSUBASHI
DO
I WOULD BE LOATH TO MAKE SUCH A SELF-DEPRECATING COMMENT, LEAGUE OF VILLAINS!

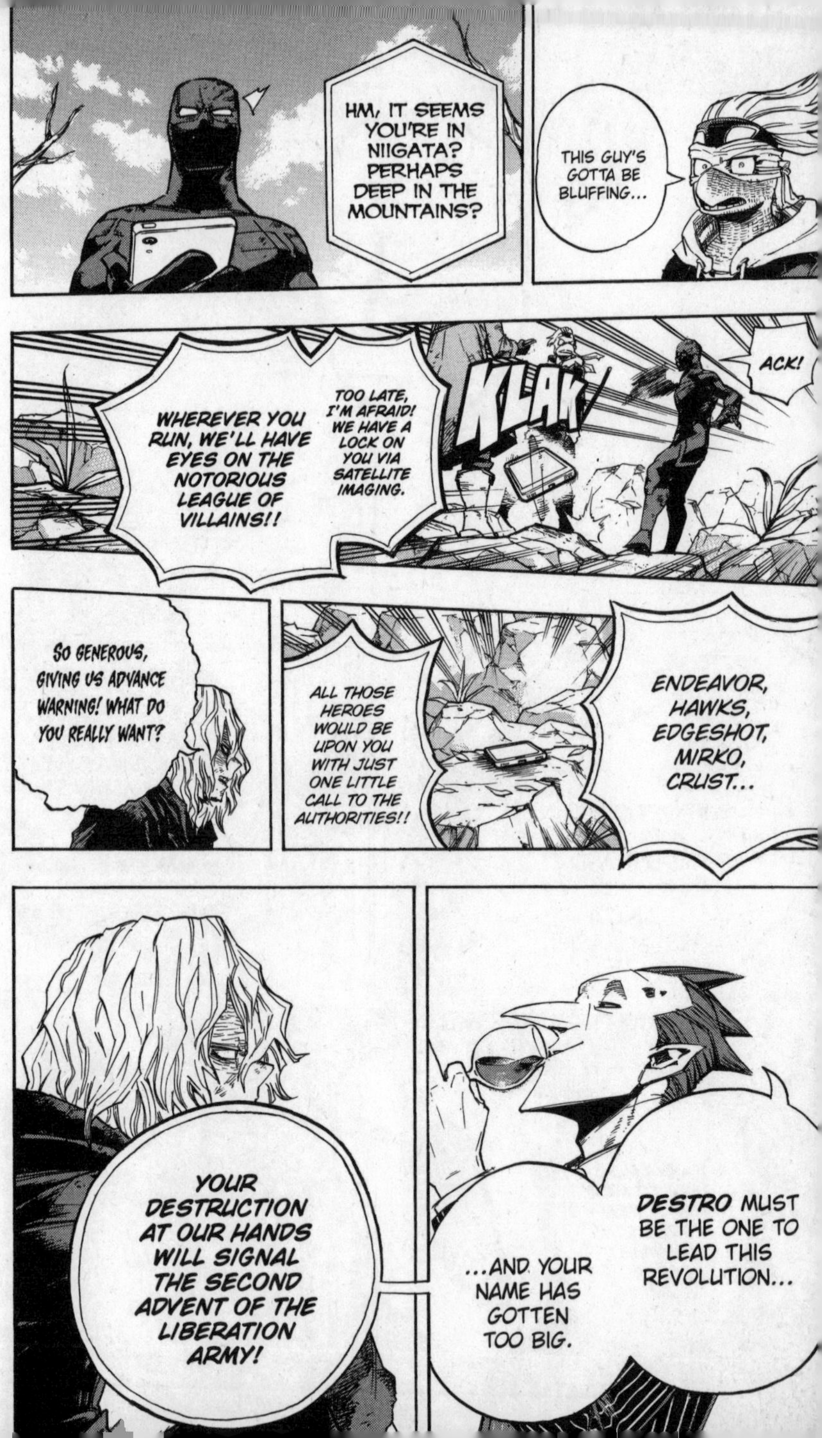
THIS GUY'S GOTTA BE BLUFFING...
HM, IT SEEMS YOU'RE IN NIIGATA? PERHAPS DEEP IN THE MOUNTAINS?
ACK!
KLAK
TOO LATE, I'M AFRAID! WE HAVE A LOCK ON YOU VIA SATELLITE IMAGING.
WHEREVER YOU RUN, WE'LL HAVE EYES ON THE NOTORIOUS LEAGUE OF VILLAINS!!
ENDEAVOR, HAWKS, EDGESHOT, MIRKO, CRUST...
ALL THOSE HEROES WOULD BE UPON YOU WITH JUST ONE LITTLE CALL TO THE AUTHORITIES!!
SO GENEROUS, GIVING US ADVANCE WARNING! WHAT DO YOU REALLY WANT?
DESTRO MUST BE THE ONE TO LEAD THIS REVOLUTION...
...AND YOUR NAME HAS GOTTEN TOO BIG.
YOUR DESTRUCTION AT OUR HANDS WILL SIGNAL THE SECOND ADVENT OF THE LIBERATION ARMY!

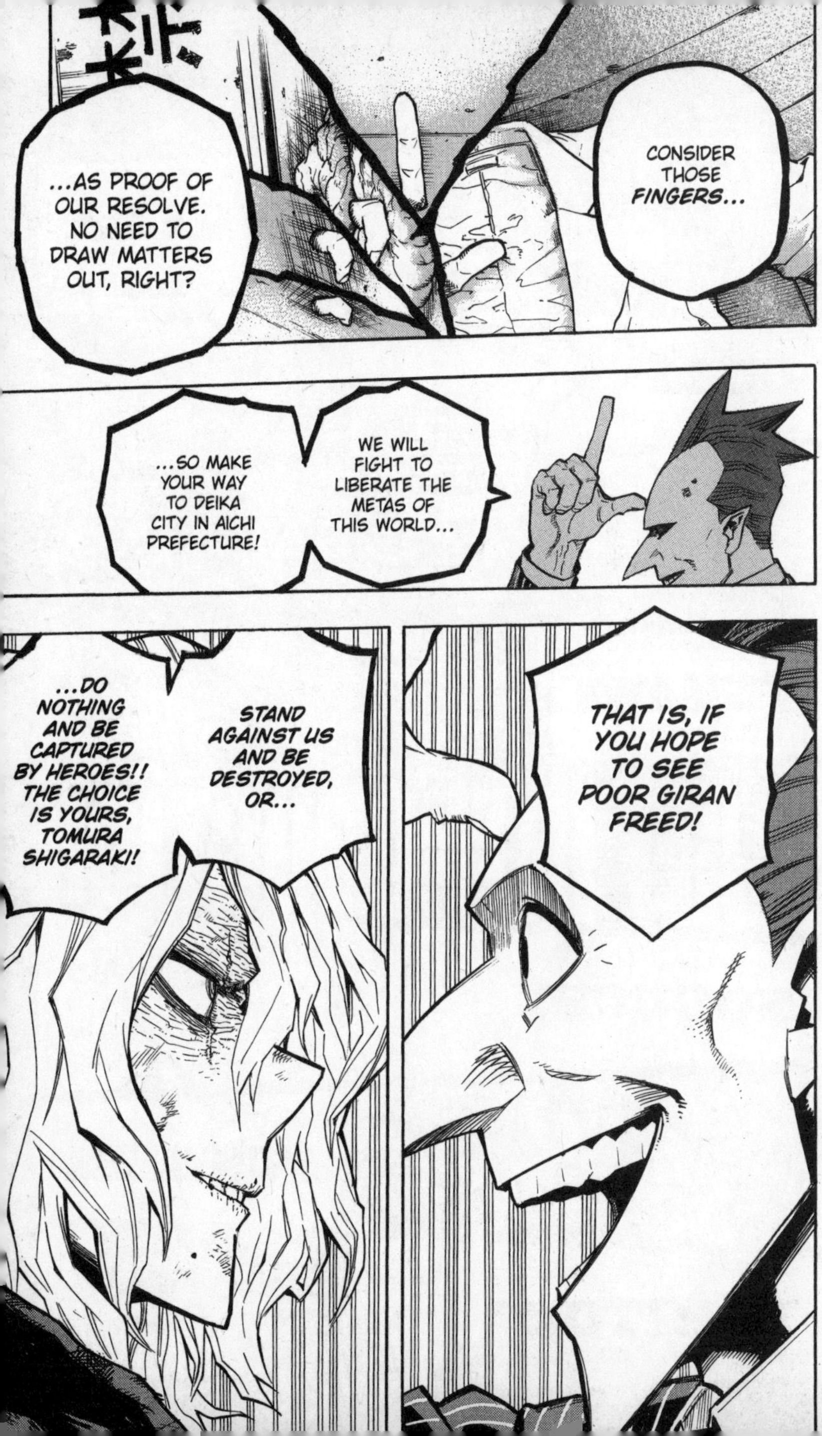
CONSIDER THOSE FINGERS...
...AS PROOF OF OUR RESOLVE. NO NEED TO DRAW MATTERS OUT, RIGHT?
WE WILL FIGHT TO LIBERATE THE METAS OF THIS WORLD...
...SO MAKE YOUR WAY TO DEIKA CITY IN AICHI PREFECTURE!
THAT IS, IF YOU HOPE TO SEE POOR GIRAN FREED!
STAND AGAINST US AND BE DESTROYED, OR...
...DO NOTHING AND BE CAPTURED BY HEROES!! THE CHOICE IS YOURS, TOMURA SHIGARAKI!

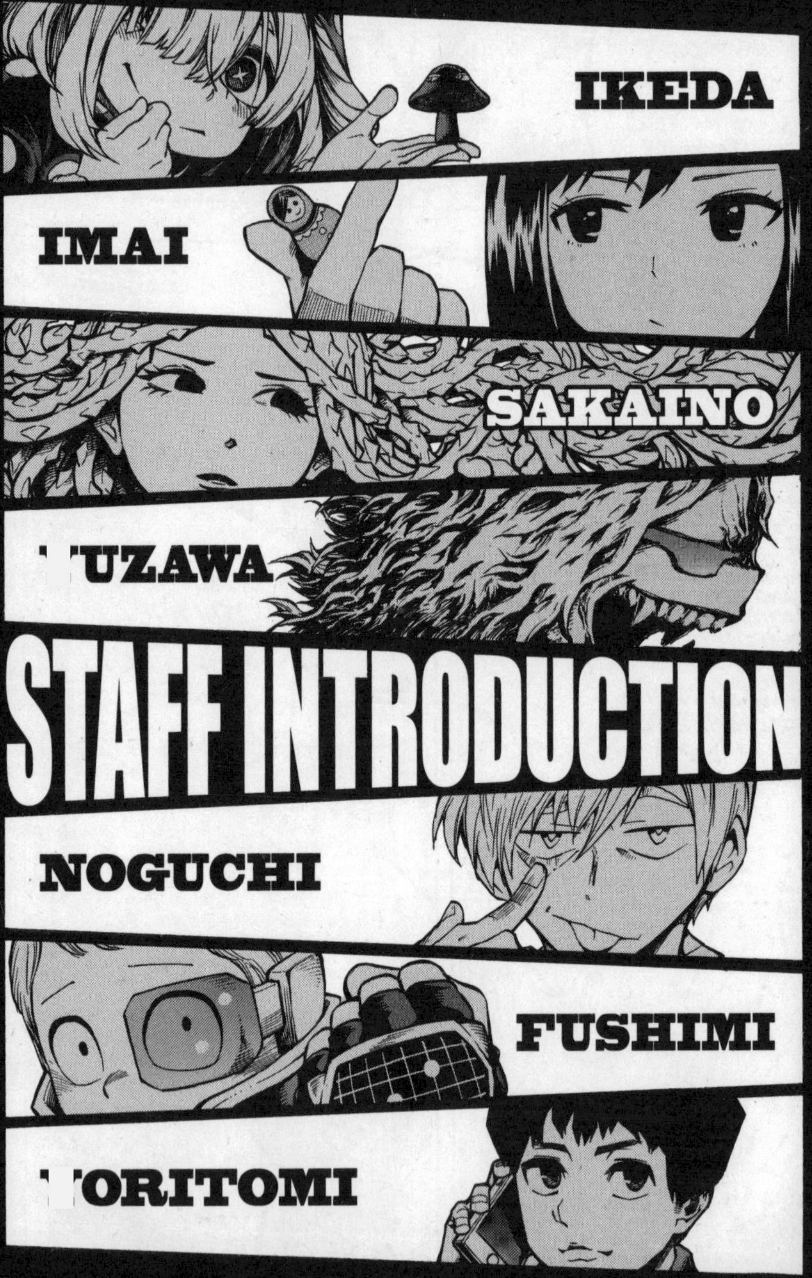
IKEDA
IMAI
SAKAINO
UZAWA
STAFF INTRODUCTION
NOGUCHI
FUSHIMI
ORITOMI

No. 224 - Revival Party

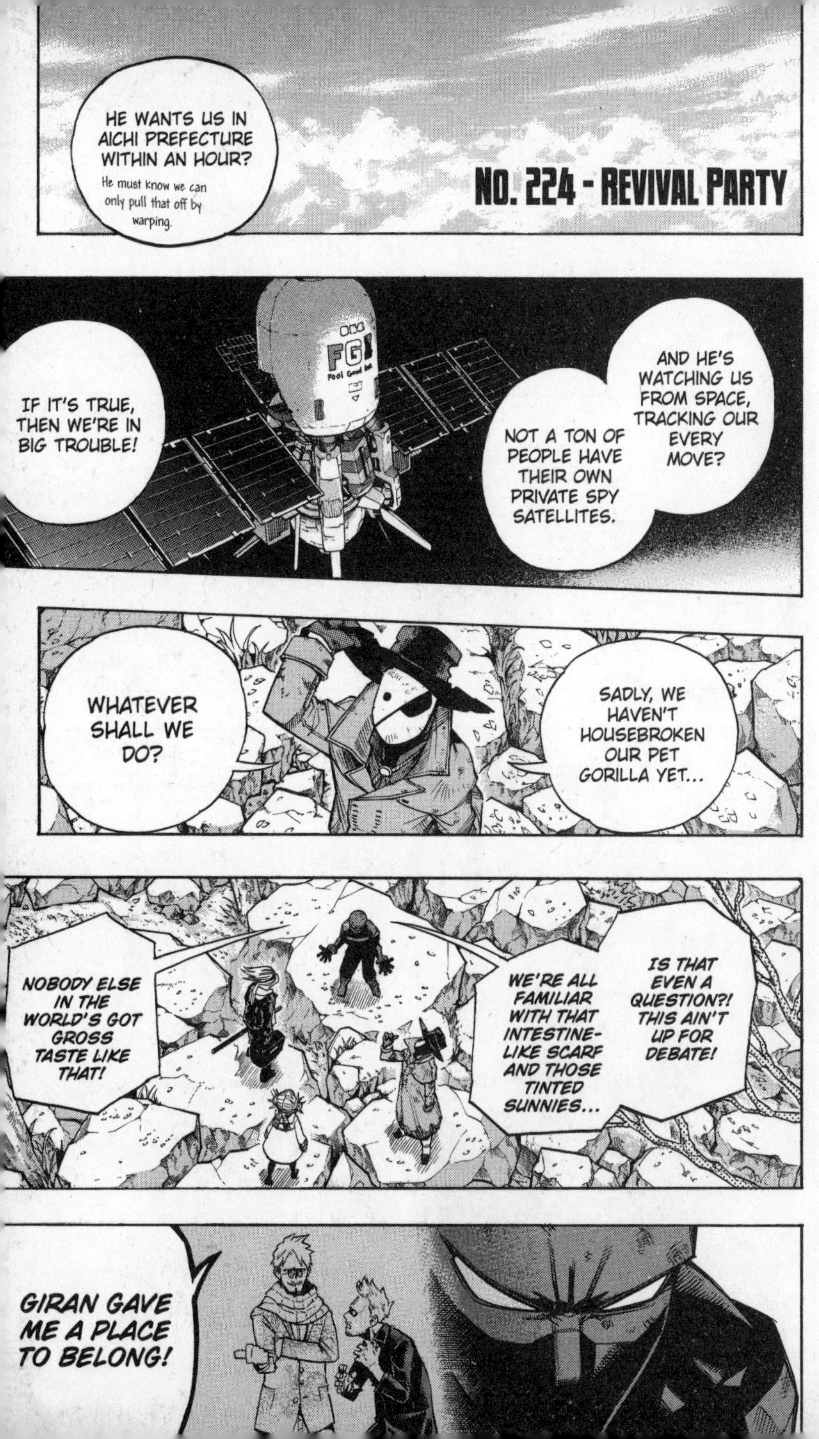
HE WANTS US IN AICHI PREFECTURE WITHIN AN HOUR?
He must know we can only pull that off by warping.
AND HE'S WATCHING US FROM SPACE, TRACKING OUR EVERY MOVE?
NOT A TON OF PEOPLE HAVE THEIR OWN PRIVATE SPY SATELLITES.
IF IT'S TRUE, THEN WE'RE IN BIG TROUBLE!
FGI
SADLY, WE HAVEN'T HOUSEBROKEN OUR PET GORILLA YET...
WHATEVER SHALL WE DO?
IS THAT EVEN A QUESTION?! THIS AIN'T UP FOR DEBATE!
WE'RE ALL FAMILIAR WITH THAT INTESTINE-LIKE SCARF AND THOSE TINTED SUNNIES...
NOBODY ELSE IN THE WORLD'S GOT GROSS TASTE LIKE THAT!
GIRAN GAVE ME A PLACE TO BELONG!

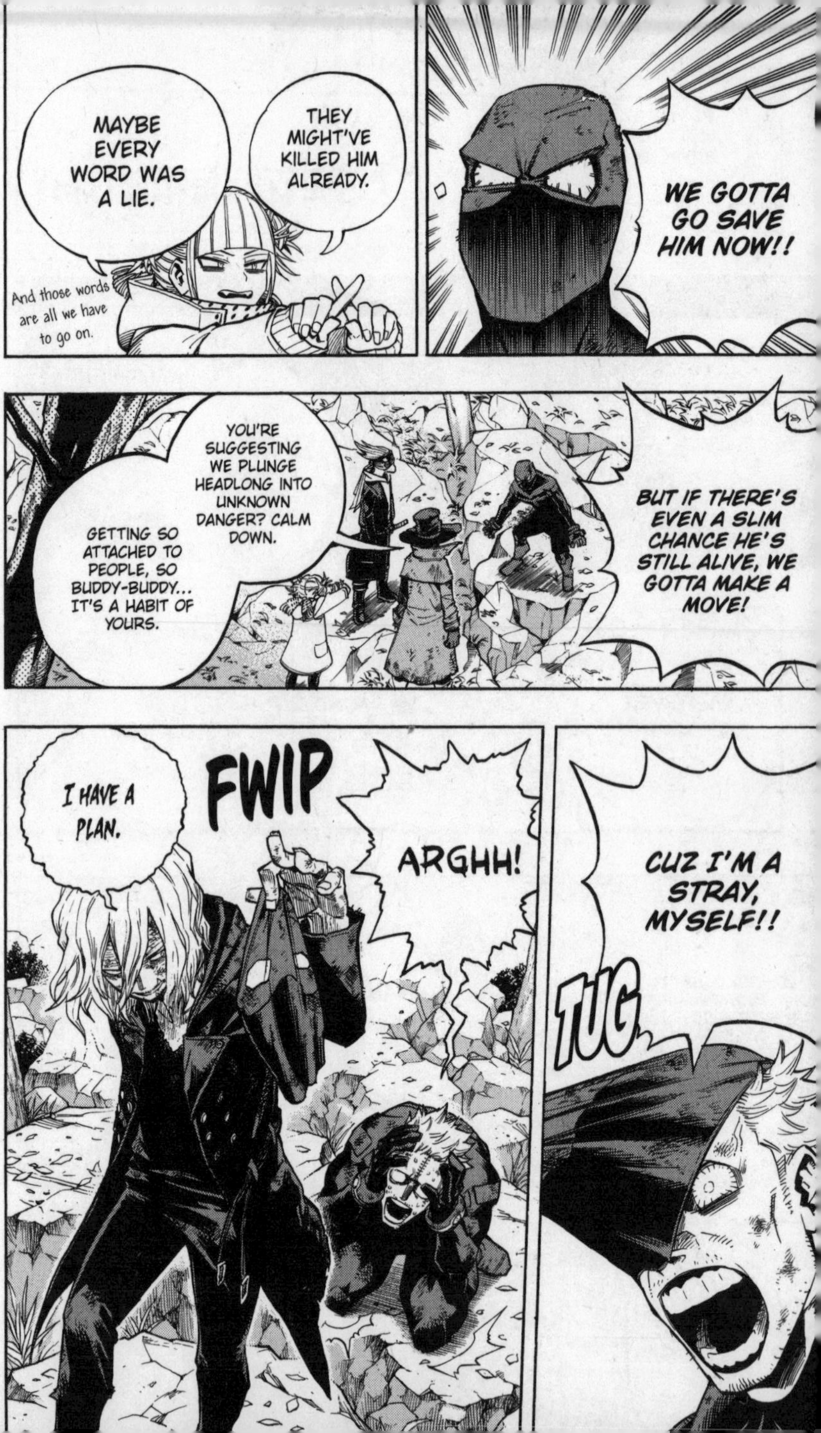
WE GOTTA GO SAVE HIM NOW!!
THEY MIGHT'VE KILLED HIM ALREADY.
MAYBE EVERY WORD WAS A LIE.
And those words are all we have to go on.
BUT IF THERE'S EVEN A SLIM CHANCE HE'S STILL ALIVE, WE GOTTA MAKE A MOVE!
YOU'RE SUGGESTING WE PLUNGE HEADLONG INTO UNKNOWN DANGER? CALM DOWN.
GETTING SO ATTACHED TO PEOPLE, SO BUDDY-BUDDY... IT'S A HABIT OF YOURS.
CUZ I'M A STRAY, MYSELF!!
TUG
ARGHH!
FWIP
I HAVE A PLAN.

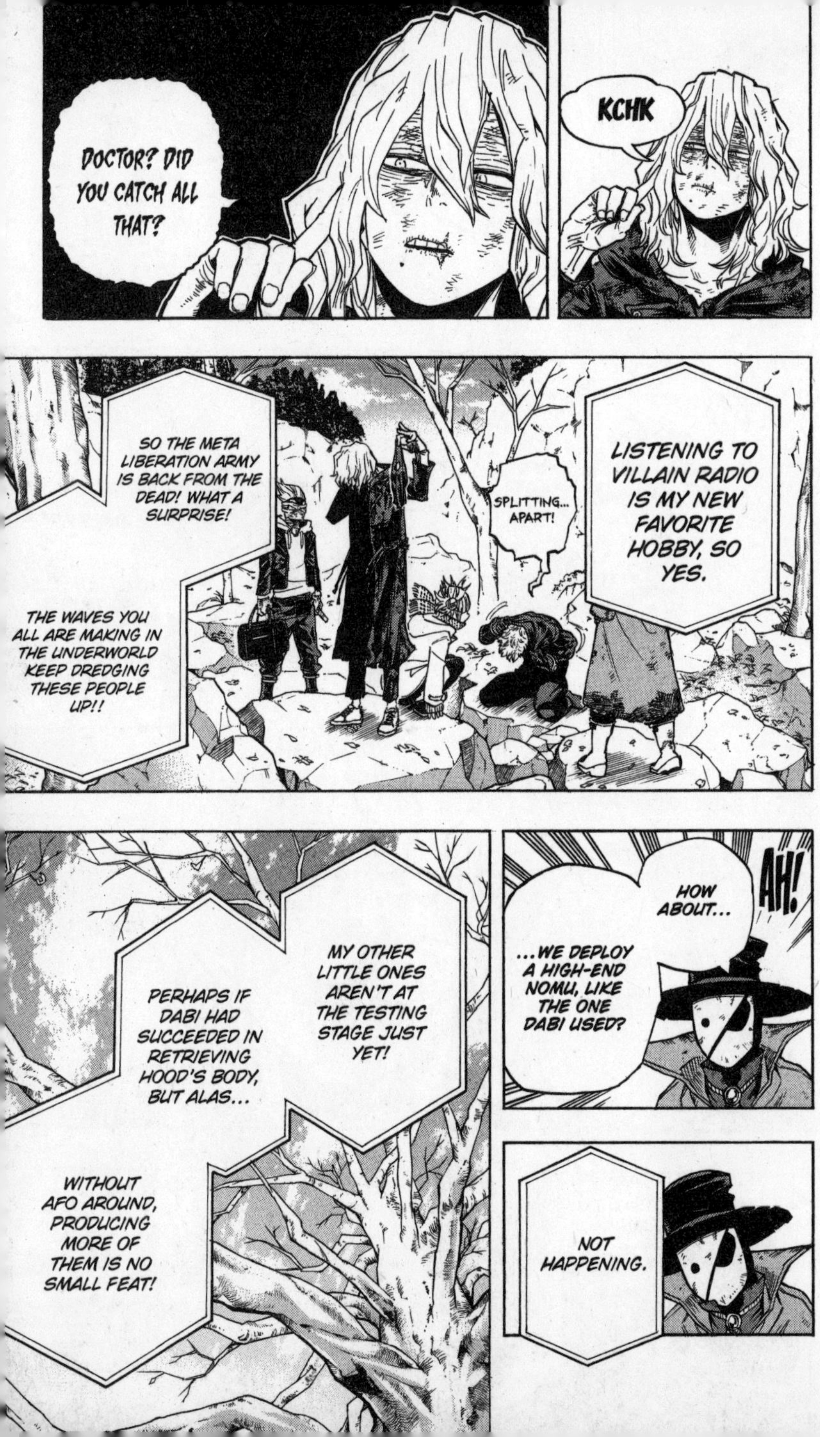
KCHK
DOCTOR? DID YOU CATCH ALL THAT?
LISTENING TO VILLAIN RADIO IS MY NEW FAVORITE HOBBY, SO YES.
SPLITTING... APART!
SO THE META LIBERATION ARMY IS BACK FROM THE DEAD! WHAT A SURPRISE!
THE WAVES YOU ALL ARE MAKING IN THE UNDERWORLD KEEP DREDGING THESE PEOPLE UP!!
AH!
HOW ABOUT...
...WE DEPLOY A HIGH-END NOMU, LIKE THE ONE DABI USED?
NOT HAPPENING.
MY OTHER LITTLE ONES AREN'T AT THE TESTING STAGE JUST YET!
PERHAPS IF DABI HAD SUCCEEDED IN RETRIEVING HOOD'S BODY, BUT ALAS...
WITHOUT AFO AROUND, PRODUCING MORE OF THEM IS NO SMALL FEAT!

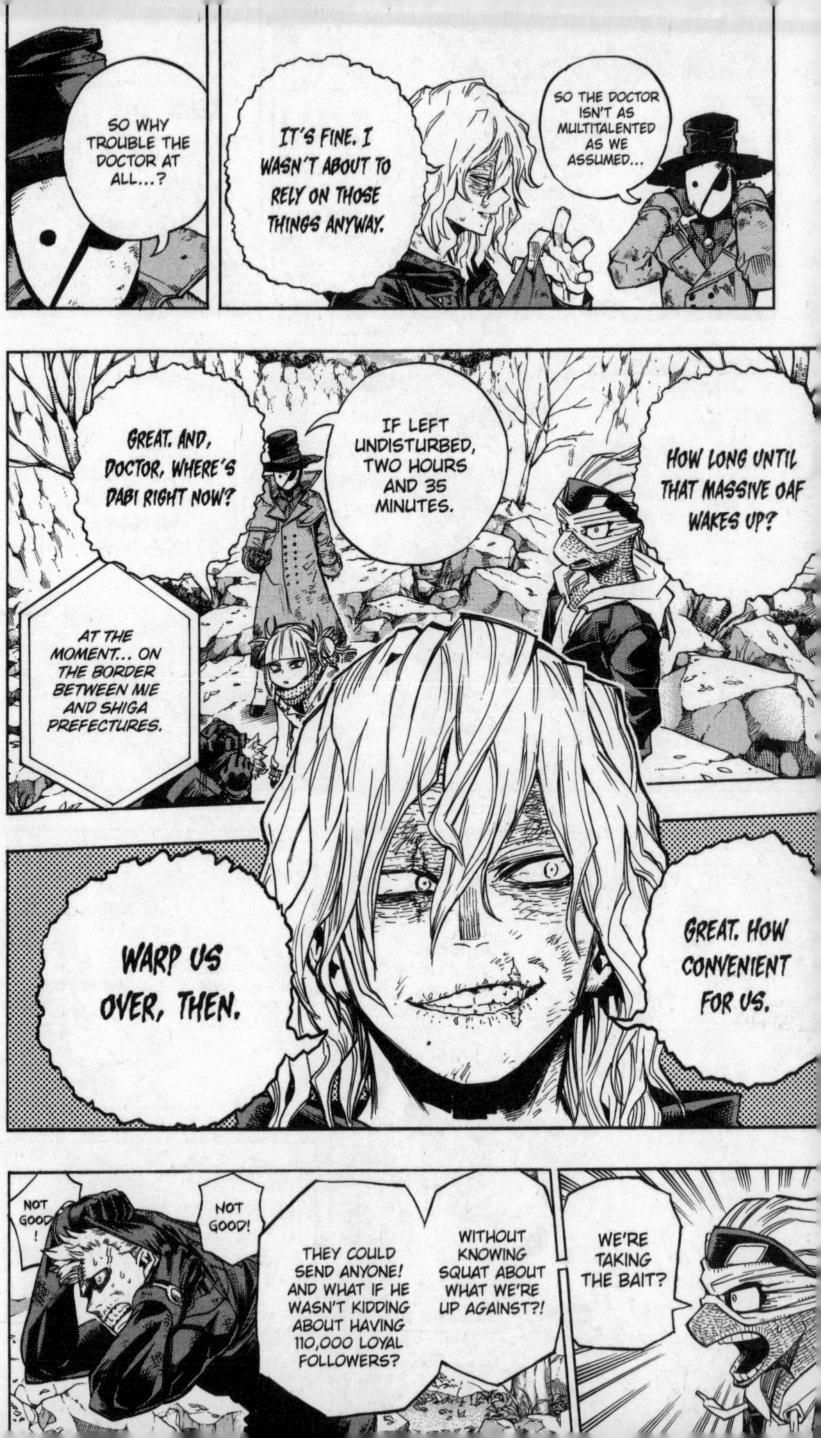
SO THE DOCTOR ISN'T AS MULTITALENTED AS WE ASSUMED...
IT'S FINE. I WASN'T ABOUT TO RELY ON THOSE THINGS ANYWAY.
SO WHY TROUBLE THE DOCTOR AT ALL...?
HOW LONG UNTIL THAT MASSIVE OAF WAKES UP?
IF LEFT UNDISTURBED, TWO HOURS AND 35 MINUTES.
GREAT. AND, DOCTOR, WHERE'S DABI RIGHT NOW?
AT THE MOMENT... ON THE BORDER BETWEEN MIE AND SHIGA PREFECTURES.
GREAT. HOW CONVENIENT FOR US.
WARP US OVER, THEN.
WE'RE TAKING THE BAIT?
WITHOUT KNOWING SQUAT ABOUT WHAT WE'RE UP AGAINST?!
THEY COULD SEND ANYONE! AND WHAT IF HE WASN'T KIDDING ABOUT HAVING 110,000 LOYAL FOLLOWERS?
NOT GOOD!
NOT GOOD!

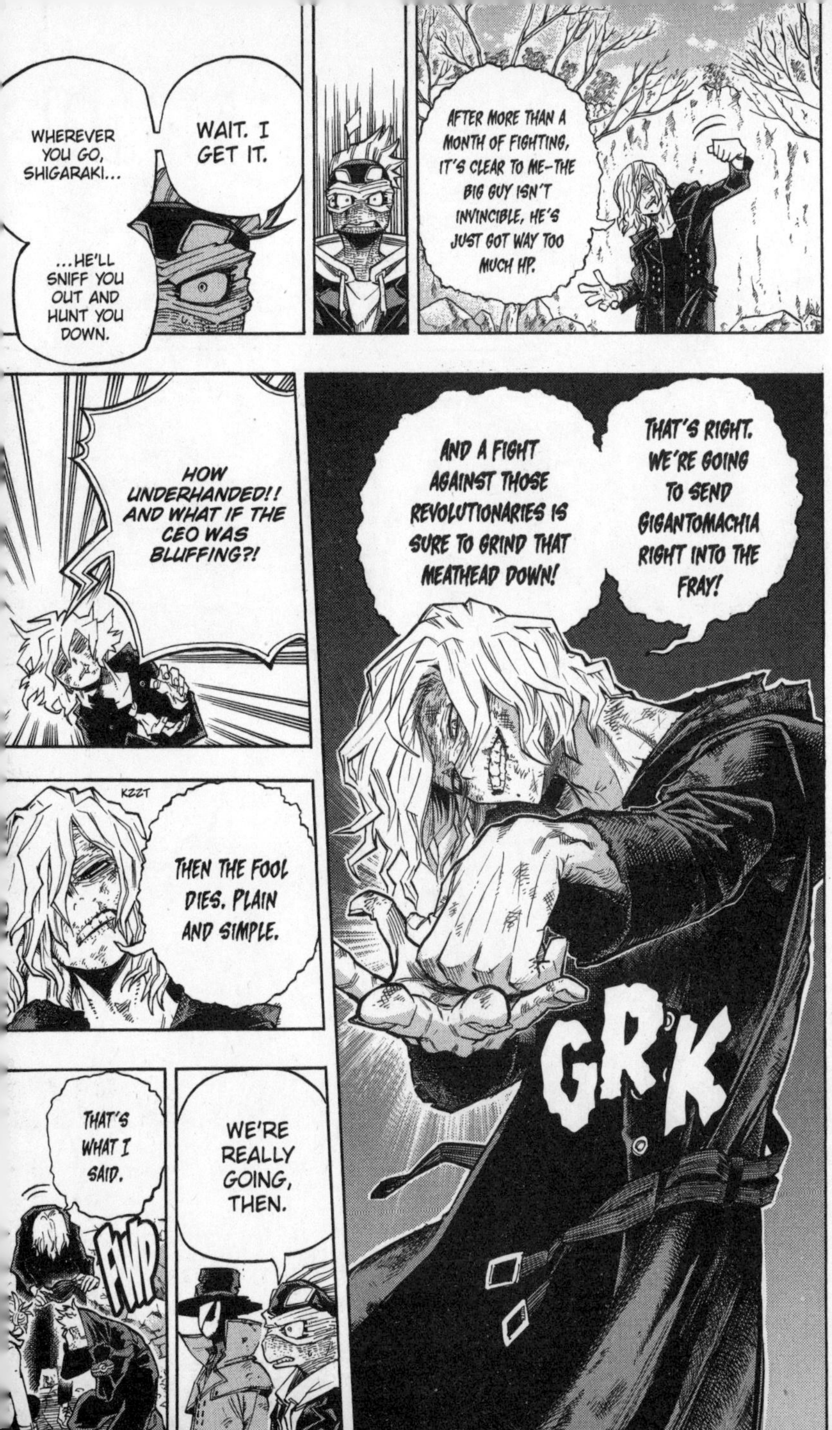

AFTER MORE THAN A MONTH OF FIGHTING, IT'S CLEAR TO ME—THE BIG GUY ISN'T INVINCIBLE, HE'S JUST GOT WAY TOO MUCH HP.
WAIT. I GET IT.
WHEREVER YOU GO, SHIGARAKI...
...HE'LL SNIFF YOU OUT AND HUNT YOU DOWN.
THAT'S RIGHT. WE'RE GOING TO SEND GIGANTOMACHIA RIGHT INTO THE FRAY!
AND A FIGHT AGAINST THOSE REVOLUTIONARIES IS SURE TO GRIND THAT MEATHEAD DOWN!
GRK
HOW UNDERHANDED!! AND WHAT IF THE CEO WAS BLUFFING?!
KZZT
THEN THE FOOL DIES. PLAIN AND SIMPLE.
WE'RE REALLY GOING, THEN.
THAT'S WHAT I SAID.
FWP

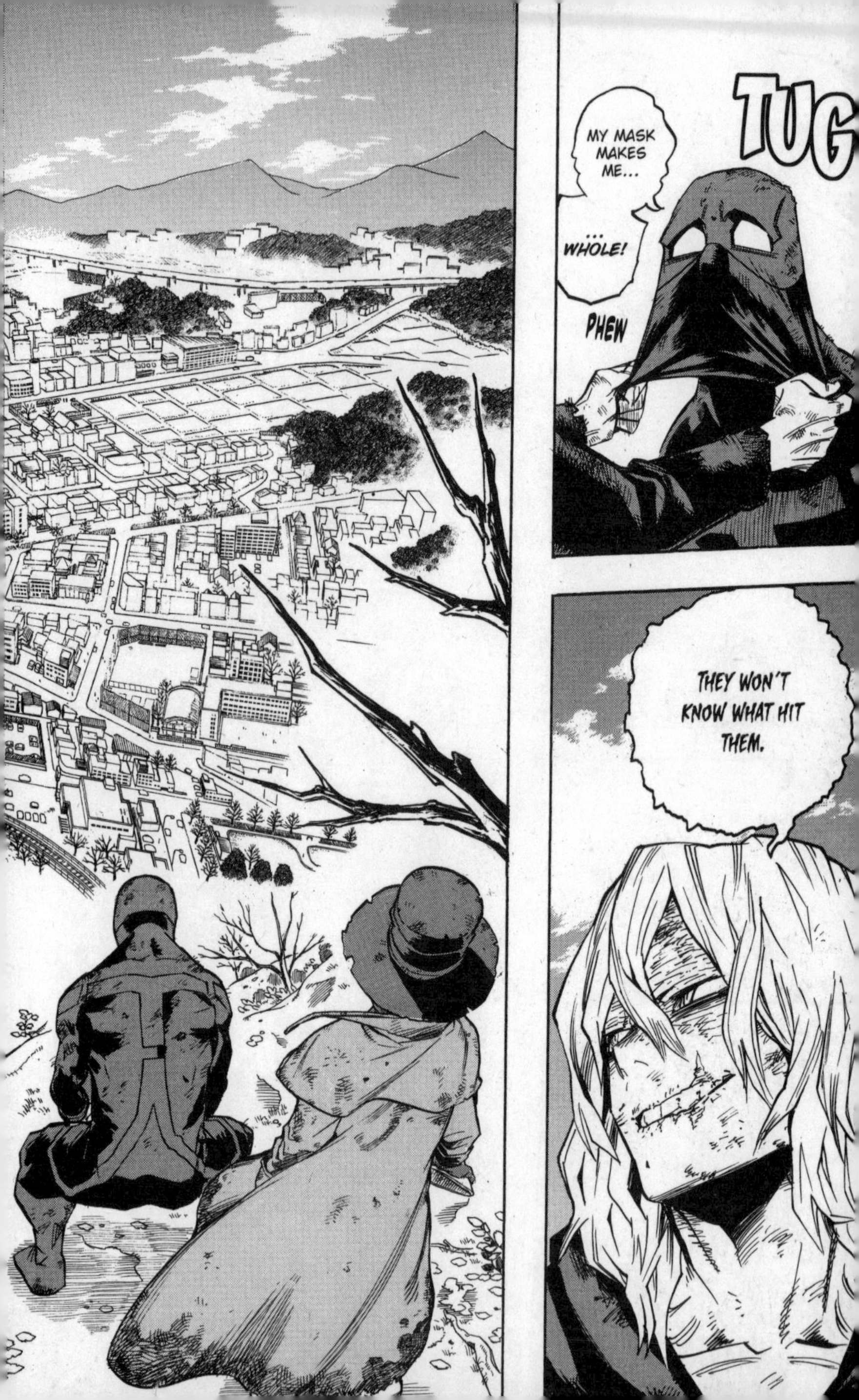
TUG
MY MASK MAKES ME...
...WHOLE!
PHEW
THEY WON'T KNOW WHAT HIT THEM.

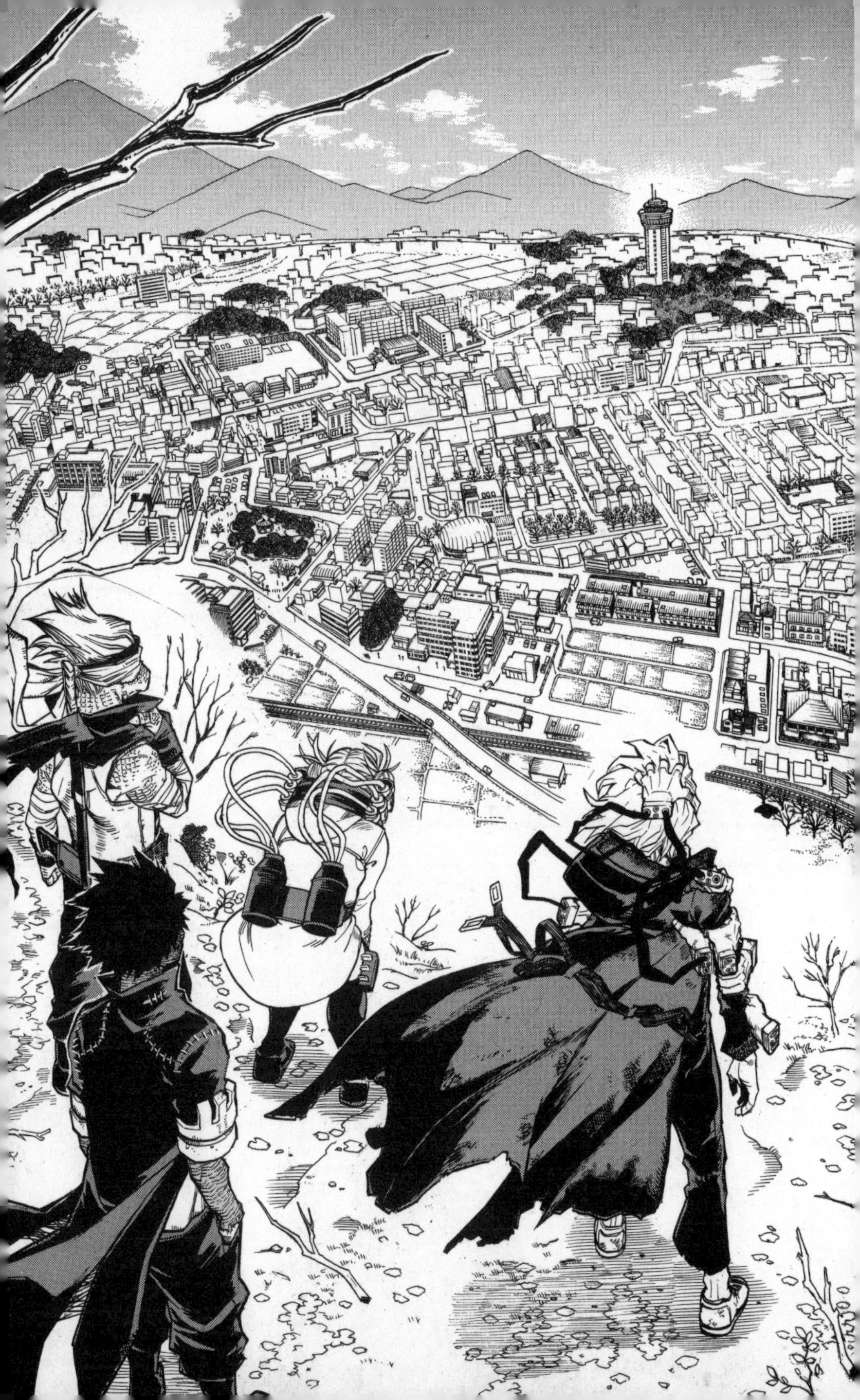

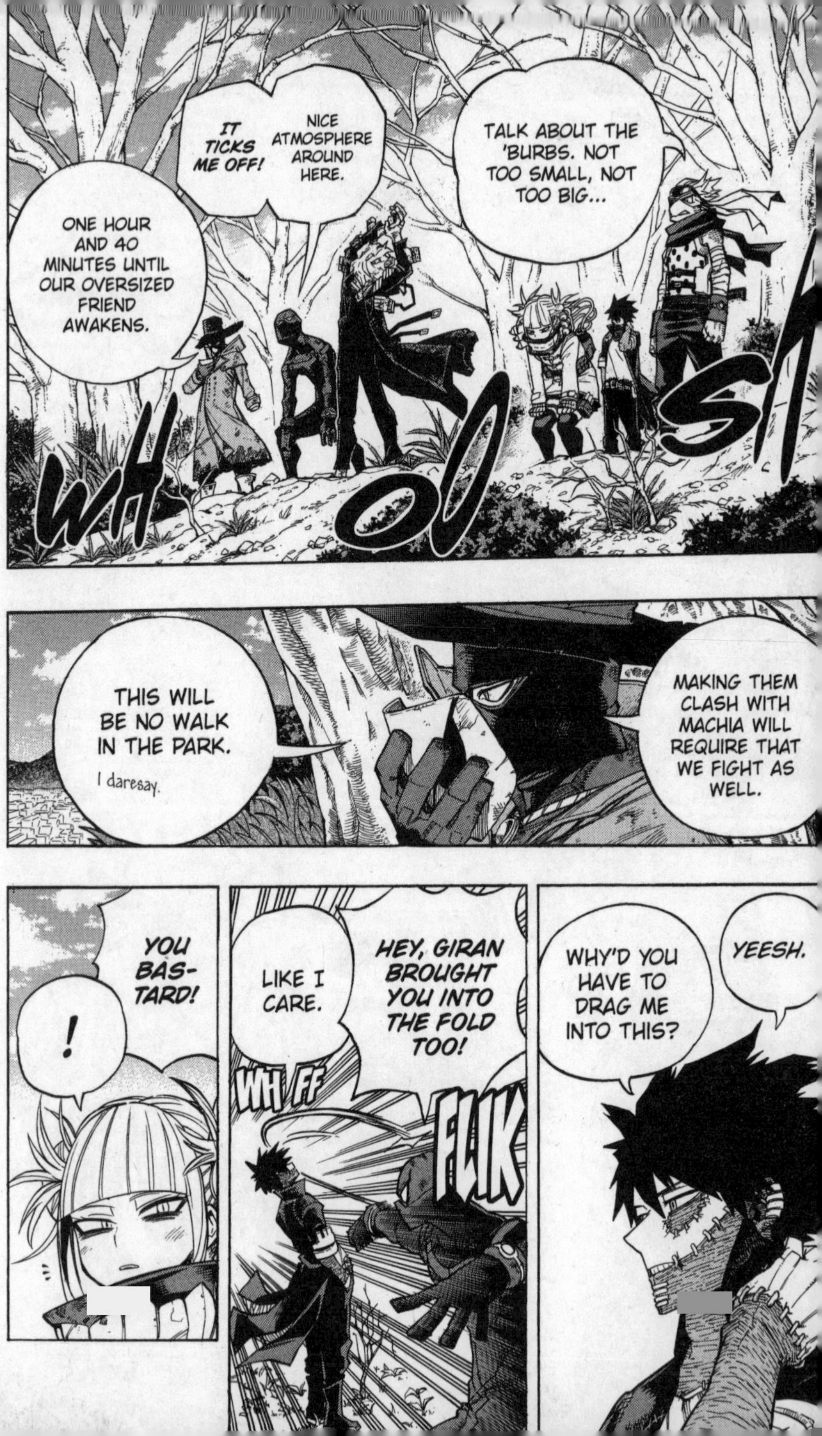
TALK ABOUT THE 'BURBS. NOT TOO SMALL, NOT TOO BIG...
NICE ATMOSPHERE AROUND HERE.
IT TICKS ME OFF!
ONE HOUR AND 40 MINUTES UNTIL OUR OVERSIZED FRIEND AWAKENS.
WHOOSH
MAKING THEM CLASH WITH MACHIA WILL REQUIRE THAT WE FIGHT AS WELL.
THIS WILL BE NO WALK IN THE PARK.
I daresay.
YEESH.
WHY'D YOU HAVE TO DRAG ME INTO THIS?
HEY, GIRAN BROUGHT YOU INTO THE FOLD TOO!
LIKE I CARE.
WHFF
FLIK
YOU BASTARD!
!

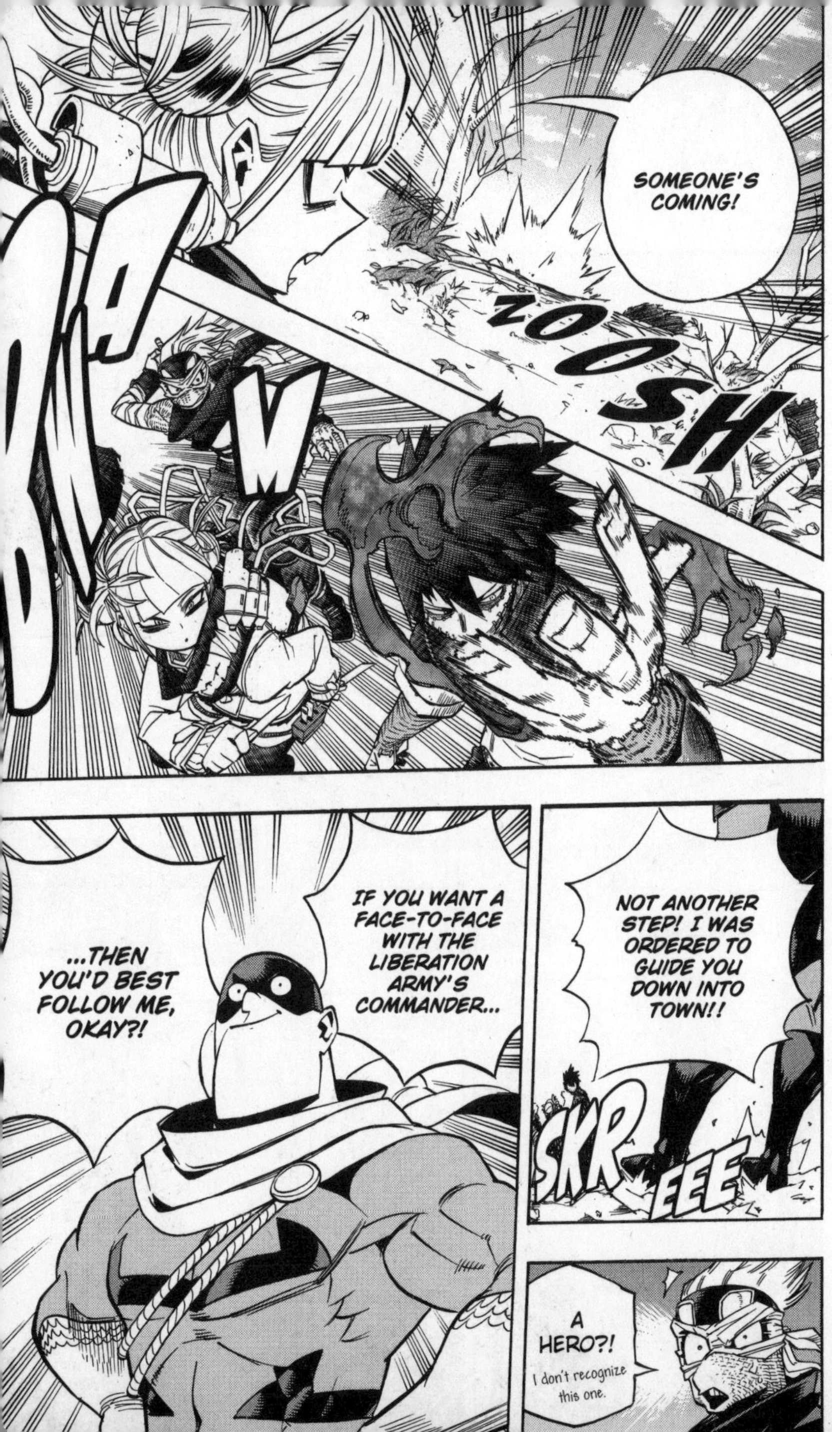
SOMEONE'S COMING!
ZOOSH
NOT ANOTHER STEP! I WAS ORDERED TO GUIDE YOU DOWN INTO TOWN!!
SKREEE
A HERO?!
I don't recognize this one.
IF YOU WANT A FACE-TO-FACE WITH THE LIBERATION ARMY'S COMMANDER...
...THEN YOU'D BEST FOLLOW ME, OKAY?!

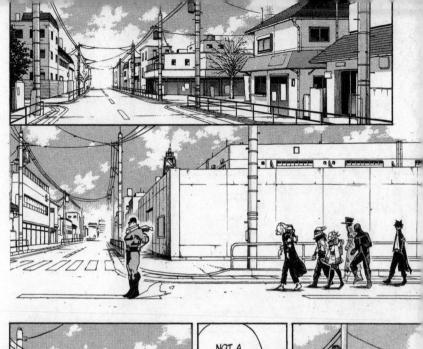

...

NOT A SOUL AROUND...

THIS WHOLE CITY, HUH?

SURE. I GET IT.

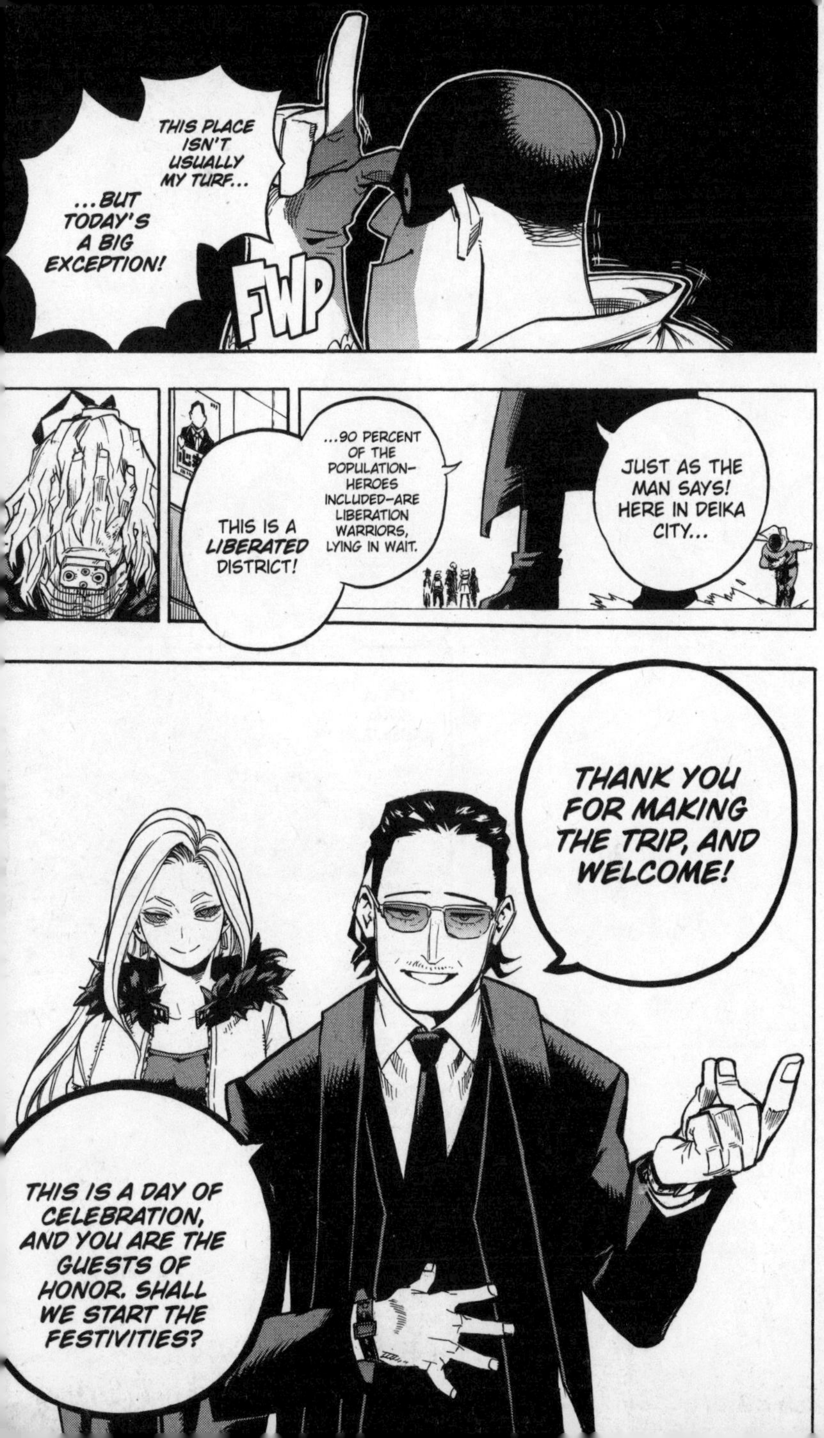
THIS PLACE ISN'T USUALLY MY TURF...
...BUT TODAY'S A BIG EXCEPTION!
FWP
JUST AS THE MAN SAYS! HERE IN DEIKA CITY...
...90 PERCENT OF THE POPULATION—HEROES INCLUDED—ARE LIBERATION WARRIORS, LYING IN WAIT.
THIS IS A LIBERATED DISTRICT!
THANK YOU FOR MAKING THE TRIP, AND WELCOME!
THIS IS A DAY OF CELEBRATION, AND YOU ARE THE GUESTS OF HONOR. SHALL WE START THE FESTIVITIES?

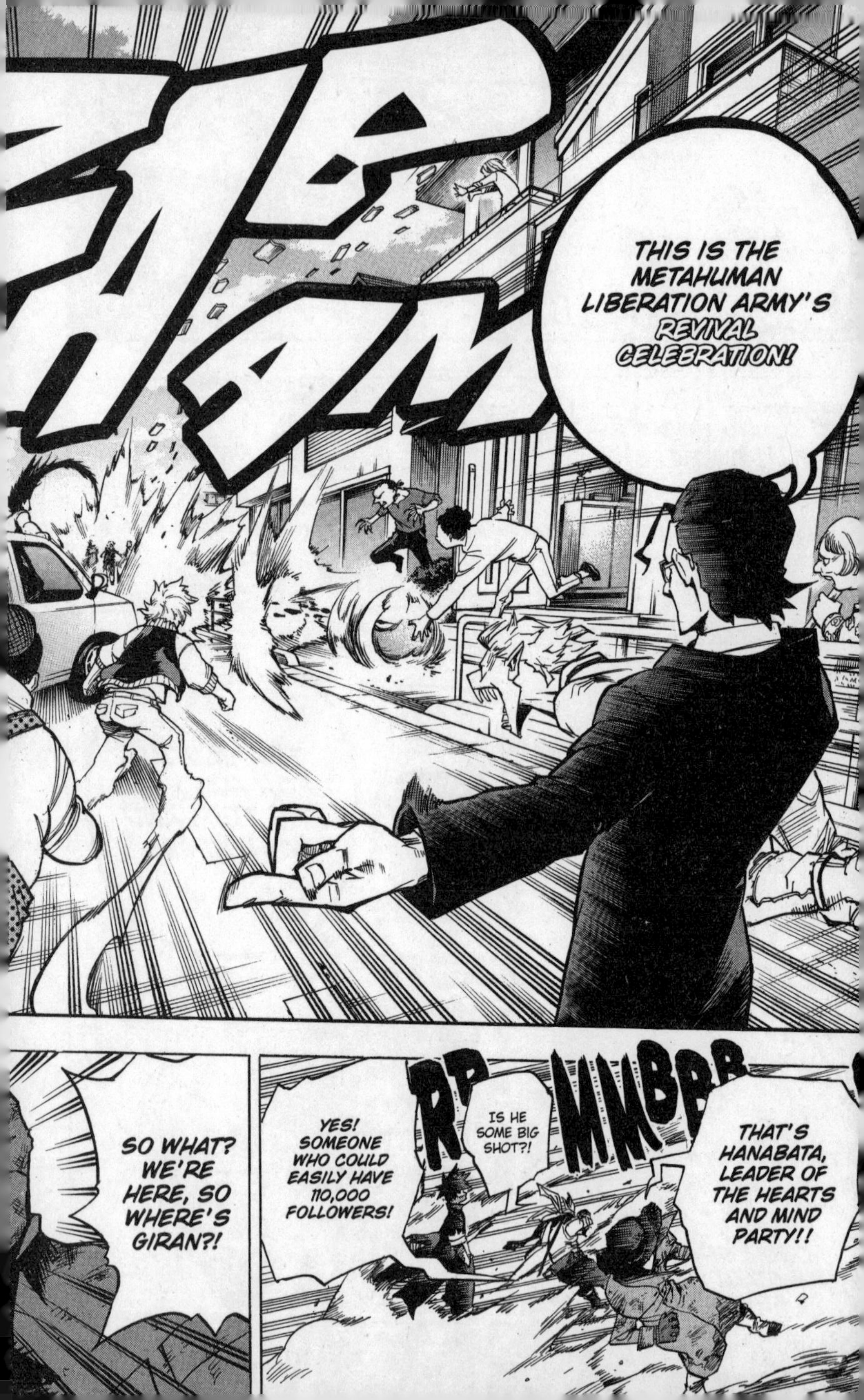
THIS IS THE METAHUMAN LIBERATION ARMY'S REVIVAL CELEBRATION!
THAT'S HANABATA, LEADER OF THE HEARTS AND MIND PARTY!!
IS HE SOME BIG SHOT?!
YES! SOMEONE WHO COULD EASILY HAVE 110,000 FOLLOWERS!
SO WHAT? WE'RE HERE, SO WHERE'S GIRAN?!

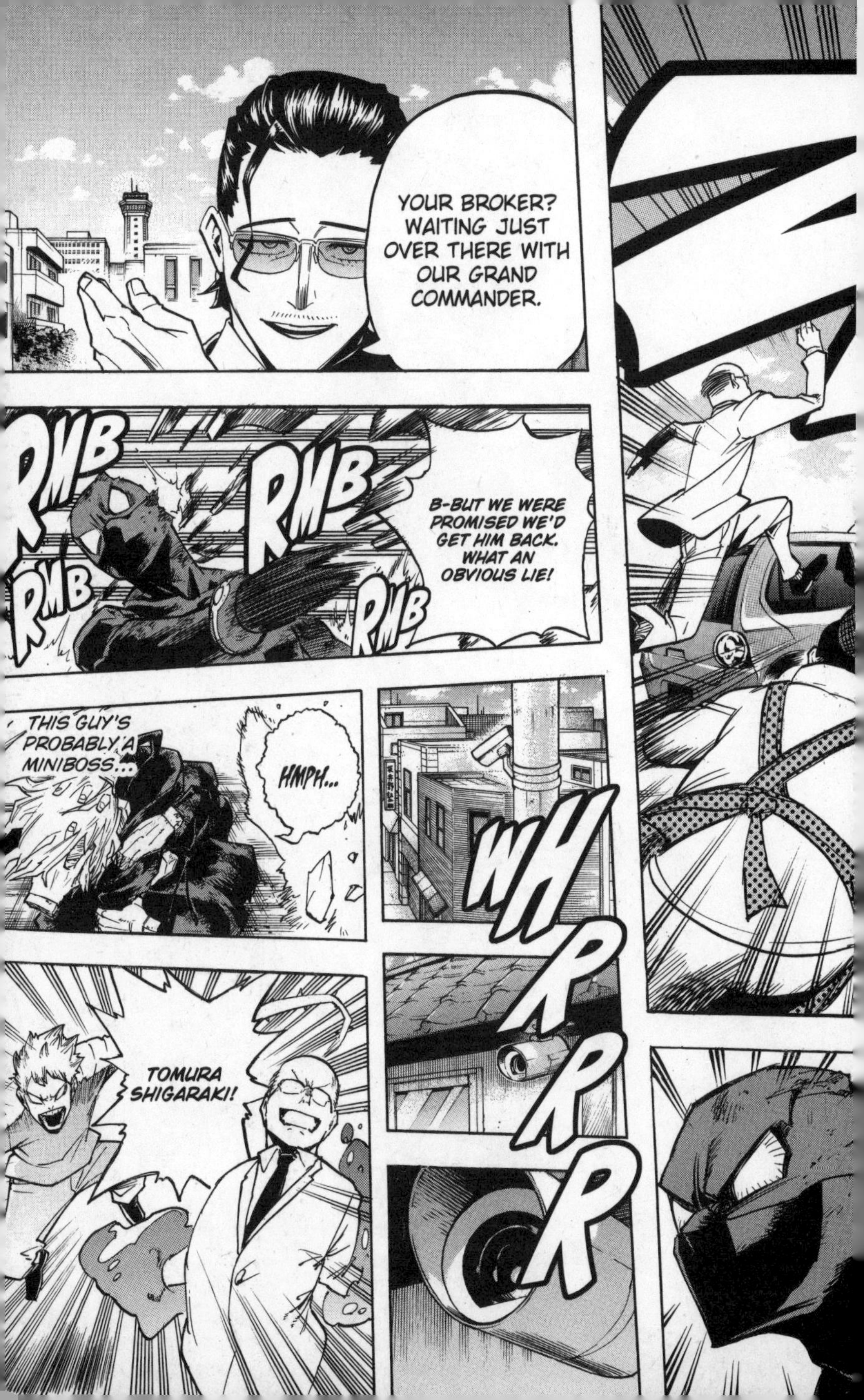
YOUR BROKER? WAITING JUST OVER THERE WITH OUR GRAND COMMANDER.
RMB
RMB
RMB
RMB
B-BUT WE WERE PROMISED WE'D GET HIM BACK. WHAT AN OBVIOUS LIE!
WHRRR
THIS GUY'S PROBABLY A MINIBOSS...
HMPH...
TOMURA SHIGARAKI!

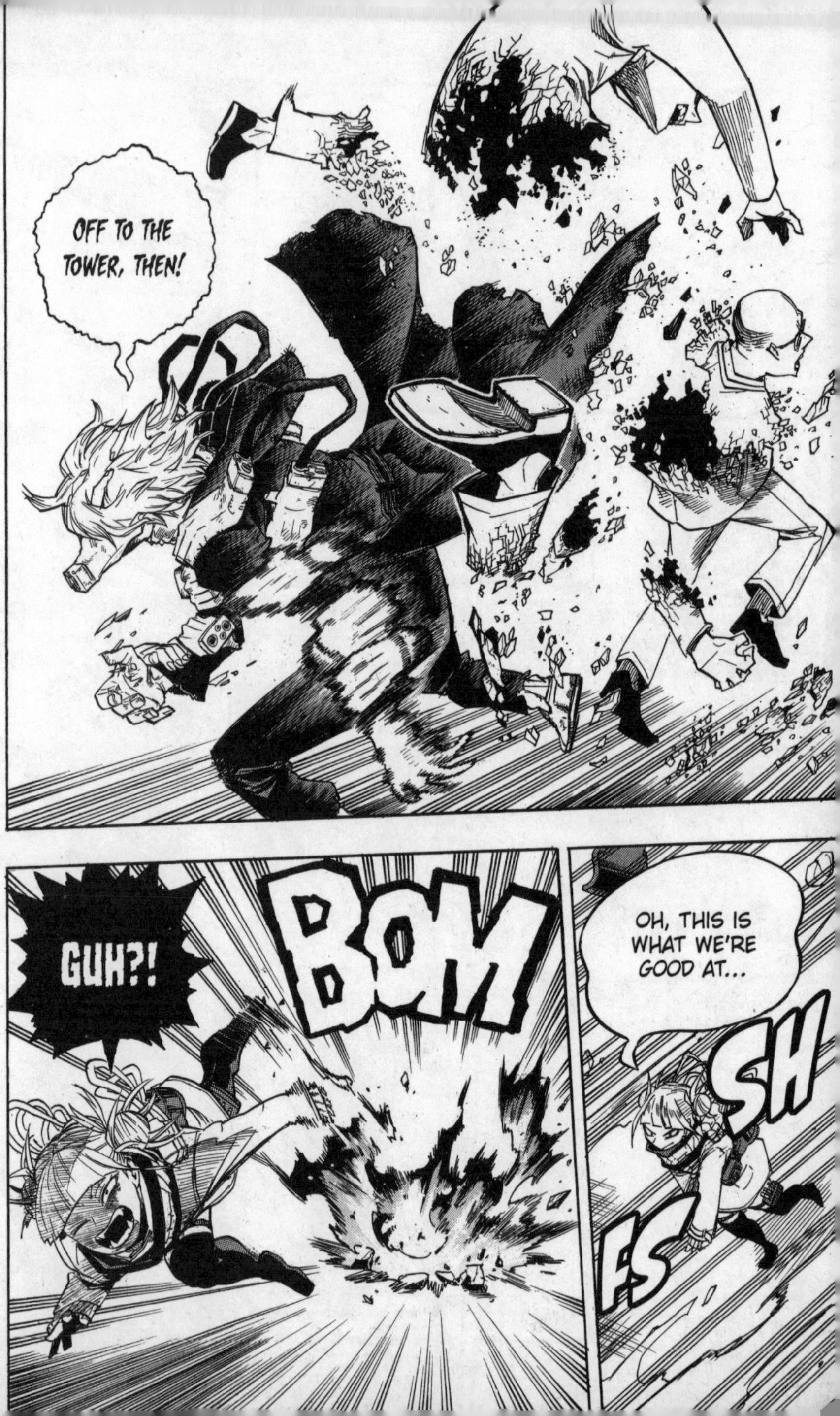
OFF TO THE TOWER, THEN!
OH, THIS IS WHAT WE'RE GOOD AT...
FSSH
BOM
GUH?!

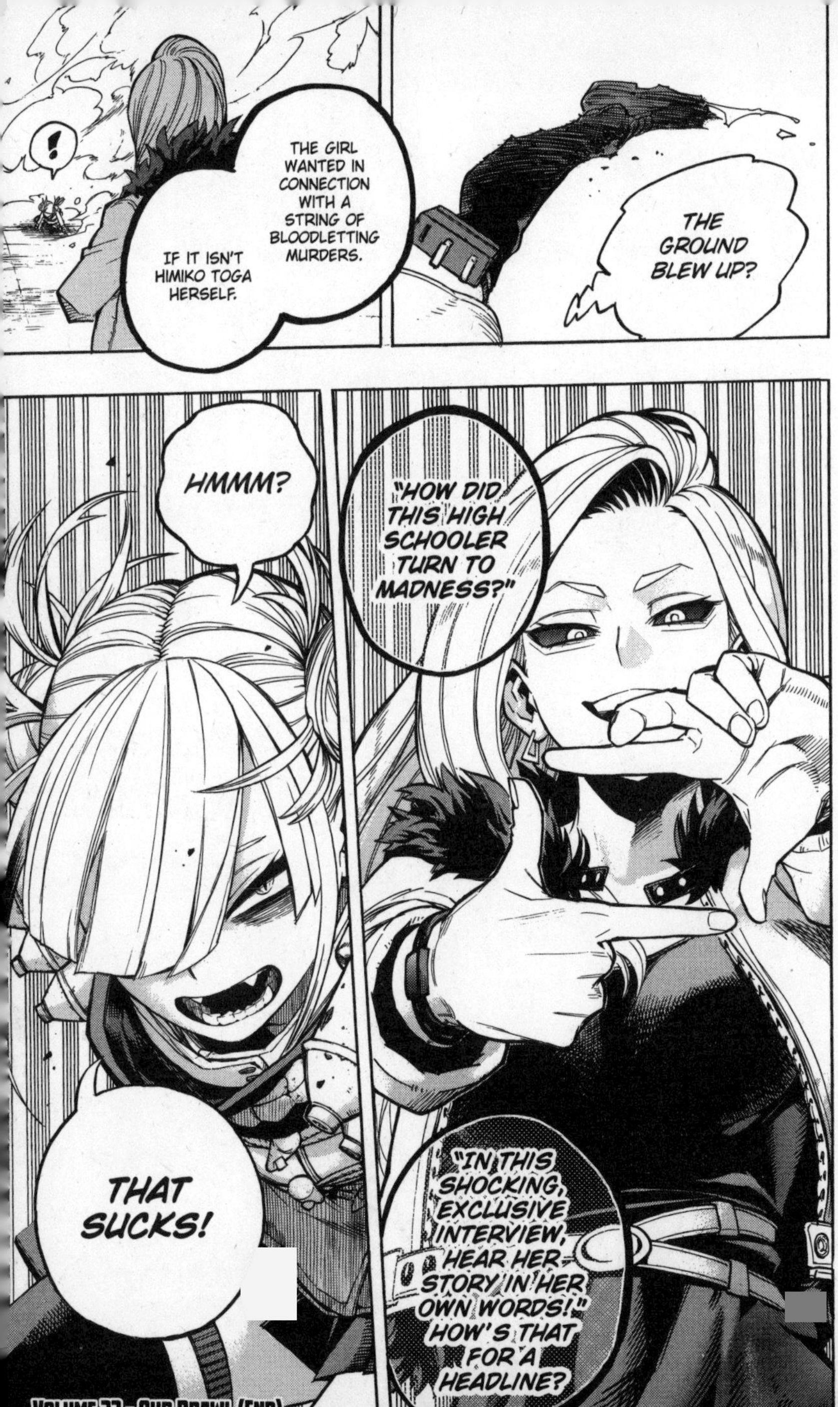
THE GROUND BLEW UP?
!
IF IT ISN'T HIMIKO TOGA HERSELF. THE GIRL WANTED IN CONNECTION WITH A STRING OF BLOODLETTING MURDERS.
"HOW DID THIS HIGH SCHOOLER TURN TO MADNESS?"
"IN THIS SHOCKING, EXCLUSIVE INTERVIEW, HEAR HER STORY IN HER OWN WORDS!" HOW'S THAT FOR A HEADLINE?
HMMM?
THAT SUCKS!

VOLUME 23 - OUR BRAWL (END)

THE VILLAINS

Back in volume 7, I made the strong claim that I would never do profile pages for the villains, because I wanted them to remain terrifying to readers. That was true then, but I'm a different Horikoshi now.

The story has evolved beyond that point, so I'm ready to start doing villain profiles.

Hooray.

VILLAINS

TOMURA SHIGARAKI [20] [TENKO SHIMURA]

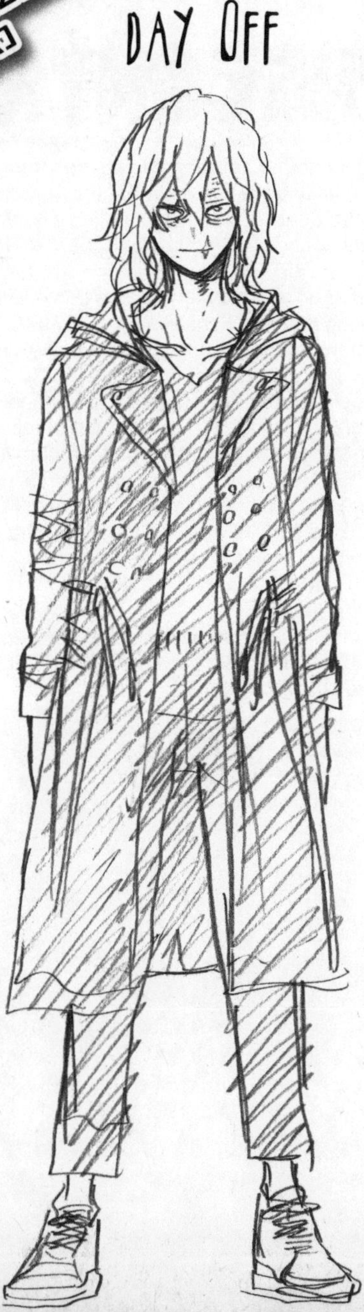
DAY OFF

Birthday: 4/4
Height: 175 cm
Favorite Thing: Nothing

THE SUPPLEMENT

When I first sketched out Shigaraki, my editor at the time said, “So his Quirk is gonna involve launching those hands, I’m guessing?” For some reason, that memory has stayed with me.

Shigaraki is based off the protagonist of my debut one-shot manga, “Tenko.” Since I thought of *My Hero Academia* as being my greatest-hits collection, from the very start I decided to toss in bits and pieces of everything I’ve ever done.

Drawing him is terrifyingly difficult. His villainy knows no bounds.

THE CONTRIBUTION

I've got another amazing contribution from a fellow artist!! Well, I might've accidentally done some strong-arming to make it happen. Sorry about that, Akutami Sensei. Yes, that's right, this contribution is from Gege Akutami Sensei, author of the hit *Jump* series ***Jujutsu Kaisen***!

It all started when Editorial came to me with a message. "You like ***JJK***, right? Because Akutami Sensei is a fan of ***MHA***. So how about you write a comment for the upcoming ***JJK*** volume's book band?" (I'm paraphrasing.)

My soul stopped evolving in middle school, and my brain stopped growing in elementary school, so my train of thought jumped the tracks over to "Art trade! We're doing an art trade!!" I mean, it made sense to me.

When I find out that an author I like also likes me, I get so excited that I end up making suggestions and creating extra work for them, without considering the consequences. Thanks for honoring my request, Akutami Sensei!! And again, sorry!!

Volume 5 of ***Jujutsu Kaisen*** was released on the same day as this book (in Japan), and it's got a drawing of the ***JJK*** characters by me in there! So please check it out!

Domain Expansion!
Anyone who gets trapped in my Western comics aesthetic...
...becomes really dramatic looking.
Direct hit!!
*Messing around, Jujutsu-style

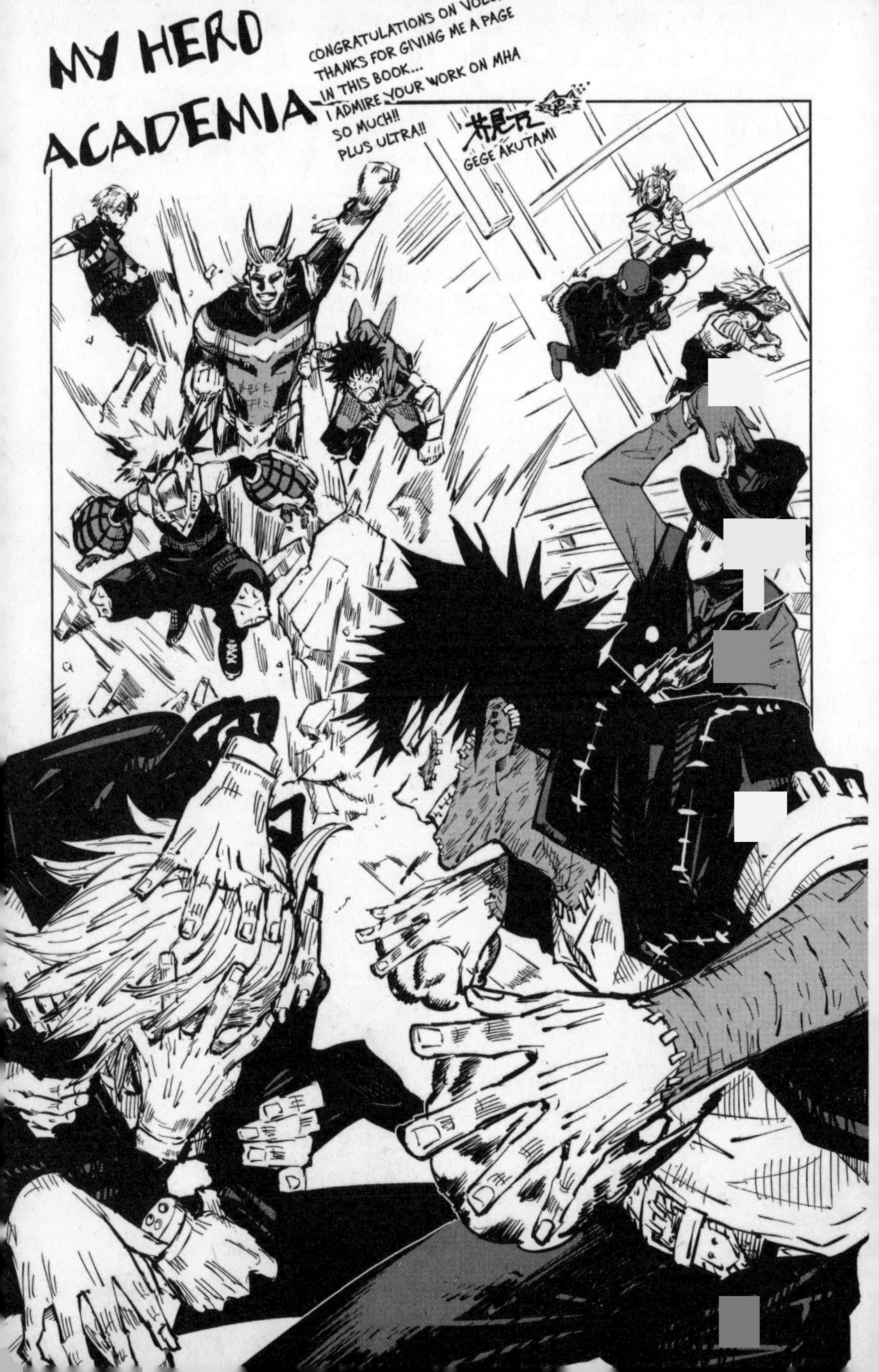
MY HERO ACADEMIA
CONGRATULATIONS ON VOLUME 23!!
THANKS FOR GIVING ME A PAGE IN THIS BOOK...
I ADMIRE YOUR WORK ON MHA SO MUCH!!
PLUS ULTRA!!
GEGE AKUTAMI

MY HERO ACADEMIA

SCHOOL BRIEFS

ORIGINAL STORY BY KOHEI HORIKOSHI

WRITTEN BY ANRI YOSHI

Prose short stories featuring the everyday school lives of My Hero Academia's fan-favorite characters!

VIZ

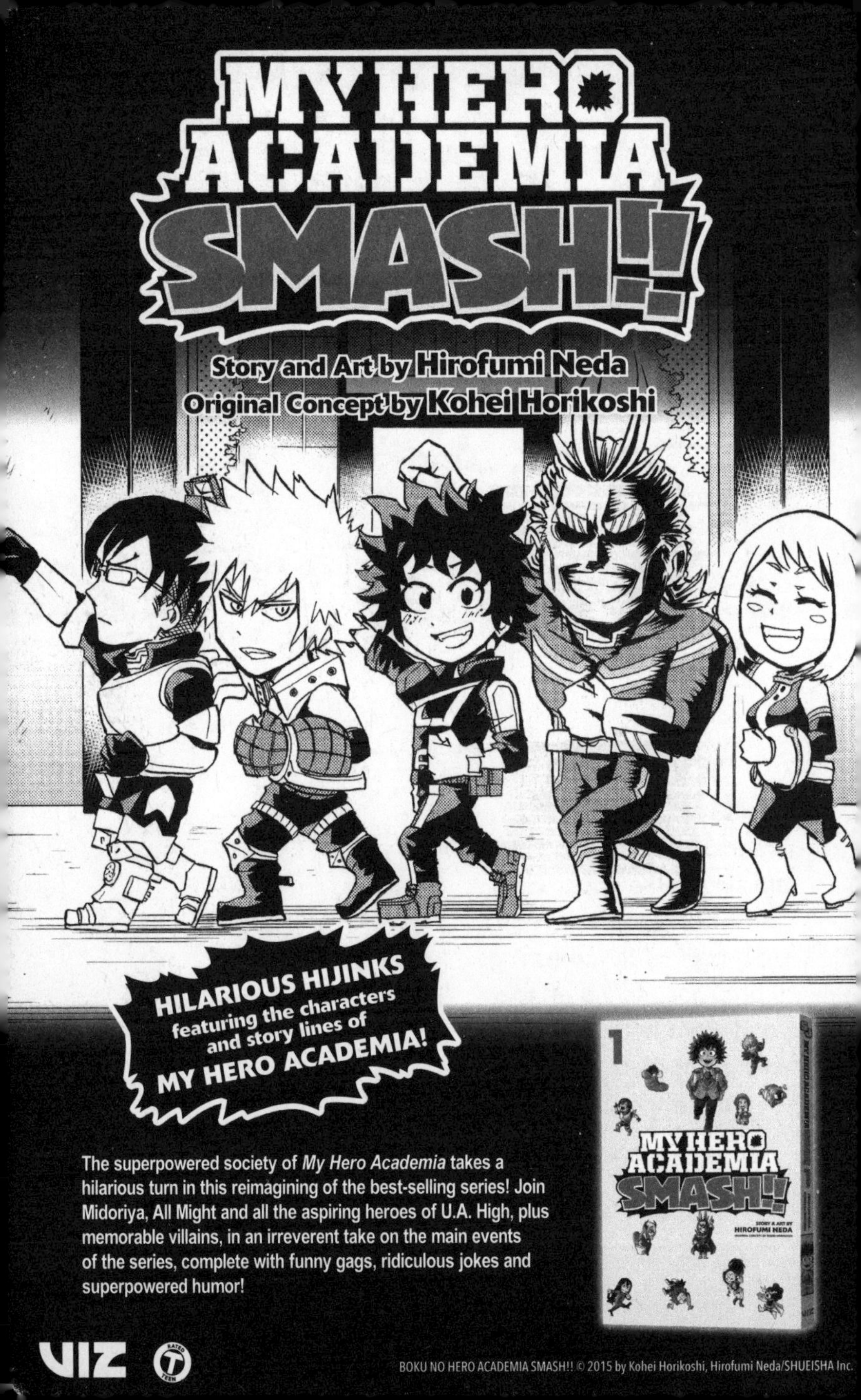
MY HERO ACADEMIA SMASH!!
Story and Art by Hirofumi Neda
Original Concept by Kohei Horikoshi
HILARIOUS HIJINKS featuring the characters and story lines of MY HERO ACADEMIA!
1
MY HERO ACADEMIA SMASH!!
STORY & ART BY HIROFUMI NEDA
The superpowered society of *My Hero Academia* takes a hilarious turn in this reimagining of the best-selling series! Join Midoriya, All Might and all the aspiring heroes of U.A. High, plus memorable villains, in an irreverent take on the main events of the series, complete with funny gags, ridiculous jokes and superpowered humor!
VIZ
RATED T TEEN
BOKU NO HERO ACADEMIA SMASH!! © 2015 by Kohei Horikoshi, Hirofumi Neda/SHUEISHA Inc.

READ THIS WAY!

MY HERO ACADEMIA

reads from right to left, starting in the upper-right corner. Japanese is read from right to left, meaning that action, sound effects and word-balloon order are completely reversed from English order.

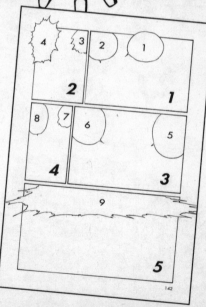